Katharina Steinbrück

Changing Consumer Law in the United Kingdom after Brexit?

A Study in Laws governing Consumer Credit and Unfair Terms in Consumer Contracts in the United Kingdom, Germany, Norway and Switzerland

Nomos

The Deutsche Nationalbibliothek lists this publication in the Deutsche Nationalbibliografie; detailed bibliographic data are available on the Internet at http://dnb.d-nb.de

a.t.: Berlin, Humboldt-Universität, Diss., 2020

ISBN 978-3-8487-8233-8 (Print)
978-3-7489-2655-9 (ePDF)

British Library Cataloguing-in-Publication Data
A catalogue record for this book is available from the British Library.

ISBN 978-3-8487-8233-8 (Print)
978-3-7489-2655-9 (ePDF)

Library of Congress Cataloging-in-Publication Data
Steinbrück, Katharina
Changing Consumer Law in the United Kingdom after Brexit?
A Study in Laws governing Consumer Credit and
Unfair Terms in Consumer Contracts in the United Kingdom,
Germany, Norway and Switzerland
Katharina Steinbrück
428 pp.
Includes bibliographic references.

ISBN 978-3-8487-8233-8 (Print)
978-3-7489-2655-9 (ePDF)

Onlineversion
Nomos eLibrary

1st Edition 2021

Meinen Eltern und Martin

Preface

This dissertation is the result of research conducted at, *inter alia*, the University of Oslo (March-April 2018 and August-October 2018), the Institute of European and Comparative Law (IECL) at the University of Oxford (November 2018 - January 2019) and the Swiss Institute of Comparative Law (ISDC) in Lausanne (April-May 2019). Please note that I used the most recent editions of literature as of the time of my research at the respective facilities. I am thankful to my supervisor Prof. Gerhard Dannemann without whose support these research stays would not have been possible. I would like to thank my supervisor at the University of Oslo, Prof. Kåre Lilleholt, as well as Prof. Mads Andenæs, Prof. Finn Arnesen, Prof. Hans Petter Graver, Prof. Ola Mestad and Ms. Eli Knotten for their support regarding my research on Norwegian law and the European Economic Area as well as Prof. Tanja Jørgensen for her help with respect to Norwegian consumer credit regulation. Furthermore, I thank Prof. Birke Häcker, Prof. Ulf Bernitz, Prof. John Cartwright, Prof. Stephen Weatherill, Prof. Simon Whittaker and Mrs. Jenny Dix for their support at the IECL during my research stay at the University of Oxford, the staff of the ISDC in Lausanne for their support regarding my research on Swiss law and Ms. Corinna Radke for her support at the Centre for British Studies at the Humboldt-University of Berlin. Moreover, I thank the Friedrich-Naumann-Foundation for Freedom for their support by offering me the Genscher Scholarship for Freedom with funds from the German Federal Ministry of Education and Research to conduct my PhD research. Last but not least, I thank Prof. Stefan Grundmann, Prof. Hans-Wolfgang Micklitz as well as Ms. Hannah Besting and Mr. Fabian Bickel for their valuable input to this dissertation and my family for their enduring support during this exciting PhD journey.

Table of Content

Abbreviations

AbzG	Deutsches Abzahlungsgesetz	German Hire-Purchase Act
ACER	European Agency for the Cooperation of Energy Regulators	
AGBG	Deutsches Gesetz zur Regelung des Rechts der Allgemeinen Geschäftsbedingungen	German Law of General Terms and Conditions
AJP	Aktuelle Juristische Praxis	
APR	Annual Percentage Rate	
AVB	Allgemeine Versicherungsbedingungen	General Terms and Conditions in insurance contracts
BaFin	Bundesanstalt für Finanzdienstleistungsaufsicht	German Federal Financial Supervisory Authority
BeckRS	beck-online.Rechtsprechung	
BGB	Deutsches Bürgerliches Gesetzbuch	German Civil Code
BGBl.	Deutsches Bundesgesetzblatt	German Federal Gazette
BKR	Zeitschrift für Bank- und Kapitalmarktrecht	
CCA	Consumer Credit Act	
CCD 1986	Council Directive 87/102/EEC of 22 December 1986 for the approximation of the laws, regulations and administrative provisions of the Member States concerning consumer credit	
CCD 2008	Directive 2008/48/EC of the European Parliament and of the Council of 23 April 2008 on credit agreements for consumers and repealing Council Directive 87/102/EEC	
CHF	Swiss Franc (Currency)	
CJEU	Court of Justice of the European Union (term used for cases from 2009 onward)	
CMA	Competition and Markets Authority	
CONC	Consumer Credit Sourcebook	
CPC	Regulation (EU) 2017/2394 of the European Parliament and of the Council of 12 December 2017 on cooperation between national authorities responsible for the enforcement of consumer protection laws and repealing Regulation (EC) No 2006/2004	

CRA 2015	Consumer Rights Act 2015	
EC	European Community	
ECJ	European Court of Justice (term used for cases until 2009)	
EEA	European Economic Area	
EEAA	Agreement on the European Economic Area	
EEC	European Economic Community	
EFTA	European Free Trade Association	
EGBGB	Einführungsgesetz zum Bürgerlichen Gesetzbuch	Introductory Act to the German Civil Code
ELKN	elklagenemnda	Norwegian Electricity Appeals Tribunal
ESA	EFTA Surveillance Authority	
EU	European Union	
EUR	Euro (Currency)	
FCA	Financial Conduct Authority	
FinDAG	Deutsches Gesetz über die Bundesanstalt für Finanzdienstleistungsaufsicht	German Law on the Federal Financial Supervisory Authority
FINKNB	finansklagenemnda bank	Norwegian Financial Appeals Tribunal for Banks
FINMA	Eidgenössische Finanzmarktaufsicht	Swiss Financial Market Supervisory Authority
FKU	forbrukerklagenemnda	Norwegian Consumer Appeals Tribunal
FOS	Financial Ombudsman Service	
FSA 2012	Financial Services Act 2012	
FSMA 2000	Financial Services and Markets Act 2000	
GBP	British Pound (Currency)	
GDP	Gross Domestic Product	
GG	Grundgesetz für die Bundesrepublik Deutschland	Basic Law for the Federal Republic of Germany
IKO	Schweizerische Informationsstelle für Konsumkredit	Swiss Information Agency for Consumer Credit
JCD	Joint Committee Decision	

JuS	Juristische Schulung	
JZ	Juristenzeitung	
KIG	Schweizerisches Konsumenteninformationsgesetz	Swiss Consumer Information Act
KG	Schweizerisches Bundesgesetz über Kartelle und andere Wettbewerbsbeschränkungen	Swiss Federal Act on Cartels and other Restraints of Competition
KKG	Schweizerisches Konsumkreditgesetz	Swiss Consumer Credit Act
KWG	Deutsches Gesetz über das Kreditwesen	German Banking Act
LG	Landgericht	German District Court
LQR	Law Quarterly Review	
MLR	Modern Law Review	
NAO	The National Audit Office	
NATO	North Atlantic Treaty Organisation	
NJW	Neue Juristische Wochenschrift	
NOK	Norwegian Crown (Currency)	
OECD	Organisation for Economic Co-operation and Development	
OFT	Office of Fair Trading	
OLG	Oberlandesgericht	German Higher Regional Court
OR	Schweizerisches Obligationenrecht	Swiss Code of Obligations
SECO	Schweizerisches Staatssekretariat für Wirtschaft	Swiss State Secretariat for Economic Affairs
T&Cs	General Terms and Conditions	
TCA	The Trade and Cooperation Agreement between the European Union and European Atomic Energy Community, of the one part, and the United Kingdom of Great Britain and Northern Ireland, of the other part	
TEC	Treaty establishing the European Community	
TFEU	Treaty on the Functioning of the European Union	
UCTA 1977	Unfair Contract Terms Act 1977	

UCTD	Council Directive 93/13/EEC of 5 April 1993 on unfair terms in consumer contracts	
UKlaG	Deutsches Gesetz über Unterlassungsklagen bei Verbraucherrechts- und anderen Verstößen	Law on injunctions in case of breaches of consumer law and other breaches
UNGCP	United Nations Guidelines on Consumer Protection	
UTCCRs 1999	Unfair Terms in Consumer Contracts Regulations 1999	
D-UWG	Deutsches Gesetz gegen den unlauteren Wettbewerb	German Act Against Unfair Competition
S-UWG	Schweizerisches Bundesgesetz gegen den unlauteren Wettbewerb	Swiss Unfair Commercial Practices Law
USD	US-Dollar (currency)	
VAG	Schweizerisches Versicherungsaufsichtsgesetz	Swiss Insurance Supervision Act
VKG	Deutsches Verbraucherkreditgesetz	German Consumer Credit Law
VSBG	Deutsches Gesetz über die alternative Streitbeilegung in Verbrauchersachen	German Law on Alternative Dispute Resolution in Consumer Matters
VuR	Verbraucher und Recht - Zeitschrift für Wirtschafts- und Verbraucherrecht	
WM	Wertpapier-Mitteilungen. Zeitschrift für Wirtschafts- und Bankrecht	
ZAG	Deutsches Gesetz über die Beaufsichtigung von Zahlungsdiensten	German Law on the Supervision of Payment Service Providers
ZBJV	Zeitschrift des Bernischen Juristenvereins	
ZEK	Schweizerische Zentralstelle für Kreditinformation	Swiss Central Agency for Credit Information
ZGB	Schweizerisches Zivilgesetzbuch	Swiss Civil Code
ZIP	Zeitschrift für Wirtschaftsrecht	
D-ZPO	Deutsche Zivilprozessordnung	German Code of Civil Procedure

S-ZPO	Schweizerische Zivilprozess-ordnung	Swiss Code of Civil Procedure

Part I: Basis of the Research

Chapter 1: Introduction

On the 23 June 2016 a majority of the British electorate voted to leave the European Union (EU) after 43 years as an EU Member State. While this decision has profound implications for relations between the United Kingdom of Great Britain and Northern Ireland (UK) and the remaining 27 EU Member States, it will also shape UK and English law[1] for the next decades. One argument brought forward by 'Brexiteers' in the campaign leading to the decisive referendum in 2016 was that many of the UK's laws were nowadays made in Brussels rather than passed by Parliament in Westminster,[2] thus, possibly constituting one reason to vote against UK Membership in the EU. It is true: much legislation has been introduced by the EU mainly regarding the integration of the internal market albeit the argument that they were passed without the consent of 'Westminster' appears misleading. For example, EU Member States assume a certain amount of discretion when implementing Directives. Another argument brought forward was the existence of alternative models to the EU, *inter alia*, in Western Europe, namely the Norwegian and Swiss model. They could possibly serve as role models for the future relationship between the UK and the EU.

This dissertation aims at answering three questions: Is European law really so foreign from UK and English law so it has to be removed from or changed within the existing regulatory system? Would the Norwegian or Swiss model of European cooperation serve as inspiration or has the UK actually moved closer to its EU partners, such as Germany, despite differing approaches to the legal system? And can regulatory approaches in Germany, Norway, and Switzerland be considered more effective and, thus,

---

1 The term 'English Law' in this work refers to the common legal system of England and Wales not including the separate jurisdictions of Scotland and Northern Ireland. For an account of the different evolution of English and Scottish Laws of Contract, cf. William James Tayler, *A treatise on the differences between the laws of England and Scotland relating to contracts: including marriage considered as a contract affecting property, and marriage settlements* and Tikus Little, *Scottish contract law essentials*.

2 Cf. i.e. Anonymous, 'Taking back control from Brussels' (*Vote Leave*) <http://www.voteleavetakecontrol.org/briefing_control.html> accessed 17 November 2019.

serve as inspiration for future regulation? In this regard, European consumer law shall serve as a sample for such an analysis. Consumer law is an area which has been shaped predominantly by European legislation in the Member States in the past decades as the EU considers consumer law an important feature of achieving internal market integration. This approach shows that consumer legislation can now be considered an important internal market feature. Stricter consumer regulation may impose more obligations on businesses and, thus, bears the potential for increased costs. Looser consumer regulation, on the other hand, leaves more room to businesses and the market itself. Consumer legislation, thus, offers an opportunity for economic (de-) regulation.

This dissertation originally presumed in 2017 that the UK would not be bound by consumer legislation without cross-border implications (such as product standards) after the departure from the EU. On the 30th December 2020 representatives of the EU (and European Atomic Energy Community) and the UK signed a cooperation and trade agreement (TCA)[3]. The TCA entered into force on the 1st May 2021.[4] The UK is now neither a member of the customs union nor the single market.[5] Neither the withdrawal agreement[6] nor the TCA contain concrete binding rules on EU non-cross border consumer legislation.[7] The parties rather recognise

> [their] respective autonomy and rights to regulate within their territories in order to achieve legitimate public policy objectives such as [...] consumer protection [...] while striving to improve their respective high levels of protection [...][8]

---

3 The Trade and Cooperation Agreement between the European Union and European Atomic Energy Community, of the one part, and the United Kingdom of Great Britain and Northern Ireland, of the other part (30 December 2020).

4 The TCA was ratified by the House of Commons on the 30th December 2020 (cf. European Union (Future Relationship) Act 2020) but was only approved by the European Parliament on the 27th April 2021 and the Council of the European Union on the 29th April 2021.

5 Northern Ireland still adheres to EU rules related to the customs union and the single market for goods while remaining part of the customs territory of the UK, cf. Protocol on Ireland/Northern Ireland (31 January 2020), Annex 2.

6 Agreement on the withdrawal of the United Kingdom of Great Britain and Northern Ireland from the European Union and the European Atomic Energy Community, 2019/C 384 I/01 (entry into force on 1 February 2020).

7 For a more detailed analysis see Chapter 14.

8 Recital 7 of the TCA, cf. also Arts. SERVIN.1.1(2), SERVIN.5.39.(1)(b), DIGIT.3, ENER.4, GRP.1(3)(f) TCA.

and desire

> that [the TCA] contributes to consumer welfare through policies ensuring a high level of consumer protection and economic well-being, as well as encouraging cooperation between relevant authorities.[9]

Even after the conclusion of the TCA this work, thus, maintains relevance and can serve as guidance for shaping future consumer legislation in the UK.

The following analysis focusses on consumer credit legislation as well as unfair terms. Consumer credit is an important economic instrument. At the same time, it bears potential for fragility due to increased consumer indebtedness. Especially since the Covid-19 health and economic crisis consumer credit may assume an increasingly important role to fund consumer spending. Thus, consumer credit regulation will also become a focus of attention for legislators. The UK can be considered a legislative 'pioneer' with respect to consumer credit legislation. The UK was the first country to introduce comprehensive consumer credit legislation in 1974 – serving as an example for the first European consumer credit legislation introduced in 1986. The UK had introduced particular consumer credit regulation – such as the Moneylenders Act 1900 – early on. The legislator has since shown an awareness for consumer credit issues. It is, hereby, thus presumed that the influence of European legislation regarding consumer credit had relatively little effect on consumer credit regulation in the UK. Furthermore, because the UK has introduced consumer credit legislation before the EU and has shown a constant awareness for consumer credit issues it is presumed that the UK will be interested in maintaining a high level of consumer protection with respect to consumer credit. *Vice versa*, the EU loses a driving force of innovative consumer credit legislation from its midst.

The second consumer legal area covered is legislation on unfair terms in consumer contracts. While legislation on unfair, mainly exclusion and limitation, clauses had already been introduced in 1977, the UK was obliged to implement legislation on unfair terms in consumer contracts under the Council Directive 93/13/EEC of 5 April 1993 on unfair terms in consumer contracts (hereinafter "Unfair Contract Terms Directive" or "UCTD" or in the respective sections the "Directive"). As will be shown, the implementation of this Directive caused quite a stir because it appears to be based on

9 Recital 12 of the TCA, cf. also Arts. DIGIT.1, DIGIT.13(1), AIRTRN.22, COMPROV.11 TCA, Annex TBT-2, Art. 3.

the civil law, specifically German, legal notion of 'good faith' which can arguably be considered foreign to English law. Thus, unlike European legislation on consumer credit, the implementation of the UCTD could constitute a foreign concept 'imposed' on English law.

The two legal areas, both concerning UK and European consumer law, can, thus, be presumed to have had different effects on UK legislation. While high standards of consumer credit legislation can be presumed to be maintained, it is more questionable whether legislation on unfair terms in consumer contracts will remain unchanged or even be repealed. In order to determine, whether the norms in question should be maintained, amended or repealed this dissertation is structured according to four parts.

Part I depicts the basis of the research. It lays out the comparative and economic methodologies as well as parameters of the research. The *moderate functional* comparative approach aims to include the background of the compared legal systems. Thus, Chapter 3 depicts the basis of the comparative analysis, including historical, economic and sociological factors influencing the UK, German, Norwegian and Swiss legal systems.

Part II depicts the status quo of consumer credit legislation in the UK, Germany, Norway and Switzerland. Each section includes a legal as well as economic and comparative analysis.

Part III portrays the status quo of regulation of unfair terms (in consumer contracts) in the UK, Germany, Norway and Switzerland from a legal and economic perspective as well as comparative analysis.

Finally, Part IV depicts the alternate European models as well as the TCA and concludes whether the German, Swiss or Norwegian models offer inspiration for amendments of regulation on consumer credit and/or unfair terms in consumer contracts and whether such changes should be implemented based on the findings of the legal, economic and comparative analysis of such regulations.

Chapter 2: Methodology

The following work uses analytic means derived from both comparative and economic legal research. This chapter sets out the concrete methodological means and parameters of the research project.

A. *Comparative Analysis*

I. Choice of Legal Systems to be compared

The comparative analyses shall portray the consequences of different political stati in Europe. While the work could have also chosen the Ukrainian or Turkish model of association with the EU, this work focusses on the Western European countries Germany, Norway and Switzerland. It is suggested that due to a presumed common core of shared historical and social developments, the depicted countries are more likely to serve as orientation for the UK rather than Ukraine and Turkey with which the UK does not share as many commonalities.

Germany is an EU Member State. The comparative analysis shall reveal whether the UK and Germany have moved closer and the same direction legally as EU Members. It will be examined how the same Directives were implemented and whether differences entailed any consequences. Germany represents a traditional civil law system which is underlied a different legal understanding than the English common law. This could lead to differences in the implementation of Directives. Furthermore, as a founding, existing and continued Member State, it can be presumed that Germany will not serve as an example comes to comparative inspiration for possible alternative regulation after the exit from the EU.

Norway is a Member State of the European Economic Area (EEA) as well as the European Free Trade Association (EFTA). It will be examined what kind of EU-norms Norway is obliged to implement through its status as an EFTA and EEA Member State and due to further treaties with the EU and whether a different or non-implementation has been effective.

Switzerland is solely a Member State of the EFTA and thus formally the least integrated country of the compared. Switzerland is (largely) not obliged to implement EU-norms automatically but only those that have been specified in bilateral treaties with the EU. It will be examined what kind of EU-norms Switzerland has implemented and whether a different or non-implementation led to an effective regulation.

II. Methodology

Prior to engaging in the actual comparative research, clear methodological parameters for the comparative analyses must be determined. The question of comparative legal methodology is discussed vividly among academia and has not yet led to a clear solution as to which approach shall prevail. Thus, this part portrays and discusses different approaches critically and concludes the approach appropriate for the following comparative analyses.

1. Presumption of Similarity

Although comparative methods go back well into ancient human history[10] modern comparative law really finds its roots in the late nineteenth century[11] when many legal codifications had just been completed[12]. The *Congrés international de droit comparé* held in Paris in 1900 marked the beginning of an effort to harmonise national laws.[13] To achieve this goal comparative legal scholars began to focus on similarities of legal systems rather than their differences.[14]

Throughout most of the twentieth century this led to a focus on a practical approach that aims to identify the functions of norms from different le-

---

10 Jan M Smits, Comparative Law and its Influence on National Legal Systems. in Mathias Reimann and Reinhard Zimmermann (eds), *The Oxford Handbook of Comparative Law*, 504; Konrad Zweigert and Hein Kötz, *Introduction to Comparative Law*, 49 et seq.

11 Roger Cotterrell, Is it so Bad to be Different? Comparative Law and the Appreciation of Diversity. in Esin Örücü and David Nelken (eds), *Comparative Law - A Handbook*, 134, 136.

12 Gerhard Dannemann, Comparative Law: Study of Similarities or Differences?. in Mathias Reimann and Zimmermann Reinhard (eds), *The Oxford Handbook of Comparative Law*, 392.

13 Ibid.; Zweigert and Kötz, *supra* note 10, 2.

14 Dannemann, *supra* note 12; Pierre Legrand, The same and the different. in Pierre Legrand and Roderick Munday (eds), *Comparative Legal Studies: Traditions and Transitions*, 245 et seq.

gal systems that are presumably similar (*functional approach*)[15] which leads to a *praesumptio similitudinis*[16]. The inherent similarity of the norms' functions is, thus, merely hidden underneath a coat of different local expressions and technicalities.[17] *Zweigert and Kötz* even emphasise that if one 'finds great differences [...] he should be warned and go back to check again'.[18]

2. Critique

The idea of an underlying general similarity of different legal systems may sound appealing especially in light of post-war efforts to maintain peace, overcome differences and foster international relations.[19] However, the functional approach has attracted much criticism.[20]

Pierre Legrand, a most outspoken critic of the functional approach, concedes that functionalists frequently ignore differences for the sake of proving similarity.[21] This accounts for a repression of differences in favour of an artificial, impossible homogeneity.[22] Instead of trying the impossible, namely showing that all legal systems are the same,[23] comparative law should focus on heterogeneity and diversity of different approaches[24].

Furthermore, *Legrand* criticises that functionalists appear to conduct their analyses from an objective standpoint but are in fact biased towards the legal systems they are rooted in.[25] This fiction produces superficial results which have no actual comparative value as they do not acknowledge

15 Cotterrell, *supra* note 11; Dannemann, *supra* note 12, 393, 394; Jaakko Husa, *A New Introduction to Comparative Law*, 182; Zweigert and Kötz, *supra* note 10, 34, 39.

16 Zweigert and Kötz, *supra* note 10, 40.

17 Dannemann, *supra* note 12, 393; Legrand, *supra* note 14, 247; Franz Werro, Comparative studies in private law - A European point of view. in Mauro Bussani and Ugo Mattei (eds), *The Cambridge Companion to Comparative* Law, 134.

18 Zweigert and Kötz, *supra* note 10, 46.

19 Werro, *supra* note 17.

20 Cotterrell, *supra* note 11, 133 et seq.; Dannemann, *supra* note 12, 395 et seq.; Husa, *supra* note 15, 183; Thomas Lundmark, *Charting the divide between common and civil law*, 16.

21 Legrand, *supra* note 14, 259.

22 Ibid. 261 et seq.

23 Ibid. 303.

24 Ibid. 272.

25 Ibid. 260, 277, 278.

the diversity of approaches to legal problems.[26] A legal comparatist must, thus, remain critically distant[27] towards both the legal system he is rooted in and the foreign legal system with which he conducts the comparison. The same criticism has been voiced by *Günter Frankenberg* and others,[28] too.

Critics suggest a *differential approach* that, contrary to the functional approach, presumes that legal systems are inherently different;[29] the functionalist approach ignores this heterogeneity[30]. The legal system according to them constitutes the product of societies' cultures.[31] Therefore, a variety of factors, i.e. history or sociology, have to be included in the comparative analysis.[32] The focus on difference shall lead to more (mutual) respect for the diversity of legal cultures.[33]

3. A "Middle Way"

Not all comparatist scholars side with either of the aforementioned theories. In fact, a middle way is possible. The assumption of function as a starting point for research does not automatically exclude aspects outside the legal system.[34] On the one hand, despite its deficiencies as a general methodological tool the presumption of similarity can be useful when comparing legal systems from the same cultural sphere as societal values, problems and their solutions are often alike.[35] On the other hand, the differential approach is not specific regarding which parameters shall be used

---

26 Ibid. 254 et seq.

27 Ibid. 252.

28 Dannemann, *supra* note 12, 396; Günter Frankenberg, 'Critical Comparisons: Rethinking Comparative Law' [1985] 26 (2) Harvard International Law Journal 411 (414, 423).

29 Cotterrell, *supra* note 11; Frankenberg, ibid., (453); Legrand, *supra* note 14, 271; Werro, *supra* note 17, 133.

30 Mathias Reimann, 'The Progress and Failure of Comparative Law in the Second Half of the Twentieth Century' [2002] 50 American Journal of Comparative Law 671 (680 et seq.).

31 cf. Cotterrell, *supra* note 11, 135; Legrand, *supra* note 14, 276 et seq.

32 cf. Cotterrell, ibid., 145, 152; Werro, *supra* note 17, 140.

33 cf. Cotterrell, ibid., 137; Legrand, *supra* note 14, 300; Werro, *supra* note 17, 136.

34 Lundmark, *supra* note 20; Ralf Michaels, The Functional Method of Comparative Law. in Mathias Reimann and Reinhard Zimmermann (eds), *The Oxford Handbook of Comparative Law*, 388.

35 Husa, *supra* note 15, 183.

and can, thus, offer only little guidance as to how to engage with comparative research.[36]

Jaakko Husa, thus, suggests a *moderate functional comparative law*.[37] Functionalism, in the sense of this approach, does not comprise a presumption of similarity, its causal explanation or the hypocritical notion of neutrality but focusses on strict comparability.[38] Function is used as a method to determine the comparability of norms and legal institutions.[39] It does not serve as a tool to include and analyse legal *cultures*.[40]

This does not, however, prevent the comparative lawyer from acknowledging similarities as well as differences and looking for explanations for them.[41] The analysis shall, thus, not be insensitive towards the societal and cultural context in which the legal framework is embedded.[42]

4. Methodology of this Dissertation

The following micro-comparative analysis[43] of consumer credit law and the law governing unfair terms in consumer contracts follows the moderate functional approach advocated by *Husa*. The comparative analysis itself shall serve to reveal similarities and differences of the respective legal systems. Historic, economic and sociological factors will be included in the respective analysis to possibly provide explanations for similar or differing legal approaches.

Function as a starting point fits the following analyses well for two reasons. First, the UK, Germany, Norway and Switzerland are all European nations with broadly similar cultures. Therefore, it is probable that similar functions for norms exist in the respective legal systems.

36 cf. Cotterrell, *supra* note 11, 147; Jaakko Husa, 'Farewell to Functionalism or Methodological Tolerance?' [2003] 67 (3) The Rabel Journal of Comparative and International Private Law 419 (441).
37 Husa, ibid., (443).
38 Ibid.
39 Ibid. (426 et seq.).
40 Ibid. (446).
41 Ibid. (443).
42 Ibid. (446).
43 For a depiction of macro- and micro-comparison, cf. Husa, *supra* note 15, 100 et seq. and Lundmark, *supra* note 20, 18.

Second, the norms to be compared – at least in the cases of the UK, Germany and Norway – derive from EU law. It can, thus, be assumed that they serve similar functions.

The concept of function as a starting point does not, however, prevent the analyses from emphasising differences. In fact, the finding of differences may prove to be a valuable element in the final assessment of the future of the discussed legislation on consumer credit and unfair terms in consumer contracts.

The following analysis will first set out 'societal factors' for each depicted legal system including a brief portrayal of historic, economic and sociological factors. The historic factors mostly focus on developments from the 19th century onward to portray differing developments in the 'modern' nation states with special regard to their place in Europe. Each section shall provide a summary of factors which will later be considered to evaluate the comparability of the depicted systems. Please note that these sections must be treated as mere summaries and cannot replace comprehensive historical, economic or social scientific assessments in the respective fields.

B. Economic Analysis

Beside the comparative analysis, economic parameters are used to determine whether respective regulation has desirable economic effects. In this light, the Chicago School 'classic' theory of law and economics, Institutional Economics and Behavioural Economics are depicted briefly to then decide which theory is best suited for the following analysis.

I. 'Classic' Law and Economics: The Chicago School

The idea of modern law and economics started at the University of Chicago which is why the 'classic' theory of law and economics is also branded the 'Chicago School'. Under the classic theory of law and economics laws are analysed according to their economic efficiency, meaning that of all regulatory options the one with the lowest effective costs for society should be chosen.[44] Under classic law and economics it is presupposed that each individual is an agent for the maximisation of his or her own satisfaction. Legal rules then merely become factors in calculating the utility of a trans-

44 Daniel H. Cole and Peter Z. Grossmann, *Principles of Law and Economics*, 73.

action for the individual. In this regard, legal rules should be viewed in light of their efficiency to rather than the fairness of the respective transaction.[45] Rather than regulation by the legislator, the classic Chicago School advocates the settlement of disputes and development of rules under the common law which from their point of view constitutes the most effective mean of regulatory intervention because common law rules already follow an economic logic.[46]

However, especially with respect to consumer law the Chicago School lacks an institutional and normative outlook. It idealises the self-regulating powers of the market as well as the judicial law-making of common law judges.[47] Modern consumer policy in European countries is nowadays not merely footed on the premise of enabling consumption but oftentimes envisages the image of a vulnerable rather than rational and circumspect consumer. Furthermore, the Chicago School is not well suited for an analysis of all four depicted legal system as only one can be classified as a common law jurisdiction while all others have relied on civil codes and regulation by the legislator. The presumption that intervention by the legislator is considered inefficient would impose a presumption of inefficiency on three of the four depicted systems.

II. New Institutional Economics

New Institutional Economists presume that the perfect market scenario envisioned by neo-classical economists does not exist. One of the problems of the Chicago School understanding of transactions is the asymmetric distribution of information between actors.[48] While acknowledging efficiency as a general theme, according to new institutional economists the market is in fact embedded in an institutional framework comprising i.e. rules,

45 Steven G. Medema, Chicago law and economics. in Ross B. Emmett (ed), *The Elgar Companion to the Chicago School of Economics*, 168.

46 Cf. Richard A. Posner, *The Problems of Jurisprudence*, 356.

47 Cole and Grossmann, *supra* note 44. With respect to considerations other than those directed at efficiency, i.e. fairness, under common law, cf. i.e. Lord Mansfield in 1766, note 1123 below.

48 Douglass C. North, 'Transaction Costs, Institutions, and Economic Performance' [1992] An International Center for Economic Growth Publication 1 (7, 14).

customs and social norms.[49] One measure for assessing efficiency – taking into account the institutional framework – are transaction costs.[50] The assessment of transaction costs can lead to the conclusion that institutional (or state) regulation provides the most efficient way to keep transaction costs at a minimum. This is especially the case where contracts would be particularly difficult to draft in the absence of a framework of norms set by the legislator.[51] Where transaction costs are high, institutions particularly matter and bear the potential of making transactions more efficient.[52] *North* goes so far to say that efficient markets are a consequence of 'institutions that provide low-cost measurement and enforcement of contracts at a particular moment'.[53] At the same time institutions should be flexible enough to allow for risk-taking and innovation, which includes 'trials and errors', thus, also providing a low-cost framework of rules in case of failure, i.e. bankruptcy laws.[54]

New Institutional Economics, thus, acknowledge regulatory intervention as long as it is fit to lower transaction costs. However, similar to the Chicago School, New Institutional Economics mainly focus on the measurable costs of transactions to determine the efficiency of a transaction. Individual factors, such as bounded rationality of consumers, do not play a key role.

III. Behavioural Economics

Behavioural Economists also criticise neo-classical economic theory for assuming an impossible perfect market scenario. However, rather than relying on external factors such as institutions to ensure the efficiency of transactions, behavioural economics focus on the individual psychological fac-

49 Cole and Grossman, ibid., 76. For an overview, cf. also Oliver E. Williamson, The Economic Analysis of Institutions and Organisations - in general and with respect to country studies, 1993, pages 12 et seq.

50 Cf. Ronald H. Coase, 'The Nature of the Firm' [1937] Economica 386 (390 et seq.).

51 Ronald H. Coase, 'The Problem of Social Cost' [1960] 3 Journal of Law and Economics 1 (16-17).

52 North, *supra* note 48, (6).

53 Ibid. (9).

54 Ibid.

tors of decision-making.[55] Beside the asymmetric distribution of information, a main problem results from the individual processing of information. Our perception and processing of information is strongly influenced by, *inter alia*, faulty memory, hindsight bias, bad probability judgments and framing (bounded rationality) which can lead to bad decision-making.[56] Such failures are not mitigated by education or experience.[57] In addition, human capacities are limited by bounded willpower – meaning that that people take actions despite knowing they are in conflict with their long-term interests – and bounded self-interest – meaning that people do not always solely act out of self-interest but also with regard to the interest of others.[58] These results lead to the conclusion that the market is not an appropriate instrument to mitigate transactional deficiencies and that government policy needs to consider behavioural findings to regulate transactions that are particularly sensitive, i.e. in the financial sector. In this regard Behavioural Law and Economics offer a mean of analysis for debiasing through law.[59]

Behavioural Economics provide a valuable tool to assess consumer transactions.[60] Nowadays, consumers are regularly confronted with complex situations and an overload of information which is difficult to process in a rational and unbiased way. Thus, behavioural insights should play a role in developing and assessing consumer-oriented legislation.

---

55 Richard H. Thaler, 'Behavioral Economics: Past, Present, and Future' [2016] 106 (7) American Economic Review 1577 (1577).

56 Daniel Kahnemann, 'New Challenges to the Rationality Assumption' [1994] 150 (1) Journal of Institutional and Theoretical Economics 18 (29); Amos Tversky and Daniel Kahnemann, 'Advances in Prospect Theory: Cumulative Representation of Uncertainty' [1992] 5 Journal of Risk and Uncertainty 297 (298); Amos Tversky and Daniel Kahnemann, 'Rational Choice and the Framing of Decisions' [1986] 59 (2) The Journal of Business 251 (257); Amos Tversky and Daniel Kahnemann, Judgment under uncertainty: Heuristics and biases. in Daniel Kahnemann, Paul Slovic and Amos Tversky (eds), *Judgment under uncertainty: heuristics and biases*, 3,11; Amos Tversky and Daniel Kahnemann, Judgments of and by representativeness. in Daniel Kahnemann, Paul Slovic and Amos Tversky (eds), *Judgment under uncertainty: heuristics and biases*, 98.

57 Daniel Kahnemann and Amos Tversky, Subjective probability: A judgment of representativeness. in Daniel Kahnemann, Paul Slovic and Amos Tversky (eds), *Judgment under uncertainty: heuristics and biases*, 46-47.

58 Cass Sunstein, Christine Jolls and Richard H. Thaler, 'A Behavioral Approach to Law and Economics' [1998] 50 Stanford Law Review 1471 (1479).

59 Christine Jolls, Behavioral Law and Economics. in Peter Diamond and Hannu Vartiainen (eds), *Behavioral Economics and Its Applications*, 137 et seq.

60 Ibid. 134-136.

IV. Methodology of this Dissertation

Based on the above depictions the economic analysis of this dissertation will be based on New Institutional and Behavioural Economics. It shall be determined whether the implemented regulation is actually fit to lower transaction costs with respect to New Institutional Economics. Behavioural insights shall serve to understand the effects of regulation in the areas of consumer credit and unfair terms and whether there exist better ways to assist with the correct processing of information. The following sections will set out (1) the consumer images used in this dissertation, (2) the parameters of effective regulation in the area of consumer credit and (3) the parameters of effective regulation in the area of unfair terms in consumer contracts.

1. Consumer Images

The consumer has long been a central theme running through economic and sociological theory.[61] *Adam Smith* famously stated that 'consumption is the sole end and purpose of all production; and the interest of the producer ought to be attended to only so far as it may be necessary for promoting that of the consumer'.[62] Consumption and *in persona* the consumer, thus, play a crucial part in the rise of capitalism and 'modern' society.[63] While historically different kinds of 'consumer cultures' can be traced back to the 14th century,[64] the roots of modern consumer culture can be traced back to England in the 18th century and the possibility of social advance of the bourgeois classes by way of a specific kind of (luxury) consumption[65]. The post-war era of the 20th century saw another spark in mass consumer culture and consumerism, meaning the 'preoccupation of society with the acquisition of consumer goods'[66]. On the one hand, consumerism embodies a policy that encourages increased consumption of

61 For a detailed depiction of the evolution of consumer culture, cf. Roberta Sassatelli, *Consumer Culture: History, Theory and Politics*, Part I.

62 Adam Smith, *An Inquiry into the Nature and Causes of the Wealth of Nations*, Book IV, Chapter VIII, recital 49.

63 Sassatelli, *supra* note 61, 10.

64 Ibid. 20.

65 Ibid. 15.

66 Cf. Anonymous, 'Consumerism' (*Lexico Dictionaries / English*) <https://www.lexico.com/en/definition/consumerism> accessed 27 August 2019.

goods to foster economic growth. On the other hand, it also relates to a movement starting in the 1950s that demands more rights and protection for consumers.[67] In this light US President John F. Kennedy introduced the Consumer Bill of Rights in 1962 which originally included the right to safety, the right to be informed, the right to choose and the right to be heard.[68] They provided the basis for the United Nations Guidelines on Consumer Protection (UNGCP) which added further consumer rights, such as the right to redress and consumer protection, to the original model.[69] From President Kennedy's speech and the succeeding UNGCP one can conclude two principle mechanisms of consumer policy: on the one hand, consumer policy aims at consumer empowerment, meaning that consumers need access to information as well as proper means of enforcement of such transparency; on the other hand, consumers require protection, i.e. by mandatory standards to ensure consumers' health and safety.

As will be depicted below, the two elements can be emphasised more or less and, thereby, reveal different consumer images. On the one hand, the consumer can be viewed as a *homo oeconomicus* who merely needs enough information to make a reasonable decision. Critics have pointed out that, in fact, consumers do not always act rationally and oftentimes afford other means of protection.[70] As has been pointed out by behavioural economists, even if they are provided with information, it is less than clear that they actually understand it or it is useful to them.[71] Furthermore, the notion that the consumer solely acts as a market participant is misleading. Con-

---

67 Anonymous, 'Basic Consumer Rights' (*Lumen Learning*) <https://courses.lumenlearning.com/boundless-business/chapter/consumer-rights/> accessed 27 August 2019.

68 Cf. President John F. Kennedy, Special message to Congress on Protecting Consumer Interest (15 March 1962), page 2.

69 Cf. the United Nations Guidelines for Consumer Protection (UNGCP) (General Assembly resolution 39/248 of the 16 April 1985, revised by the General Assembly resolution 70/186 of the 22 December 2015).

70 Cf. i.e. Peter Cartwright, The consumer image within EU law. in Christian Twigg-Flesner (ed), *Research Handbook on EU Consumer and Contract Law*, 204; on the notion of the 'confident consumer' Christian Twigg-Flesner, The Importance of Law and Harmonisation for the EU's Confident Consumer. in Dorota Leczykiewicz and Stephen Weatherill (eds), *The Images of the Consumer in EU Law: Legislation, Free Movement and Competition Law*, 183-202.

71 Stefan Grundmann, Targeted Consumer Protection. in Dorota Leczykiewicz and Stephen Weatherill (eds), *The Images of the Consumer in EU Law: Legislation, Free Movement and Competition Law*, 235; Twigg-Flesner, ibid., 188 et seq.

sumers act at multiple levels, i.e. as citizens and members of society.[72] On the other hand, the consumer can be viewed as vulnerable and in need of protection from abuse which reflects a consumer image that is rather oriented at improving consumer *welfare* and protection from harm.

The following work will use these two 'extreme' consumer definitions. On the one hand, it will speak of the rational consumer, a *homo oeconomicus*, who only makes rational decisions that benefit him or her. He or she is circumspect and takes all relevant considerations into account before deciding. He or she is also able to process all available information adequately and balance all (non-) economic factors as long as he or she is provided with enough information to make a decision.

On the other hand, this work will speak of the vulnerable consumer. The vulnerable consumer lacks the circumspect abilities of the rational consumer. He or she is not able to process all the information required to make a reasoned decision. It is, thus, more likely that he or she will weigh several factors incorrectly and unconsciously make a decision to his or her detriment. For vulnerable consumers the provision of enough information does not suffice. They either need thorough guidance or must be protected from concluding certain agreements to ensure their (economic) well-being.

The following chapters will reveal which consumer image underlies each measure of regulation. And whether the consumer image underlying national legal measures fits in with the consumer image put forward by the European Union.

2. Consumer Credit

Consumer credit fulfils several economic functions. Consumption crucially depends on financial services and consequently the availability of capital resources. Among savings such availability includes (consumer) credit. On the one hand, a consumer credit agreement can benefit both the creditor and the borrower. The creditor makes a profit of lending money to a borrower and charging interest. The borrower profits from consumer credit because he or she is able to buy desired consumer goods. On the other hand, the producer of the goods purchased by the borrower profits from

72 Hans-W. Micklitz, The Consumer: Marketised, Fragmentised, Constitutionalised. in Dorota Leczykiewicz and Stephen Weatherill (eds), *The Images of the Consumer in EU Law: Legislation, Free Movement and Competition Law*, 23-26.

the enhanced purchase power of the borrower. If the demand for products rises, the production grows which in turn benefits economic growth. In a perfect scenario, consumer credit, thus, fulfils a very important function with respect to demand and supply of goods. The costs of credit will be regulated by a functioning market in which consumer act freely and with circumspection. Institutional regulation would not appear necessary.

Under such a perfect scenario the transaction costs can be assumed to be rather low. Assuming that the consumer is rational and circumspect he or she will understand the consumer credit agreement which entails the main rights and obligations of both parties. One element of transaction costs comprises the drafting of the agreement on behalf of the creditor. If the creditor is allowed to presume that the borrower is a rational and circumspect consumer who understands all rights and obligations of the agreement, the transaction costs for drafting the agreement are presumably low. The creditor can also include the costs for drafting and administering the credit in the calculation of the interest rate which as another element of transaction costs must be borne by the borrower.

However, especially in light of insights regarding consumer behaviour reality looks different and requires institutional intervention. Behavioural economics show that consumers are not rational and circumspect economic actors but are often subject to bounded rationality.[73] Such bounded rationality includes a lack of information and adequate information processing capability.[74] In addition, underlying 'tacit assumptions'[75] as well as unjustified overoptimism[76] can taint the consumer's decision. This can lead to two alternative scenarios: under the less likely scenario the creditor takes the consumer's lack of rationality into account and informs the borrower adequately while maintaining the same conditions and accepting higher transaction costs and reduced profit. Under the more likely scenario, however, the creditor will not change the offer or even worse take actual advantage of the consumer's lack of capabilities. For example, if the creditor changes the interest rates so they appear rather low in the first year of re-

73 Cf. Oren Bar-Gill, Consumer Transactions. in Eyal Zamir and Doron Teichman (eds), *The Oxford Handbook of Behavioral Economics and the Law*, 466.

74 Melvin A. Eisenberg, Behavioral Economics and Contract Law. in Eyal Zamir and Doron Teichman (eds), *The Oxford Handbook of Behavioral Economics and the Law*, 443.

75 Ibid. 444.

76 Ibid. 446; Paul Ali, Ian Ramsay and Cate Read, 'Behavioural Law and Economics: Regulatory Reform of Consumer Credit and Consumer Financial Services' [2014] 43 Common Law World Review 298 (312); Bar-Gill, *supra* note 73, 474.

payment and increase rapidly in the second year so the consumer effectively pays more in total interest[77] the transaction costs are higher on behalf of the consumer. Now one could argue that, nevertheless, functioning competition will sort this problem out. However, even if there existed competitors who took the bounded rationality into account, their products would likely become more expensive because transaction costs on behalf of the creditor increase. Consumers, however, will often not be able to comprehend the benefit they receive in return for the increased price. Due to inherent bias they will likely choose the apparently cheaper offer because they do not foresee the negative consequences such an offer could entail afterwards.[78] In the end, competition will be distorted to the detriment of both honest creditors and consumers.[79]

Increased transaction costs remain on behalf of the consumer. If he or she must pay more interest on the credit it is likely that he or she will not be able to consume as much. This has a negative effect on demand and supply and, thus, the whole economy. Furthermore, an 'irrational' consumer will likely not be able to assess the possibility of default under the consumer credit agreement due to overoptimism.[80] A defaulting consumer will create more transaction costs for the creditor, i.e. by possible forfeiture proceedings as well as the whole economy because the consumer will oftentimes not be able to spend money in the foreseeable future. A loose financial policy and bulk of unsecured credit that may not be repaid means the stability of the financial market is consequently also at risk. Consumer credit policy must, thus, aim at both, the availability of financial resources and cautionary measures to prevent the overindebtedness of consumers which could destabilise financial markets.

Institutional intervention helps to lower and manage transaction costs in both scenarios. Under the perfect scenario, institutional intervention could contribute to lowering transaction costs for the creditor by providing standard consumer credit agreements and help to lower transaction costs for the borrower by introducing information duties relating to advertisement as well as the consumer credit agreement so the borrower can easily and effectively compare different credit offers and make an informed decision without losing too much time in the process.

---

77 For an exemplary calculation, cf. Bar-Gill, ibid., 468.

78 Ali, Ramsay and Read, *supra* note 76, (311-312).

79 For the inadequacy of competition as a compensatory mean, cf. Bar-Gill, *supra* note 73, 468.

80 Ibid. 474.

With respect to the second imperfect scenario, institutional intervention appears necessary. Transaction costs are considerably higher for all parties involved. Furthermore, behavioural insights show that consumers oftentimes are not capable of processing the consequences entailed in entering a credit agreement without being given adequate and easily understandable information. Rather than prohibiting the issue of consumer credit, behavioural economists advocate the implementation of information duties regarding both the product itself and the personal use of the product, thus, providing personalised information to the individual consumer.[81] This means that the information provided to the consumer must include all conditions under the consumer credit agreement and information on how the consumer can cope with the obligations that come with it, i.e. by gathering information on the individual consumer's creditworthiness. The information must, furthermore, be easily comprehensible for the consumer.[82] A consumer who is well informed regarding the product as well as his or her own abilities will be able to consume confidently. Under an information policy guided by responsible lending, i.e. tailored to the consumer's individual needs, the risk of default is minimised which benefits the individual consumer's financial well-being as well as the general financial stability.

Moreover, consumer credit does not only serve the function of fostering economic growth through consumption but is also considered a mean of social inclusion. The availability of financial resources allows socially disadvantaged citizens to participate in consumption and, thus, in society.[83] However, credit consumption also makes this group all the more vulnerable in case of default and consequently leads to an even greater social *exclusion*.[84] Thus, consumer credit policy should not aim at an ever more liberal credit policy to achieve social inclusion but focus on responsible (and sometimes even restrictive) lending and financial education. Thereby, both micro- and macro-economic risks of consumer credit lending are minimised.

---

81 Ibid. 478-480; Ali, Ramsay and Read, *supra* note 76.

82 Bar-Gill, ibid., 481.

83 Guido Comparato, The Design of Consumer and Mortgage Credit Law in the European System. in Hans-W. Micklitz and Irina Domurath (eds), *Consumer Debt and Social Exclusion in Europe*, 12; more generally Vanessa Mak, Financial services and consumer protection. in Christian Twigg-Flesner (ed), *Research Handbook on EU Consumer and Contract Law*, 317, 321.

84 Comparato, ibid.

This work will focus on pre-contractual information duties and the creditor's duties relating to consumers' access to credit. The former aims at enabling the consumer to make an informed decision on taking out credit. The latter shall ensure that the creditor assesses the consumer's creditworthiness before lending; a prerequisite to responsible lending. The two focus points, thereby, resemble the consumer related aims of Directive 2008/48/EC of the European Parliament and of the Council of 23 April 2008 on credit agreements for consumers and repealing Council Directive 87/102/EEC (hereinafter the "Second Consumer Credit Directive" or "CCD 2008"). They, furthermore, strongly influence if and when credit is taken out and granted and are, thus, closely connected to the degree of (over-) indebtedness of the compared jurisdictions. An analysis of the European Directives' implementation and the actual micro-economic effects offers the opportunity to examine and relate their economic consequences. The following work will, therefore, focus on the practical impacts of consumer credit regulation to assess its effectiveness.

Consumer credit regulation will be held effective if consumer credit is generally available but at the same time the volume of (unsecured) consumer credit compared to the overall credit volume of the depicted economy and the default rates of consumers are low. While this model entails the risk that disadvantaged consumers may be less likely to be granted unsecured credit, the risks for both the individual consumer as well as the overall financial systems are lowered and consumer credit can make a positive impact on individual consumption in general. It is assumed that such a scenario can only be achieved if a policy of responsible and restrictive lending is implemented.

3. Unfair Terms in Consumer Contracts

Under a perfect economic scenario, a rational consumer would negotiate all terms of a contract with the trader. Because both parties would be knowledgeable and circumspect regarding the subject-matter and circumstances of the contract it can be presumed that the outcome will reflect a balance of interests of the parties. As a first amendment of the perfect scenario it must, however, nowadays be acknowledged that in an era of mass consumption the terms of consumer contracts are rarely individually negotiated. Today non-negotiated general terms and conditions (T&Cs) provided by the trader are the usual way of contracting.

If the trader and the consumer had to negotiate all contract terms individually, they would have to invest a lot of time in everyday dealings. The transaction costs are, thus, presumably high for both parties in the phase of negotiation. After the individually tailored contract is concluded both parties would know exactly about their rights and obligations under the agreement which could mean that the contract will presumably be adhered by both parties so secondary costs, i.e. for non-compliance with the contract, will unlikely arise. However, the presumption with respect to secondary transaction costs is not a guarantee.

Under the 'perfect T&Cs scenario' both parties would save time and transaction costs. The trader can use the same form of terms for each transaction. Both parties can conclude contractual agreements quickly. While T&Cs are not usually fit to the individual needs of each customer it can be presumed under the image of a rational consumer that he or she has read the T&Cs, understands the advantages and disadvantages, knows of his or her rights and realises whether such T&Cs are detrimental to him or her; thus, transaction costs in the form of secondary costs are presumably low. This scenario is especially beneficial for the rational consumer as he or she compares different offers and T&Cs, thereby, foresees possible transaction costs for him or her (i.e more detrimental T&Cs would justify a lower price) and in this light makes the best individual choice available to him or her. There also exists flawless competition under the perfect scenario, so the consumer has a wide range of choice of T&Cs and respective offers. Competitors with 'bad T&Cs', meaning that they charge high prices and offer bad contractual conditions, will not be chosen, consequently unsuccessful and removed from the market.

However, as has been shown with respect to consumer credit, a perfect scenario cannot be presumed. Most consumer transactions involving T&Cs must be considered an 'imperfect scenario' for different reasons. While one could argue that consumers could still have a choice between more expensive competitors who use fair terms that do not shift all the risks associated with the contract to the consumer, it is unlikely that the consumer will assess the T&Cs associated with an offer elaborately.[85] Consumers are often not capable of processing the extensive small print of T&Cs. In fact, studies have shown that most consumers do not read the

85 Ernst A. Kramer, Konsumentenschutz als neue Dimension des Privat- und Wettbewerbsrechts. in Ernst A. Kramer (ed), *Zur Theorie und Politik des Privat- und Wirtschaftsrechts: Beiträge aus den Jahren 1969-1996*, 186; Ludwig Raiser, 'Vertragsfreiheit heute' [1958] 13 (1) JZ 1 (3).

small print.[86] At the same time their decisions are also influenced by tacit assumptions as well as overoptimism regarding their own abilities. Even if the consumers were to be provided with all relevant information, it is likely that they will still base their decision on the price rather than taking into account possible advantages of paying a higher price for less detrimental T&Cs.[87] Ultimately most consumers will choose the offer at the lowest price rather than evaluating closely which risks the offer entails for them due to bounded rationality.[88] He or she will in most cases neither be interested nor intellectually equipped to enter lengthy contractual negotiations when buying consumer goods.[89] Under this scenario it is likely that the user of T&Cs will exploit the weak position of the consumer. The use of T&Cs to the benefit of the trader will one-sidedly reduce transaction costs to the benefit of him or her. This could motivate other traders to reduce their transaction costs which brings us to the second problem: a 'race to the bottom' with respect to the consumer friendliness of terms and possible monopolisation by use of unfair terms. With the emergence of mass production and consumption it becomes virtually impossible for the consumer to negotiate the terms of the individual agreement. This creates the danger of a parallel law of T&Cs that is dictated by businesses and bears the potential to exploit consumers who must accept those T&Cs in order to gain access to consumer goods, leaving them in a vulnerable position.[90] Unregulated T&Cs, thus, bear the risks of, on the one hand, leaving the consumer vulnerable and, on the other hand, allowing for disruptions of the market, i.e. a race to the bottom to gain an advantage ahead of com-

---

86 Cf. i.e. Yanis Bakos, Florencia Marotta-Wurgler and David R. Trossen, 'Does Anyone Read the Fine Print? Consumer Attention to Standard-Form Contracts' [2014] 43 (1) The Journal of Legal Studies 1 (23).

87 Cf. the 'Fair Terms Campaign' led by the CMA, https://fairterms.campaign.gov.uk/. Regarding price asymmetries due to the use of unfair terms, cf. Hans-Bernd Schäfer and Patrick C. Leyens, Judicial Control of Standard Terms and European Private Law. in Pierre Larouche and Filomena Chirico (eds), *Economic Analysis of the DCFR*, 99 et seq.

88 With respect to unfair terms in particular, cf. Michael G. Faure and Hanneke A. Luth, 'Behavioural Economics in Unfair Contract Terms - Cautions and Considerations' [2011] 34 Journal of Consumer Policy 337 (348 et seq.).

89 Kramer, *supra* note 85, 185-186; Hans-W. Micklitz, Unfair Terms in Consumer Contracts. in Norbert Reich and others (eds), *European Consumer Law*, recital 3.1.

90 Cf. Hans Großmann-Doerth, Selbstgeschaffenes Recht der Wirtschaft und staatliches Recht (1933). in Uwe Blaurock, Nils Goldschmidt and Alexander Hollerbach (eds), *Das selbstgeschaffene Recht der Wirtschaft*, 77 referring to the 'self-created law of business' ('selbstgeschaffenes Recht der Wirtschaft', Translation by author); Raiser, *supra* note 85, (7).

petitors and consequently the risk of a unjust monopolies based on unfair contract terms.[91] This leads to a distortion of competition which consequently leads to a lack of fair choice for consumers as well a loss of consumer confidence. Furthermore, products would be sold at higher prices and worse conditions. These factors would lead to higher transaction costs for the individual consumer as well as society as whole. At the same time consumers may lose trust in the market because they enter into a transaction of which they unknowingly bear risks they would not normally expect to bear.[92] In the absence of classic contractual negotiations in which both parties can act autonomously[93] and facing the depicted risks of consumer vulnerability and market failure, the legislator may introduce mechanisms to regulate unfair contract terms. Especially with the emergence of mass production and consequently the mass production of T&Cs embodied in standard contracts, regulation of unfair terms appears necessary.[94]

Regulation of T&Cs and unfair terms in consumer contracts bears the advantage that the legislator creates bottom rules for all traders, thus, benefiting traders who offer products with fair terms at higher prices as well as consumers who are protected from certain kinds of unfair terms. From a New Institutional Economics perspective, regulation in the area of T&Cs would focus on information disclosure, thus, ensuring that terms are provided in an open and comprehensible way. However, Behavioural Economics show that the mere provision of information does not suffice as consumers oftentimes do not actually read unfair terms. If the main problem is the ignorance of consumers, it may be necessary to implement stricter forms of overall term control,[95] such as by administrative authori-

91 George Akerlof, 'The Market for 'Lemons': Quality Uncertainty and the Market Mechanism' [1970] 84 Quarterly Journal of Economics 488-500; Michael Schillig, 'Inequality of bargaining power versus market for lemons: legal paradigm change and the Court of Justice's jurisprudence on Directive 93/13 on unfair contract terms' [2008] 33 (3) European Law Review 336 (341 et seq.).

92 In this regard, cf. the 'Fair Terms Campaign' led by the CMA, *supra* note 87.

93 Cf. Kramer, *supra* note 85; Raiser *supra* note 85.

94 Friedrich Kessler, 'The Contracts of Adhesion - Some Thoughts about Freedom of Contract Role of Compulsion in Economic Transactions' [1943] 43 Columbia Law Review 629 (631); Kramer, *supra* note 85, 184 et seq.; Raiser *supra* note 85, (3, 7).

95 Faure and Luth, *supra* note 88, 354.

ties[96] or consumer organisations[97]. While such a measure could also be viewed as too paternalistic,[98] such regulation can contribute to a reduction of transaction costs as it prevents too many individual proceedings against unfair terms in which individual consumers and the opponent businesses would have to invest resources. If businesses only need to fear individual court proceedings with *inter partes* effect it is easy for them to incorporate these transaction costs in the price for the offered product. In contrast administrative decisions can unfold *erga omnes* effect and thereby affect *all* businesses that use the respective unfair term. Respective sanctions against businesses that do not follow the guidelines also bear the potential for a preventative effect on the business concerned as well as competitors.[99] Thus, an administrative or alternative dispute resolution structure with *erga omnes* competencies outside the judicial system constitutes a more effective mean of consumer protection than the provision of individual legal proceedings.

These measures can, furthermore, have a positive impact on consumer confidence as consumers could rely on terms being fair rather than having to fear that they are detrimental to them. Collective enforcement, furthermore, oftentimes constitutes the most efficient mean to achieve justice with respect to possible damages claims regarding the use of unfair terms as large organisations and public authorities will have more resources and information at their disposal than the individual consumer.[100]

Furthermore, certain terms could be blacklisted, thus, declared inapplicable if those terms are in any case inacceptable to the consumer. However, it must be considered whether this approach leads to welfare restrictions for consumers who would otherwise read and re-negotiate such terms.[101] If such lists are accepted, they can serve as a guideline for businesses which can, thereby, save time in drafting their T&Cs. Regulation

---

96 Cf. Arthur Leff, 'Unconscionability and the Crowd-Consumers and the Common Law Tradition' [1970] 31 University of Pittsburgh Law Review 349 (357-358).

97 For a detailed economic analysis regarding enforcement of consumer law by consumer organisations, cf. Roger van den Bergh, Enforcement of consumer law by consumer associations. in Michael Faure and Frank Stephen (eds), *Essays in the Law and Economics of Regulation: In Honour of Anthony Ogus*, 279-305.

98 Cf. Anthony Ogus, *Costs and cautionary tales Economic insights for the law*, 250-252.

99 Cf. Dieter Hart, 'Allgemeine Geschäftsbedingungen und Justizsystem' [1971] 4 (3) Kritische Justiz 269 (277).

100 Cf. van den Bergh, *supra* note 97, 282 et seq.

101 Cf. Faure and Luth, *supra* note 88, 343.

should tackle the information imbalance as well as the ignorance of consumers, thus, providing for both duties regarding the concrete drafting of terms as well as collective term control.

The following work will mainly focus on the systematic implementation and enforcement of legislation on unfair terms in consumer contracts. This work assumes that an emphasis on collective and administrative measures constitutes a more effective mean to prevent consumers from suffering harm through unfair terms. Administrative bodies are often well-equipped to search for unfair terms and enter into a dialogue with their users to remove them from the market and, thus, benefit all consumers. Furthermore, an investigation by a public authority will oftentimes appear more convincing than by private individuals or organisations as it is attributed public character by the addressees and decisions can bear *erga omnes* effect. Collective proceedings are, furthermore, held to be more effective than individual proceedings because individuals are oftentimes deterred from initiating long and costly court proceedings. Collective proceedings, on the other hand, can help multiple consumers who – if represented by a public or private body – do not have to bear the individual procedural risks. It will be shown, however, that the EU parameters on effectiveness may deviate from this work's (see Chapter 9).

Chapter 3: Comparative Basis

This chapter lays out the comparative basis of the research. Each compared legal system will be portrayed including historic, economic and sociological factors. Please note that such sections cannot replace and in-depth analysis in each field. At the end of each section the comparability with the UK and the other respective compared systems will be evaluated to set out the basis for the comparative analysis.

A. *United Kingdom*

I. Society and Traditions

The following section shall briefly outline historic, economic and sociological factors that have shaped the UK and shall be considered later in the comparative analysis.

Historic Factors

The UK is a constitutional monarchy and one of the oldest Parliamentary democracies in the world. Historically the (modern) United Kingdom has mainly been shaped by continuity and its history as the leader of the British Empire. Politically the UK has developed gradually and continuously into a Parliamentary democracy and constitutional monarchy since the mid-17th century.[102] Unlike its European neighbours it has been spared from the turmoil resulting from the battles of extreme ideologies of the 19th century (such as communism and fascism) that led continental Europe into wars and destruction. Nevertheless, the UK has been part of (modern) European history,[103] especially as an Ally in the two World Wars and from 1973 to 2019 as a member of the EU. However, the UK's outlook has not been limited to the European continent. Once the largest empire in the world, the UK took the role of an imperial and colonial world power from the 17th century onward.[104] While the empire has now dissolved,

---

102 Cf. Peter Wende, *Grossbritannien 1500-2000*, 33 et seq.

103 Cf. ibid. 88 et seq.

104 Ibid. 94 et seq.

the UK keeps its worldwide outlook as part of (and with HM Queen Elizabeth II as leader of) the Commonwealth.

The continuity and world outlook are also reflected in the English law. The common law itself is a representation of continuity. As a world leader the UK 'exported' the common law system to various Commonwealth nations and, thereby, remains legally influential until today. The continuity is also reflected in the unwritten British constitution as the result of a gradual evolution toward Parliamentary democracy unlike the written continental constitutions which mainly resulted as the aftermath of conflicts and wars.

Economic Factors

The UK was one of the first countries to undergo the Industrial Revolution starting in the late 18th century. Throughout the 19th and until the mid-20th century the British economy continued to be shaped by the secondary sector.[105] The Industrial Revolution and mass production of goods not only shaped the economy but also brought with them an increase in wealth and consequently the growth of a consumer culture.[106] However, since the mid-20th century the secondary sector has undergone decline while the tertiary sector has seen a stark increase. Nowadays, the traditional secondary sector economic activities, such as coal mining and associated production activities, i.e. steel production, only comprised 17.93% of the UK's GDP while services made up for 70.56% in 2017.[107] While the Greater London area had always been a strong economic centre, the focus has shifted even more to the City and away from the industrially shaped North of England. Today, the largest contribution to the GDP comes from the services sector in based in London, especially international finance based in the City of London.[108] Thereby grows a dependence on international cooperation as the functioning of international financial services only works if cross-border access to foreign financial markets is ensured. Beside the economic growth resulting from the Industrial Revolution, the UK has traditionally had a strong merchant fleet. Especially in

105 Cf. ibid. 7 et seq.

106 Cf. John Benson, *The Rise of Consumer Society in Britain 1880-1980*, 11 et seq.

107 H. Plecher, 'United Kingdom: Distribution of gross domestic product (GDP) across economic sectors from 2007 to 2017' (*statista*, 9 August 2019) <https://www.statista.com/statistics/270372/distribution-of-gdp-across-economic-sectors-in-the-united-kingdom/> accessed 9 November 2019.

108 For a depiction of this development, cf. Stephan Schieren, *Großbritannien: Eine Einführung in das politische System*, 212-213.

light of the rise of the global British Empire, the British merchant fleet became one of the largest in the world by the 19th century.[109] Still, the British economy is export dependent[110] with the EU as its main trading partner (48% of all exports)[111] which makes functioning international trade relations all the more important.

The rise of the service economy has also brought about large income disparities between rural and urban regions. According to OECD data the UK is the country with the sixth largest disparities in this regard.[112] Generally, the UK is one of the countries with the highest Gini coefficients among OECD countries (0.351).[113] This means that while in the UK the GDP per capita (USD 46,010) may be above average it is neither distributed equally throughout the regions nor society.

Sociological Factors

Through immigration, especially from other Commonwealth countries, the UK has turned into a diverse society.[114] Especially London, draws an international community with its international service-oriented economy. Nevertheless, UK society also remains firmly divided along class lines[115] partly because, unlike in many continental countries such as Germany, in the past centuries no (civil) wars or (ideologically motivated) revolutions have caused a shift of capital. Instead, some British have been able to accumulate wealth and hand it down to future generations while not a lot of redistribution took place. Thereby, social class divides have been mani-

---

109 Wende, *supra* note 102, 10 et seq.

110 Bruno Urmersbach, 'Die 20 größten Exportländer weltweit im Jahr 2018 (in Milliarden US-Dollar)' (*statista*, 21 May 2019) <https://de.statista.com/statistik/daten/studie/37013/umfrage/ranking-der-top-20-exportlaender-weltweit/> accessed 9 November 2019.

111 Office for National Statistics, 'Who does the UK trade with?' (*Office for National Statistics*, 3 January 2019) <https://www.ons.gov.uk/businessindustryandtrade/internationaltrade/articles/whodoestheuktradewith/2017-02-21> accessed 9 November 2019.

112 OECD, Regions and Cities at a Glance – United Kingdom (5 March 2019). See also Schieren, *supra* note 108, 213.

113 OECD, 'OECD Income Distribution Database (IDD): Gini, poverty, income, Methods and Concepts' (*OECD*) <http://www.oecd.org/social/income-distribution-database.htm> accessed 9 November 2019.

114 On the history of immigration to the UK since 1850, cf. Colin Holmes, The impact of immigration on British Society 1870-1980. in Theo Barker and Michael Drake (eds), *Population and Society in Britain 1850-1980*, 172 et seq.

115 For an overview of the evolution of the British class system, cf. Wende, *supra* note 102, 17 et seq.

fested.[116] Thus, British society is caught in a constant struggle between a relatively manifested class system and the challenges to offer socially elevating opportunities to those who have not benefited from the centuries-long accumulation of wealth as well as immigrants who join the system. Nevertheless, as of 2017 the interpersonal trust rate (Annex 1, Figure 2) as well as trust in the police and the government (Annex 1, Figures 3 and 4) remain above OECD average. Especially, the interpersonal trust rate indicates that despite the possible tensions along different societal lines, the UK remains an open society. The Brexit vote in 2016, however, has likely changed the situation, creating yet another and most divisive societal line in addition to, *inter alia*, divisions along regions, classes and economic well-being.

Conclusion: Relationship with Europe and Consequences for the Legal System

The common law is both a result of and dependent on the continuous historical and political development of the UK. In relation to Europe, the UK has not been involved in the integration process as much as other continental European nations, such as France and Germany. This may provide one explanation for the departure of the UK from the EU. The UK does not define its role regionally but under the impression as the former leader of the British Empire. The UK image of sovereignty may, thus, be characterised as a 'freedom to' perform certain (expansionist) actions. Economically, the UK and especially London are a global market place especially with respect to global finance. The economy is, thus, dependent on providing a legal framework that attracts global economic players and investors. Legal rules are not attributed distributive character. Nevertheless, in light of several societal division lines, the law must also address several social group interests. The law's task is to strike a fine balance between concurring economic and sociological interests while not neglecting the continuous nature of the English common law.

II. Sources of (Private) Law

As in most legal systems, English private law derives from different sources. For the purposes of this work, the focus rests on common law and equity, statutory provisions and European Law.

---

116 Ibid. 21.

1. Common Law and Equity

The main source of private and especially contract law rests with common law. There exists no comprehensive legislative code governing contract law in general but rules are developed on a case-by-case basis. Such development *inter alia* benefited from the continuous historic development in the UK.[117] Based on traditions and experience it uniquely shaped society and the way of life in common law countries.[118]

Under traditional common law, contracts are not sorted into different categories but are, as a general rule, all subjected to the same regime of control and enforcement. They can, however, be classified according to certain features, such as the parties, the form or their effect.[119] Beside common law, the law of equity was developed as a corrective mainly governing relationships involving trusts and fiduciary duties. Equity's influence on the common law has been fairly limited.[120] Its impact can be exemplified in the doctrine of undue influence[121] or the doctrine of unconscionability which are described in more detail below.[122] However, case-law shows that equitable intervention in common law is restricted.[123] The two main guiding principles of English contract law are *freedom of contract* and the *binding force of contracts*, thereby, following a vision of contract law as an expression of the parties' free wills.[124]

Under the principle of *freedom of contract*, it is assumed that the law's role is restricted to enforcement of the parties' agreement. The parties' wills are expressed in the agreement and judicial interference by way of normative interpretation is undesirable.[125] While this position was especially predominant in the 19th century, it remains relevant today even though judicial interpretation has become more interventionist when it

---

117 Cf. also Franz Wieacker, *Privatrechtsgeschichte der Neuzeit unter Berücksichtigung der deutschen Entwicklung*, 497 referring to an uninterrupted development since the Norman conquest.

118 Ibid. 498.

119 Simon Whittaker, Chapter 1: Introductory. in Hugh Beale (ed), *Chitty on Contracts* (Volume 1), recitals 1-102 et seq.

120 Ibid., recital 1-003.

121 Hugh Beale, Chapter 8: Duress and Undue Influence. in Hugh Beale (ed), *Chitty on Contracts* (Volume 1), recitals 8-058-059.

122 Ibid. recital 8-132.

123 Ibid.

124 Whittaker, *supra* note 119, recital 1-030.

125 Ibid. recital 1-031.

comes to contractual interpretation.[126] Especially with respect to commercial contracts, freedom of contract remains the prevalent doctrine,[127] as it was well summarised extra-judicially by Goff LJ (as he then was):

> We are there to help businessmen, not to hinder them; we are there to give effect to their transactions, not to frustrate them; we are there to oil the wheels of commerce, not to put a spanner in the works, or even grit in the oil.[128]

The principle of *binding force of contracts* complements the principle of contractual freedom in order to safeguard the expectations of the party.[129] Traditionally, common law does not focus on the enforcement of primary obligations under an agreement but entitles to damages in case of a breach of obligations.[130] This approach, however, has been subject to modifications especially due to the influence of equity and (European) statutory regulation.[131] Under both principles the courts still show reluctance to hold a contract invalid due to unfairness or inequality of bargaining power.[132]

All these findings show that the English common law is generally founded on a liberal theory of contract which does not allow for much equitable interference. In relation to the description of British Society (see above) the findings also tell us that the common law of contract does not aim to fulfil distributive social functions. In light of Goff LJ's (as he then was) extra-judicial statement, the common law of contract rather serves the well-functioning of economic transactions. The analysis in the following

126 Ibid. recitals 1-036 et seq.

127 Ibid. recital 1-032, with reference to *Homburg Houtimport BV v Agrosin Private Ltd (The Starsin)* [2003] 2 All ER 785 at [57] per Lord Bingham ('Commercial men must be given the utmost liberty of contracting.'); *Transocean Drilling UK Ltd v Providence Resources plc (The GSF Arctic III)* [2016] EWCA Civ 372 at [28] per Moore-Bick LJ ('The principle of freedom of contract, which is still fundamental to our commercial law, requires the court to respect and give effect to the parties' agreement.').

128 Robert Goff, 'Commercial Contracts and the Commercial Court' [1984] Lloyd's Maritime and Commercial Law Quarterly 382 (391).

129 Whittaker, *supra* note 119, recital 1-041.

130 Ibid.; Patrick S. Atiyah, *An Introduction to the Law of Contract*, 37; Oliver Wendell Holmes, *The Common Law*, 300.

131 Beale, *supra* note 121, recital 8-132 et seq.; Whittaker, *supra* note 120, recitals 1-041, 1-043.

132 Ibid. recitals 1-032, 1-042, cf. also *National Westminster Bank plc v Morgan* [1985] 1 All ER 821 at 830 per Lord Scarman arguing against Lord Denning MR in *Lloyds Bank Ltd v Bundy* [1974] 3 All ER 757 at 765.

sections will reveal whether and how far principles of common law have been influenced by European developments.

2. Statutes

Parliamentary statutes provide another source of contract law.[133] While the common law had served as the predominant source of contract law for the most of English legal history, statutory provisions have gained more significance in the past two centuries, thereby diminishing the importance of 'pure' common law with regard to general contract law and especially with respect to specific contracts.[134] The common law still dominates the rules governing contracts in general. However, statutory provisions tend to regulate the contractual context. In most situations one is, thus, confronted with an interplay of common law rules and statutory provisions.[135] Statutes typically address a particular issue instead of laying down general principles underlying a certain area of the law.[136] The provisions are drafted in a detailed manner to address problems as precisely as possible.[137] Statutes, furthermore, include a range of definitions to allow for a uniform application of such terms.[138] Furthermore, the Interpretation Acts 1850, 1889 and 1978 provide further guidance on the meaning of certain statutory provisions.

Since the 18th century the starting point for legal interpretation has been the literal meaning of a provision to explore the intention of the legislator.[139] Since then different emphases could be noted: while until the 1830s courts strongly considered flexible notions of justice,[140] interpretation shifted to a more restricted and literal approach from the 1830s until the early 20th century[141]. Similarly, with respect to contract law rules courts did not intervene based on notions of equity or justice but stuck with the

133 *The Prince's Case* (1606) 8 Co Rep 13b, 77 ER 496.
134 Whittaker, *supra* note 120, recitals 1-005-008.
135 Ibid. recital 1-004.
136 JA Clarence Smith, 'Legislative Drafting: English and Continental' [1980] 1 (1) Statute Law Review 14 (15).
137 Ibid. (21 et seq.).
138 Francis Bennion, *Understanding Common Law Legislation*, 58-62.
139 Bennion, ibid., 35-36; Stefan Vogenauer, *Die Auslegung von Gesetzen in England und auf dem Kontinent (Band II)*, 669 et seq., 781, 965.
140 Vogenauer, ibid., 685 et seq., 692 et seq., 777, 779.
141 Ibid. 795 et seq., 871 et seq., 885 et seq., 953 et seq.

literal interpretation of contracts.[142] Since the second half of the 20th century a purpose-oriented approach prevails.[143] The interpretation of the statute's wording is thereby accompanied by a purposive construction, meaning that the decision-making body must consider the goals pursued by Parliament taking into account principles deriving from legal and public policy including obligations under international treaties.[144] Courts today similarly show more willingness to intervene in contractual relationships based on notions of equity and justice.[145]

3. European Law

Until the exit from the European Union was bound by EU Primary and Secondary Legislation. Under Section 2 European Communities Act 1972 the UK was obliged to implement obligations arising under the European Treaties.[146] While EU Regulations have had direct effect under English Law, EU Directives had to be implemented into English law by way of a national legislative Act. European law has, thereby, had profound effect on the areas of contract law which concern European cooperation, especially in the areas of competition and consumer law.[147] In the past the UK's approach to EU Directives' implementation underwent change. They were first known to pursue an elaborative approach, meaning that EU legislation was evaluated and implemented according to legal tradition. This approach changed, however, to a 'copy-out' approach pursued by other Member States under which EU legislation is transposed without much national legislative intervention and oftentimes by means of delegated le-

142 Ibid. 961-962.

143 Ibid. 963 et seq., 1235-1236.

144 Bennion, *supra* note 138, 37-39, 89-95.

145 Vogenauer, *supra* note 139, 1248 et seq.

146 'The European Communities Act 1972, as it has effect in domestic law or the law of a relevant territory immediately before [the 31 January 2020], continues to have effect in domestic law or the law of the relevant territory on and after [the 31 January 2020 … until the 31 December 2020]', cf. Section 1A European Union (Withdrawal) Act 2018, Section 39 European Union (Withdrawal) Act 2020.

147 Cf. Whittaker, *supra* note 120, recitals 1-011-013. In addition, the development of legislation on fundamental rights, i.e. the Charter of Fundamental Rights of the European Union, have influenced English contract law. These developments are, however, not covered by this dissertation.

gislation instead of primary Parliamentary legislation.[148] Accordingly, EU legislative acts have mostly not been incorporated into existing statutes but passed as separate legislative instruments containing the same or very similar sounding provisions as the Directive they stem from.[149] This approach has ensured that EU legislation is transposed into English law as accurately and completely as possible.[150]

B. Germany

I. German Society

The following sections provide an overview of societal factors and structures underlying the German legal system. An understanding of these factors and structures is necessary in order to conduct a comparative analysis. German society is shaped by unique and reciprocal historic, economic and social factors that have to be considered to gain a full understanding of the law, its background and application. The unique combination of these factors provides a guideline as to how societal factors have influenced legal developments in Germany.

Historic Factors
The modern German unified state goes back to the founding of the German Empire (*Deutsches Kaiserreich*) in 1871. The German Empire was dominated by conservative forces with only limited powers of Parliament and civil rights in contrast to broad powers of aristocracy and ultimately on behalf of the *Kaiser*.[151] The first democratic German state was only founded in 1918 (the *Weimarer Republik*).[152] However, even though the

148 Jean-Pierre Duprat and Helen Xanthaki, Legislative Drafting Techniques/ Formal Legistics. in Ulrich Karpen and others (eds), *Legislation in Europe: A Comprehensive Guide for Scholars and Practitioners*, 123; Bernhard Steunenberg and Wim Voermans, *The transposition of EC directives: a comparative study of instruments, techniques and processes in six member states*, 36-37.

149 Steunenberg and Voermans, ibid.

150 Ibid.

151 Cf. Thomas Nipperdey, *Deutsche Geschichte 1866-1918: Machtstaat vor der Demokratie (Band II)*, 85 et seq.

152 Thomas Nipperdey, *Deutsche Geschichte 1800-1866: Bürgerwelt und starker Staat*, 314 et seq. Regarding the 'late German democracy', cf. Rainer Geißler, *Die Sozialstruktur Deutschlands*, 26.

new constitutional order appeared promising, for example by including civil and basic rights as well as the women's right to vote, it turned out fragile in light of economic and political crises in the 1920s and early 1930s.[153] The constitutional deficiencies of the Weimar Constitution as well as these crises eventually led to the catastrophic rise of national socialism in Germany. The unimaginable atrocities imposed by the regime on minorities and dissenters only ended with the end of World War II and liberation by the Allied Forces in 1945, known as *Stunde Null* ('zero hour') in an almost completely destroyed Germany.

In 1949, the Federal Republic of Germany (West Germany) and, shortly afterwards, the socialist German Democratic Republic (East Germany) were founded. West Germany was given a modern constitution, the Basic Law for the Federal Republic of Germany (*Grundgesetz für die Bundesrepublik Deutschland*, hereinafter "GG"), based on fundamental rights, most importantly human dignity (Art. 1 GG) and democratic values which are guaranteed under an eternity clause (Art. 79 Section 3 GG). The 'two Germanies' were only reunited and became sovereign in 1990 under the Two Plus Four Agreement.

West Germany's first chancellor, Konrad Adenauer, immediately sought an integration with the Western Allies. His efforts were manifested in the Petersberg Agreement under which West Germany committed to 'pursue liberty, tolerance and humanity and to eradicate all traces of Nazism from German life and institutions and to halt any revival of totalitarian efforts' and in return was allowed to resume diplomatic contacts and signed the Marshall agreement with the United States of America which fuelled economic growth in the 1950s and 1960s in Germany. Under Adenauer's reign West Germany sought to establish firm bonds with the West (*Westbindung*), for example by becoming a founding member of the European Coal and Steel Community, the predecessor of the EU (1951), a NATO member (1955) and looking for reconciliation with France (Élysée Treaty on French-German cooperation, 1963).[154] The European and Western integration was received positively by the population and led to economic post-war prosperity in West Germany.[155] Thus, post-war (West) Germany

---

153 For a detailed overview, cf. Eberhard Kolb and Dirk Schumann, *Die Weimarer Republik (Oldenbourg Grundriss der Geschichte, Band 16)*.

154 Cf. Rudolf Morsey, *Die Bundesrepublik Deutschland: Entstehung und Entwicklung bis 1969 (Oldenbourg Grundriss der Geschichte, Band 19)*, 67-69.

155 Ibid. 28.

found renewed independence only through integration and cooperation and today is firmly integrated in Europe (and the Western world).[156]

Economic Factors

In the course of the 19th century German society not only underwent an intellectual and political but also an industrial revolution. Starting with the coal and steel production and later, among others, a growing metal processing and chemical sector, the German industry grew rapidly from the mid-19th century onward.[157] As a response to social as well as economic challenges a number of legislative instruments were introduced, including laws on health insurance as well as the German Civil Code (*Bürgerliches Gesetzbuch*, hereinafter "BGB").[158] While in the 1870s the German Empire's industrialised economy was much less developed than the British, it overtook Great Britain in all relevant sectors by the end of the 19th century.[159] Until today the industry and manufacturing sector still produces a relatively large share of the German GDP (25.8%). The largest share is generated by the services sector (68.2%).[160] While the most prominent German manufacturers are large global group companies, small and medium sized oftentimes family owned businesses (*Mittelstand*) form the backbone of the German economy.[161]

156 Regarding a more detailed account of German history 1969-1990, cf. Andreas Rödder, *Die Bundesrepublik Deutschland 1969-1990 (Oldenbourg Grundriss der Geschichte, Band 19A)*.

157 Thomas Nipperdey, *Deutsche Geschichte 1866-1918: Arbeitswelt und Bürgergeist (Band I)*, 226 et seq.

158 For an overview, cf. Werner Abelshauser, *Deutsche Wirtschaftsgeschichte: Von 1945 bis zur Gegenwart*, 31.

159 Nipperdey, *supra* note 157, 278-279. Cf. also Gregor Schöllgen and Friedrich Kiessling, *Das Zeitalter des Imperialismus (Oldenbourg Grundriss der Geschichte, Band 15)*, 26 et seq.

160 Cf. Statista, 'Anteil der Wirtschaftssektoren an der Bruttowertschöpfung in Deutschland im Jahr 2018' (*Statista*, 20 August 2019) <https://de.statista.com/statistik/daten/studie/36846/umfrage/anteil-der-wirtschaftsbereiche-am-bruttoinlandsprodukt/> accessed 6 October 2019.

161 In 2017 99.5% of all businesses were small or medium sized generating EUR 2.331 billion and employing 17.49 million people with taxable income subject to social security, cf. Institut für Mittelstandsforschung Bonn, 'Unternehmensbestand' (*Institut für Mittelstandsforschung Bonn*) <https://www.ifm-bonn.org/statistiken/unternehmensbestand/#accordion=0&tab=0> accessed 6 October 2019.

The German economy is not based on the ideals of a free but rather a *social* market economy.[162] State intervention in light of social welfare policies ensures a balance of social interests. With a GDP of USD 53,749,- per capita Germany ranges 12th compared to other OECD countries (see Annex 1, Figure 1) with a lower-average Gini coefficient (0.294) as of 2016[163]. Beside the principles of the social market model, Germany's economic system can also be characterised as a corporative market economy. This means that businesses benefit from a diverse and close-knit network of economic institutions that enable economic actors to cooperate effectively.[164] The corporative and cooperative market structure has an 'autonomous and self-administrative status' with 'traditionally high moral expectations regarding business behaviour'.[165] Rather than an invisible hand as *Smith* envisaged it, German business is, thus, guided by a clearly 'visible hand', for example by Art. 14 GG which does not only provide for property rights but also that '[property] entails obligations [and its] use shall also serve the public good'.[166]

The cooperative network in combination with a highly skilled workforce enables German business to be world leaders in highly specified and high-quality product markets.[167] The German economy is heavily export dependent ranking third in the world only behind China and the USA with respect to the export volume in 2018.[168] Among the top 20 trading partners of Germany only three are not located in Europe.[169] This makes close ties with Germany's European partners all the more important.

Nevertheless, the German economy has undergone several crises in the 20th century. In light of the (traumatising) economic developments of the first half of the 20th century,[170] German private households approach economic matters conservatively: sceptical towards stock investments[171] and

---

162 For the beginnings, cf. Abelshauser, *supra* note 158, 186 et seq.

163 OECD, *supra* note 113.

164 Abelshauser, *supra* note 158, 481 et seq.

165 Ibid. 482.

166 Ibid. 453.

167 Ibid. 485.

168 Urmersbach, *supra* note 110.

169 Statistisches Bundesamt, Außenhandel: Rangfolge der Handelspartner im Außenhandel der Bundesrepublik Deutschland (2018) 2.

170 Such as the inflation crisis (1919), the Great Depression (1929) and total destruction in World War II (1945).

171 Cf. Abelshauser, *supra* note 158, 507.

relying on savings accounts.[172] The reunification of Germany also constitutes a challenge for German society (see below) as well as the economy. Even 30 years after Germany's reunification productivity levels of the East German states have not reached the levels of the West German states.[173] Beside the complicated division between East and West Germany there also exists a notable divide between the productivity levels of North and South Germany.[174] Such divides are also reflected in Germany's seventh rank among OECD countries with respect to regional disparities.[175]

It can be summarised that Germany is a strong global economic player which heavily relies on exports by predominantly small and medium sized businesses producing specialised high-quality products. Furthermore, while Germany is a market economy it is also highly regulated both by businesses themselves (corporative market economy) and the state (social market economy). Meanwhile, German economic strength is not found equally throughout Germany but along East-West and North-South division lines.

Sociological Factors

While German political unification took place 30 years ago, social divisions continue to exist. Beside differences in wealth, division lines can also be drawn along North-South and especially East-West lines. While the North-South division can be explained mainly in economic terms (see above), the East-West divide is more complex as it goes back to historical, cultural and sociological developments of the two German states which ex-

172 Cf. also specifically on the development (consumer) lending in Germany, Rebecca Belvederesi-Kochs, Moral or Modern Marketing? *Sparkassen* and Consumer Credit in West Germany. in Jan Logemann (ed), *The Development of Consumer Credit in Global Perspective: Business, Regulation and Culture*, 41-62; Jan Logemann, 'Americanization through Credit? Consumer Credit in Germany, 1860s–1960s' [2011] 85 (3) Business History Review 529-550; Silke Meyer, Economic Agents and the Culture of Debt. in Jan Logemann (ed), *The Development of Consumer Credit in Global Perspective: Business, Regulation and Culture*, 223-241 (who also points recent changes toward taking out more credit, thus, causing greater indebtedness, see also below).

173 Cf. Beauftragte der Bundesregierung für die neuen Bundesländer, Jahresbericht der Bundesregierung zum Stand der Deutschen Einheit 2019 (August 2019), pages 20-21.

174 Ibid. page 21 (only taking into account the West German states). See also Karl Friedrich Bohler and Bruno Hildenbrand, Nord-Süd. in Stephan Lessenich and Frank Nullmeier (eds), *Deutschland - eine gespaltene Gesellschaft*, 234-255.

175 OECD, Regions and Cities at a glance – Germany (5 March 2019).

isted until 1990.[176] Beside the geographical division lines, Germany is a nation comprised of a heterogenous society.[177] One factor for such heterogeneity and pluralism is Germany's sheer population size which as of the 1 June 2019, amounted to 83.073 million and, thereby, makes Germany the largest country in the EU population-wise.[178] In addition, the pluralism, *inter alia*, derives from the historical influence of several ideological movements as well as, nowadays, increasing migration movements toward Germany from within and outside the EU.[179] Meanwhile, the interpersonal trust rates are low ranking at the end of a scale of OECD countries (Annex 1, Figure 2) while trust rates are high with respect to the government (Annex 1, Figure 4) and above OECD average with respect to the police (Annex 1, Figure 3). The low interpersonal trust rates can be explained with the heterogeneity of German society. In this light, inclusive government and administrative policies and as well as an inclusive function of the law become all the more relevant to enable peaceful and cooperative coexistence in society. The higher trust rates in the government and police constitute positive indicators in this regard.

Conclusion: Relationship with Europe and Consequences for Legal System

It can be summarised that both historically and economically European cooperation is important for Germany. Only by way of the ever-closer European integration process was Germany able to rebuild its reputation after 1945. Therefore, the German understanding of sovereignty can nowadays be understood as a 'freedom with' its (European) neighbours. This also means that it can be expected that Germany implements European legislation loyally. Sociologically, Germany can be characterised as a heterogenous, pluralist and sometimes divided society. In this regard, government actions and consequently legal norms must be inclusive to accommodate various views. Germany follows the economic model of a social market

176 Michael Gehler, *Deutschland: Von der Teilung bis zur Einigung 1945 bis heute*, 477 et seq.; Geißler, *supra* note 152, 455 et seq.; Karl-Siegbert Rehberg, Ost-West. in Stephan Lessenich and Frank Nullmeier (eds), *Deutschland - eine gespaltene Gesellschaft*, 209-233.

177 Cf. for the pluralisation of German society, Geißler, ibid. 121 et seq.

178 Statistisches Bundesamt, 'Bevölkerungsstand' (Destatis - Statistisches Bundesamt, 2 October 2019) <https://www.destatis.de/DE/Themen/Gesellschaft-Umwelt/Bevoelkerung/Bevoelkerungsstand/Tabellen/zensus-geschlecht-staatsangehoerigkeit-2019.html;jsessionid=27F71E6A61A501E0C6DDD1C7E43CF22D.internet741> accessed 14 October 2019.

179 Geißler, *supra* note 152, 267 et seq.

economy. This approach entails distributive measures and a regulatory economic approach. Thus, legal norms can be instrumentalised as distributive tools. At the same time, legal rules must be balanced to retain the position as a global economic leader. Beside the sociological and economic considerations, the values embodied in Germany's constitution as the countervision to national-socialist ideology underlies all legal principles.

II. German Legal Institutions, Drafting and Method

The following section provides a general introduction to German legal institutions, drafting and interpretation of norms.

1. Institutions and Drafting Method

Germany is a federal democratic republic. It is a confederation (*Bund*) consisting of 16 states (*Länder*). Beside the federal Parliament (*Bundestag*) and the federal government (*Bundesregierung*), there exist 16 state Parliaments (*Landtage*) and state governments (*Landesregierungen*). Laws are made both on the federal level and on the state level. However, most areas are legislated on the federal level (Arts. 73, 74 GG). The areas of private law covered by this dissertation belong to the federal legislating competence. Nevertheless, federal laws have to be passed by the federal Parliament as well as the representative chamber of the states (*Bundesrat*). The German court system is divided into five branches: ordinary courts (responsible for private and criminal matters), administrative courts, labour courts, social courts and finance courts. While the lower courts are administered on the state level, there also exists one federal court for each branch (Art. 95 Section 1 GG). Furthermore, there exists a Federal Constitutional Court (*Bundesverfassungsgericht*) according to Arts. 92 to 94 GG.

Germany is a traditional codified civil law country.[180] The civil law tradition mainly goes back to Roman legal principles.[181] Continental civil law jurisdictions typically adapted principles of the *corpus iuris civilis* which were further developed by commentators and experts.[182] In line with this tradition, writing by legal academia is still an important factor that is frequently considered by German courts today. Unlike the common law which is founded on traditions, practical reasoning and continuity, civil law is founded on general ideas and principles.[183] It is thereby more abstract than the common law and had less impact on the development of public life and practical morals in respective societies.[184]

At the core of German law lie five principle legal codes: a civil law code (BGB), a criminal code (*Strafgesetzbuch*), a civil procedure code (*Zivilprozessordnung*, hereinafter "D-ZPO"), a criminal procedure code (*Strafprozessordnung*) and a commercial code (*Handelsgesetzbuch*). Beside these basic general codes there exist further specific laws which are drafted in a more detailed manner. Under German law, the courts are only meant to apply but not to create the law.[185] Accordingly, there also does not exist a doctrine of precedence and *stare decisis* under German law.[186] Nevertheless, a court will consider previous – especially federal – case-law to ensure legal certainty and consistency.[187]

For the purposes of this dissertation, the most important legal code to consider is the BGB. After the modernisation of the law of obligations (*Schuldrechtsmodernisierung*) in 2002 it now contains provisions on both the regulation of unfair terms (in consumer contracts) and consumer credit.

180 As opposed to the uncodified i.e. Scottish civil law system with similar roots in Roman law, cf. for a detailed account of the position of Scottish law between the common law and civil law doctrines, Thomas Mackay Cooper, 'The Common and the Civil Law A Scot's View' [1950] 63 (3) Harvard Law Review 468-475. Cf. also Vogenauer, *supra* note 139, 665.

181 For an overview of the influence of Roman law on German law, cf. Ulrich Eisenhardt, *Deutsche Rechtsgeschichte*, recitals 173 et seq.; Wieacker, *supra* note 117, 497. For a general overview of differences between common and civil law, cf. Birke Häcker, 'Das englische Common Law – Eine Einführung' [2014] JuS 872-876.

182 Eisenhardt, ibid., recitals 188 et seq., 210 et seq.; Wieacker, ibid., 500.

183 Wieacker, *supra* note 117, 498.

184 Ibid. 500.

185 For an overview of judge-made law in Germany, cf. Heinrich Honsell, Einleitung. in Herbert Roth (ed), *Staudinger BGB*, recitals 209 et seq.

186 Cf. ibid. recitals 226 et seq.

187 Cf. ibid. recital 229.

The BGB was introduced in 1900. At the time its main purpose was the unification of German private laws.[188] The BGB is mainly founded on liberal ideas and at the time did not concern distributive justice.[189] Instead, the BGB serves as a rather technical tool to ensure the functioning of legal dealings (*Rechtsverkehr*). The BGB is intentionally drafted in an abstract and technical manner by jurists for jurists.[190] The BGB is divided into five parts and based on the principles of freedom of contract including the principle to conclude (*Abschlussfreiheit*) and design (*Gestaltungsfreiheit*) contracts as well as making a will freely (*Testierfreiheit*), the principle of property including possession (*Besitz*) and ownership (*Eigentum*) and the principle of abstraction (*Abstraktionsprinzip*) which distinguishes between the obligation (*Verpflichtungsgeschäft*) and the transfer of rights (*Verfügungsgeschäft*).

While contract law in the BGB mainly follows the principle of freedom of contract, it is also founded on the principle of good faith (*Treu und Glauben*) pursuant to §§ 157 and 242 BGB.[191] Good faith comprises various general principles underlying legal dealings including socio-ethical principles. General clauses such as § 138 BGB and § 242 BGB mainly serve to allow the judge to consider all the circumstances of the case without being limited to the technical norms of the BGB.[192] As they are formulated in an abstract manner and it is nearly impossible to subsume concrete technical features under which a jurist could subsume specific cases, they are of subsidiary and exceptional character and do not normally arise as claims in front of the courts. As a general principle § 242 BGB underlies all private law and – as will be shown below – can be used by judges to develop new legal instruments.[193]

188 Ibid. recital 19.

189 Cf. Otto von Gierke who criticised the lack of 'socialist oil' in the draft of the BGB, Otto von Gierke, *Die soziale Aufgabe des Privatrechts*, 13; Honsell, ibid., recital 65. It is questionable whether modern consumer law constitutes such a drop of 'socialist oil', cf. Hans-W. Micklitz, 'Do Consumers and Businesses Need a New Architecture of Consumer Law? A Thought Provoking Impulse' [2013] 32 (1) Yearbook of European Law 266 (282).

190 Honsell, ibid., recital 68.

191 Ibid. recitals 70 et seq.

192 Ibid. recital 71.

193 Cf. Wieacker, *supra* note 117, 527.

2. Interpretation of Norms

The interpretation of norms is based on the canones developed by *Carl Friedrich von Savigny*. The starting point is the grammatical and logical interpretation, meaning the wording and phrasing of the norm.[194] As a second step the historical element must be considered, meaning the intention of the legislator at the time of the introduction of the norm.[195] The third step demands a systematic interpretation, meaning that the norm must be interpreted taking into account the surrounding norms and its systematic standing within the code.[196] Lastly, the reason behind the norm (*ratio legis*) must be considered under a teleological interpretation of the norm.[197]

Beside these traditional principles of interpretation, more modern principles have emerged in the 20th century. Norms must, furthermore, be interpreted in accordance with the constitution (*verfassungskonforme Auslegung*), European law (*europarechtskonforme Auslegung*) and with regard to international law (*völkerrechtsfreundliche Auslegung*, see Art. 25 GG). In addition, norms deriving from European law must be interpreted in accordance with European principles to ensure uniform application.[198] With respect to the interpretation in accordance with the constitution the German Federal Constitutional Court held in the *Lüth* decision that private law norms must be interpreted in light of the constitution and the basic rights contained therein.[199] In this regard, the BGB's general clauses (such as § 242 BGB) open the way for an interpretation of private law in light of constitutional values.[200]

---

194 Carl Friedrich von Savigny, *System des heutigen Römischen Rechts (Band 1)*, 213-214.

195 Ibid. 214.

196 Ibid.

197 Ibid. 216-217.

198 Carsten Herresthal, 'Die richtlinienkonforme und die verfassungskonforme Auslegung im Privatrecht' [2014] JuS 289 (290 et seq.); Franz Jürgen Säcker, Einleitung BGB. in Franz Jürgen Säcker and others (eds), *Münchener Kommentar zum Bürgerlichen Gesetzbuch (2018)*, recitals 146 et seq.

199 German Federal Constitutional Court, order of the court on the 15 January 1958 (Lüth), reference number: 1 BvR 400/51, BVerfGE 7, 198 at [32].

200 Ibid. at [27]. For further details on interpretation in accordance with the constitution, cf. Herresthal, *supra* note 198, (295 et seq.).

3. Access to Justice and Alternative Dispute Resolution

In Germany disputes are usually settled by way of court procedure (see §§ 253 et seq. D-ZPO). However, there also exist some alternate means of dispute resolution. According to § 278 D-ZPO the judge shall at any point in the proceedings consider an 'amicable solution' to the dispute (Section 1). Thus, all court hearings shall be preceded by conciliation hearings (Section 2). Thereby, the court offers the parties the opportunity of a settlement at the court. Furthermore, the court may suggest a 'mediation or other alternative conflict resolution procedures' to the parties (§ 278a D-ZPO).

Beside these means provided by the German Code of Civil Procedure there also exist arbitration bodies (*Schlichtungsstellen*). These arbitration bodies include a general arbitration body for consumers (i.e. *Allgemeine Verbraucherschlichtungsstelle des Zentrums für Schlichtung* or *Außergerichtliche Streitbeilegungsstelle für Verbraucher und Unternehmer*) as well as sector specific ones such as the ombudsman for private banks or the arbitration body for energy (*Schlichtungsstelle Energie*).[201] Unless the complaint is clearly abusive the proceedings are free of charge for consumers. Only specific consumer arbitration bodies (*Verbraucherschlichtungsstellen*) are obliged to publish an annual activity report according to § 34 Section 1 of the Law on Alternative Dispute Resolution in Consumer Matters (*Gesetz über die alternative Streitbeilegung in Verbrauchersachen*, hereinafter "VSBG").

III. Comparability

In the next step, it must be evaluated whether the societal conditions and connected legal framework and traditions of the UK and Germany are comparable.

With respect to the relationship with Europe, Germany appears to be more favourable to European integration than the UK.

Regarding the historic factors, it must be noted that UK and German modern history differ considerably. While the UK is marked by relatively continuous developments, the modern unified German state only emerged in the 19th century. Shaken by wars and crises it can be said that German history has been discontinuous. These developments are also reflected in the continuous common law tradition and the BGB which was introduced

201 For a full list, cf. Bundesamt für Justiz, Liste der Verbraucherschlichtungsstellen (as of 26 March 2021).

as a unifying factor. Such unification appears to have been achieved easier through a rather technical and abstract framework. While being based on the same liberal notion of freedom of contract, unlike the common law of contract, the BGB law of contract is based on the principle of good faith rather than being subject to occasional equitable intervention. Nevertheless, both private legal systems acknowledge notions of fairness in private law.

As to the economic factors, the approaches of the UK and Germany differ. While the UK is marked by an internationalised economy and liberal approach, Germany pursues the social market economy model which allows for more intervention. Nevertheless, Germany must also balance economic interests to remain a strong global economic player. While the inequality factor is considerably higher in the UK, both countries show large regional disparities which also contribute to social divisions. Both countries have heterogenous and pluralist societies. Sociologically, the divisions have differing roots in both countries. Nevertheless, both societies are tasked with balancing the interests of several social groups to manage and overcome divisions. In this light, the laws of both countries should, *inter alia*, be based on inclusive considerations. The rather interventionist German economic approach may provide a more fertile ground for such policies than the liberal UK approach.

It can, thus, be summarised that there exist notable differences regarding all factors between the UK and Germany. Nevertheless, sociologically both countries face the similar task of managing and overcoming societal divisions. Thus, the laws must be drafted inclusively. Furthermore, both countries have undergone the Industrial Revolution in the 19th century and face similar challenges as largely post-industrial societies. The wealth remains at a relatively stable high level which enables individual consumption and makes consumer law regulation necessary. It must be noted, however, that the legal approaches, i.e. with respect to good faith, may differ.

C. *Norway*

I. Norwegian Society

The following sections provide an overview of societal factors and structures underlying the Norwegian legal system. An understanding of these factors and structures is necessary in order to analyse and explain Norwegian legal institutions and developments especially in comparison with other legal systems. Norwegian society is shaped by unique and reciprocal historic, economic and social factors that have to be considered to gain a full understanding of the law, its background and application. The unique combination of these factors provides a guideline as to how societal factors have influenced legal developments in Norway. This is especially true in light of Scandinavian Legal Realism (see below).

Historic Factors

For centuries Norway had been part of state unions with Denmark (1397-1814) and Sweden (1814-1905), thus being placed under the rule of foreign governments. Only in 1905 Norway finally became an independent nation state with a constitution that had, however, already been introduced on the 17 May 1814.[202] Above all sovereignty and independence are central themes for Norwegians. This is not only exemplified by the fact that the date of the original ratification (17 May) still is the Norwegian national day, but also by the continuous use of the original constitution which is the second oldest written constitution that is still in use in the world (after the United States of America's constitution). The constitution of 1814 is, thus, well entrenched in Norwegian identity and culture.[203] Furthermore, in contrast to Great Britain, where nation building took place through expansion, and Germany, where it took place through expansion, integration and unification, the Norwegian nation state was founded through separation[204] and, thereby, defines its independence and sovereignty as freedom from foreign rule ('freedom from'). Since the end of World War II and occupation by the German Nazi regime Norway has formed a close bond with the Western Allies, i.e. by becoming a founding member of NATO.[205] Norway is interested in maintaining a close defence cooperation under NATO, especially considering Norway's small population and location at the European periphery.[206] Norway's historic develop-

---

202 For a detailed account of the making of the Norwegian constitution and way to independence, cf. William B. Warner, Eirik Holmøyvik and Mona Ringvej, The Thing That Invented Norway. in Karen Gammelgaard and Eirik Holmøyvik (eds), *Writing Democracy - The Norwegian Constitution 1814-2014*, 21-42 and Georg-Christoph von Unruh, *Eidsvoll: Das norwegische Grundgesetz von 1814 als konstitutionelles Modell.*

203 Warner, Holmøyvik and Ringvej, ibid., 36.

204 Bjarne Hodne, *Norsk Nasjonalkultur - En kulturpolitisk oversikt*, 25.

205 Ibid. 160.

206 Sieglinde Gstöhl, *Reluctant Europeans: Norway, Sweden and Switzerland in the Process of Integration*, 34.

ment since the 19th century can, thus, be characterised by a wish for sovereignty and independence from foreign rule.

Economic Factors

For many centuries Norway's economy was dominated by the primary sector (agriculture) and considered poor.[207] Economic evolution to becoming a modern Western European economy only began in the beginning of the 20th century after the achievement of nationhood.[208] Since then the gap between Norway and then more developed European countries has gradually narrowed[209] until Norway eventually overtook most other European countries with respect to the GDP per capita. As of 2018 Norway had a GDP of USD 65,515 per capita, the fourth highest among OECD countries (cf. Annex 1, Figure 1). While the population between 1900 and 1999 doubled, the GDP rose 25-fold in the same time span.[210] As of 2018 Norway leads the United Nation's Human Development Index as the country with the highest overall quality of life.[211] Different factors have influenced this economic success story.

It should be noted that the Norwegian economy profited from the lack of destruction that hit other European countries during wars in the 19th and 20th century. The economy could, thus, grow steadily.[212] Furthermore, Norway benefited from a peaceful transition into nationhood. While a forceful revolution would have borne the risk of destroying existing structures, i.e. with respect to the administration, the peaceful and democratic transition that took place could benefit from existing structures and knowledge that were created and accumulated during the unions with Denmark and Sweden. This peaceful transition also made it easier to enter into a relationship of mutual recognition and cooperation with the Scandinavian neighbours. The acknowledgement of cultural bonds and respect for each other, have created a realm of peace and prosperity.[213]

207 Erling Røed Larsen, The Norwegian Economy 1900-2000: From Rags to Riches - A brief history of economic policymaking in Norway. in Statistisk Sentralbyrå (ed), *Economic Survey 4/2001*, 27.

208 Ibid. 27, 29.

209 Tor Jakob Klette, Økonomisk Vekst. in Steinar Holden and others, *En strategi for sysselsetting og verdiskaping*, 756.

210 Larsen, *supra* note 208, 25.

211 Selim Jahan and others, *Human Development Indicators and Indices: 2018 Statistical Update*, 22.

212 Larsen, *supra* note 208, 23.

213 Cf. ibid.

Originally the Norwegian economy was dominated by agriculture in the sense of exploitation of natural resources such as water for hydropower energy production, timber or wood and the export of such unrefined resources by shipping.[214] The focus on these two sectors has not changed until today. Norwegian growth, thus, highly depends on the availability and technology to exploit natural resources.[215] This is especially true since oil wells were found on Norway's West Coast in the 1960s.[216] While the dependence on exhaustible natural resources can turn out to be a curse rather than a gift to a country,[217] Norway's story is different. The Norwegian government soon decided to instate the Government Pension Fund Global and to invest profits from the oil business for the future so that Norwegian society as a whole benefits from the wealth that the oil exploitation brought in the long run.[218] Since the Fund invests in stocks, the Norwegian government has become a global player in the market, currently said to own at least 1% of the value of all listed companies in the world.[219]

The strategy with respect to the distribution of oil profits reflects economic policies that generally characterise the Norwegian economy and labour market. Throughout the 20th century they have focussed on democracy, education and public power.[220] The fact that the policies are not predominantly aimed at the private individual but rather the progress of the whole society shows that equality is a core Norwegian value.[221] This is exemplified by the fact that Norway has the most compressed wage structure in the world, meaning that the gap between wages is narrow.[222] The Gini coefficient is one of the lowest among OECD countries (0.262) as of

214 Ibid. 29.

215 Ibid. 26.

216 Per Morten Schiefloe, Kapittel 20: Norge og oljen. in Ivar Frønes and Lise Kjølsrød (eds), *Særtrykk av Det norske samfunn (bind 1, 2, og 3) for BSS130 - Samfunnsstruktur i endring, Universitetet i Stavanger*, 140-142.

217 Larsen, *supra* note 208, 33.

218 Ibid.; Schiefloe, *supra* note 216, 159-162.

219 Eli Moen, Norway: Raw Materials Refinement and Innovative Companies in Global Dynamics. in Peer Hull Kristensen and Kari Lilja (eds), *Nordic Capitalisms and Globalization - New Forms of Economic Organization and Welfare Institutions*, 149.

220 Larsen *supra* note 208, 32.

221 Ibid.

222 Ibid.; however, there has been a slight rise of income inequality since the 1990s, cf. Simen Markussen and Knut Røed, Kapittel 17: Ulikhet og sosial mobilitet. in Ivar Frønes and Lise Kjølsrød (eds), *Særtrykk av Det norske samfunn (bind 1, 2, og 3) for BSS130 - Samfunnsstruktur i endring, Universitetet i Stavanger*, 61-85.

2016.[223] The careful policies, drafted to benefit the many, not the few, result from the omnipresence of the Nordic welfare state model in Norway which can be traced back to the process Norwegian nation building.[224] Once Norway achieved independence from Sweden, their policies had been directed at the possibility of participating in society, through the reduction of inequality and increase of social mobility, the provision of public education for everyone and the establishment of public health institutions.[225] Along political party lines and across society these values are accepted and promoted. Unlike Great Britain, Norway has pursued a coordinated market economy approach from the beginning, relying on government intervention to regulate the market.[226] From an economic point of view Norwegian society can, thus, be summarised as egalitarian when it comes to wealth distribution, providing broad social security and promotion mechanisms and focussing on the exploitation and export of natural resources. By sharing the nation's wealth, an atmosphere of security, identity and belonging is created.[227]

Sociological Factors

Norwegian society can be said to be divided along several cultural lines which have influenced political outcomes. It is, furthermore, characterised by a culture of compromise, relative homogeneity and high trust rates in public institutions as well as on an interpersonal level.

Norwegian trust rates with respect to the government and the police as well as on an interpersonal level are high (cf. Annex 1, Figures 2 to 4). Remarkably, Norway scores among the top five countries in each category. A high trust rate in the government eases the government's capacity to implement certain policies.[228] A high trust rate in the police shows that people are satisfied with the justice system. A high interpersonal trust rate shows that people feel comfortable and safe in the country they reside. Interpersonal trust leads to a positive market environment. It can, further-

223 OECD, *supra* note 113.

224 Svein Bjørkås, Kapittel 17: Fra enhetskultur til kulturell pluralisme?. in Ivar Frønes and Lise Kjølsrød (eds), *Det norske samfunn*, 453.

225 Olli Kangas, Joakim Palme and Markus Kainu, Kapittel 29: The Nordic welfare-state model. in Ivar Frønes and Lise Kjølsrød (eds), *Særtrykk av Det norske samfunn (bind 1, 2, og 3) for BSS130 - Samfunnsstruktur i endring, Universitetet i Stavanger*, 41; Larsen *supra* note 208, 30.

226 Larsen, ibid., 24.

227 Ibid. 36.

228 OECD, *How's Life? 2017: Measuring Well-being*, 184.

more, be assumed that the chances for conflict are low if people trust each other. Historically, the high interpersonal trust rates are rooted in the formerly predominant farmers' community. People had to cooperate and share to survive in the rough Norwegian environment. The basis for this cooperation lied in a high degree of trust among each other.[229] Moreover, the government policies promoting equality constitute a contributing factor to the high trust rates. In a country, where leading policies promote the sharing of wealth rather than 'rugged' individualism, it appears easier to trust the opposite.

The small[230] and rather homogenous Norwegian population also contributes to the high trust rates. Despite immigration movements Norwegian society can still be described as homogenous. While equality lies at the heart of Norwegian values, the tolerance for social deviation has been rather little, partly due to the fact that Norway for most of its history was a mono-religious Christian-Protestant society[231] and Norwegian nation building that is still present in contemporary Norwegian society.[232] This leads to strong forces of conformity and assimilation.[233] Whether this changes due to increasing migration movements[234] is yet to be seen. However, as the Norwegian public has become more critical towards immigration movements and especially emphasises the immigrants' duty to integrate,[235] one can assume strong assimilation forces in this regard. While one cannot deny that especially Norway's urban population has become more diverse in a globalised setting, Norwegian society is still homogenous especially when it comes to well established values, such as equality.[236]

229 Hodne, *supra* note 204, 42.

230 As of the 1 January 2019 the Norwegian population amounted to 5,328,212 people, cf. Statistisk sentralbyrå, 'Population and population changes' (*Population*, 22 February 2019) <https://www.ssb.no/en/befolkning/statistikker/folkemengde/aar-per-1-januar> accessed 12 November 2019.

231 Pål Repstad, Kapittel 15: Privat og forankret – Religion og livssyn i dagens Norge. in Ivar Frønes and Lise Kjølsrød (eds), *Det norske samfunn*, 385.

232 Bjørkås, *supra* note 224, 452.

233 Larsen *supra* note 208, 28, 35.

234 For statistics, cf. Grete Brochmann, Kapittel 6: Innvandring til Skandinavia – Velferdsstater i pluralismens tid. in Ivar Frønes and Lise Kjølsrød (eds), *Særtrykk av Det norske samfunn (bind 1, 2, og 3) for BSS130 - Samfunnsstruktur i endring, Universitetet i Stavanger*, 134-135.

235 Ibid. 146-148.

236 Cf. also Pia Letto-Vanamo and Ditlev Tamm, Nordic Legal Mind. in Pia Letto-Vanamo, Ditlev Tamm and Bent Ole Gram Mortensen (eds), *Nordic Law in European Context*, 8-9.

This relative homogeneity and shared values of honesty, cooperation and acceptance further lead Norwegian society to be anti-conflictual and compromise driven. This may result in less conflicts to require solutions by the judiciary.[237]

Beside a high degree of homogeneity, however, Norway also reveals several cleavages along cultural lines. As a centralised state, a large part of the economic activity takes place around the nation's capital Oslo.[238] One first divide can, thus, be traced along the rural and the urban population, more precisely between the East and the South- and North-Western periphery.[239] Language-wise this societal cleavage is reflected in and reinforced by the languages spoken in the respective regions. While the East is dominated by *bokmål*, *nynorsk* is the prevalent language in Western Norway.[240] Furthermore, there exists a fundamental religious counter-culture especially in the South and West of the country which has been leading abstinence movements.[241] The East and especially Oslo on the contrary have been rather secularised, again exemplifying the centre-periphery cleavage in Norway.[242] Such can also be seen in the outcomes of political votes both in elections and referenda and constrains the possibility of supranational integration.[243] It must be pointed out that the centre-periphery cleavage is not necessarily one of those 'left behind' and the progressive cosmopolitan elite.[244] It is rather one about attitude, as historically the peripheral population has been depicted and sees itself as 'defenders of Norwegian democracy, culture and values against [urban] forces of centralisation [...]', thus, playing a crucial role in Norwegian societal development.[245]

Conclusion: Relationship with Europe and Consequences for the Legal System

It has been shown that historically, Norway is characterised by a strong wish for (maintaining) sovereignty and independence, while economically,

237 Larsen, *supra* note 208, 28. The anti-conflictual character of Norwegian society may also be exemplified by the avoidance of open conflicts at the constitutional assembly at Eidsvoll, cf. von Unruh, *supra* note 202, 13-14.

238 Gstöhl, *supra* note 206, 32.

239 Ibid. 30.

240 Ibid. 31.

241 Ibid.

242 Ibid.

243 Ibid. 30-31.

244 For example, Norway has the lowest regional disparities among OECD countries, cf. OECD, Regions and Cities at a Glance – Norway (5 March 2019).

245 Marianne Sundlisæter Skinner, 'Norwegian Euroscepticism: Values, Identity or Interest' [2012] 50 (3) Journal of Common Market Studies 422 (426).

Norway is characterised by a coordinated market economy dependent on natural resources and export with a strong focus on equality and the fair distribution of wealth. Sociologically, Norwegian society may be characterised as homogenous, trusting and anti-conflictual, however, also divided along centre-periphery lines. As for the legal system, sociological factors indicate that there exists a high degree of interpersonal trust as well as a tendency to avoid conflicts. This entails that less conflicts require adjudication. A shared set of values in a rather homogenous society also makes it easier to find solutions that suit all parties. This also opens the door for individual, rather than formalised legal solutions (cf. also below).[246] Moreover, high trust rates in state organs make acceptance of their decisions, including those of the judiciary, more likely.

As for the relationship with the rest of Europe and the EU especially, this means that it is unlikely that Norway will become an EU Member State as Membership would entail a formal loss of sovereignty. However, as Norway's economy is export dependent, there exist strong interests in maintaining good (trade) relationships with European partners. Furthermore, as a comparatively small nation state Norway is dependent on and interested in international cooperation, such as under NATO. As for further European integration, the long struggle for independence and repeated exposition to foreign rule as well as societal cleavages along centre-periphery lines (what *Sollohub* calls the 'double dose' of counter-culture identification[247]) make further supranational integration at the expense of sovereignty appear unlikely.

II. Norwegian Legal Institutions, Drafting and Method

1. Institutions and Drafting Method

Norway is a constitutional monarchy with a central government. Legislation is passed by the National Parliament (*Stortinget*). The courts are not

246 Unlike i.e. in Germany, where the BGB is specifically drafted as a technical tool for the resolution of conflicts.

247 Maria Sollohub, *National Identity and the Norwegian EC Debate*, 34.

specialised due to concerns regarding the judges' regard for the legal systems' overriding principles.[248]

The Norwegian legal system is based on a civil law approach but also bears some common law elements.[249] This means that there is no strict doctrine of precedent. However, due to the comparatively low number of codified legislation as well as the use of short norms and general principles rather than detailed codification, the application of norms in the individual case bears a lot of importance.[250] A comprehensive civil code, as i.e. in France or Germany, does not exist. The Contracts Act of 1918 (*avtaleloven*)[251] offers a basic account of contract law with respect to formation and validity of contracts. More detailed regulations are contained in legislative acts referring to the specific legal area in question, i.e. the Sales Act (*kjøpsloven*)[252] or the Consumer Sales Act (*forbrukerkjøpsloven*)[253].

2. Scandinavian Legal Realism

Norwegian legal theory and practice are profoundly influenced by Scandinavian Legal Realism.[254] Also referred to as the 'Uppsala School' and thereto founded by Axel Hägerström it is characterised by a rejection of a normative and metaphysical categorisation of the law.[255] While the term

---

248 Norges domstoler, 'Tingrettene' (Norges Domstoler) <https://www.domstol.no/no/Om-domstolene/De-alminnelige-domstolene/Tingrettene/> accessed 17 November 2019.

249 Ulf Bernitz, 'What is Scandinavian Law? Concept, Characteristics, Future' [2007] 50 Scandinavian Studies in Law 13 (20, 28); Giuditta Cordero-Moss, 'Ulike trekk ved norsk og engelsk kontraktsrett' [2016] 51 (5) Jussens Venner 276 (277); Zweigert and Kötz, *supra* note 10, 277.

250 Bernitz, ibid., (20-21).

251 *Lov om avslutning av avtaler, om fuldmagt og om ugyldige viljeserklæringer (avtaleloven)* (31 May 1918). The Act is a result of Nordic legislative cooperation as a mean to ensure a homogenous legal system in Scandinavia. Similar Acts of Parliament were adopted in Denmark and Sweden in 1915, in Finland in 1929 and in Iceland in 1936. Cf. also Letto-Vanamo and Tamm, *supra* note 236, 3-4.

252 *Lov om kjøp (kjøpsloven)* (13 May 1988).

253 *Lov om forbrukerkjøp (forburkerkjøpsloven)* (21 June 2002).

254 Anders C. Stray Ryssdal, *Economic Analysis of Law & Scandinavian Legal Realism - A Theory of Fact (Draft Edition)*, 23 with reference to Torstein Eckhoff as the leading Norwegian legal methodologist; Letto-Vanamo and Tamm, *supra* note 236, 13.

255 Cf. Jes Bjarup, 'The Philosophy of Scandinavian Legal Realism' [2005] 18 (1) Ratio Juris 1 (2); Jes Bjarup, *Reason, Emotion and the Law - Studies in the Philoso-*

'Scandinavian Legal Realism' comprises differing approaches to legal science,[256] one of its most prominent common features is the claim that the law must evolve in reciprocal accordance with societal developments.[257] Legal science shall, thus, enter into a dialogue with social sciences and societal reality to attribute meaning to otherwise 'empty' words of legal norms.[258] In light of this, Norwegian legal realists have attributed a lot of weight to a broad discretionary realm of judges' decision-making powers.[259] As a consequence, rather than as a closed conceptual science, Norwegian law is viewed as embedded in the circumstantial reality of its society. Rather than fitting case scenarios into certain legal schemes and concepts, jurists are concerned with appropriate and pragmatic solutions for individual cases, thereby, considering various factors (also see the concept of *reelle hensyn* below).[260]

3. Interpretation of Norms

Contractual freedom and validity form the basis of Norwegian private law. The principles go back to the King Christian V's Norwegian law[261] from 1687 which constituted the first formal regulation of contract law. In Book 5 Chapter 1 Art. 2 it reads

> All voluntary contracts that are made between mature persons or that have been consented to by such, be they purchase, sale, gift, [...] mortgage, loan, rent, commitments, engagement and others of which they know the name which are not against the law or honour shall keep their word and clauses as they were entered into.[262]

---

phy of Axel Hägerström, 425; Rune Slagstad, 'Norwegian Legal Realism since 1945' [1991] 35 Scandinavian Studies in Law 215 (216).

256 Cf. Bjarup (2005), ibid., (10 et seq.); Ryssdal, *supra* note 254, 23; Johan Strang, 'Two Generations of Scandinavian Realists' [2009] 32 (1) Retfærd 62-82.

257 Ryssdal, *supra* note 254, 20.

258 Cf. Bjarup (2005), *supra* note 255, (7); Slagstad, *supra* note 255, (221); Carsten Smith, *Bankrett og Statsstyre*, 597-599.

259 Ibid. 21.

260 Cf. Ryssdal, *supra* note 254, 46-47; Slagstad, *supra* note 255, (229-230, 232).

261 *Kong Christian Den Femtis Norske Lov* (15 April 1684).

262 Alle Contracter som frivilligen giøris af dennem, der ere Myndige, og komne til deris Lavalder, være sig Kiøb, Sal, Gave, Mageskifte, Pant, Laan, Leje, Forpligter, Forløfter og andet ved hvad Navn det nævnis kand, som ikke er imod Loven,

As the courts play a prominent role in Norway's legal system, it is important to understand their methodological approach when it comes to interpreting norms. Norwegian legal methodology is oriented at the interpretation by the Norwegian Supreme Court.[263]

The influential Norwegian Legal Realist *Torstein Eckhoff* first published the results of a study of the methodology used by the Norwegian Supreme Court in 1971. His book *Rettskildelære* depicts the legal sources (*rettskildefaktorer*) as well as the underlying principles (*rettskildeprinsippene*) to interpret norms and cases.[264] The legal sources include the wording of the written law (*lovtekster*), preparatory works from the law-making process (*lovforarbeider*), the courts' legal practice (*rettspraksis*), other authorities' legal practice (*andre myndigheters praksis*), private legal practice (*privates praksis*), (academic) legal opinions (*rettsoppfatninger*) and 'policy considerations' (*reelle hensyn*).[265] If written legal sources exist, one takes the wording of the norm in question as a starting point and then considers especially Parliamentary preparatory works and the Norwegian Supreme Court's case-law.[266] The preparatory works are especially important due to a sentiment of 'loyalty towards the law-maker'.[267]

Another important factor in decision-making is *reelle hensyn*. While the character and scope of *reelle hensyn* are disputed,[268] it may be described as a

> [...] heterogenic group of arguments that can be considered relevant when one shall answer a legal question. It is a 'legal category' of arguments that is not directly connected to the law, preparatory works, customary law, legal practice or other clearly distinguishable categories. Simple 'policy considerations' can be heavy arguments that determine legal solutions, while others can appear as weak with indefinite or limited weight as a legal source.[269]

---

eller Ærbarhed, skulle holdis i alle deris Ord og Puncter, saasom de indgangne ere (Translation by author).

263 Ola Mestad, § 2 Rettens kilder og anvendelse. in Kåre Lilleholt (ed), *Knophs Oversikt over Norsk Rett*, 4.

264 Cf. Torstein Eckhoff and Jan Helgelsen, *Rettskildelære*.

265 Ibid. 23.

266 Ibid. 161 (referring to the importance of the Norwegian Supreme Court's judgments) Mestad, *supra* note 263, 5, 8-9, 11.

267 Eckhoff and Helgelsen, *supra* note 264, 71-74.

268 For an overview and discussion on the character, scope and role of *reelle hensyn*, cf. Sverre Blandhol, *De Beste Grunner - Reelle hensyn i juridisk argumentasjon*.

269 Asbjørn Kjønstad, Reelle hensyn som rettskilde. in Ole Kristian Fauchald and others (eds), *Dog fred er ej det beste: Festskrift til Carl August Fleischer på hans 70-*

The considerations may include, among many others, legal traditions, general legal principles, the economic reality of each case, thriving towards a harmonised legal system, a balanced contractual relationship, fairness or a consideration of the implications of the case's outcome.[270] *Reelle hensyn*, thereby, reflects the ideas of Scandinavian Legal Realism of a deconstructive, honest, pragmatic approach to law.[271] *Eckhoff* himself encouraged that it should be the goal of jurisprudence to lay open the actual considerations concerning a case instead of hiding them behind a curtain of formality and phrases.[272]

While some may criticize *reelle hensyn*, i.e. for causing a lack of legal certainty (*rettssikkerhet*),[273] the concept must be seen in light of the above described societal prerequisites in Norway. Norwegian society is still a rather homogenous society.[274] Combined with a small population, a flexible concept such as *reelle hensyn* seems more practical than in other countries. It offers a pragmatic and individual use of arguments in each individual case and leaves courts with a broad discretion. This, in combination with a lack of detailed legislation and frequent use of general principles, leads to an increased importance of case-law in the development of legal concepts and Norwegian legal methodology.

årsdag (26 august 2006) 358: 'Reelle hensyn er en heterogen gruppe av argumenter som kan anses som relevante når man skal ta stilling til rettsspørsmål. Det er en «restkategori» av argumenter som ikke direkte kan knyttes til lov, lovforarbeider, sedvanerett, rettspraksis og andre klarere avgrensbare kategorier. Enkelte reelle hensyn kan være tungtveiende argumenter som determinerer rettslige løsninger, mens andre kan ha preg av svake normer med ubestemt eller begrenset rettskildemessig vekt' (Translation by author). This quote reflects the opinion of one legal scholar and may be disputed by others, i.e. cf. Morten Kinander, 'Trenger man egentlig 'reelle hensyn'?' [2002] (4) Lov og Rett 224-241; Blandhol, *supra* note 268. For matters of simplicity this piece uses the aforementioned definition of the concept of *reelle hensyn*.

270 Kjønstad, ibid., (358-359).

271 Cf. Ryssdal, *supra* note 257, 21 et seq., 40.

272 Eckhoff and Helgelsen, *supra* note 264, 396-399; cf. also Carl August Fleischer, *Rettskilder og juridisk metode*, 376.

273 Blandhol, *supra* note 268, 54-55.

274 Cf. Kjønstad, *supra* note 269, 378.

4. Alternative Dispute Resolution

Another important, albeit not necessarily unique, factor in Norwegian law-making are institutions for dispute resolution and consumer protection outside the court system.

The Consumer Authority (*forbrukertilsynet*)[275] was established in the 1970s and controls marketing practices as a supervisory body.[276] The Consumer Authority can furthermore bring cases on behalf of consumers to the Market Council (*Markedsrådet*), which settles disputes between consumers and businesses.[277] While the Consumer Authority's task is to *balance* interests in the marketplace, the government funded independent Consumer Council (*forbrukerrådet*) solely pursues consumer interests and i.e. gives advice in consumer cases.[278]

It is common to settle disputes in front of tribunals (*nemndene*), i.e. the Consumer Appeals Tribunal (*forbrukerklageutvalget*, FKU), rather than to take action in front of the courts. Tribunals can be composed of lawyers and/or layman. As opposed to courts' judgments, decisions are often drafted in a short manner, sometimes lacking thorough legal reasoning. Part of the success may be the societal background of Norway. In a country with high interpersonal trust rates and a high degree of homogeneity decisions of non-court tribunals may be more easily acceptable.[279]

In many cases the tribunals are a very quick and effective way to settle especially smaller disputes that would otherwise eventually not reach the courts. Claimants do not require representation and incur lower or no costs as the procedure in front of tribunals itself takes place free of charge.[280] This makes the alternative settlement options popular and leads to two consequences: on the one hand, there exists a readily available consumer protection system to settle disputes. On the other hand, many consumer related disputes do not reach the courts so the development of case-law (as will also later be shown) depends on a relatively small number of court cases.

---

275 Formerly known as the Consumer Ombudsman.

276 Kjersti Graver, 'A study of the Consumer Ombudsman institution in Norway with some references to the other Nordic countries I: Background and description' [1986] 9 (6) Journal of Consumer Policy 1 (1-2).

277 Ibid. (2).

278 Ibid. (4).

279 Letto-Vanamo and Tamm, *supra* note 236, 8-9.

280 Cf. i.e. the *forbrukerklageutvalget*'s website: http://www.forbrukertvistutvalget.no/om-forbrukerklageutvalget/, accessed 17 November 2019.

III. The "Norwegian Model" (EEA-Membership)

Unlike the other neighbouring Nordic countries[281] Norway is neither a Member State of the EU nor of the customs union. In fact, three attempts to join the EEC (European Economic Community) and EC (European Community) failed. The first application process was stopped when France opposed the UK joining the EEC 1967. Consequently, Norway that had applied together with the UK withdrew its application.[282] The second attempt to join the EEC in 1972 was stopped by the negative outcome of the first referendum on EEC Membership.[283] The third attempt was stopped yet another time by the negative outcome of the second referendum on EC Membership in 1994.[284] The Norwegian people have, thus, voiced their reservation regarding EU Membership several times. Instead of an 'ever closer union'[285] in the shape of supranational institutions and treaties, Norway has chosen (formal) independence of their state organs.[286]

This does not, however, mean that Norway is not interested in European cooperation. In fact, Norway was one of the founding members of the EF-

---

281 Denmark became a member in 1972. Sweden and Finland followed in 1995.

282 Fredrik Bøckmann Finstad, Norway and the EEA. in Finn Arnesen and others (eds), *Agreement on the European Economic Area - A Commentary*, recital 4; Sven Norberg and Martin Johansson, The History of the EEA Agreement and the First Twenty Years of Its Existence. in Carl Baudenbacher (ed), *The Handbook of EEA Law*, 11-12; Fredrik Sejersted, Del I - Bakgrunn og hovedtrekk. in Fredrik Sejersted, Finn Arnesen and others (eds), *h*, 33.

283 53.5 % voted against EEC Membership, Anonymous, 'The 1994 Referendum on Norwegian Membership of the EU' (*Statistisk Sentralbyrå*, 6 March 1995) <https://www.ssb.no/a/histstat/nos/nos_c235.pdf> accessed 17 November 2019, page 19.

284 52.2 % voted against EC Membership, ibid.

285 cf. Solemn Declaration on European Union, Stuttgart, 19 June 1983, Bull. EC 6-1983, page 25; cf. John Erik Fossum and Hans Petter Graver, *Squaring the circle on Brexit - Could the Norway Model Work?*, XI.

286 Erik O. Eriksen, Despoiling Norwegian Democracy. in Erik O. Eriksen and John Erik Fossum (eds), *The European Union's Non-Members - Independence under hegemony?*, 77; Fossum and Graver, ibid., 42; Tor-Inge Harbo, 'The European Economic Area Agreement: A Case of Legal Pluralism' [2009] 78 Nordic Journal of International Law 201 (203); Peter-Christian Müller-Graff, Norway in the Dynamics of European Legal Integration. in Holger Hestermeyer and others (eds), *Coexistence, Cooperation and Solidarity: Liber Amicorum Rüdiger Wolfrum*, 2022-2025; Fredrik Sejersted, Between Sovereignty and Supranationalism in the EEA Context – On the Legal Dynamics of the EEA-Agreement. in Peter-Christian Müller-Graff and Erling Selvig (eds), *The European Economic Area - Norway's Basic Status in the Legal Construction of Europe*, 44, 67-68.

TA in 1960[287] showing that the country has particular interest in European ties. In the 1970s and 1980s Norway was involved in several trade agreements with the EEC through its EFTA Membership and even adapted EEC rules on a voluntary basis to secure access to the internal market.[288] In addition to the EEA Agreement of 1994 Norway has concluded further agreements with the EEC, EC and EU respectively. In total there exist 130 associating agreements between the EU and Norway including those on the internal market, the Schengen agreement and several agreements on asylum, foreign and security policy.[289] Norway has thereby adapted around 75% of its policies according to EU-cooperation.[290]

Norway's legal status in the European framework is mainly governed by its membership in the EFTA and the EEA.

1. EFTA

The EFTA was founded with the Stockholm Convention in 1960 beside the Rome Treaty of 1957. It was supposed to form a looser alternative to the supranational institutional model of the latter[291] and thus constituted a defensive reaction to the formation of the EEC[292]. It is the EFTA's goal to promote open market access among its Member States as well as through multi- and bilateral agreements.[293] While measures under the Vaduz Convention which replaced the Stockholm Convention in 2002[294] resemble

---

287 Fredrik Bøckmann Finstad, Norway and the EEA. in Finn Arnesen and others (eds), *Agreement on the European Economic Area - A Commentary*, recital 4; cf. Preamble of the Convention establishing the European Free Trade Association.

288 Finstad, ibid., recital 5.

289 Eriksen, *supra* note 286; Fossum and Graver, *supra* note 285, 41.

290 Eriksen, ibid., 85; Fredrik Sejersted and others, *Utenfor og innenfor – Norges avtaler med EU,* 790.

291 Finstad, *supra* note 287, recital 4; Sejersted, Fredrik Sejersted, Del I - Bakgrunn og hovedtrekk. in Fredrik Sejersted and others (eds), *EØS-Rett*, 32.

292 Sven Norberg and Martin Johansson, The History of the EEA Agreement and the First Twenty Years of Its Existence. in Carl Baudenbacher (ed), *The Handbook of EEA Law*,11; Christoph Vedder, The EEA in the Union's Legal Order. in Finn Arnesen and others (eds), *Agreement on the European Economic Area - A Commentary*, recital 7.

293 Preamble and Art. 2 Vaduz Convention.

294 The Vaduz Convention incapsulates the evolution of a 'common market' among the EFTA Member States oriented at the integration provided in the EEA Agreement, cf. Vedder, *supra* note 292, recital 22.

the regulations and especially four freedoms of the internal market of the EU, thus creating a similar relationship among the EFTA countries as with the EU according to the Agreement on the European Economic Area (EEAA)[295], they do not entail the same obligations as under full EU Membership. The EFTA was originally never meant to set up a common market but merely aims at removing internal barriers as its Member States see fit.[296] The EFTA Membership bears importance for Norway's relationship with Switzerland as a non-member of the EEA and especially the negotiation of Free Trade Agreements with countries outside the EU.[297]

2. EEA

The EFTA had originally been designed as an alternative to the EEC.[298] However, from the beginning in the 1960s the EFTA states and the EEC worked on bringing the EFTA Member States and the internal market together, i.e. by alignment of technical and inspection standards.[299] This development of continuous and growing cooperation ended in negotiations which would result in the EEA Agreement between the EEC and then EFTA states Austria, Finland, Sweden, Norway, Iceland and Liechtenstein[300] which came into effect in 1994. Its goal is to create 'a dynamic and homogenous European Economic Area'.[301] The EEA Agreement, thereby, provides that the EFTA Member States have to adhere to EU rules on the four freedoms and competition law to gain access to the common market.[302] Furthermore, the agreement intends a close cooperation on 'other fields, such as research and development, the environment, education and

295 Vedder, *supra* note 292, recital 22.

296 Thomas Pedersen, *European Union and the EFTA Countries - Enlargement and Integration*, 21.

297 Sejersted, *supra* note 291, 36. Cf, also Anonymous, 'Free Trade Agreements and Trade Relations by Country' (*EFTA*) <http://www.efta.int/free-trade/free-trade-agreements> accessed 17 November 2019 and Anonymous, 'EFTA Trade Statistics' (*EFTA*) <http://trade.efta.int/#/overview/EFTA/WORLD/2017/HS2> accessed 17 November 2019.

298 Norberg and Johansson, *supra* note 292, 12-13; Pedersen, *supra* note 296, 20.

299 Norberg and Johansson, ibid.

300 Vedder, *supra* note 292, recital 13; Switzerland did not join due to the negative outcome of a referendum on the matter (see below page 112 et seq.). Austria, Sweden and Finland acceded to the EU in 1995.

301 Preamble and Art. 6 EEAA.

302 Art. 1 Section 2 lit. (a)-(e) EEAA; cf. also Sejersted, *supra* note 291, 34.

social policy' as well as consumer protection tourism and culture ('horizontal policies').[303] It also includes a principle of loyalty regarding the fulfilment of the parties' obligations under the agreement.[304] It does not include cooperation in the fields of agriculture and fishery, the Monetary Union or justice and home affairs[305] and the EFTA countries are not part of the customs union[306]. Furthermore, the EFTA countries can still conclude trade agreements with other states.[307] In addition to the legal commitments, Norway must contribute ca. EUR 870 million per year within the scope of different European programmes to secure access to the internal market for the period 2014-2020.[308]

Implementation of Norms

As of 2019, ca. 12,200 EU Acts have been implemented into the EEA Agreement.[309] As of 2008, ca. 28% of Norwegian laws were amended in light of EU law.[310]

---

303 Art. 1 Section 2 lit. (f) EEAA; Fossum and Graver, *supra* note 285, 42.

304 Art. 3 EEAA.

305 Fossum and Graver, *supra* note 285, 42; Sieglinde Gstöhl, The European Union's Different Neighbourhood Models. in Erik O. Eriksen and John Erik Fossum (eds), *The European Union's Non-Member - Independence under hegemony?*, 21.

306 EFTA Court judgment E-2/97, *Mag Instrument Inc. v California Trading Company Norway, Ulsteen (Mag Lite)* [1997] recital 25.

307 Ibid. recital 27.

308 Agreement between the Kingdom of Norway and the European Union on a Norwegian Financial Mechanism for the period 2014-2021, Official Journal of the European Union L 141/11 (28 May 2016); Utenriksdepartement, 'Financial Contributions' (Norway and the EU) <https://www.norway.no/en/missions/eu/areas-of-cooperation/financial-contribution/> accessed 17 November 2019.

309 Storting Library, The Storting and the EEA Agreement – Factsheet from the Storting Library (July 2019), page 1.

310 69.7% Directives and 17.5% Regulations. Cf. Sejersted and others, *supra* note 290, 795. The low number of implemented regulations can be explained by the large number of EU regulations in the area of agriculture which is excluded from EEA cooperation.

The EEA Agreement itself can be viewed as a treaty *sui generis* under international law[311] which does not confer legislative powers to the EEA.[312] Thus, not all legislative acts of the EU have to be implemented into the EFTA states national legislation. Whether or not an EU legislative act shall also bind the EFTA states is decided upon by the EEA Joint Committee after an assessment of possible 'horizontal challenges to the EEA Agreement'.[313] The EU legislative act must then be incorporated into the EEA Agreement by way of an EEA Joint Committee Decision according to Arts. 98, 102 EEAA which is binding on the contracting parties pursuant to Art. 104 EEAA. As a general premise legislative acts under EEA law, unlike EU Regulations for EU Member States, do not have direct effect on Norwegian law.[314] As no legislative power was conferred to EEA organs,

---

311 cf. EFTA Court judgment E-9/97, *Sveinbjörnsdóttir* [1998] recital 59; Fredrik Sejersted, Between Sovereignty and Supranationalism in the EEA-Context – On the Legal Dynamics of the EEA-Agreement. in Peter-Christian Müller-Graff and Erling Selvig (eds), *The European Economic Area – Norway's Basic Status in the Legal Construction of Europe*, 44; for a critical view on the EEA's character as a legal order, cf. Finn Arnesen, Is the EEA a Federal Legal Order?. in Peter-Christian Müller-Graff and Erling Selvig (eds), *European Law and National Constitutions*, 69-82 and Finn Arnesen, EEA - a "distinct legal order of its own"?. in Trond Solvang (ed), *SIMPLY 2016: Scandinavian Institute of Maritime Law Yearbook (MarIus nr 482)*, 111-131.

312 cf. EFTA Court judgment E-4/01, *Karlsson* [2002] recital 26; Henrik Bull, 'The EEA Agreement and Norwegian Law' [1994] 5 (12) European Business Law Review 291 (291-292); Finstad, *supra* note 287, recitals 18, 36; Fossum and Graver, *supra* note 285, 70; Hans Petter Graver, 'Mission Impossible: Supranationality and National Legal Autonomy in the EEA Agreement' [2002] 7 European Foreign Affairs Review 73 (76, 90); Harbo, *supra* note 286; Sejersted, *supra* note 291, 195. Pål Wennerås, Attorney General of Norway. in Carl Baudenbacher (ed), *The Handbook of EEA Law*, 216.

313 Marthe Kristine Fjeld Dystland Fredrik Bøckmann Finstad and Ida Sørebø, Part II: The Agreement on the European Economic Area. in Finn Arnesen and others (eds), *Agreement on the European Economic Area - A Commentary*, Art. 102 recital 9.

314 Norwegian Supreme Court, *Finanger I* [2000] Rt. 2000, 1811 (1826) per Judge Flock; Sejersted, *supra* note 311, 56-57. However, note that the Norwegian Supreme Court has acknowledged that international law itself (including EEA law) can serve as a primary source of law cf. Norwegian Supreme Court, *Finanger I* [2000] Rt. 2000, 1811 (1827). This creates a 'factual direct effect' for many EEA legislative acts, cf. Arnesen and Stenvik, *supra* note 334, 54, 62-63. Also note that in Liechtenstein EEA law inheres direct effect due to a monist approach towards international law, cf. Christian Frommelt and Sieglinde Gstöhl, *Rapport #18 – Liechtenstein and the EEA: the Europeanization of a (very) small state*, 23.

consequently, the EFTA states have not changed the constitutional rules on the implementation of new laws. Thus, every legislative act must be incorporated according to the individual EFTA state's national law-making procedure.[315]

Norway pursues a dualist approach to transform and implement international rules into Norwegian law. This approach also applies to rules introduced under EEA law.[316] The EEA Agreement itself was implemented under § 26 Section 2 of the Constitution of the Kingdom of Norway (*Kongeriket Norges Grunnlov*) by way of the EEA Act (*EØS-loven*)[317]. EEA legislative acts are mostly implemented through administrative regulations by way of clauses that delegate legislative powers to the administration.[318] Where such clauses do not exist or are insufficient the respective EEA legislative act has to be implemented by way of an Act of Parliament.[319] Most Directives are transformed by amending existing legislation. As of 2012, 174 out of a total 600 Acts of Parliament (29%) and 1,000 out of a total 11,000 administrative regulations (ca. 9%) in various legal areas contained EU law elements.[320] In the period 1992-2019 only 46 of the *Storting*'s bills on matters relating to the implementation of European law were not passed unanimously[321] which, *inter alia*, hints at a depoliticization of the relationship

315 EFTA Court judgment E-4/01, *Karlsson* [2002] recital 28; Georges Baur, Decision-Making Procedure and Implementation of New Law. in Carl Baudenbacher (ed), *The Handbook of EEA Law*, 63; Dystland, Finstad and Sørebø, *supra* note 313, Art. 103 recital 2; Fossum and Graver, *supra* note 285, 68 and 70.

316 Arnesen and Stenvik, *supra* note 334, 52; Bull, *supra* note 312, (292); Finstad, *supra* note 287, recital 18; Graver, *supra* note 312, (82).

317 *Lov om gjennomføring i norsk rett av hoveddelen i avtale om Det europeiske økonomiske samarbeidsområde (EØS) m.v. (EØS-loven)*, No. 109, 27 November 1992.

318 Bull, *supra* note 312, (293); Finstad, *supra* note 287, recital 30; Sejersted and others, *supra* note 290, 120, 128 and 230.

319 Bull, ibid. For criticism regarding the Parliamentary procedures of the *Europautvalg*, cf. Fossum and Graver, *supra* note 285, 90 et seq.; John Erik Fossum and Cathrine Holst, Norsk konstitusjonell debatt og europeisk integrasjon. in John Erik Fossum and Erik Oddvar Eriksen (eds), *Det Norske paradoks: om Norges forhold til Den europeiske union*, 206 et seq. And with respect to an apparent democratic deficit, cf. Erik Oddvar Eriksen, 'EØS, Norge og demokratiet' [2009] 35 (3) Kritisk Juss 230 (230); Kristen Ringdal, Velgernes argumenter. in Anders Todal Jenssen and Henry Valen (eds), *Brussel midt imot*, 51 (stating the importance of considerations of self-rule in the referenda).

320 Sejersted and others, *supra* note 290, 122, 127 and 128.

321 Storting Library, *supra* note 309, page 2.

with the EU[322]. While in many EU Member States EU matters raise constitutional and democratic questions,[323] the Norwegian focus is a pragmatic one on what is best for the Norwegian people and businesses[324].

Regarding the interpretation of the incorporated act, Norwegian courts use the *principle of presumption* according to which it is presumed that the respective piece of legislation shall conform with the state's international obligations. Thus, when interpreting the incorporated or transformed national rule the courts shall take into account the original regulation or directive.[325]

Role of and Application by the Courts

After the ECJ dismissed the idea of a joint 'EEA Court' which would have ruled cases both for the EC/EU and the EFTA side due to incompatibility with Community law[326] the EFTA Court was established beside the ECJ. According to the EEA Agreement the EFTA Court must interpret obligations under the EEA Agreement in conformity with the ECJ/CJEU's case-law 'given prior to the date of signature of [the] Agreement' if the respective norm is 'identical in substance' with EC/EU rules.[327] As to future case-law the EFTA Court decided in the *L'Oreal* case that obligations under the EEA Agreement must be interpreted 'in line with new case law of the ECJ regardless of whether the EFTA Court has previously ruled on the

322 Fossum and Graver, *supra* note 285, 90; Fossum and Holst, *supra* note 319, 205-212.

323 Fossum and Holst, ibid., 209.

324 Ibid. 208. Also exemplified by the 'ACER' dispute, cf. Nina Berglund, 'Sparks fly over the EU energy union' (*NewsinEnglish.no - Views and News from Norway*, 12 March 2018) <http://www.newsinenglish.no/2018/03/12/sparks-fly-over-eu-energy-union/> accessed 17 November 2019 and Harald Breievne, 'One of ten norwegians say yes to Acer' (*Norway Today - Small and Big News from Norway*, 16 March 2018) <http://norwaytoday.info/news/one-ten-norwegians-say-yes-acer/> accessed 17 November 2019.

325 Bull, *supra* note 312, (295); Graver, *supra* note 312, (77); for a more detailed account of the principle of presumption cf. Arnesen and Stenvik, *supra* note 334, 64-71.

326 ECJ Opinion 1/91 (14 December 1991), ECR I-6079 (I-6101 et seq.); Fredriksen, Halvard Haukeland Fredriksen, Part VII: Institutional provisions – Chapter 3: Homogenity, surveillance procedure and settlement of disputes. in Finn Arnesen and others (eds), *Agreement on the European Economic Area - A Commentary*, Art. 105 recitals 2, 3.

327 Art. 3 SCA, Art. 6 EEAA; i.e. EFTA Court judgment E-1/94, *Restamark* [1994] recital 24.

question'.[328] This conformity constitutes a presumption that can be rebutted[329] but results in a very but not entirely similar case-law of the EFTA Court and the CJEU[330].

The Supreme Court of Norway (*Norges Høyesterett*) holds that the EFTA Court's decisions (cf. Art. 3 Surveillance and Court Agreement (SCA), Arts. 1 and 6 EEAA) must be attributed significant weight (*vesentlig vekt*)[331] and should usually be followed unless 'special circumstances' suggest otherwise.[332] As for now two categories of such 'special circumstances' can be envisaged: (1) cases which deviate from CJEU case-law[333] and (2) cases in which the courts find that the legislator did not intend to be bound under international law. The Norwegian courts must not interpret obligations under international law against the will of the legislator.[334]

The relationship between the EFTA Court and Norwegian Courts is shaped through § 51a *domstolloven* which refers to the request for the EFTA Court's advisory opinion under Art. 34 SCA. As the advisory opinions, according to the wording of Art. 34 SCA, do not formally bind Norwegian courts, the relationship has been described as a 'partnership' rather than

---

328 Joint EFTA Court judgments E-9/07 and E-10/07, *L'Oreal* [2008] recital 29.

329 EFTA Court judgment E-2/06, *ESA v Norway* [2007] recital 59; Pål Wennerås, Part III: The Agreement on ESA and EFTA Court. in Finn Arnesen and others (eds), *Agreement on the European Economic Area - A Commentary*, Art. 3 recital 8.

330 see i.e. EFTA Court judgment E-28/15, *Jabbi* [2016] recitals 62, 68, 71; Joint Cases E-9/07 and E-10/07, *L'Oreal* [2008] recitals 27, 28; ECJ Opinion 1/92 (10 April 1992), ECR I-2825 (I-2841); Fredriksen, *supra* note 326, Art. 105 recitals 6; Pål Wennerås, Part II: The Agreement on the European Economic Area. in Finn Arnesen and others (eds), *Agreement on the European Economic Area - A Commentary*, Art. 6 recital 20. Cf. also the deviating case-law in EFTA Court judgment E-8/00, *LO* [2002], EFTA Court judgment E-14/15, *Holship* [2016] and ECJ judgment C-67/96, *Albany International BV v Stichting Bedrijfspensioenfonds Textielindustrie (Albany)* [1999] as an example for the EFTA Court not following ECJ/CJEU case-law.

331 Norwegian Supreme Court, *Storebrand Skadeforsikring AS v Veronika Finanger (Finanger I)* [2000] Rt. 2000, 1811 (1820) per Judge Flock.

332 Norwegian Supreme Court, *Holship Norge AS v Norsk Transportarbeiderforbund* [2016] HR 2016, 2554, recital 77.

333 i.e. Norwegian Supreme Court, *STX OSV AS and others v Staten v/Tariffnemnda (STX)* [2013] Rt. 2013, 258.

334 Cf. Norwegian Supreme Court, *Oljearbeidernes Fellessammenslutning v Staten v/ Kommunal- og arbeidsdepartement (OFS)* [1997] Rt. 1997, 580 (585, 590); Finn Arnesen and Are Stenvik, *Internasjonalisering og juridisk metode - Særlig om EØS-rettens betydning i norsk rett*, 50. As to the importance of Parliamentary preparatory works, see the description of Norwegian methodology, 77 et seq.

hierarchical with the EFTA Court as court of last instance.[335] Unlike Art. 267 TFEU, Art. 34 SCA does not create an obligation for national courts to refer cases to the EFTA Court. Furthermore, the EFTA Court's ruling is merely advisory. According to the wording to Art. 34 SCA the national courts are not strictly bound by the ruling.[336] It is, thus, not clear whether the EFTA Court's advisory opinions (should) have actual binding effect. On the one hand, it must be taken into account that from a teleological point of view the EFTA states did not intend to transfer sovereignty to EFTA institutions. This includes their independent judiciaries.[337] Thus, it would be contrary to their intentions to grant the EFTA Court a position similar to that of the CJEU which would allow it to – in fact – become a court of last instance on EEA law matters.[338] On the other hand, the duty of loyalty according to Art. 3 EEAA must be considered.[339] If the national courts were to be exempted from a duty to refer cases to the EFTA Court which shall ensure homogeneity in the EEA, the goal of a homogenised area within the EEA could be undermined.

Between 2003 and March 2015 the Norwegian Supreme Court did not ask for the EFTA Court's advisory opinion in a single case.[340] Prior to this period the Norwegian courts had already been rather reluctant to refer cases to the EFTA Court. While in the years 1994-2010 out of 716 cases at Norwegian courts 261 involved decisive EEA law, only about 10%[341] of these cases were forwarded to the EFTA Court according to § 51a *domstolloven*.[342] Of those 10% of cases only two referrals were made by the

335 EFTA Court judgment E-18/11, *Irish Bank* [2012] recital 57.

336 Per Christiansen, Part III: The Agreement on ESA and EFTA Court. in Finn Arnesen and others (eds), *Agreement on the European Economic Area - A Commentary*, Art. 34 recital 28.

337 Cf. recital 15 of the Preamble to the EEA Agreement.

338 Cf. Halvard Haukeland Fredriksen, 'One Market, Two Courts: Legal Pluralism vs Homogeneity in the European Economic Area' [2010] 79 Nordic Journal of International Law 481 (486-488) on the EFTA Court's position in the EEA.

339 Christiansen, *supra* note 336, Art. 34 recital 28.

340 Carl Baudenbacher, The Relationship Between the EFTA Court and the Court of Justice of the European Union. in Carl Baudenbacher (ed), *The Handbook of EEA Law*, 160.

341 Cf. for a list of cases, Halvard Haukeland Fredriksen, The two EEA Courts: a Norwegian perspective. in EFTA Court (ed), *Judicial protection in the European economic area: international conference by the EFTA Court on 17 June 2011*, 199-201.

342 Sejersted, *supra* note 291, 169-170.

Norwegian Supreme Court.[343] Thus, even though acceptance of the EFTA Court's judgments has been indicated,[344] the courts do not seem to require many cases to be forwarded despite the increasing relevance of EEA norms in Norwegian law.

Different explanations for this are brought forward:[345]

1. Neither the court nor the parties involved want to bear the prolonged trial or the increased procedural costs.[346]
2. Due to the emphasis on oral proceedings in Norwegian procedural law questions regarding EEA law are usually raised at a later point in the court proceedings.[347]
3. The lack of the Norwegian courts' awareness for EEA legal issues.[348]
4. Some parties' preference for their cases to be handled at Norwegian courts only.[349]

A number of cases further illustrate the difficult relationship between Norwegian courts and authorities and the EFTA Court:

Similar to the ECJ in *Francovich*, the EFTA Court acknowledged the principle of state liability for incorrect implementation of EEA law by the EFTA states under (unwritten) EEA law in the Icelandic *Sveinbjörnsdóttir* case despite the opposition of the Icelandic, Norwegian and Swedish gov-

343 EFTA Court judgment E-1/99, *Storebrand Skadeforsikring AS v Veronika Finanger (Finanger I)* [1999] and EFTA Court judgment E-3/02, *Paranova v Merck & Co., Inc. and Others (Paranova)* [2003]. Two other cases (EFTA Court judgment E-5/97, *European Navigation* [1998] and the *Jet-ski* case) were withdrawn or eventually did not make it before the EFTA Court proceedings began, cf. Fredriksen, *supra* note 341, 196.

344 i.e. in both cases the Norwegian Supreme Court followed the EFTA Court's advisory opinions, cf. Norwegian Supreme Court, *Finanger I* [2000] Rt. 2000, 1811 and Norwegian Supreme Court, *Paranova AS v Merck & Co Inc, Merck, Sharp & Dohme B.V. og MSD (Norge) AS (Paranova)* [2004] Rt. 2004, 904.

345 Cf. Arnfinn Bårdsen, 'Noen refleksjoner om Norges Høyesterett og EFTA-domstolen' [2013] 52 (8) Lov og Rett 535 (542-543); Thomas Christian Poulsen, Norwegian Courts. in Carl Baudenbacher (ed), *The Handbook of EEA Law*, 271.

346 Ibid.; Halvard Haukeland Fredriksen, *Rapport #3 - EU/EØS-rett i norske domstoler*, 92.

347 Bårdsen, *supra* note 345, (542); Poulsen, *supra* note 345, 271.

348 Ibid.

349 Namely the Office of the Attorney General for Civil Affairs as the representative of the government in civil proceedings, cf. ibid. and Fredriksen, *supra* note 346, 95.

ernments as well as the EU Commission.[350] In the Icelandic *Karlsson* case the EFTA Court later confirmed this judgment against the Norwegian government's concerns[351] by emphasising that the state liability was a distinct one from the state liability under EU law.[352] The Norwegian Supreme Court later acknowledged the principle of state liability under EEA law in the *Finanger II* case.[353] This development is seen by some as not just an interpretation in line with the CJEU's case-law where necessary but a quasi-adoption of EU law in an area that was regarded distinct from EU law.[354] Commentators saw this as an indication of the EFTA Court's willingness to accord with CJEU case-law instead of focussing on the EEA Agreement's distinctness.[355] Furthermore, it has been derived that the EFTA Court rather focusses on an 'effect-oriented' implementation[356] of the homogeneity principle than the Contracting Parties' intentions.[357] Thus, the establishment of a separate court for the EFTA states to the EEA Agreement which was intended to preserve their autonomy turns out to have quite the opposite effect.[358]

The Norwegian *STX* case[359] concerned the interpretation of the Posted Workers Directive (Directive 97/71/EC). The Borgarting Court of Appeal had referred the case to the EFTA Court which offered an advisory opinion

---

350 Ibid. (744-745); EFTA Court judgment E-9/97, *Sveinbjörnsdóttir* [1998] Report for the Hearing, recitals 52-91, 94-100 (equivalent of ECJ judgment C-479/93, *Francovich* [1995]).

351 EFTA Court judgment E-4/01, *Karlsson* [2002] Report for the Hearing recitals 51-85.

352 EFTA Court judgment E-4/01, *Karlsson* [2002] recital 25-30.

353 Norwegian Supreme Court, *A v Staten v/Justisdepartementet (Finanger II)* [2005] Rt. 2005, 1365.

354 The CJEU case-law's argument in ECJ judgment C-479/93, *Andrea Francovich v Italian Republic (Francovich)* [1995] and ECJ judgment C-148/84, *Deutsche Genossenschaftsbank v SA Brasserie du Pêcheur (Brasserie de Pecheur)* [1985] was based on the elements of direct effect and supranationality under EU law which are absent under EEA law, cf. Halvard Haukeland Fredriksen, 'The EFTA Court 15 years on' [2010] 59 (July 2010) International and Comparative Law Quarterly 731 (738, 750); EFTA Court judgment E-4/01, *Karlsson* [2002] Report for the Hearing recitals 54 (brought forward by the Government of Norway); Opinion of the Advocate General in ECJ Case C-321/97, *Ulla-Brith Andersson and Susanne Wåkerås-Andersson v Svenska staten (Andersson)* [1999] recitals 37-54.

355 Fredriksen, *supra* note 354, (739-740, 743, 745, 749-750).

356 Ibid. (738).

357 Ibid. (744-745).

358 Ibid. (756-758).

359 Norwegian Supreme Court, *STX* [2013] Rt. 2013, 258.

on the case.[360] The Borgarting Court of Appeal did not decide according to the EFTA Court's advisory opinion.[361] The claimants (STX) appealed against the decision to the Norwegian Supreme Court and demanded that in case the Norwegian Supreme Court would not agree with the EFTA Court another advisory opinion would have to be requested.[362] The Norwegian Supreme Court, despite disagreeing with the EFTA Court, did not seek a further advisory opinion but confirmed the Borgarting Court of Appeal's judgment. It thereby emphasised that it

> shall not accept the EFTA Court's opinion without due examination; it has the authority as well as the duty to consider independently whether and to what extent this is warranted. In this light, I cannot see that the Supreme Court is formally prevented from relying on a different opinion. However, because significant importance must be attributed to the opinion, special reasons would be required for the Supreme Court to diverge.[363]

The Norwegian Supreme Court emphasised that it deviated from the EFTA Court's decision because it did not find the ruling to be in line with previous CJEU jurisdiction.[364] The judgment shows that the Norwegian Supreme Court sees itself independent from the EFTA Court.[365] The EFTA Court's reaction to the judgment was not welcoming. Carl Baudenbacher as President of the EFTA Court criticised the decision as 'a wrong use of Norwegian law instead of EEA law' as well as the Norwegian Supreme Court's 'misunderstanding of the Directive's legal character and the CJEU's legal practice'.[366]

---

360 EFTA Court judgment E-02/11 *STX Norway Offshore AS m.fl. v Staten v/ Tariffnemnda (STX)* [2013].

361 Borgarting Court of Appeal, *STX* [2012] LB-2010-60176-2.

362 Norwegian Supreme Court, *STX* [2013] Rt. 2013, 258, recital 17.

363 Ibid. recital 94 (per Judge Matheson). Translation taken from Astrid O Eidesen, The Norwegian Experience of the EEA Judiciary. in EFTA Court (ed), *The EEA and the EFTA Court - Decentred Integration*, 138.

364 Norwegian Supreme Court, *STX* [2013] Rt. 2013, 258, recitals 44-49.

365 Fredriksen, Halvard Haukeland Fredriksen, The Troubled Relationship between the Supreme Court of Norway and the EFTA Court - Recent Developments. in Peter-Christian Müller-Graff and Ola Mestad (eds), *The Rising Complexity of European Law*, 36.

366 Carl Baudenbacher, 'EFTA-domstolen og dens samhandling med de norske domstolene' [2013] 52 (8) Lov og Rett 515 (528).

In the Norwegian *Jonsson* case[367] (20 March 2013) the EFTA Court stated *obiter dictum* that cases concerning EEA law shall be referred to it. It, furthermore, underlined that

> [t]hereby unnecessary mistakes in the interpretation and application of EEA law are avoided and the coherence and reciprocity in relation to rights of EEA citizens, including EFTA nationals, in the EU are ensured.[368]

In Norway this part of the EFTA Court's advisory opinion was seen as a direct critical reply to the Norwegian Supreme Court's judgment in *STX*, thus, implying that the Norwegian Supreme Court committed an 'unnecessary mistake' by not following the EFTA Court's prior advisory opinion.[369] In the Liechtenstein *Koch* case[370] the EFTA Court again emphasised *obiter dictum* that

> effective judicial protection [...] can only be achieved if EEA/EFTA and EU nationals and economic operators enjoy equal access to the courts in both the EU and EFTA pillars of the EEA to ensure their rights which they derive from the EEA Agreement.[371]

In its decision *Fosen Linjen*[372] the Frostating Court of Appeal decided not to follow an EFTA Court advisory opinion[373] in the case and instead followed the Norwegian Supreme Court's and CJEU case-law explicitly referring to the Norwegian Supreme Court's decision in *STX*.[374] The case was referred to the Norwegian Supreme Court which asked for another advisory opinion from the EFTA Court. On the 1 August 2019 the EFTA Court reversed its previous decision in *Fosen Linjen I*.[375] In its final decision on

367 EFTA Court judgment E-3/12, *Staten v/Arbeidsdepartementet v Stig Arne Jonsson (Jonsson)* [2013].

368 Ibid. recital 60; Fredriksen, *supra* note 365, 24.

369 Fredriksen, ibid.

370 EFTA Court judgment E-11/12, *Beatrix Koch, Dipl. Kfm. Lothar Hummel and Stefan Müller v Swiss Life (Liechtenstein) AG (Koch)* [2013].

371 Ibid. recital 117; Fredriksen, *supra* note 365, 25.

372 Frostating Court of Appeal, *Fosen-Linjen AS v Atb AS (Fosen Linjen)* [2018] LF-2015-187242.

373 EFTA Court judgment E-16/16 *Fosen-Linjen AS v Atb AS (Fosen Linjen I)* [2017].

374 Frostating Court of Appeal, *Fosen Linjen* [2018] LF-2015-187242, pages 22-23.

375 EFTA Court judgment E-7/18 *Fosen Linjen AS v AtB AS (Fosen Linjen II)* [2019]. For criticism on the procedure, cf. Carl Baudenbacher, 'Fosen Fiasco – Now the ball is in the Norwegian Supreme Court's field' (*anbud365.no*, 5 July 2019)

the case, the Norwegian Supreme Court accepted the EFTA Court's second decision.[376]

The relationship between Norwegian courts and the EFTA Court is, thus, conflicted. Norwegian courts appear inclined to follow the CJEU's case-law rather than the EFTA Court's in order to meet the principle of homogeneity.

3. Conclusion

It can be concluded that through the EEA Agreement Norwegian businesses and consumers are able to fully participate in the European internal market without fully giving up sovereignty. However, the EEA Agreement thereby does not offer much leeway to deviate from European norms included under the EEA Agreement. Due to the structural imbalance of the EEA it is hardly possible to veto the implementation of new legislation into national law. Furthermore, the mandatory implementation of EEA law does raise questions. On the one hand, there seems to exist a lack of democratic control when it comes to incorporating EU legislative acts into national law. On the other hand, there exist conflicts between the Norwegian national courts and the EFTA Court.

IV. Comparability

In a next step the comparability of Norwegian societal factors and legal system with the UK's and Germany's societal and legal factors must be evaluated. Due to the topic of this dissertation the focus lies on the comparability between Norway and the UK.

With respect to their relationship with Europe, the UK and Norway are historically shaped in different ways. While the UK defines its sovereignty as a 'freedom to' implement certain policies, Norway has – at least since the 19th century – sought a 'freedom from' foreign rule. Thus, the reluctance to stay in and respectively join the supranational EU are based on different historic foundations. Norway's focus, furthermore, appears to be more directed at Europe and especially the neighbouring Scandinavian

---

<https://www.anbud365.no/regelverk/fosen-fiasco-now-the-ball-is-in-the-norwegian-supreme-courts-field/> accessed 16 August 2019.

376 Norwegian Supreme Court, *AtB AS v Fosen-Linjen AS* [2019] HR-2019-1801-A.

countries rather than a global network such as the Commonwealth. Thus, the UK and Norway pursue different policy objectives in this regard. Nevertheless, both countries aim at a position outside of the EU while maintaining good trade relations with EU Member States.

Compared to Germany, Norway also differs in its approach to European cooperation. While Germany, *inter alia*, defines its sovereignty and freedom through European integration and membership in the EU ('freedom with'), Norway is more reluctant to give up sovereignity because of its past experience as a part of Denmark and Sweden.

Norway's EEA-Membership may well be explained by its past. At the same time there exists a struggle between maintaining sovereignty and keeping close relations with European partners. The Norwegian model mainly works for Norway because the process has been depoliticised and legal integration takes place in a consensual, rather technical way. It is questionable whether such a way of 'silent' implementation is possible in the UK which is a lot less compromise driven and shaped more by societal divisions. Furthermore, the UK would become more of a rule-taker than a rule-maker and would still be bound by CJEU case-law despite the EFTA Court's apparent willingness to deviate from such in some cases. The relationship between the UK and the EFTA Court could prove equally as difficult as that between the EFTA Court and Norway.

Historically, Norway and the UK differ fundamentally. While both countries have experienced European history, they have done so in very different ways. The main difference is probably borne by the fact that the UK was a colonial power while Norway had been a part of Denmark and Sweden and occupied by Germany. Like the UK, however, Norway is located at the European periphery unlike Germany in the geographic centre. Therefore, both countries have been relatively spared from destruction by wars throughout the past centuries. All three countries have in common that they have seeked Western political integration during and since the end of World War II.

Unlike the UK, Norway pursues a coordinated market economic approach which is rather comparable to the social market economic policy in Germany. Instead of a focus on the individual and wealth maximisation, the Norwegian approach focusses on social mobility and the reduction of inequalities. Such policies are enabled by the income generated from Norwegian oil dwelling which is invested for the benefit of the whole society and turned the Government Pension Fund Global into a global player. While UK economic growth has slowed down in the 20th century, Norway's GDP has been growing rapidly. And unlike the UK, the Norwegian model is not dependent on providing for a global financial market place but specifically relies on government intervention.

The Norwegian economic policy goals are also reflected in the sociological factors. Despite divisions along cultural lines, Norwegian society can be said to be homogenous, i.e. indicated by very high trust rates on all levels, sharing similar values such as the disapproval of inequality. In this regard the small egalitarian Norwegian society differs starkly from the larger and more heterogenous UK and Germany.

These factors also influence the Norwegian legal system. The interpretation and application of legal norms in light of Scandinavian Legal Realism are eased by factors that indicate a homogenous and egalitarian society. If the parties to a dispute found their beliefs on the same basis of values, it is more likely for them to accept a judgment that is not merely based on the application of legal norms but takes into account various outside factors including 'policy considerations'. For example, in Germany the formality that is despised by Scandinavian Legal Realists was considered a positive mean to achieve legal unification in Germany. In this light, it may also be said for Germany that the formality of the law also creates legal certainty (*Rechtssicherheit*) as it is easier for the parties of the disputes to accept a judgment based on formal legal considerations rather than individual notions of 'justice' which may not accord with the parties' own concepts of justice (heterogeneity of value sets). In Norway, however, individual considerations may prove to be a more acceptable mean especially because it is likely that the parties base their notions of justice on a similar set of values.

The Norwegian legal concepts, thereby, also differ from the concept of the English common law despite the similar foundation on freedom of contract. While formally Norwegian law may be considered closer to the common law conceptually than German law because it relies a lot more on case-law, the material considerations are contrasted. As has been shown, the interpretative means of English common law of contract are mainly restricted to the interpretation of the agreement of the parties rather than considering outside factors or even the broad notion of 'fairness'. Such considerations would have to be clearly defined. Equitable intervention remains the exception. Norwegian law, however, explicitly allows for such intervention. Social and fairness considerations are common.

Regarding the structure of dispute resolution mechanisms, Norway and the UK reveal similarities with respect to the offer of alternative dispute resolution bodies and administrative consumer protection which are not as common in Germany (see also below). However, the availability of alternative dispute resolution appears broader in Norway where such bodies exist for several economic branches and have been a well-established feature of the legal system for many years. Also, the rationales behind alternative dispute resolution in the UK and Norway may differ. While in the UK they appear to offer a cheap and effective way to resolve disputes (economic rationale), it is likely they are also rooted in the high interpersonal trust rates and homogeneity in Norway (sociological rationale). Independent courts are especially necessary where the parties require and expect absolute neutrality. In societies with low interpersonal trust rates such neutrality is achieved by independent state institutions. Where interpersonal trust rates are higher, it appears likely that the parties may also accept the decision of an alternative tribunal.

D. Switzerland

I. Swiss Society

The following sections provide an overview of societal factors and structures underlying the Swiss legal system. As with the previously depicted legal systems, an understanding of these factors and structures is necessary in order to conduct a comparative analysis. Swiss society is shaped by unique and reciprocal historic, economic and social factors that have to be considered to gain a full understanding of the law, its background and application. The unique combination of these factors provides a guideline as to how societal factors have influenced legal developments in Switzerland.

Historic Factors

Swiss history is characterised by the struggle to achieve a federal nation state that can represent Swiss interests, i.e. on the international stage, while at the same time maintaining a high degree of independence at the cantonal level. As a consequence, Swiss societal and economic developments have progressed at a slow but steady pace.[377]

The original Swiss Confederation was established 1291 by the Swiss Charter of Confederation (*Bundesbrief*) which guaranteed mutual assistance against internal and external aggression.[378] The Confederate members remained largely independent did not show much interest in the in-

377 Leonhard Neidhart, *Die politische Schweiz - Fundamente und Institutionen*, 132 et seq.; Jonathan Steinberg, *Why Switzerland*, 38.

378 Patricia Egli, *Introduction to Swiss Constitutional Law*, 7.

terests of the whole Confederation.[379] Since the conclusion of the Westphalian Peace Treaty (1648)[380] Switzerland pursues a neutral approach to foreign policy to ensure independence and sovereignity of the country which was formally acknowledged by the other European powers at the Congress of Vienna in 1815 and guaranteed by the Paris Charter.[381] After a brief civil war in 1847 (*Sonderbundkrieg*), a new constitution was introduced in 1848 which made Switzerland the first federal state in Europe.[382] It was characterised by a balance of self- and shared-rule, meaning that only where cooperation was held necessary, powers were transferred to the federal state while most of the competences rested with the cantons.[383] A revised constitution was adopted in 1874 which introduced a stronger element of centralisation.[384] It granted federal competences in the fields of legal unification of civil and criminal law, a single Swiss market as well as a unified army, created a stronger federal judiciary and included a catalogue of fundamental citizens' rights.[385] The constitution also introduced the citizens' right to demand referenda[386] which underlined the status of Switzerland as a semi-direct democracy. While the federal order largely remains the same until today, the constitution underwent ca. 150 partial revisions until the next total revision in 1999.[387]

During the two World Wars Switzerland was able to maintain its neutrality and establish itself as a neutral location for international confe-

---

379 Andreas Kley, *Verfassungsgeschichte der Neuzeit - Grossbritannien, die USA, Frankreich, Deutschland und die Schweiz*, 209.

380 Alexander Misic and Nicole Töpperwien, *Constitutional Law in Switzerland*, recital 8.

381 Ibid. recital 10; Steinberg, *supra* note 377, 42. Neutrality was reaffirmed in the Treaty of Versailles (1919) and the London Declaration (1920).

382 Egli, *supra* note 378, 9; Misic and Töpperwien, ibid., recitals 12, 13.

383 Egli, ibid.; Kley, *supra* note 379, 232; Misic and Töpperwien, ibid., recital 13. Areas such as foreign policy, customs, currency, unified measurements or the postal sector were attributed to the federal level, while taxing and law-making powers in areas such as labour or trade law remained with the cantons.

384 Misic and Töpperwien, ibid., recital 14.

385 Egli, *supra* note 378, 10; Kley, *supra* note 379, 241; Misic and Töpperwien, ibid., recitals 15, 17. Under the constitution of 1848 the Swiss Federal Court only had very limited powers, cf. Kley, ibid., 233. The new role under the 1874 constitution included the protection of citizens' constitutional rights and unified application of the law, cf. Kley, ibid., 255-257; Misic and Töpperwien, ibid., recital 18.

386 Kley, ibid., 243-244; Misic and Töpperwien, ibid., recital 16.

387 Misic and Töpperwien, ibid., recital 19.

rences and institutions; a reputation that lasts until today.[388] Despite international organisations' seats in Switzerland, the country has been reluctant to join such due to fears of loss of the status of neutrality.[389] While Switzerland had already participated in several UN programs since the end of World War II, it only joined the UN as a member in 2002. It only joined the Council of Europe in 1963 and the ECHR in 1974 and has been reluctant when it comes to European cooperation ever since.[390]

Swiss history has, thus, been characterised by slow but gradual development, i.e. with respect to international developments[391]. The country has benefited from the early acknowledgement of a status of neutrality and has, therefore, been spared from rapid societal changes and revolutions. Internally the country has been shaped by regional pluralism which is reflected in strong elements of federalism and direct democracy. The slow pace of societal change and compromise oriented involvement of regions have contributed to, on the hand, a high degree of stability as well as, on the other hand, a strong sense of awareness with respect to the maintenance of devolved competences on behalf of the cantons.

Economic Factors

Switzerland was one of the first European countries to undergo and benefit from industrialisation in the 19th century.[392] Until today Switzerland remains a wealthy country with a thriving economy especially in the areas of pharmaceuticals, banking and production of luxury goods. As of 2018,

388 Kley, *supra* note 379, 268-270; Neidhart, *supra* note 377, 160.

389 Kley, ibid., 299.

390 Ibid. 300.

391 International developments were frequently acknowledged but, if at all, mostly adopted in a much weaker form due to the scrutiny the policies faced by way of referenda, cf. Alfred Kölz, *Neuere Schweizerische Verfassungsgeschichte - Ihre Grundlinien in Bund und Kantonen seit 1848*, 675.

392 Steinberg, *supra* note 377, 171, 176. The Swiss economy could be characterised as a middle-way between the British (specialised with respect to consumer goods) and German (specialised with respect to future technologies and iron processing industry) industrial models, cf. David Gugerli, Luigi Lorenzetti, Margrit Müller, Jakob Tanner and Ulrich Woitek, Teil 1: Wirtschaftliche Entwicklung, Demographie und Technologie. Einleitung. in Patrick Halbeisen, Margrit Müller and Béatrice Veyrassat (eds), *Wirtschaftsgeschichte der Schweiz im 20. Jahrhundert*, 47; Margrit Müller and Ulrich Woitek, Teil 1: Wirtschaftliche Entwicklung, Demographie und Technologie. 1.1: Wohlstand, Wachstum und Konjunktur. in Patrick Halbeisen and others (eds), *Wirtschaftsgeschichte der Schweiz im 20. Jahrhundert*, 96.

Switzerland shows the third highest GDP per capita (USD 68,079) among OECD countries (cf. Annex 1, Figure 1) with a lower-average Gini coefficient (0.296) as of 2015[393]. It ranks second on the Human Development Index.[394] The economy has been and still is extremely export oriented. In this regard, the pluralism of languages and regional cultures, which are difficult to manage internally, constitute a unique advantage externally. Communication between the French-Swiss and French, the German-Swiss and Germans and Austrians and the Italian-Swiss with Italians is eased by the lack of language barriers as well as cultural proximity.[395] Furthermore, the internal pluralism of culture and language has been used as a motor rather than a source of division.[396] Beside the usefulness of multilingualism in foreign trade relations, the cantons' internal competition has led to a diversification of the economy that has contributed to its innovative power and stability.[397]

Lacking natural resources,[398] the Swiss are forced to manufacture products efficiently. This led to an early high degree of specialisation.[399] Furthermore, a lot of public and private investments have been directed at education, research and development.[400] From the 19th century onward the level of education among the Swiss population has been above average.[401] The strong focus on education, innovation, thus, qualified labour and asso-

393 OECD, *supra* note 113.

394 Jahan and others, *supra* note 211, 22.

395 Neidhart, *supra* note 377, 116.

396 Manuel Hiestand, Margrit Müller and Ulrich Woitek, Teil 3: Wohlstandsverteilung und regionale Entwicklung. 3.3: Partizipation der Kantone und Regionen. in Patrick Halbeisen and others (eds), *Wirtschaftsgeschichte der Schweiz im 20. Jahrhundert*, 761.

397 Ibid. 811; Misic and Töpperwien, *supra* note 380, recitals 277, 278; Neidhart, *supra* note 377, 132-133.

398 David Gugerli and Jakob Tanner, Teil 1: Wirtschaftliche Entwicklung, Demographie und Technologie. 1.3: Wissen und Technologie. in Patrick Halbeisen and others (eds), *Wirtschaftsgeschichte der Schweiz im 20. Jahrhundert*, 265. Only 5.8% of the country can be used for habitation and infrastructure while 25.5% are classified as 'unproductive', cf. Steinberg, *supra* note 377, 180-181.

399 Ibid. 173.

400 As of 2017 Switzerland leads OECD countries with respect to (mainly private) investments in the area of research and development and shows the highest innovation performance, cf. OECD, *OECD Economic Surveys: Switzerland*, 41-42; Steinberg, ibid., 171.

401 Müller and Woitek, *supra* note 392, 92.

ciated efficient use of resources is exemplified by the growth of the luxury industry.[402]

Due to a lack of destruction during European or cantonal wars, the economy could grow gradually and today is one of the most stable in the world.[403] Swiss growth rates run slowly but gradually.[404] One explanation lies in the decentralised federal Swiss political system. Most taxing and economic steering powers lie with the cantons.[405] Furthermore, policy developments are exposed to the 'danger of referenda', so it takes time and compromise to implement policies that could fuel the economy.[406]

Switzerland introduced collective measures of social security late compared to its European neighbours. While regulatory measures with respect a to safety in the workplace had been implemented on a federal level by the end of the 19th century,[407] effective collective social security measures were only introduced after World War II.[408] Generally workers' conditions have not only been improved by unilateral actions by employers or unions but an underlying sense of industrial peace, cooperation and compromise between workers and employers.[409]

Switzerland has provided fertile ground for the establishment of 'big players' especially in the banking and pharmaceutical industries. Some of these companies' revenues exceed the federal budget.[410] Still the Swiss administration is able to control them with efficient bureaucratic means as well as constant exchange between business leaders and government agencies.[411] Apart from the 'Swiss giants' the Swiss economy is dominated by medium-sized businesses which are, as mentioned above, highly spe-

402 Steinberg, *supra* note 377, 180 et seq.

403 Gugerli, Lorenzetti, Müller, Tanner and Woitek, *supra* note 392, 30; Steinberg, ibid., 172.

404 Cf. Müller and Woitek, *supra* note 392, 204.

405 Hiestand, Müller and Woitek, *supra* note 396, 762.

406 Steinberg, *supra* note 377, 114.

407 Cf. Brigitte Studer, Teil 4: Die schweizerische Variante des Kapitalismus. 4.3: Ökonomien der sozialen Sicherheit. in Patrick Halbeisen and others (eds), *Wirtschaftsgeschichte der Schweiz im 20. Jahrhundert*, 925, 929.

408 Ibid. 925.

409 Bernhard Degen, Teil 4: Die schweizerische Variante des Kapitalismus. 4.2: Arbeit und Kapital. in Patrick Halbeisen and others (eds), *Wirtschaftsgeschichte der Schweiz im 20. Jahrhundert*, 903. Dispute resolution agencies installed by cantons contributed to the development of appeasing rather than escalating conflicts, ibid. 883-884. However, the social partnership was not as distinct as in Scandinavian countries, ibid. 909.

410 Steinberg, *supra* note 377, 191.

411 Ibid.

cialised and innovative.[412] These businesses also profit from an efficient bureaucracy which eases regulatory certainty and foreseeability when it comes to investments.

The Swiss economy is one of the strongest and most stable in the world thanks to slow and gradual growth since the 19th century. Due to a lack of resources the Swiss have focussed their economic activity on trade and innovation. Rather than a universal welfare state, Switzerland developed a fragmented system of social security measures. Decentralisation has diversified the economy and limits the federal state's means of intervention. A compromise driven labour policy has led to high wages regulated by collective agreements as well as a relatively even distribution of wealth among Swiss citizens, although slight cantonal differences continue to exist[413].

Sociological Factors

Swiss societal phenomena are closely intertwined with the decentralised semi-direct democratic political system.[414] The society uniquely combines elements of pluralist cultural features that cause internal distance as well as geographical features that at the same time produce an inherent nearness.

Swiss nation building proceeded differently from that of other European countries. Rather than a force for internal unification, the Swiss cantons formed a convenient partnership against foreign invasion. In combination with its policy of neutrality the Swiss Confederation has not had to suffer a violation of its external and internal borders or foreign rule for centuries.[415] Thus, internally a fragmented system of culturally diverse regions continued to exist partly because there was no reason to unite against foreign aggressors. As there was no need to change the *status quo*, this fragmentation has since been reflected in a strong sense of federalism and subsidiarity in all federal constitutions. Due to the strong position of the cantons, they – rather than the federal state – serve as a mean of identification.[416] The fact that an integrative process of evaluation of a variety of interest groups by which the majority of people feel included (*Konkor-*

412 Ibid.

413 Regional disparities in Switzerland are low, cf. OECD, Regions and Cities at a Glance – Switzerland (5 March 2019).

414 Paolo Dardanelli, Federalism: institutional adaptation and symbolic constraints. in Clive H. Church (ed), *Switzerland and the European Union - A close, contradictory and misunderstood relationship*, 23.

415 With the exception of the establishment of the 'Helvetic Republic' (1789-1813). Neidhart, *supra* note 377, 129.

416 Steinberg, *supra* note 377, 307.

danz)[417] precedes compromise-oriented decision-making in addition to devolved competences of local authorities also explains that the Swiss show the highest trust rate in their government (Annex 1, Figure 4) and relatively high trust in the police (Annex 1, Figure 3) among OECD countries. The compromise-shaped coexistence in Switzerland appeases regional differences.

The regional sourcing of identity is reinforced by the pluralism of Swiss official languages: German, French, Italian and Romansch. In addition, especially in the German-speaking part of Switzerland, a variety of regional and communal dialects further diversify the issue of regional identity.[418] Despite the lingual pluralism, Swiss citizens rarely speak two of the official languages fluently.[419] This makes communication difficult and leads to harder borders between the regions. As it is easier to communicate and perceive culture in one's mother tongue, affiliation has grown toward the respective foreign neighbouring country rather than the internal neighbouring region.[420] Thereby, the lingual barriers have also caused differing cultural developments. The fragmentation of the Swiss cultural landscape has emphasised a sense of 'smallness' while at the same time producing cultural enlargement through pluralism.[421] Thus, the homogeneity created by the nearness of community life and heterogeneity caused by cultural pluralism frequently coincide in Switzerland.[422] In combination with the element of concordance there exists a strong awareness for differences and willingness to compromise to avoid conflicts.[423]

At the same time, one cannot neglect the fact that both geographic[424] and population[425] wise Switzerland is a small country. The small size and lack of resources make cooperation between citizens and institutions indis-

417 Ibid. 84.

418 Neidhart, *supra* note 377, 117; Steinberg, ibid., 141-143, 147.

419 Neidhart, ibid., 113.

420 Ibid.

421 Ibid. 118-119.

422 Ibid. 82.

423 Ibid. 119.

424 41.285 km^2, Swiss Federal Statistical Office, 'Überblick Schweiz' (*Federal Statistical Office*) <https://www.bfs.admin.ch/bfs/de/home/statistiken/raum-umwelt/bodennutzung-bedeckung/ueberblick-schweiz.html> accessed 13 April 2019.

425 The Swiss population amounts to 8.542.300 people as of 2018, cf. Swiss Federal Statistical Office, 'Bevölkerungsentwicklung 2018: Provisorische Ergebnisse' (*Federal Statistical Office*, 9 April 2019) <https://www.bfs.admin.ch/bfs/en/home/statistics/population/effectif-change.assetdetail.7926998.html> accessed 13 April 2019.

pensable[426] and create nearness among actors[427] which is also emphasised by a relatively high interpersonal trust rate (Annex 1, Figure 2). Due to the absence of aristocracy, decision-making processes have developed from the 'bottom up' rather than the 'top down'.[428] The strong element of direct democracy that derives from this concept, engages the individual citizen and recognises their individuality amidst the nearness and pressure of conformity caused by the necessity to cooperate.[429]

The depicted features of direct democracy, federalism and concordance are interdependent. The concept of direct democracy does not only serve to recognise the individual but also contributed to the appeasement of different layers of government on and in between the federal, cantonal and communal levels and, thereby, strengthened federalism.[430] In addition, the compromise-oriented principle of concordance strengthened federal cooperation.[431] In turn it also resulted from the principle of direct democracy which allows the influence of a variety of actors on different levels. Meanwhile, federalism ensures stability and maintains the pluralism of regional cultures.

It can, thus, be summarised that Swiss identity is mainly shaped regionally. Society is bound together by common features and values, such as democracy and compromise, rather than commonalities such as language.[432] This leads to regional confinement as well as federal pluralism.

Conclusion: Relationship with Europe and Consequences for Legal System

Historically, Switzerland is characterised by slow but stable and gradual development focussed on federalism that ensures regional autonomy internally and neutrality to ensure the nation's integrity externally. Economically, Switzerland is characterised by a focus on trade and innovation which leads to a strong dependence on exports as well as on the import of foreign and highly skilled labour. Sociologically, Swiss society may be characterised by the coincidence of communal homogeneity and federal plur-

---

426 Neidhart, *supra* note 377, 227.
427 Ibid. 91.
428 Ibid. 137; Thomas Cottier and Rachel Liechti, Schweizer Spezifika: Direkte Demokratie, Konkordanz, Föderalismus und Neutralität als politische Gestaltungsfaktoren. in Fritz Breuss, Thomas Cottier and Peter-Christian Müller-Graff (eds), *Die Schweiz im europäischen Integrationsprozess*, 44.
429 Neidhart, ibid., 89, 225 et seq.
430 Cottier and Liechti, *supra* note 428, 41.
431 Ibid. 45.
432 Cf. also Dardanelli, *supra* note 414, 19.

alism, the importance of cooperation and compromise as well as a strong identification with the intrinsic features of the political system, such as direct democracy, federalism and concordance.

As for the relationship with the rest of Europe and the EU especially, this means that it is unlikely that Switzerland will become an EU Member State as Membership could restrict the elements of direct democracy and cantonal autonomy. However, because Switzerland's economy is extremely export dependent, it is crucial to maintain open trade relationships with the EU.

II. Swiss Legal Institutions, Drafting and Method

1. Institutions and Drafting Method

Switzerland is a federal semi-direct democracy. As has been explained above, competences are allocated according to the principle of subsidiarity, meaning that only where it is considered necessary, competences are assigned to the federal state. All other competences remain with the 26 cantons. The regulation of private law lies with the federal legislator.[433] As a civil law country there exists a distinction between private and administrative courts.[434] The Swiss Federal Court (*Schweizerisches Bundesgericht*) is the highest court of the Confederation (cf. Art. 188 Section 1 Swiss Constitution).

Switzerland is a civil law country. The main body of private law is codified in the Swiss Code of Obligations originally introduced in 1881 and revised on 1911 (*Obligationenrecht*, hereinafter "OR")[435] and in the Swiss Civil Code introduced in 1907 (*Schweizerisches Zivilgesetzbuch*, hereinafter "ZGB").[436] The Code of Obligations is considered the fifth part of the Civil Code.[437] Further legislation on private law is included in special legal acts such as the Swiss Consumer Credit Act 1993 (*Konsumkreditgesetz 1993*,

433 Art. 122 Section 1 Swiss Constitution.

434 Misic and Töpperwien, *supra* note 380, recital 237.

435 The OR includes provisions on contract law, trade law and corporate law.

436 The ZGB includes provisions on the law of persons, family law, inheritance law and property law. Generally, the ZGB ist drafted in a less complex manner than the BGB, cf. Wieacker, *supra* note 117, 490-494.

437 Cf. the title of the revised OR 'Federal Act on the Amendment of the Swiss Civil Code (Part Five: The Code of Obligations)'. At the same time the ZGB recurs to the OR for general provisions on contract law (Art. 7 ZGB).

hereinafter "KKG 1993") or the Unfair Commercial Practices Law (*Bundesgesetz gegen den unlauteren Wettbewerb*, hereinafter "S-UWG"). It, thereby, resembles the German legal order of private law. Unlike German private law, however, Art. 1 Section 2 ZGB specifically includes judge-made law by providing that

> [in] the absence of a provision, the court shall decide in accordance with customary law and, in the absence of customary law, in accordance with the rule that it would make as legislator.[438]

Until the beginning of the 21st century Swiss consumer protection policy remained fragmented and weakly organised.[439] For a long time governmental regulatory measures stood beside the industries' soft-law approaches of self-regulation.[440] This may be explained with the liberal orientation of the existing main bodies of codified private law (ZGB and OR). Social measures, such as labour law, were only added gradually.[441] Since 1981 consumer protection is integrated in the Swiss Constitution.[442] The constitutional principle shows that the legislator realised an imbalance in business-consumer relationships and wishes to recreate a fair balance.[443] The first comprehensive consumer law instruments were introduced in the 1980s and 1990s and influenced by European and international law.[444] Since the failed accession to the EEA, the influence of European consumer law by way of autonomous adaptation has decreased.[445] However, as the history of consumer credit legislation exemplifies, a struggle long continued to exist between liberal tendencies and the introduction of new consumer protection measures.

---

438 Kann dem Gesetz keine Vorschrift entnommen werden, so soll das Gericht nach Gewohnheitsrecht und, wo auch ein solches fehlt, nach der Regel entscheiden, die es als Gesetzgeber aufstellen würde. (Translation by Swiss Federal Council).

439 Jakob Tanner und Brigitte Studer, Teil 3: Wohlstandsverteilung und regionale Entwicklung. 3.1: Konsum und Distribution. in Patrick Halbeisen and others (eds), *Wirtschaftsgeschichte der Schweiz im 20. Jahrhundert*, 692-694.

440 Ibid. 692.

441 Marlis Koller-Tumler, Marlis Koller-Tumler, Einführung in die Grundlagen des privatrechtlichen Konsumentenschutzes. in Ernst A. Kramer (ed), *Schweizerisches Privatrecht, Band 10: Konsumentenschutz im Privatrecht*, 13.

442 Formerly Art. 31 Swiss Constitution (1874); now Art. 97 Swiss Constitution (1999).

443 Koller-Tumler, *supra* note 441, 35.

444 Ibid. 36 et seq., 43 et seq.

445 Ibid. 53 et seq.

2. Interpretation of Norms

Similar to the other legal systems depicted in this work, the principles of freedom of contract,[446] and specifically free will, mutual trust, equivalence of consideration and *pacta sunt servanda*[447] form the basis of Swiss contract law. Art. 2 Section 1 ZGB specifically includes a duty to act according to good faith.

The interpretation of norms draws back to Art. 1 Section 1 ZGB which provides that

> [the] law applies according to its wording or interpretation to all legal questions for which it contains a provision.[448]

Similar to German law,[449] Savigny's *canones* – grammatical, systematic, historical and teleological interpretation – form the basis of norm interpretation under Swiss law.[450] However, Swiss private law is constructed in a less formal and complex manner.[451] According to the Swiss Federal Court there exists no hierarchy of interpretative elements but a '(pragmatic) methodological pluralism', meaning that the weight attributed to each interpretative method depends on the individual case.[452] Its interpretative approach has been summarised by the Swiss Federal Court as follows:

> [It requires] the factually correct decision in a normative framework, directed at a satisfactory result based on the ratio legis. In that regard the Swiss Federal Court follows a pragmatic methodological pluralism and rejects to subject the interpretative elements to a hierarchical prioritising order.[453]

---

446 Arts. 11, 19 Section 1 OR.

447 Ernst A. Kramer, *Juristische Methodenlehre*, 104.

448 Das Gesetz findet auf alle Rechtsfragen Anwendung, für die es nach Wortlaut oder Auslegung eine Bestimmung enthält. (Translation by Swiss Federal Council).

449 Cf. pages 68 et seq. above. However, regarding differences between the German and Swiss codifications see Wieacker, *supra* note 117, 491-494.

450 Kramer, *supra* note 447, 60.

451 Wieacker, *supra* note 117, 493-494.

452 Cf. Swiss Federal Court, *X. v Bundesamt für Polizeiwesen* [1984] BGE 110 Ib 1 (8); Swiss Federal Court, *SBG v BK Vision AG* [1995] BGE 121 III 219 (225); Susan Emmenegger and Axel Tschentscher, Art. 1 ZGB. in Heinz Hausheer and Hans Peter Walter (eds), *Berner Kommentar zum schweizerischen Privatrecht, Band I: Einleitung und Personenrecht (Art. 1-9 ZGB)*, recital 194.

453 Swiss Federal Court (1995), ibid.: 'Gefordert ist die sachlich richtige Entscheidung im normativen Gefüge, ausgerichtet auf ein befriedigendes Ergebnis aus

While this approach has been criticised for barely providing an opportunistic mean to reach a desired result,[454] it has also been praised for providing flexibility necessary to deal with complex situations of everyday life which cannot be grasped by the static hierarchical application of principles.[455] The systematic element includes the unity of the legal order (*Einheit der Rechtsordnung*) and thereby requires that the Swiss Constitution's basic rights (Art. 35 Swiss Constitution) and international law must be considered (Art. 5 Section 4 Swiss Constitution).[456] The teleological and historical elements include a euro compatible interpretation if it was the legislator's aim to create provisions parallel to EU law.[457] Beside the classic interpretative canones, Swiss courts frequently use comparative elements as an aid to interpret norms, especially in the areas of international and European law.[458]

In case a Swiss court reaches the conclusion that there does not exist a provision that fits the case in front of them, Art. 1 Section 2 Option 1 ZGB provides that 'the court shall decide according to customary law' (see above). Art. 5 Section 2 ZGB therefore especially refers to cantonal customs. 'In the absence of customary law' the court must decide as the legislator would (Art. 1 Section 2 Option 2 ZGB, *modo legislatoris*). Unlike the interpretative closing of gaps by way of using an analogy or teleological reduction,[459] this option must only be applied in case there do not exist any legal or customary norms that could be applied to the case. Where such provisions do not exist, the court is empowered to law-making.[460] The Swiss Federal Court has rarely made use of this competence.[461] Previous

---

der ratio legis. Dabei befolgt das Bundesgericht einen pragmatischen Methodenpluralismus und lehnt es namentlich ab, die einzelnen Auslegungselemente einer hierarchischen Prioritätsordnung zu unterstellen.' (Translation by author).

454 Among others Kramer, *supra* note 447, 133. For an overview cf. Emmenegger and Tschentscher, *supra* note 452, recital 198.

455 Emmenegger and Tschentscher, ibid., recitals 201-204. And for an overview ibid., recitals 199-200.

456 Ibid. recitals 264, 276 and 282 et seq.

457 Swiss Federal Court, *Eidgenössisches Volkswirtschaftsdepartement v Swisscom (Schweiz) AG and Swisscom (Schweiz) AG v Wettbewerbskommission* [2011] BGE 137 II 199, recital 4.3.1; Emmenegger and Tschentscher, ibid., recitals 300 et seq.; Kramer, *supra* note 447, 322 et seq.

458 Emmenegger and Tschentscher, ibid., recitals 314 et seq.

459 For a detailed account, cf. Emmenegger and Tschentscher, 452, recitals 376-413; Kramer, *supra* note 447, 191 et seq.

460 Kramer, ibid., 249.

461 Emmenegger and Tschentscher, *supra* note 452, recital 447.

case-law indicates that the weighing of interests, legal system conformity, current legislative proposals, comparative law, the context of the case and justice considerations feature in the decision-making process under Art. 1 Section 2 Option 2 ZGB.[462]

Lastly, courts 'shall follow the established doctrine and case-law' (Art. 1 Section 3 ZGB). The provision includes contributions and monographs from legal and non-legal academia.[463] It encourages a critical assessment of sources[464] and thereby creates a dialogue between judicial practice and academia. The provision does not establish a *stare decisis* principle in Swiss law as previous case-law is not formally binding.[465] The reference to previous case-law rather aims at a critical engagement with previous decisions which can lead to a new assessment of the respective legal position.[466]

3. Access to Justice and Alternative Dispute Resolution

According to Art. 97 Section 3 Swiss Constitution the cantons must provide for a 'a conciliation procedure or simple and rapid court procedure' with respect to consumer cases. This requirement is realised with the mandatory conciliation procedure at a conciliation authority (*Schlichtungsbehörde*) or Justice of Peace (*Friedensrichter*) prior to eventual court proceedings.[467] If the case is not settled by the conciliation authority, the claimant must bear the costs (Art. 207 S-ZPO). According to Art. 212 S-ZPO the conciliation authority may make a legally binding decision relating to small claims (up to CHF 2,000). Otherwise the proceedings end with a settlement (Art. 208 S-ZPO) or a proposed judgment (Art. 210 S-ZPO) if the parties reach an agreement. If the case cannot be settled, the conciliation authority will authorise the parties to proceed to court (Art. 209 S-ZPO). For claims with a value in dispute of less than CHF 30,000, Art. 243 S-ZPO provides for simplified proceedings especially relating to formality (cf. Art. 244 S-ZPO).

Switzerland does not offer a comprehensive system of alternative dispute resolution institutions for consumers. Beside the duty to consult a concilia-

462 Ibid. recitals 456-463.
463 Ibid. recitals 475, 476.
464 Ibid. recital 479.
465 Ibid. recital 490.
466 Ibid.
467 Cf. Arts. 197 et seq. (conciliation authority), 213 et seq. (mediation) Swiss Code of Civil Procedure (*Schweizerische Zivilprozessordnung*, hereinafter "S-ZPO").

tion authority before taking a case to court, ombudsman institutions exist for certain sectors. They are set up and organised privately.[468] Most ombudsman institutions are free of charge for the consumer and, thus, become increasingly attractive for Swiss consumers.[469] For example, the Swiss Banking Ombudsman settled 1,926 cases in 2018.[470] However, the ombudsman institutions have received criticism for a lack of impartiality and a lack of transparency especially because the ombud is dependent on being elected by the respective industry association as well as considered a stakeholder for the consumer.[471] They are currently not regulated and institutionalised by the legislator.[472] While some ombudsman institutions publish past and present cases in front of them, no comprehensive database for ombudsman case-law exists.[473] It is, thus, difficult to assess the actual impact of consumer protection norms with respect to these cases.

III. The "Swiss Model" (Bilateral Agreements)

Switzerland is the one of the few Western European countries that is not associated with the EU by way of full or EEA membership.[474] Full membership has been and is a contested issue due to Switzerland's foreign policy position of neutrality.[475] An ever-closer political union could endanger this position which is key to protecting Swiss national integrity. Prior to joining the Organisation for European Economic Cooperation (predeces-

468 Koller-Tumler, *supra* note 441, 92; Isaak Meier and David Siegwart, 'Ombudsstellen für Konsumentenstreitigkeiten' [2012] 21 (11) AJP 1523 (1524).

469 Meier and Siegwart, ibid., (1526, 1541).

470 Swiss Banking Ombudsman, Jahresbericht 2018, page 9.

471 Meier and Siegwart, *supra* note 468, (1529, 1537-1539). The ombud is not (formally) bound by any instructions from the industry association, cf. ibid. (1529).

472 For a critical view and suggestions for improvement in this regard, cf. ibid. (1541, 1544).

473 For a critical view and suggestions for improvement in this regard, cf. ibid. (1542). The Swiss Banking Ombudsman publishes case-law with respect to consumer credit law which will be included later in the analysis (see below).

474 Others include the Principality of the Valleys of Andorra, the Principality of Monaco, the Republic of San Marino and the Vatican City State.

475 Marius Vahl and Nina Grolimund, *Integration ohne Mitgliedschaft - Die bilateralen Verträge der Schweiz mit der Europäischen Gemeinschaft*, 11. However, cf. for a different opinion, Daniele Ganser and Georg Kreis, Swiss neutrality: incompatible with EU membership?. in Clive H. Church (ed), *Switzerland and the European Union - A close, contradictory and misunderstood relationship* (Routledge 2007), 52-78.

sor organisation of the OECD) in 1948, the Swiss had listed requirements that had to be fulfilled in order to accept membership in a European organisation: (1) No change in neutral policy, (2) Preservation of autonomy in economic policy making and (3) Maintenance of national autonomy in trade policy.[476]

As an export-oriented small country in the centre of Europe, Switzerland cannot neglect its dependence on its European neighbours who are all members of the EU or the EEA. Thus, economically Switzerland has traditionally been interested in maintaining good relationships with its European neighbours, i.e. as a founding member of EFTA.[477] While membership in the EU remains rather unlikely, membership in the EEA had been considered but was eventually rejected by the Swiss people in a referendum as well as the majority of cantons in 1992.[478] Switzerland has, thereby, become a 'special case' (*Sonderfall*)[479] not only with respect to its unique history in Europe but also in light of its position in the European framework. The negative outcome of the referendum did not put an end to Swiss-European cooperation but marked the starting point for the 'Bilateral Model'.

Switzerland's legal status in the European framework is mainly governed by its membership in the EFTA and in several bilateral agreements with the EU.

---

476 Laurent Goetschel, The wider setting of Swiss foreign policy. in Clive H. Church (ed), *Switzerland and the European Union - A close, contradictory and misunderstood relationship*, 176.

477 Preamble of the Vaduz Convention.

478 50.3% of participants in the referendum and 14 cantons and 4 half-cantons out of 26 cantons rejected EEA membership, cf. Bundeskanzlei, 'Volksabstimmung vom 06.12.1992' (*Volksabstimmungen*, 15 April 2019) <https://www.bk.admin.ch/ch/d/pore/va/19921206/index.html> accessed 16 April 2019, Matthias Oesch, *Switzerland and the European Union - General Framework, Bilateral Agreements, Autonomous Adaptation*, recital 32.

479 The expression encapsulates the unique combination of societal, cultural, economic and political features that shape Swiss identity, cf. Steinberg, *supra* note 377, 307. Christa Markwalder Bär, Die europapolitischen Optionen der Schweiz. in Fritz Breuss, Thomas Cottier and Peter-Christian Müller-Graff (eds), *Die Schweiz im europäischen Integrationsprozess*, 111.

1. EFTA

The supranational orientation of the European project, starting with the European Coal and Steel Community prevented Switzerland from taking part due to concerns with respect to its neutrality and sovereignty.[480] Instead it is a founding member of the EFTA which features are depicted above (see pages 84 et seq. above) and remains the only member that is not an EEA Member State at the same time.

2. Agreements with the European Union

Today Switzerland is associated with the EU by way of over 120 bilateral agreements.[481] In the following the most prominent treaties are depicted.

Free Trade Agreement (1972)

The Free Trade Agreement[482] was negotiated by the EFTA and subsequently implemented bilaterally between each of the then EFTA Member States and the EU.[483] Until today it forms the basis of trade relations between Switzerland and the EU.[484] It aims to

(a) to promote through the expansion of reciprocal trade the harmonious development of economic relations between the European Economic Community and the Swiss Confederation and thus to foster in the Community and in Switzerland the advance of economic activity, the improvement of living and employment conditions, and increased productivity and financial stability,

(b) to provide fair conditions of competition for trade between the Contracting Parties,

480 Oesch, *supra* note 478, recital 26.

481 Christine Kaddous, § 20 Die Zusammenarbeit zwischen der EU und der Schweiz. in Armin Hatje and Peter-Christian Müller-Graff (eds), *Enzyklopädie Europarecht: Europäisches Organisations- und Verfassungsrecht*, recital 7; Oesch, ibid., recital 40.

482 Agreement between the European Economic Community and the Swiss Confederation (22nd July 1972), Official Journal L 300, 31/12/1972 P. 0189 – 0280.

483 Matthias Oesch, *Europarecht - Band I: Grundlagen, Institutionen, Verhältnis Schweiz-EU*, recital 896.

484 Kaddous, *supra* note 481, recital 12; Oesch, *supra* note 478, recital 43.

(c) to contribute in this way, by the removal of barriers to trade, to the harmonious development and expansion of world trade [485]

and therefore, includes the removal of customs duties,[486] the removal of quantitative restrictions[487] and other discriminatory measures[488].

Bilateral Agreements I (1999)

After the Swiss rejection of EEA membership Switzerland and the EU looked for alternatives to at least partially remove trade barriers and achieve closer cooperation. The first package of sectorial bilateral agreements ('Bilateral Agreements I') was introduced in 1999 and came into force in Switzerland in 2002. The package contains seven separate agreements that differ with respect to nature and content. It includes agreements on free movement of persons,[489] technical barriers to trade,[490] public procurement,[491] trade in agricultural products,[492] overland transport,[493] scientific and technological cooperation[494] and air transport[495].

Under the Bilateral Agreements I Switzerland was granted decision shaping rights, meaning that they can take part in preparatory committee meetings regarding the introduction of new legislative measures relating to the respective agreements. However, Switzerland does not have any

485 Art. 1 Free Trade Agreement 1972.

486 Art. 3 Free Trade Agreement 1972.

487 Art. 13 Free Trade Agreement 1972.

488 Cf. Art. 18 Free Trade Agreement 1972.

489 Agreement between the European Community and its Member States, of the one part, and the Swiss Confederation, of the other, on the free movement of persons, Official Journal L 114, 30/04/2002 P. 0006 – 0072.

490 Agreement between the European Community and the Swiss Confederation on mutual recognition in relation to conformity assessment, Official Journal L 114, 30/04/2002 P. 0369 – 0429.

491 Agreement between the European Community and the Swiss Confederation on certain aspects of government procurement, Official Journal L 114, 30/04/2002 P. 0430 – 0467.

492 Agreement between the European Community and the Swiss Confederation on trade in agricultural products, Official Journal L 114, 30/04/2002 P. 0132 – 0368.

493 Agreement between the European Community and the Swiss Confederation on the Carriage of Goods and Passengers by Rail and Road, Official Journal L 114, 30/04/2002 P. 0091 – 0131.

494 Agreement on Scientific and Technological Cooperation between the European Communities and the Swiss Confederation, Official Journal L 114, 30/04/2002 P. 0468 – 0480.

495 Agreement between the European Community and the Swiss Confederation on Air Transport, Official Journal L 114, 30/04/2002 P. 0073 – 0090.

voting rights and is, thus, barred from EU decision making. The Bilateral Agreements I are connected by so called 'guillotine-clauses'. They can only come into force and end together.[496] If one agreement is terminated all other agreements also cease to apply.[497] Thereby, the EU prevents Switzerland from 'cherry picking' certain agreements.[498]

Bilateral Agreements II (2004)

A further package of nine sectorial bilateral agreements was passed in 2004. The dates of coming into force differ.[499] They include agreements on taxation of savings,[500] fight against fraud,[501] cooperation with respect to MEDIA,[502] the environment,[503] statistics,[504] pensions of former employees

496 Astrid Epiney, Beate Metz and Benedikt Pirker, *Zur Parallelität der Rechtsentwicklung in der EU und in der Schweiz - ein Beitrag zur rechtlichen Tragweite der "Bilateralen Abkommen"*, 97.

497 Kaddous, *supra* note 481, recital 4.

498 Oesch, *supra* note 483, recital 899.

499 Ibid. recital 901.

500 Agreement between the European Community and the Swiss Confederation providing for measures equivalent to those laid down in Council Directive 2003/48/EC on taxation of savings income in the form of interest payments, Official Journal L 385, 29/12/2004 P. 0030 – 0049 and Official Journal L 153, 07/06/2006 P. 0383 – 0402. Entry into force in 2005.

501 Cooperation Agreement between the European Community and its Member States, of the one part, and the Swiss Confederation, of the other part, to combat fraud and any other illegal activity to the detriment of their financial interests, not in force yet.

502 Agreement between the European Community and the Swiss Confederation in the audiovisual field, establishing the terms and conditions for the participation of the Swiss Confederation in the Community programme MEDIA 2007, Official Journal L 303, 21/11/2007 P. 0011 – 0023. Entry into force in 2006.

503 Agreement between the European Community and the Swiss Confederation concerning the participation of Switzerland in the European Environment Agency and the European Environment Information and Observation Network, Official Journal L 090, 28/03/2006 P. 0037 – 0047. Entry into force in 2006.

504 Agreement between the European Community and the Swiss Confederation on cooperation in the field of statistics, Official Journal L 090, 28/03/2006 P. 0002 – 0020. Entry into force in 2007.

of the EU,[505] education and vocational training,[506] processed agricultural products[507] and cooperation with respect to the Schengen and Dublin Agreements[508]. The Bilateral Agreements II are not connected by way of 'guillotine-clauses'. However, the Schengen and Dublin agreements are connected due to their interdependent nature.[509]

Agreements after 2004

Since 2004 Switzerland and the EU have continued their cooperation mainly in the area of joint policing, international crime and justice.[510] Furthermore, Switzerland agreed to pay CHF 1 billion within five years to reduce economic and social inequality in Europe in a memorandum of understanding in 2006 (*Kohäsionsmilliarde*).[511] Until 2017 Switzerland has contributed CHF 1.3 billion to such cohesion projects.[512]

Institutional Agreement

The fragmented bilateral agreements are constructed statically meaning that they do not adapt to additional European legal developments. The

505 Agreement between the Swiss Federal Council and the Commission of the European Communities with a view to avoiding the double taxation of retired officials of the institutions and agencies of the European Communities resident in Switzerland, not published in the Official Journal. Entry into force in 2005.

506 Agreement between the European Union and the Swiss Confederation establishing the terms and conditions for the participation of the Swiss Confederation in the 'Youth in Action' programme and in the action programme in the field of lifelong learning (2007-2013), Official Journal L 087, 07/04/2010 P. 0009 – 0018. Entry into force in 2011.

507 Agreement between the European Community and the Swiss Confederation amending the Agreement between the European Economic Community and the Swiss Confederation of 22 July 1972 as regards the provisions applicable to processed agricultural products, Official Journal L 023, 26/01/2005 P. 0019 – 0048. Entry into force in 2005.

508 Agreement between the European Union, the European Community and the Swiss Confederation on the Swiss Confederation's association with the implementation, application and development of the Schengen acquis, Official Journal L 053, 27/02/2008 P. 0052 – 0079. Entry into force in 2008;
Agreement between the European Community and the Swiss Confederation concerning the criteria and mechanisms for establishing the State responsible for examining a request for asylum lodged in a Member State or in Switzerland, Official Journal L 053, 27/02/2008 P. 0052 – 0017. Entry into force in 2008.

509 Oesch, *supra* note 483, recital 901.

510 Cf. Kaddous, *supra* note 481, recital 61 et seq.; Oesch, ibid., recital 902.

511 Oesch, ibid.

512 Oesch, *supra* note 478, recital 316.

harmonisation and cooperation agreements do not provide means to add future legislative measures.[513] Furthermore, the agreements lack dispute resolution institutions. The EU has criticised this situation and suggested to introduce a new and dynamic institutional framework.[514] On the 7 December 2018 the draft text of the 'Institutional Agreement' was published by the Swiss Federal Council, underwent consultations but was eventually rejected by the Swiss side on the 26 May 2021.[515]

The Institutional Agreement should ensure a more dynamic adaptation of European legislation.[516] It only applied to bilateral agreements that deal with access to the European Single Market.[517] The Free Trade Agreement 1972 was to be revised to ensure compatibility with the new agreement.[518] The agreement aimed to ensure homogenous interpretation of European norms as well as the timely addition of new legislative measures to the bilateral *acquis* (dynamic adaptation[519]).[520] Furthermore, the agreement contained a 'guillotine-clause' providing that if one bilateral agreement mentioned in the Institutional Agreement was terminated, all other agreements and the Institutional Agreement would subsequently also be terminated.[521]

The introduction of the Institutional Agreement was a highly contested issue in Switzerland.[522] The main points of criticism were (1) the potential alignment, i.e. lowering, of labour law standards and (2) the possibility of

513 Epiney, Metz and Pirker, *supra* note 496, 97-98.

514 Cf. Council conclusions on EU relations with EFTA countries, 3060th General Affairs Council Meeting, Brussels (14 December 2010), recitals 48, 49; Council conclusions on a homogeneous extended single market and EU relations with Non-EU Western European countries, General Affairs Council meeting, Brussels (16 December 2014), recital 44.

515 Bundesrat, Bericht betreffend die Verhandlungen über ein institutionelles Abkommen zwischen der Schweiz und der EU (26 May 2021).

516 Art. 1 Section 3 Draft Institutional Agreement.

517 Art. 2 Draft Institutional Agreement.

518 Recital 4 Preamble of the Draft Institutional Agreement.

519 Cf. Astrid Epiney, 'Der Entwurf des Institutionellen Abkommens Schweiz – EU: Überblick und erste Einschätzung' [17th December 2018] Jusletter recital 22.

520 Art. 4, 5, 12 Draft Institutional Agreement.

521 Art. 22 Section 2 Draft Institutional Agreement, cf. also Epiney, *supra* note 519, recitals 51, 52.

522 Cf. Markus Notter, 'Institutionelles Rahmenabkommen - ein europapolitischer Zwischenruf' [2019] 21 (1) EUZ - Zeitschrift für Europarecht 4-9.

a 'foreign court'[523], i.e. the CJEU, gaining competence to adjudicate Swiss law.[524] As for point (1), Protocol 1 to the Institutional Agreement included exceptions to the mechanism of dynamic adaptation to acknowledge the specifics of the Swiss labour market.[525] As for point (2), disputes under the Institutional Agreement must first be brought in front of an arbitration court. The CJEU only would have been called upon if the dispute had involved the interpretation of EU norms (see below).[526] The Draft Institutional Agreement had generally been perceived benevolently by academics[527] and the Swiss people[528], who eventually would have decided whether or not to enter the agreement in a referendum. Especially in light of Swiss dependence on access to European markets, an agreement appears inevitable. Furthermore, Switzerland would benefit from the increased transparency and clarity entailed in the mechanism of dynamic adaptation as well as new dispute resolution provisions at least as much as the EU.[529]

a. Implementation of European Norms

Switzerland pursues a monistic approach with respect to international law.[530] This means that no further act of implementation is required after ratification. However, only self-executing norms can be relied upon by in-

---

523 The notion of 'foreign judges in the valleys' has its roots in the medieval beginnings of the Swiss Confederation, cf. Wolfgang Ernst, 'Fremde Richter – damals und heute' [2013] 22 (9) AJP 1374-1377. It has subsequently been (ab-)used by anti-EU campaigners, cf. also the popular initiative 'Swiss law instead of foreign judges' (*Schweizer Recht statt fremde Richter*) (2018).

524 Michael Ambühl and Daniela Scherer, 'Zum Entwurf des Institutionellen Abkommens: Auf der Suche nach einem Interessenausgleich' [4th February 2019] Jusletter recital 24.

525 Cf. also Astrid Epiney and Lena Hehemann, 'Die Tragweite des Institutionellen Abkommens im Bereich der Arbeitnehmerentsendung' [8th April 2019] Jusletter recital 45.

526 Art. 10 Section 3 Draft Institutional Agreement.

527 Epiney, *supra* note 519, recitals 53 et seq.; with suggestions for improvement Ambühl and Scherer, *supra* note 524, 2-14.

528 Anonymous, 'Die Mehrheit der Schweizer Stimmbevölkerung unterstützt das institutionelle Abkommen' (*Presseportal.ch*, 31 March 2019) <https://www.presseportal.ch/de/pm/100002276/100826461> accessed 17 April 2019.

529 Ambühl and Scherer, *supra* note 524, recital 31.

530 Misic and Töpperwien, *supra* note 380, recital 803; Egli, *supra* note 378, 16.

dividuals in judicial proceedings whereas non-self-executing provisions require a transformation into national law.[531]

European norms are integrated into Swiss law in different ways. On the one hand, Switzerland is bound by bilateral agreements. On the other hand, norms are adapted by way of 'autonomous adaptation' (*autonomer Nachvollzug*) on a voluntary basis without being bound by international obligations.

Bilateral Agreements

Upon ratification, bilateral agreements become part of Swiss law. Some agreements fall under the competence of the cantons and must, therefore, be implemented into cantonal law.[532] As pointed out above, the bilateral agreements are different in nature. With respect to the implementation of the agreements and possibly subsequent European legislation there exist two types of agreements: static and dynamic ones.

All bilateral agreements except the Schengen and Dublin agreements are static agreements. They are classic treaties under public international law and only oblige Switzerland to implement existing legislative measures but do not include any such duties with respect to future legislative developments. Thus, Switzerland is free (not) to implement future changes to the bilateral agreements. The non-implementation of additional legislative measures does not entail any negative consequences.[533] However, as Switzerland is interested in the well-functioning of the agreements, the authorities check for legislative changes regularly.[534]

Thus, the bilateral agreements are formally treaties under international law preserving the Swiss autonomous decision making with respect to the advancement of agreements. Thereby, Switzerland is theoretically free to refrain from adopting new EU legislation in both static and dynamic arrangements. In most cases, however, Switzerland would adopt new legislative measures to ensure the well-functioning of the agreements.

---

531 Egli, ibid., 16; Kaddous, *supra* note 481, recital 85.

532 For a detailed depiction of the implementation of EU in the cantons, cf. Stephan Kux, Die Umsetzung der bilateralen Abkommen in den Kantonen. in Fritz Breuss, Thomas Cottier and Peter-Christian Müller-Graff (eds), *Die Schweiz im europäischen Integrationsprozess*, 169-182.

533 Matthias Oesch, 'Die bilateralen Abkommen Schweiz-EU und die Übernahme von EU-Recht' [2017] 26 (5) AJP 638 (639).

534 Ibid. Some agreements require Swiss authorities to inform themselves regarding new relevant legal developments, i.e. Art. 4 Section 4 statistics agreement.

Institutional Agreement

Under the Institutional Agreement, a dynamic approach would have been adopted with respect to the agreements covered by the Institutional Agreement (cf. Chapter 4 of the Draft Institutional Agreement). Similar to the Schengen and Dublin Agreements the Institutional Agreement provided for Swiss involvement in European legislative procedures.[535] Switzerland would have had to implement respective legislation within a maximum period of three years.[536] There still would not have existed a duty to implement EU legislative measures on behalf of Switzerland;[537] the agreement would not have introduced an automatic adaptation of EU law[538]. If Switzerland had failed to implement necessary legislative measures, the Institutional Agreement and all associated agreements would have been terminated.[539]

Autonomous Adaptation

Beside its obligations under international law, Switzerland voluntarily adapts European legal instruments by way of autonomous adaptation. In 1988 the Federal Council found in its 'Report on the Swiss position in the European Integration Process' that

> [our] goal has to be to secure the *greatest compatibility of our legislation with the legislation of our European partners* in the areas of cross-border significance (and only there). [...] This pursuit of parallelism is not motivated by the introduction of an automatism to adopt European law, but by the prevention of unwanted and unnecessary legal differences, which hamper the aspired mutual recognition of legislation on a European level.[540]

---

535 Art. 12 Draft Institutional Agreement.

536 Arts. 13, 14 Draft Institutional Agreement.

537 Epiney, *supra* note 519, recital 21.

538 Ibid. recital 22.

539 Art. 22 Section 2 Institutional Agreement.

540 Swiss Federal Council, Bericht über die Stellung der Schweiz im europäischen Integrationsprozess, 24 August 1988, Bundesblatt, 140. Jahrgang, Band III, 249 (380): 'Unser Ziel muss sein, in Bereichen von grenzüberschreitender Bedeutung (und nur dort) eine *grösstmögliche Vereinbarkeit unserer Rechtsvorschriften mit denjenigen unserer europäischen Partner* zu sichern. [...] Es geht bei diesem Streben nach Parallelität nicht darum, das europäische Recht automatisch nachzuvollziehen, wohl aber darum, zu verhindern, dass ungewollt und unnötigerweise neue Rechtsunterschiede geschaffen werden, welche die grundsätzlich ange-

Subsequently, Art. 141 Section 2 lit. a Federal Act on the Federal Assembly (*Bundesgesetz über die Bundesversammlung*) was introduced which provides that for each new bill the impact on the relationship with the EU must be assessed. While the provision does not introduce a binding force of EU law on the Swiss legislator, it does imply that any deviation from EU law must be justified.[541] Since then a number of European legal measures have been adapted by the Swiss legislator. Today the adapted provisions do not only relate to 'areas of cross-border significance' but to various areas of regulation (*spill over* effect).[542] One prominent example of autonomous adaptation is the 'Swisslex' package passed in 1993. Formerly known as 'Eurolex' and meant as a preparatory legislative package for accession to the EEA, it was reduced to 27 modifications and renamed 'Swisslex' after EEA membership had been rejected.[543] Among others the 'Swisslex' package includes the introduction of the Swiss Consumer Credit Act 1993 (KKG 1993) drafted according to the First Consumer Credit Directive. Another example is provided by the adaptation of the *Cassis de Dijon* decision.[544] Beside introducing measures outside the bilateral agreements the principle of autonomous adaptation has contributed to an eased process of adapting advanced measures under the bilateral agreements.[545]

b. Role and Application by the Courts

The interpretation of the legal measures adopted by the Swiss legislator play an important role in assessing the impact of EU law on the Swiss legal

strebte gegenseitige Anerkennung der Rechtsvorschriften auf europäischer Ebene behindern.' (Translation by Oesch, *supra* note 478, recital 325).

541 Oesch, *supra* note 483, recital 933.

542 Ibid. recital 935.

543 Clive H. Church, Continuities within change: the background of Swiss relations with Europe. in Clive H. Church (ed), *Switzerland and the European Union - A close, contradictory and misunderstood relationship*, 196; Roy Gava and Frédéric Varone, Chapter 11: So Close, Yet So Far? The EU's Footprint in Swiss Legislative Production. in Sylvain Brouard, Olivier Costa and Thomas König (eds), *The Europeanization of Domestic Legislatures - The Empirical Implications of the Delors' Myth in Nine Countries*, 201; Oesch, *supra* note 478, recital 327; Vahl and Grolimund, *supra* note 475, 13.

544 Francesco Maiani, 'Legal Europeanization as Legal Transformation: Some Insights from Swiss "Outer Europe"' [2008] EUI Working Paper MWP No 2008/32, page 4; Oesch, *supra* note 483, recitals 946 et seq.

545 Vahl and Grolimund, *supra* note 475, 59.

system. Theoretically the CJEU and the Swiss courts adjudicate the bilateral agreements independently from one another. Thus, diverging case-law on the agreements remains a possibility.[546]

The Swiss Federal Court interprets the bilateral agreements according to Arts. 31 to 33 Vienna Convention.[547] International law must be considered by the Swiss Federal Court as a federal authority (Art. 5 Section 4 Swiss Constitution) and takes precedence over national provisions.[548]

With respect to agreements that do not explicitly refer to the CJEU's case-law, the Swiss Federal Court distinguishes treaties according to their integration purpose similar to the CJEU.[549] It has, however, also pointed out that it takes notice of the CJEU's case-law regarding parallel provisions.[550] Furthermore, it can be assumed that European legal concepts must be considered if the agreement contains direct references to European legislative measures.[551] With respect to agreements that explicitly refer to the ECJ's case-law before the 21 June 1999, the Swiss Federal Court, as of now, has only dealt with the agreement on the free movement of persons.[552] It distinguishes between the case-law prior to the 21 June 1999 which is binding (*Befolgungspflicht*)[553] and the case-law after the 21 June 1999 which must be considered (*Beachtungsgebot*)[554]. Until today the Swiss Federal Court has not deviated from the case-law falling into the latter cat-

546 Kaddous, *supra* note 481, recital 114.

547 Cf. Swiss Federal Court, *C. v Caisse de compensation des banques suisses ainsi que Tribunal des assurances du canton de Vaud (H 31/06)* [2008] BGE 133 V 329, recital 8.4.

548 Cf. Swiss Federal Court, *A. v Schweizerische Bundesanwaltschaft, Eidgenössisches Justiz- und Polizeidepartement und Schweizerischen Bundesrat* [1999] BGE 125 II 417 (425). With respect to the agreement on free movement of persons, cf. Swiss Federal Court, *A.A. und B.A. gegen Migrationsamt und Sicherheitsdirektion des Kantons Zürich* [2015] BGE 142 II 35, recitals 3.2, 3.3.

549 Cf. with respect to the Free Trade Agreement 1972, Swiss Federal Court, *Bosshard Partners Intertrading AG v Sunlight AG* [1979] BGE 105 II 49 (59-60).

550 Swiss Federal Court, *Bosshard Partners Intertrading AG v Sunlight AG* [2005] BGE 131 II 271, recital 10.3.

551 Epiney, Metz and Pirker, *supra* note 496, 181.

552 Oesch, *supra* note 478, recital 75.

553 Swiss Federal Court, *X. and Mitb. v Migrationsamt und Sicherheitsdirektion des Kantons Zürich* [2013] BGE 139 II 393, recital 4.1.1.

554 Ibid.; Swiss Federal Court, *X. and Y. v Sicherheitsdirektion und Regierungsrat des Kantons Zürich* [2009] BGE 136 II 5, recital 3.4.

egory[555] but developed a 'dynamic adaptation' of CJEU case-law[556]. Deviations would require a compelling reasoning.[557]

Institutional Agreement

Art. 4 Section 2 Draft Institutional Agreement provided that provisions relating to EU law contained in the Institutional Agreement or related agreements must be interpreted in light of CJEU case-law before or after the conclusion of the respective agreement to ensure a uniform interpretation and application of the Institutional Agreement and related agreements (cf. Art. 1 Section 3 Draft Institutional Agreement). This would have entailed a duty to interpret the respective agreements in light of the CJEU's past, present and future case-law.

Autonomous Adaptation

The principle of autonomous adaptation entails a euro compatible interpretation of legislative measures that have been adapted from the *acquis communitaire*. Otherwise, the goal of eliminating barriers between the Swiss and European markets could not be achieved.[558] However, a euro compatible interpretation does not entail that the courts are bound by the CJEU's case-law.

3. Europeanisation without Membership?

Appreciating both the association by way of bilateral agreements as well as the internal policy of autonomous adaptation, one could assume that the Swiss legal system has been Europeanised without membership in the EEA or EU. This trend of 'rule-taking' is criticised for possibly putting Swiss legislative autonomy at risk.[559]

---

555 Oesch, *supra* note 478, recital 74.

556 Oesch, *supra* note 483, recital 920.

557 Ibid. An example for a reasoned deviation is provided by cases relating to EU citizenship, cf. Epiney, Metz and Pirker, *supra* note 496, 165-166 with reference to Swiss Federal Court, *X. and Mitb. v Migrationsamt Kanton Aargau* [2009] BGE 136 II 329, recital 2.3.

558 Maiani, *supra* note 544, 12 et seq.; Oesch, *supra* note 478, recital 355; Oesch, ibid., recital 941. Cf. for an example Swiss Federal Court, *Öffentliche Arbeitslosenkasse des Kantons Solothurn v Metallbau X. GmbH* [2003] BGE 129 III 335, recital 6.

559 Oesch, *supra* note 478, recital 349.

A study of 186 legislative acts enacted between 1996 and 2005 showed that 48.38% of laws showed a 'medium or high degree of Europeanisation' and found that similar numbers could be established for the European influence on Austrian laws.[560] A study of 107 bills enacted between 2004 and 2007 found that 55% of bills related to EU law. 66.5% of bills included partial adaptations of EU law, while 30% constituted complete adaptations. Regarding the legislative purpose, only 5.6% of bills were introduced with the sole objective of EU law adaptation.[561] A study of Swiss legislative measures enacted between 1987 and 2007 shows a growing influence of EU law on Swiss law.[562] While the areas of immigration and integration and foreign trade were mostly influenced by bilateral agreements, the areas of domestic commerce, education and culture stand out as areas were Swiss legislation was influenced by autonomous adaptation.[563] A study relating to changes to Swiss federal legislation between 1990 and 2010 finds that 13.29% of a total of 1144 Swiss federal law reforms amounted to full adaptations of EU law, 6.99% amounted to partial adaptations and 14.42% were at least compatible with EU law.[564] In combination with other findings, *Jenni* concludes that Switzerland is a case of *differentiated European integration*[565] which entails that despite not being a member of the EU Switzerland is part of the European integration process.[566]

All studies, despite having different focusses, show that in the past decades Switzerland has adopted an increasing amount of European legislation. This reflects the Swiss interest in maintaining close ties with its European neighbours and ensuring access to the European markets. It is true that the increasing adaptation of European measures inheres the risk of a democratic deficit, turning Switzerland into a mere 'rule taker'. However, the studies show that most adaptations of European law are classified as partial. This means that although these legislative measures contain a European footprint, they are essentially 'Swiss made'. Furthermore, the bilateral intergovernmentalist structure of the Swiss-EU cooperation pre-

---

560 Ali Arbia, *The Road not Taken Europeanisation of Laws in Austria and Switzerland 1996-2005*, 66 et seq.

561 Emilie Kohler, 'Influences du droit européen sur la législation suisse: analyse des années 2004 à 2007' [31 August 2009] Jusletter recital 33.

562 Gava and Varone, *supra* note 543, 212-213.

563 Ibid. 213.

564 Sabine Jenni, *Switzerland's Differentiated European Integration - The Last Gallic Village?*, 67.

565 Ibid. 249.

566 Ibid. 259-260.

vents an automatism of legislative adaptation. Thereby, Switzerland is free to adopt rules where it sees fit but is not forced to submit to a supranational law-maker or supervisory authority.

4. Conclusion

The relationship between Switzerland and the EU is governed by intergovernmentalist agreements under public international law. None of them include means of automated adaptation of European legislation or supranational (supervisory) institutions. Thereby, Switzerland preserves its (law-making) autonomy. Under most agreements Swiss courts are not obliged to consider the CJEU's case-law. However, Switzerland is also dependent on the well-functioning of Swiss-EU relations. Therefore, in practice the Swiss legislator and authorities voluntarily adopt advancing legislative measures to ensure the functioning of the bilateral agreements and Swiss courts consider CJEU case-law where necessary. Furthermore, the Swiss have adopted a policy of autonomous adaptation and introduced the interpretative principle of euro compatibility regarding European legislative measures that are not included in the bilateral agreements in acknowledgement of the importance of maintaining good relations with their European neighbours. Of the countries compared in this work, Switzerland is the least integrated country in the European framework. The basis of co-operation with the EU is fragmented and static and, thus, requires Swiss voluntary efforts to maintain it. Thus far, the bilateral agreements have functioned well, however, the Institutional Agreement would have stabilised the relationship between Switzerland and the EU.

IV. Comparability

In a next step it must be evaluated whether the Swiss societal factors and legal system are comparable with the societal factors and legal system of the UK, Germany and Norway. Due to the aim of this dissertation the focus lies on the comparability between Switzerland and the UK.

With respect to the relationship with the rest of Europe it can be noted that similarly to the UK and Norway there exist reservations against joining the EU in Switzerland. However, they are founded on different concerns rather comparable with those in Norway. Similar to Norwegians, the Swiss fear interference from the 'outside'. However, in addition they are mostly concerned about the erosion of the carefully balanced 'interior' Swiss federalism and concordance. Under the Swiss system notions of federalism and direct democracy have played a key role in Swiss constitutional history ('freedom for'). It is likely, this carefully balanced system cannot be preserved in case of EU membership. Thus, while both in the UK and Switzerland notions of sovereignty play a role in rejecting EU membership, they are based on different arguments.

The Swiss model of cooperation with the EU is underlied by the Swiss wish to maintain neutrality. While the model may seem attractive for the UK as it is based almost solely on international treaties rather than a supranational organisation, the previous negotiation of an Institutional Agreement indicates an intended closer cooperation between Switzerland and the EU. Furthermore, by way of autonomous adaptation Switzerland has voluntarily adopted European rules to maintain a good and functioning relationship with its European partners. The Swiss model, thereby, shows that even under a bilateral model the UK will not be free from 'looking over the pond' and adopt EU legislation where necessary even without being under an obligation to do so. It is, thus, advisable to keep an eye on countries such as Germany, which for example shaped their consumer credit legislation almost entirely according to EU law, to evaluate whether rules should be adopted voluntarily to ensure smooth cooperation with European partners.

The historic developments in Switzerland differ from those in the UK, Germany and Norway. Unlike the UK and Germany, Switzerland is a relatively small country which has stayed out of the conflicts in the 19th and 20th century. It established a federal democracy early on and enabled slow but steady growth. Unlike Norway, it rarely had to suffer occupation and could, thus, develop relatively independently.

Nevertheless, at the centre of Europe Switzerland depends on its European neighbours and is economically well-connected especially due to its multicultural society. It also profits from its location and has made the most of a lack of own resources. Unlike Norway, Switzerland does not pursue an approach of interventionist economic policies but remains decentralised. With respect to the notion of a welfare state, it, thus, comes closest to the UK. The most important economic task of the state is seen in providing an effective administration for the economy to prosper.

Sociologically, the Swiss multiculturalism and multilingualism can hardly be compared to any other country. Similar to Norway, however, Swiss culture can be described as compromise-oriented and rather anticonflictual which results in high trust rates. Despite the pluralism which in the UK and Germany can be seen as a factor of division, there exists a rather peaceful cohabitation in Switzerland, also likely to be caused by the small size and rough landscape of the country which requires the citizens' cooperation.

As for the legal system, Switzerland comes closest to the German civil law system which can be explained by the cultural nearness of the countries. Both systems explicitly rely on the duty of good faith and use similar interpretative methods. Nevertheless, the ZGB is based on a different premise than the BGB as it rather emphasises accessibility over technicality. Moreover, Swiss private law also includes the feature of *modo legislatoris* which is closer associated with the common law concept of private law. Furthermore, the underlying values of the Swiss private legal system are similar to those underlying the English common law of contract. Unlike Norway and the UK, there does not exist a comprehensive administrative system involving collective consumer claims. The only options of alternative dispute resolution are provided by private actors.

Part II: Consumer Credit Status Quo

Chapter 4: European Legislation on Consumer Credit

This section first introduces the European approach to consumer protection regulation and then focusses on the European Directives concerning consumer credit (together hereinafter the "Consumer Credit Directives"), namely Council Directive 87/102/EEC of 22 December 1986 for the approximation of the laws, regulations and administrative provisions of the Member States concerning consumer credit (hereinafter the "First Consumer Credit Directive" or "CCD 1986") and the Second Consumer Credit Directive.

A. *Consumer Protection Regulation: Rationale and European Developments*

The consumerist developments depicted at the beginning did not pass by the European legislator. However, it took them a while until consumer policy was officially integrated into the treaties and, thus, turned into a policy objective. When the Treaty of Rome was signed in 1957 consumer policy was rather mentioned as a side note.[567] The EEC's attitude only shifted in the 1970s together with a stronger focus on social policy.[568] However, the policy objective of consumer protection was not seen as a goal in itself. Rather, in light of consumerism (or European 'producerism'[569]), it was seen as an element of internal market policy. Consumer policy harmonisation would reduce national barriers to an open internal market.[570] Only with the Maastricht Treaty in 1992 a separate policy objective of consumer policy was inserted (Art. 169 TFEU, ex Art. 153 TEC). Several questions arise and have been thoroughly discussed as to how consumer protection is realised in the EU which shall not be subject to this work. Instead the focus lies on three areas which shall provide an overview

---

567 Paolisa Nebbia, *Unfair contract terms in European law: a study in comparative EC law*, 4-5.

568 Ibid. 5-6. Stephen Weatherill, Consumer Policy. in Paul Craig and Gráinne De Búrca (eds), *The Evolution of EU Law*, 844-845.

569 Cf. Micklitz, *supra* note 72, 29; James Q. Whitman, 'Consumerism Versus Producerism: A Study in Comparative Law' [2007] 117 (3) Yale Law Journal 340 (348-349).

570 Weatherill, *supra* note 568, 838.

of the rationale behind and implementation of EU consumer policy and legislation: (1) the rationale and general categorisation of consumer policy measures, (2) an overview of the consumer image underlying EU consumer policy and (3) an overview of the discussion of minimum and maximum harmonisation measures.

The two main elements of consumer policy are enshrined in Art. 169 Section 1 TFEU which provides that

> [in] order to promote the interests of consumers and to ensure a high level of consumer protection, the Union shall contribute to protecting the health, safety and economic interests of consumers, as well as to promoting their right to information, education and to organise themselves in order to safeguard their interests.

The policy objective shall also be considered when adopting measures under Art. 114 TFEU (cf. Art. 169 Section 2 lit. (a) TFEU) and more generally 'in defining and implementing other Union policies and activities' (Art. 12 TFEU, ex Art. 153 Section 2 TEC). The Commission has reiterated – most recently in their 'New Deal for Consumers in 2018[571] – that European consumer policy is still closely related to the (improved) functioning of the internal market.[572] However, an emphasis on 'better monitoring and regulation' reveals that the EU is also concerned with the welfare of consumers. This makes European consumer policy (producerism) distinct from US consumer policies (consumerism).[573] Unlike the European model, US consumerism solely aims at improving market efficiency in the interest of consumers, i.e. by providing for information duties or offering class actions against mandatory rule infringements.[574] Compared to the US model the European one appears more fragmented. Rather than presupposing that the consumer *always* acts as a rational *homo oeconomicus*, the European consumer legislation reveals a more pluralist consumer image, ranging from the rational consumer[575] to an emerging image of the vulnerable con-

571 European Commission, A New Deal for Consumers, COM(2018) 183 final (11 April 2018), page 1.

572 European Commission, EU Consumer Policy strategy 2007-2013: Empowering consumers, enhancing their welfare, effectively protecting them, COM(2007) 99 final (13 March 2007), page 4.

573 Whitman, *supra* note 569, (340); Micklitz, *supra* note 72, 29.

574 Micklitz, ibid., 29-30.

575 Cf. i.e. Directive 2005/29/EC of the European Parliament and of the Council of 11 May 2005 concerning unfair business-to-consumer commercial practices in the internal market (Unfair Commercial Practices Directive), Recital 18.

sumer[576]. The variety of consumer images leads to different types of legislative instruments and consequently a fragmented consumer policy.

The prevalent consumer image under EU law, however, remains the rational consumer.[577] According to the CJEU in *Gut Springenheide* such consumers are 'reasonably well-informed and reasonably observant and circumspect'.[578] The definition is not meant as a pure empirical standard but embodies a normative concept.[579] Nevertheless, the categorisation reflects a consumer image oriented at free movement and an open internal market[580] and close to that of a rational *homo oeconomicus*. Under this consumer image, information duties should usually suffice to create a level playing field between businesses and consumers.[581]

However, EU legislation occasionally also reveals the image of a 'weak consumer' in need of substantive protection and equipment with rights.[582] One example which will also be discussed more thoroughly as part of this work is the Unfair Contract Terms Directive. The UCTD does not merely aim at informing the consumer about (unfair) terms of the contract but allows for a substantive control of terms by the judiciary (as for CJEU case-law, see below). It, thereby, provides an example of consumer *protection from* unfair practices as well as *empowerment to* engage in the (internal) market.[583] In this light, Recital 19 of the Unfair Commercial Practices Directive also provides that

> [where] certain characteristics such as age, physical or mental infirmity or credulity make consumers particularly susceptible to a commercial practice or to the underlying product and the economic behaviour only of such consumers is likely to be distorted by the practice in a way that the trader can reasonably foresee, it is appropriate to ensure that they are adequately protected by assessing the practice from the perspective of the average member of that group.

---

576 Cf. i.e. Recital 19 of the Unfair Commercial Practices Directive.

577 Vanessa Mak, The Consumer in European Regulatory Private Law. in Dorota Leczykiewicz and Stephen Weatherill (eds), *The Images of the Consumer in EU Law: Legislation, Free Movement and Competition Law*, 384. Also cf. Recital 18 of the Unfair Commercial Practices Directive.

578 ECJ judgment C-210/96, *Gut Springenheide and Rudolf Tusky v Oberkreisdirektor des Kreises Steinfurt – Amt für Lebensmittelüberwachung* [1998] recital 31.

579 Mak, *supra* note 577, 385.

580 Ibid. 386, 388.

581 Cartwright, *supra* note 70, 203; Grundmann, *supra* note 71, 234; Mak, ibid. 387.

582 Mak, ibid., 389.

583 See also ibid. 390-392.

While this provision leaves plenty of room for interpretation,[584] it indicates a concern for the diverse interests and requirements of consumers. However, by acknowledging the pluralism of consumer interests, the task of ascertaining the rationale behind and scope of consumer legislation becomes increasingly difficult and fragmentised.[585] While the official rationale behind consumer policy remains the functioning of the internal market, the legislator[586] as well as the CJEU move toward substantive protection measures in some areas of consumer protection (such as the UCTD) which also benefit the rational consumer[587] and erode the less than clear distinction of consumer types further. A solution could lie in a further and clearer classification of consumer types[588] or a differentiation according to substantive risks rather than consumer types[589].

Beside the problem of determining the scope of consumer protection with respect to the consumer image, EU Consumer Directives unfold different harmonising effects.[590] On the one hand Directives can have minimum harmonisation effect. This means that the Directive sets a minimum standard ('the floor') and Member States still have the opportunity to go beyond what is envisaged by the EU (*gold-plating Directives*). On the other hand, Directives can have maximum harmonisation effect. This means that the Member States may not go beyond what the (scope of the) Directive provides ('the floor and the ceiling').[591] In the past, minimum harmonisation Directives had been the common mean of consumer policy measures (see i.e. the UCTD).[592] However, more recently the EU legislator has moved toward a maximum harmonisation standard with respect to consumer protection (see i.e. the Unfair Commercial Practices Directive or the Second Consumer Credit Directive). The focus on maximum harmonisation shall serve to remove barriers for trade within the internal market, such as more stringent consumer protection in some Member States, and

---

584 Cartwright, *supra* note 70, 212 et seq.

585 Cf. also Micklitz, *supra* note 72, 32 et seq.

586 For example, the Consumer Rights Directive, cf. Grundmann, *supra* note 71, 230-231 who is critical of consumer protection appearing to be an end in itself.

587 Mak, *supra* note 577, 391-392, 399.

588 Ibid. 383, 400.

589 Grundmann, *supra* note 71, 224.

590 For a detailed overview of European means of harmonisation, cf. Constanze Lippstreu, *Wege der Rechtsangleichung im Vertragsrecht: Vollharmonisierung, Mindestharmonisierung, optionales Instrument*.

591 European Commission, Green Paper on the Review of the Consumer *Acquis* (2007/C 61/01), C 61/6.

592 Ibid.

to increase consumer confidence in cross-border purchases.[593] At the same time EU legislation shall itself provide a high standard of consumer protection.[594] The move toward maximum rather than minimum harmonisation has been received with concerns.[595] It is questionable whether the best consumer protection standard[596] or an increased volume of cross-border trade[597] can be achieved this way.

Beside issues within the area of consumer law, its relation to another key area of EU regulation, namely competition law, cannot be disregarded. Both consumer and competition law pursue the goal of a functioning internal market. On the one hand, competition law provides the consumer with a proper range of options instead of just one monopolist supplier. On the other hand, consumer law – understood in its market dimension – ensures an acceptable quality for and informative choice on behalf the consumer.[598] Consumer and competition law, thus, complement each other.[599] Both legal areas relate to the internal market and especially due to EU competition law's increased emphasis on consumer welfare the two areas develop in a converging way.[600] Despite persistent and fundamental differences between competition and consumer law,[601] consideration of competition law principles and measures can, thus, provide a useful tool when looking at EU consumer policy.

---

593 Ibid. C 61/4, C 61/6, C 61/9.

594 Ibid. C 61/2; European Commission (2007), *supra* note 572, page 7.

595 Cf. i.e. Geraint Howells, Europe's (Lack of) Vision on Consumer Protection: A Case of Rhetoric Hiding Substance?. in Dorota Leczykiewicz and Stephen Weatherill (eds), *The Images of the Consumer in EU Law: Legislation, Free Movement and Competition Law*, 431-446 with further references; Lippstreu, *supra* note 590, 335, 339, 343; Vanessa Mak, 'Review of the Consumer Acquis: Towards Maximum Harmonization?' [2009] (1) European Review of Private Law 55-73; generally critical of increased consumer confidence through European harmonisation Twigg-Flesner, *supra* note 70, 197 et seq.

596 Mak, ibid., (65 et seq.).

597 Howells, *supra* note 595, 432.

598 Neil W. Averitt and Robert H. Lande, 'Consumer Sovereignty: A Unified Theory of Antitrust and Consumer Protection Law' [1997] 65 Antitrust Law Journal 713 (713-714).

599 Albertina Albors-Llorens, 'Competition and Consumer Law in the European Union: Evolution and Convergence' [2014] 33 (1) Yearbook of European Law 163 (164).

600 Ibid. (176 et seq.).

601 Ibid. (190).

As *Weatherill* puts it, EU consumer policy has rather 'evolved as a spillover' and, thus, 'lacks planned theoretical underpinning'.[602] The main common goal pursued by EU action is the functioning of the internal market rather than targeted consumer protection under Art. 169 TFEU, even if it results in substantive protection, i.e. by way of interpretation by the CJEU. An analysis of the depicted problems shall not be the focus of this work but rather serve as an introduction to tensions that have arisen in the course of the introduction and implementation of European Directives that shall be covered by this work. The following analysis allows us to discover possible differences between the First (minimum) and Second (partial maximum) Consumer Credit Directives as well as the minimum Unfair Contract Terms Directive.

B. Consumer Credit Regulation

The First Consumer Credit Directive was introduced in 1986. It was followed by the Second Consumer Credit Directive which repealed the First Consumer Credit Directive in 2008. The analysis will focus on provisions relating to pre-contractual information and access to credit (Arts. 5 to 9 CCD 2008).

I. Rationale behind European Consumer Credit Regulation

Beside the general rationales behind consumer credit, European consumer credit policy is predominantly concerned with the removal of barriers to the internal market in the field of financial instruments ('inclusion in the market').[603] To the EU this is especially important because financial markets – at least when it comes to private lending – have remained largely national[604] because of consumers' presumed distrust in foreign financial institutions, i.e. because of languages. Most consumers simply feel more comfortable with a financial institution seated in their home country and region.

602 Weatherill, *supra* note 568, 845.

603 Comparato, *supra* note 83, 16.

604 Peter Rott, Consumer Credit. in Norbert Reich and others (eds), *European Consumer Law*, recital 5.1.

As will be shown below, the European Consumer Credit Directives focus on promoting informed consumer decisions and credit assessment rather than substantive responsible lending which would entail lending restrictions where the granting of credit can have detrimental consequences for and overindebtedness of the consumer.[605] However, merely informing consumers often is not enough. In many instances consumers cannot comprehend the information and conditions associated with financial products correctly (with only a short amount of time available) and further cannot evaluate all of the entailed consequences at the time of the conclusion of the contract.[606] As has been pointed out, rather overoptimism about their financial situation can motivate consumers to agree to credit agreements which overburden them economically.[607] Suggestions for improvement have been brought forward, such as the inclusion of mandatory debt counselling or penalties on lenders who do not act responsibly.[608] These policies would presume a vulnerable consumer image rather than following a market oriented approach that the EU pursues. As of now, EU consumer credit legislation provides an example of regulation that is targeted at the rational consumer. Such a regulatory approach is not effective under the parameters set out for this work. As has been proposed above and taking into account insights from behavioural economics the vulnerability of consumers needs to be considered. I, therefore, agree with suggestions for respective reform that have been brought forward.

II. Legislative Developments

The European Union has introduced two major Consumer Credit Directives[609] which are depicted in the following sections.

---

605 Irina Domurath, A Map of Responsible Lending and Responsible Borrowing in the EU and Suggestions for a Stronger Legal Framework to Prevent Over-Indebtedness of European Consumers. in Hans-W. Micklitz and Irina Domurath (eds), *Consumer Debt and Social Exclusion in Europe*, 161 et seq.

606 Vanessa Mak and Jurgen Braspenning, '*Errare humanum est*: Financial Literacy in European Consumer Credit Law' [2012] 35 (3) Journal of Consumer Policy 307-332; Rott, *supra* note 604.

607 Domurath, *supra* note 605, 160; Mak and Braspenning, ibid., (324).

608 Domurath, ibid., 166 et seq.

609 Two further Directives had been introduced to adjust the calculation of interest rates, cf. Council Directive 90/88/EEC of 22 February 1990 amending Directive 87/102/EEC for the approximation of the laws, regulations and administrative provisions of the Member States concerning consumer credit and Directive

1. Directive 87/102/EEC (The First Consumer Credit Directive)

The first Directive on consumer credit was introduced to the EEC in 1986. It is based on the principles of a functioning, meaning the removal of barriers in the, internal market and the consumer information paradigm.[610] The First Consumer Credit Directive applied to 'agreement[s] whereby a creditor grants or promises to grant to a consumer a credit in the form of a deferred payment, a loan or other similar financial accommodation'. The consumer was defined as 'a natural person who, in transactions covered by this Directive, [was] acting for purposes which can be regarded as outside his trade or profession' (Art. 1 Section 2 lit (a)). Several kinds of credit were excluded in Arts. 1 and 2 Consumer Credit Directive. It focussed on the provision of information (Arts. 3 and 5) and formal (Art. 4) and information (Art. 6) requirements.

While the European legislator was praised for adopting a functional approach to the definition of credit,[611] it also turned out inefficient due to the low consumer protection level and minimum harmonisation character.[612] Consequently, Member States had introduced their own national provisions which gold-plated the Directive.[613] Furthermore, the credit market had undergone rapid changes that could not be captured by the First Consumer Credit Directive.[614] The European Commission admitted that the Directive had failed to fulfil expectations because consumer credit provisions across the EC remained fragmentised. No harmonisation or removal of barriers had taken place.[615] The critical report also introduced

---

98/7/EC of the European Parliament and of the Council of 16 February 1998 amending Directive 87/102/EEC for the approximation of the laws, regulations and administrative provisions of the Member States concerning consumer credit.

610 Cf. Recitals 4 and 10 CCD 2008.

611 Rott, *supra* note 604, recital 5.2. Unlike Manfred Westphal, The EU Financial Services Policy and its Effect on Consumer Law. in Michelle Kelly-Louw and others (eds), *The Future of Consumer Credit Regulation: Creative Approaches to Emerging Problems*, 79.

612 Rott, ibid.; Westphal, ibid.

613 Cf. the overview in European Commission, Report on the operation of Directive 87/102/EEC, COM (95) 117 final (11 May 1995), pages 64 et seq. The United Kingdom (page 73-74) and Germany (pages 66-67) are mentioned as 'gold-plating Member States'. Norway (page 75) is also mentioned as an EEA Member State under the obligation to implement the Directive.

614 Ibid. Recitals 4, 14.

615 Ibid. Recitals 11 and 12.

ideas for a revised Consumer Credit Directive and especially considered concerns regarding the increasing problem of overindebtedness.[616]

2. Directive 2008/48/EC (The Second Consumer Credit Directive)

Following the negative assessment of the First Consumer Credit Directive, the first proposal for a new consumer credit Directive was introduced in 2002[617] which suggested a maximum harmonisation measure[618] including the principle of responsible lending[619]. The proposal was, on the one hand, criticised for the maximum harmonisation aim due to a fear of ensuing lower consumer protection standards[620] and, on the other hand, for a wide and 'overprotective' approach which placed too many burdens on the credit industry.[621] Consequently, the broad responsible lending provisions in the first proposal were removed from the next amended proposal.[622] The maximum harmonisation paradigm remained a disputed issue throughout the legislative procedure[623] but was eventually partially adopted (Art. 22 Section 1 CCD 2008).

Scope

The Second Consumer Credit Directive still only covers credit to consumers (Art. 1). A consumer is defined as 'a natural person who, in transactions covered by this Directive, is acting for purposes which are outside his trade, business or profession' (Art. 3 lit (a)). While some definitions have been added, the ones that had already existed under the First Consumer Directive largely remain the same (cf. Art. 3 CCD 2008). Several exemp-

616 Ibid. pages 93 et seq.

617 European Commission, Proposal for a Directive of the European Parliament and of the Council on the harmonisation of the laws, regulations and administrative provisions of the Member States concerning credit for consumers, COM (2002) 443 final (11 September 2002).

618 Ibid. page 6.

619 Ibid. pages 15 et seq.

620 Westphal, *supra* note 611, 80.

621 Rott, *supra* note 604, recital 5.3.

622 Cf. European Commission, Amended proposal for a Directive of the European Parliament and of the Council on credit agreements for consumers amending Council Directive 93/13/EC, COM (2005) 483 final (23 November 2005), page 31.

623 Westphal, *supra* note 611, 81.

tions are listed in Art. 2 Sections 2 (total exemptions), 3-4 (mandatory partial exemptions) and 5-6 (optional partial exemptions).

Information Duties

The Second Consumer Credit Directive provides for advertisement (Art. 4) as well as pre-contractual (Arts. 5, 6) information duties. Art. 5 Section 1 provides that the consumer must receive 'information needed to compare different offers in order to take an informed decision [...] in good time before [he or she] is bound by any credit agreement' on a 'durable medium'. Compared to the First Consumer Credit Directive the list of mandatory information has been extended. Art. 5 Section 6 requires Member States to 'ensure that creditors and, where applicable, credit intermediaries provide adequate explanations to the consumer, in order to place the consumer in a position enabling him to assess whether the proposed credit agreement is adapted to his needs and to his financial situation'. Handing out the written information, thus, does not suffice. In this respect the CJEU has emphasised that the given information must be personalised.[624] 'Suppliers of goods or services acting as credit intermediaries in an ancillary capacity' are exempted from information duties under Arts. 5 and 6 according to Art. 7.

Duties relating to Access to Credit

In addition to enabling the consumer to take an informed decision, creditors are also obliged to assess the applicant's creditworthiness. According to Art. 8 Section 1

> Member States shall ensure that, before the conclusion of the credit agreement, the creditor assesses the consumer's creditworthiness on the basis of sufficient information, where appropriate obtained from the consumer and, where necessary, on the basis of a consultation of the relevant database.

Another assessment of creditworthiness must occur in case of an increase of credit (Art. 8 Section 2). Art. 9 shall ensure that Member States enable for non-discriminatory cross-border access to relevant databases (Section 1). Furthermore, the consumer must be informed of the consultation of a database in case of rejection (Section 2). With respect to the assessment of creditworthiness the CJEU has held that Art. 8 Section 1 allows for

624 CJEU judgment C-449/13, *CA Consumer Finance SA v Ingrid Bakkaus, Charline Bonato, née Savary, Florian Bonato* [2014] recital 49.

an assessment to be carried out solely on the basis of information provided by the consumer without requiring the creditor to verify those.[625] Such a policy deviates sharply from the strict requirements under the Mortgage Credit Directive (see below). However, the CJEU has since also held that the penalty for not carrying out a creditworthiness assessment must be effective and dissuasive[626] and that a national rule can provide that credit must be denied in case of a negative outcome of the assessment of creditworthiness[627]. The CJEU has, furthermore, pointed out that the consumer cannot waive the assessment of creditworthiness by being granted the consumer credit under the condition that it was presumed that a creditworthiness assessment was conducted.[628] The CJEU sees the duty to assess the consumer's creditworthiness in line with the duty to provide personalised information and, thus, as a (combined) mean to protect the individual consumer from the dangers of overburdening credit.[629]

3. Further Directives which affect Consumer Credit Regulation

While the Second Consumer Credit Directive remains the focus of this work, it must not be neglected that several other European legislative instruments influence the (consumer) credit and financial markets. When it comes to the Directive's aim to foster *cross-border* lending, the EU legislative instruments on cross-border credit transfers and payments[630] are an important addition to consider. These instruments aim at harmonising and removing barriers to cross-border financial transactions, such as

625 Ibid. recitals 37-39.

626 CJEU judgment C-565/12, *LCL Le Crédit Lyonnais SA v Fesih Kalhan* [2014] recitals 43, 44.

627 CJEU judgment C-58/18, *Michel Schyns v Belfius Banque SA*, [2019] recitals 47-49 (with reference to the Mortgage Credit Directive in recital 46).

628 CJEU judgment C-449/13, *CA Consumer Finance SA v Ingrid Bakkaus, Charline Bonato, née Savary, Florian Bonato* [2014] recital 31.

629 Cf. ibid., recital 44.

630 Directive (EU) 2015/2366 of the European Parliament and of the Council of 25 November 2015 on payment services in the internal market, amending Directives 2002/65/EC, 2009/110/EC and 2013/36/EU and Regulation (EU) No 1093/2010, and repealing Directive 2007/64/EC; Regulation (EC) No 924/2009 of the European Parliament and of the Council of 16 September 2009 on cross-border payments in the Community and repealing Regulation (EC) No 2560/2001.

charges, within the EU. Furthermore, the Payment Accounts Directive[631] regulates payment account fees and rules and includes a guarantee for consumers to open basic accounts. Both instruments bear the potential to affect the Second Consumer Credit Directive. When it comes to marketing credit, the Distance Marketing of Financial Services Directive[632] which aims to 'approximate the laws, regulations and administrative provisions of the Member States concerning the distance marketing of consumer financial services' and includes further pre-contractual information duties in the special case of distance contracts (Art. 3). More generally practices under the Unfair Commercial Practices Directive (see Arts. 5-7) can become relevant.

While the Second Consumer Credit Directive explicitly excludes mortgage agreements (Art. 2 Section 2 lit. a), the Mortgage Credit Directive[633] which was passed after the Second Consumer Credit Directive provides guidance as to the EU's possible future attitude toward consumer credit. The Mortgage Credit Directive refers to the Second Consumer Credit Directive (i.e. many definitions in Art. 4 refer to the Second Consumer Credit Directive) and explicitly states that the two Directives should build a consistent and coherent framework for credit regulation.[634] However, the Mortgage Credit Directive also goes further than the Second Consumer Credit Directive. The advertising as well as pre-contractual information must include warnings regarding exchange rate fluctuations (Art. 11 Section 2 lit. (j)) as well as (general) risks relating to the credit agreement (Arts. 11 Section 6, 13 Section 1 lit. (n)). The Mortgage Credit Directive also provides for an assessment of creditworthiness (Art. 18) which specifically states that such shall not rely predominantly on the value of the mortgaged property but the consumer's ability to repay the credit (Section 3). The consumer and his or her individual abilities rather than the security

631 Directive 2014/92/EU of the European Parliament and of the Council of 23 July 2014 on the comparability of fees related to payment accounts, payment account switching and access to payment accounts with basic features.

632 Directive 2002/65/EC of the European Parliament and of the Council of 23 September 2002 concerning the distance marketing of consumer financial services and amending Council Directive 90/619/EEC and Directives 97/7/EC and 98/27/EC.

633 Directive 2014/17/EU of the European Parliament and of the Council of 4 February 2014 on credit agreements for consumers relating to residential immovable property and amending Directives 2008/48/EC and 2013/36/EU and Regulation (EU) No 1093/2010.

634 Ibid. Recital 20.

move to the centre of attention of the creditworthiness assessment (Recital 55). Such focus is combined with the obligation that a negative assessment outcome should lead to the denial of the credit application (Recital 57, Art. 18 Section 5 lit. (a)). The Mortgage Credit Directive, thus, includes more elaborate and strict provisions on responsible lending in the form of a creditworthiness assessment. Finally, the Unfair Contract Terms Directive is relevant when it comes to consumer credit. Beside the Second Consumer Credit Directive's preventative measures, the UCTD provides for a control mechanism of the concluded credit agreement. The Directive and a variety of cases that concern both unfair terms and consumer credit agreements will be discussed below.

In 2018 the European Commission initiated an evaluation of the Second Consumer Credit Directive. After previous consultations regarding the Second Consumer Credit Directive in 2014 and 2017 which among other findings stated that oftentimes information duties were not adhered by[635] the Commission started a new round of evaluation targeted at the effectiveness, efficiency, coherence, relevance and EU added value to the Directive[636]. An EU-wide public consultation conducted between the 14 January and 8 April 2019 revealed that most respondents still only applied for credit in their home Member States.[637] Furthermore, only half of the respondents were aware of pre-contractual information duties.[638] The overall response to European consumer credit regulation was positive, highlighting a higher consumer protection standard.[639] Gold-plating policies in Member States were criticised for hindering harmonised credit access.[640] Suggestions for improvement included lowering the minimum credit sum, punishing non-compliance and adapting consumer credit legislation to digitalisation and modern forms of lending, such as crowdfunding.[641] Furthermore, the Commission found that the unclear wording of Art. 8 of the Directive has led to a fragmented implementation which needs to be im-

635 European Commission, Evaluation Road Map regarding the Evaluation of the consumer credit directive, Ares(2018)3472049 (29 June 2018), page 1.

636 Ibid. page 2.

637 European Commission, Evaluation of the Consumer Credit Directive (Directive 2008/48/EC) Summary report - public consultation, Ares(2019)3218540 (16 May 2019), page 2.

638 Ibid. page 3.

639 Ibid. pages 4-5.

640 Ibid. page 6.

641 Ibid.

proved.[642] A revised Directive proposal is due to be published in the second quarter of 2021.[643]

642 European Commission, Report from the Commission to the European Parliament and the Councilon the implementation of Directive 2008/48/EC on credit agreements for consumers, COM(2020) 963 final (5 November 2020), pages 6-7, 12.

643 Ibid. page 12.

Chapter 5: Consumer Credit in the United Kingdom

The following chapter depicts the development of consumer protection law with respect to consumer credit legislation under English law. The analysis is divided into developments prior to the UK's Membership in the EEC, EC and EU respectively, and developments as a Member State. As it is difficult to determine a change of developments along periodic timelines, the criteria for allocating legal developments within the former or the latter time period shall be oriented at material legislative developments. This means that the Consumer Credit Act 1974 (CCA 1974) will be discussed under developments prior to joining the EEC despite the UK having already joined the EEC in 1972 because the CCA 1974 goes back to national legislative efforts dating before the UK became a Member State. However, the focus first shifts to the development of consumer law in general, specifically when and whether consumer law came into existence as a legal category under English law, its historic and present significance and influence on English private and contract law in particular.

A. *General Developments under English Law*

Today 'consumer law' describes a category of private law and includes a wide range of private legal regulatory measures. However, the legal area is still relatively young compared to the long-standing history of English private law. This section, outlines the emergence of consumer law under common law and statutory law as well as its significance for contract law until today.

I. Common Law

As has been pointed out above, the original position under common law is shaped by two guiding principles: *freedom to contract* and the *binding force of contracts*.[644] It can generally be said that a comprehensive line of case-law specifically targeted at consumer protection has not been developed by

644 Cf. Common Law and Equity above.

English courts. Protection measures have been introduced at a general level, rather than specifically targeting the business-consumer relationship.[645] Such a broad rather than specifically targeted development of case-law may also be explained by the continuous development of UK history. This continuity is reflected in the development of the common law. Broader rather than narrowly defined doctrines open up the possibility of continuous development across several legal areas.

One area of such protection measures is the influence of equitable doctrines. Broadening the previously defined category of consumer law (see above), measures that can be considered relevant for consumer protection as we define them today are those which target abusive relationships or an inequality of bargaining power in contractual relationships. While a general doctrine of inequality of bargaining power as suggested by Lord Denning MR in *Lloyds Bank Ltd v Bundy*[646] has not been adopted,[647] the equitable doctrines of undue influence and unconscionability were introduced to tackle such situations.

Under the *doctrine of undue influence* a contract can be set aside because of an abuse of relationship and the underlying equitable principle that no contracting party should retain an advantage from committing a wrongful act.[648] The doctrine focusses on the circumstances under which the abused party's consent was achieved rather than the disadvantage the party had to suffer eventually.[649] It, thereby, aims to ensure that the bargaining process is free from unconscionable exploitation by one party. In the more recent case of *Royal Bank of Scotland v Etridge (No. 2)*[650] such instances were exemplified with 'taking of an unfair advantage', 'misuse of influence' and 'abuse of trust and confidence'.[651] Without going into the specifications re-

645 Simon Whittaker, Chapter 38: Consumer Contracts. in Hugh Beale (ed), *Chitty on Contracts* (Volume 2), recital 38-001.

646 [1974] 3 All ER 757 at 765.

647 *National Westminster Bank Ltd. v Morgan* [1985] 1 All ER 821 at 830 per Lord Scarman.

648 Beale, *supra* note 121, recital 8-059; *Allcard v Skinner* [1886-90] All ER Rep 90 at 99 per Lindley LJ. See also at 93 per Cotton LJ ('public policy') and at 103 per Bowen LJ ('public policy and fair play').

649 Cf. *CIBC Mortgages Ltd v Pitt* [1994] 4 All ER 433. Unlike *National Westminster Bank Ltd. v Morgan* [1985] 1 All ER 821 at 829 per Lord Scarman.

650 [2001] 4 All ER 449 at [9], [10] and [32] per Lord Nicholls.

651 Beale, *supra* note 121, recital 8-059.

lating to cases of presumed and actual undue influence[652], the doctrine exemplifies that English law does pay attention to the parties' positions in the bargaining process and allows for intervention in harsh cases.

Under the *doctrine of unconscionability* contracts can be set aside because of harsh unconscionable bargains to the detriment of one contracting party.[653] It shall protect 'poor and ignorant [men]'[654], thus, suffering from a weak bargaining position, from unconscionable, oppressive bargains that the other contracting party willingly exploited.[655] This includes the case where a weaker party did not know about or could not understand detrimental clauses of a contract, i.e. due to the lack of language capability.[656] This, again, exemplifies that the common law has ensured weaker party protection under harsh circumstances, albeit not specifically targeting consumer-trader situations.

While the common law has allowed for measures of weaker party protection in extraordinary situations, the courts have not developed specific doctrines to benefit 'consumers' as such.

II. Legislative Action

Concrete consumer protection measures were introduced by legislative action. The legislator thereby reacted to developments of the modern industrialised society and the rise of consumerism as explained above (see pages 131 et seq.). While the legislator had intervened in private legal relationships where it was held necessary before, the first targeted consumer legislation emerged in the second half of the 20th century.[657] In the following,

---

652 Cf. *Barclay's Bank plc v O'Brien* [1994] 4 All ER 417 at 423 per Lord Browne-Wilkinson; *Allcard v Skinner* [1886-90] All ER Rep 90 at 93 per Cotton LJ; Beale, ibid., recital 8-062.

653 Beale, ibid., recital 8-132.

654 *Fry v Lane* (1880) 40 Ch.D. 312 at 322 per Kay J.

655 *Strydom v Venside Ltd.* [2009] All ER (D) 135 (Aug) per Blair J; *Boustany v Pigott* (1995) 69 P. & C.R. 298 at 303 per Lord Templeman (Privy Council); Beale, *supra* note 121, recital 8-135.

656 Cf. *Schwartz v Barclays Bank plc* [1995] Lexis Citation 2066 per Millett LJ. As to the introduction and exploitation of unfair terms, cf. also *Boustany v Pigott* (1995) 69 P. & C.R. 298 at 303 per Lord Templeman (PC) and *Multiservice Bookbinding Ltd. and others v Marden* [1978] 2 WLR 535 at 549-550 per Browne-Wilkinson J.

657 Whittaker, *supra* note 645, recital 38-002.

this work focusses on two prominent areas of such legislative intervention: consumer credit legislation and legislation on unfair terms.[658]

B. Consumer Credit Legislation

By entering the EEC in 1973 the UK came under an obligation to implement European legislative measures (Section 2 Subsection 1 European Communities Act 1972). The legislative developments which have been depicted above impacted Consumer Credit Legislation. The following section depicts the changes that the area of consumer credit legislation underwent before and after joining the EEC.

I. Consumer Credit Legislation before 1986

The history of early forms of consumer credit in Great Britain starts in the 18th century together with the Industrial Revolution and increasing demand for consumer goods.[659] Once a working-class problem, developments in the 19th and 20th century turned different forms of lending – which are now considered consumer credit under the CCA 1974 – into an issue across society, paving the way for intensive regulation from the turn of the 20th century onward. As one of the first countries undergoing Industrial Revolution and encountering respective issues concerning consumer lending, the UK became a forerunner in modern consumer credit legislation.

1. Early Legislation on Hire-Purchase, Pawnbroking and Moneylending

In 1896 there existed essentially three credit instruments available for working-class people, entailing that they involved the purchase of goods and a relatively small amount of money: not paying (right away), meaning

658 The sections are divided into categories 'before and after joining the EEC' although technically the CCA 1974 and UCTA were introduced *after* the UK entered the EEC in 1972. However, work on these legislative instruments had started before, so in fact they constituted national legislation which was introduced largely uninfluenced by European legislation.

659 Cf. an early law on pawnbroking in 1757, Rosa-Maria Gelpi and François Julien-Labruyère, *The History of Consumer Credit: Doctrines and Practices*, 127.

small credit by local stores and hire-purchase agreements, pawning and borrowing.[660] While borrowing in general was seen negatively as admitting to poverty,[661] lending was soon also viewed as a necessity to aid economic growth by enabling workers to purchase luxury articles[662]. Beside the deferred payments at local stores which were mainly based on trust within the personal relationship between the trader and the buyer, the 'tallymen' trade emerged.[663] Through building personal relationships, the tallymen were often in a position to exploit the vulnerable position of their customers, by both collecting information on their creditworthiness,[664] deferring payments and eventually inducing them to borrow from a tallyman and, thus, becoming financially dependent[665].

In the course of the 19th century, stores started to offer hire-purchase sales mainly for luxury goods.[666] A sharp rise in hire-purchase was noted in the decades after World War I[667] and hire-purchase replaced pawning and small credit from local stores as the main source of consumer credit[668]. While hire-purchase allowed working-class and middle-class citizens luxury consumption, it also bore the risk of high interest rates and repossession.[669] In this light, the legislator passed the Hire Purchase Act 1938 (later revised by the Hire Purchase Act 1965 and amended by the Advertisements (Hire-Purchase) Act 1967) to protect vulnerable customers and regulate, *inter alia*, when repossessions could take place. Furthermore, the Act included information duties with respect to the price, interest rate and instalments.[670]

660 Paul Johnson, *Saving and spending: the working-class economy in Britain, 1870-1939*, 144.
661 Gelpi and Julien-Lebruyère, *supra* note 659, 126.
662 Johnson, *supra* note 660, 150.
663 Ibid. 153-154.
664 Ibid.
665 Sean O'Connell, *Credit and Community: Working-Class Debt in the UK since 1880*, 28.
666 Johnson, *supra* note 660, 155 et seq.
667 Ibid. 157. 1 million hire-purchase agreements in 1891 compared to 21 million in 1921, cf. Gelpi and Julien-Lebruyère, *supra* note 659, 130.
668 Steven Finlay, *Consumer Credit Fundamentals*, 26.
669 Johnson, *supra* note 660, 156-157.
670 UK Parliament, 'Hire Purchase Act 1938' (parliament.uk) <https://www.parliament.uk/about/living-heritage/transformingsociety/electionsvoting/case-study-radical-politicians-in-the-north-east/from-the-parliamentary-collections/education-act-1944/> accessed 17 September 2019.

Long before hire-purchase, pawning had been a common way to acquire money. By the end of the 19th century several legislative Acts had already been passed on pawnbroking. They included, *inter alia*, Acts in 1757, 1784, 1800, 1872 and 1900 (later revised by the Pawnbrokers Act 1960) which regulated, *inter alia*, the obligations arising under pawnbroking, the maximum interest and period of repayment. One of the reasons for the relatively early regulation of pawnbroking were certainly the large number of pledges, thus, the very frequent use of pawnbrokers to borrow money.[671] For the even less fortunate who did not own goods that they could offer a pawnbroker, moneylending was the only remaining option.[672] From 1854 onward, with the introduction of the Bill of Sale Act and the abolition of usury laws, moneylending was left completely unregulated.[673] The Moneylenders Act 1900 (revised by the Moneylenders Act 1927) marked a u-turn. Rather than further liberalising the market, it aimed at regulating this area, i.e. by registration duties, to protect customers from fraudulent behaviour and excessive interest rates.[674] It is especially notable that courts had the power to redraft moneylenders' 'harsh and unconscionable' contracts.[675] Nevertheless, the mandatory provisions were often ignored by private lenders.[676] However, the problem was reduced with the growth of hire-purchase agreements offered by larger lenders by the beginning of the 20th century.[677]

The depicted early forms of consumer credit reflect an increased social mobility in 19th century Britain.[678] Early industrialisation was the pre-requisite for a rapidly growing credit market. Starting with small credit from local stores to pawnbroking to the evolution of modern forms of credit, such as hire-purchase, the lending culture adapted to the evolving culture

---

671 In 1870 150 million pledges were registered in Great Britain meaning ca. 60,000 pledges per year for London pawnbrokers alone, cf. Johnson, *supra* note 660, 168.

672 Ibid. 188.

673 Finlay, *supra* note 668, 21; Gelpi and Julien-Lebruyère, *supra* note 659, 127; O'Connell, *supra* note 665, 133.

674 Johnson, ibid., 189; O'Connell, *supra* note 665, 134 et seq.

675 O'Connell, ibid., 137.

676 Especially after the introduction of higher lincensing fees with the Moneylenders Act 1927, cf. ibid. 132.

677 Cf. Gelpi and Julien-Lebruyère, *supra* note 659, 130-131.

678 Gelpi and Julien-Lebruyère, ibid., 128, 131 with reference to Lord Geoffrey Crowther, Consumer Credit: Report of the Committee Vol. 1 ('Crowther Report') (Her Majesty's Stationery Office 1971), page 44.

of mass consumption throughout most social classes.[679] The development of new forms of credit urged the legislator to adopt new measures of regulation.[680] However, the depicted developments also show that regulation of what is now known as consumer credit had at that point not been a foreign concept to the legislator. Legislation intended to protect customers – not necessarily working-class citizens – had been introduced from the 18th century onward. The availability of credit had been acknowledged as an important factor to foster individual consumption and consequently economic growth.[681]

2. The 'Crowther Report'

In the beginning of the 1950s more regulation on instalment credit was introduced, i.e. introducing a mandatory down payment and maximum repayment periods.[682] However, by the end of the 1950s following the Radcliffe Report (1959), credit regulation was reduced[683] while such would still have been necessary in light of the growing number of unsecured credit in the area of mail orders as well as the rise of credit cards[684]. In light of the ongoing developments, a Committee under the leadership of Lord Geoffrey Crowther was set up in 1968 to investigate the plurality of legislative instruments that had been introduced with respect to different kinds of consumer credit.[685] In the final report the Commission generally found that consumer credit has a positive impact on society, as it contributes to the social mobility of people.[686] It, furthermore, revealed a consumer image comparable to that of the European rational consumer. The report suggested that rather than restricting the access to credit 'to protect the relatively small minority who get into difficulties', freedom of choice should

679 Gelpi and Julien-Lebruyère, *supra* note 659, 130-131.
680 Ibid. 131.
681 Cf. Johnson, *supra* note 660, 150.
682 Gelpi and Julien-Lebruyère, *supra* note 659, 131.
683 Ibid.
684 Finlay, *supra* note 668, 26.
685 Gelpi and Julien-Lebruyère, *supra* note 659, 132. For a detailed description of the Crowther Report and its impact on the Consumer Credit Act 1974, cf. Stuart Aveyard, Paul Corthorn and Sean O'Connell, *The Politics of Consumer Credit in the UK, 1938-1992*, 170 et seq.
686 Crowther Report, *supra* note 678, page 141.

be preserved[687] and 'the state should interfere as little as possible'[688]. The Committee, thus, suggested to introduce information duties and consumer education programmes.[689] However, the Committee also noted social inequality when it comes to consumer credit; namely, that such financial instruments often affect those who cannot afford to pay the total amount in cash at once.[690] Thus, future consumer credit legislation should both encourage competition and comprehensive consumer protection, i.e. by the introduction of interest rate ceilings.[691] The Crowtherian approach reflects a regulatory approach that mainly aims at serving the overall positive effects of consumer credit for the economy by creating clear a set of rules for the market. Consumer law is seen as a tool for the market as well as the individual consumer.

3. The Consumer Credit Act 1974

Based on the 'Crowther Report' a *single* Consumer Credit Act was introduced in 1974 that repealed the Pawnbrokers Acts 1872-1960, the Hire Purchase Act 1965, the Advertisements (Hire-Purchase) Act 1967 and the Moneylenders Acts 1900 and 1927.[692]

Overview

The CCA 1974 established a supervision and licensing system governed by the Director General of Fair Trading (now Competition and Markets Authority, hereinafter "CMA") (Parts I and III CCA 1974) and at the same time governs contractual relationships in the area of hire-purchase agreements, lending (Parts II to VII) and pawnbroking (Part VIII). The first version of the CCA 1974 defined a 'consumer credit agreement' as 'a personal credit agreement by which the creditor provides the debtor with credit not exceeding £5,000' (Section 8 Subsection 2 CCA 1974).[693] A 'personal credit agreement' is defined as 'an agreement between an individual ("the debtor") and any other person ("the creditor") by which the creditor pro-

687 Ibid. page 153.
688 Ibid. page 151.
689 Aveyard, Corthorn and O'Connell, *supra* note 685, 173.
690 Crowther Report, *supra* note 678, page 357.
691 Aveyard, Corthorn and O'Connell, *supra* note 685, 170, 173-174.
692 Section 192 Subsection 3 lit. (b) in connection with Schedule 5 CCA 1974.
693 The maximum amount was later eliminated by the Consumer Credit Act 2006 (see below).

vides the debtor with credit of any amount' (Section 8 Subsection 1 CCA 1974). Credit and hire businesses must attain a licence before they can lend consumer credit (Section 21 CCA 1974). Such a licence is only granted to persons 'fit to engage in activities covered by the licence' (Section 25 CCA 1974).

Pre-Contractual Information Duties

The original CCA 1974 already included pre-contractual information duties with respect to advertisement (Sections 44, 45 CCA 1974)[694] and the specific credit agreement (Section 55 Subsection 1 CCA 1974). For example, 'advertisement [should convey] a fair and reasonably comprehensive indication of the nature of the credit or hire facilities offered by the advertiser and of their true cost to persons using them'.[695] The disclosure duties with respect to the individual agreement were later specified with separate Disclosure Regulations.[696]

Calculation of the Total Charge for Credit and APR

The CCA 1974 was the first legislative instrument to introduce rules on the information and calculation of the total charge for credit which had to be included prominently in advertisements (Section 44 Subsection 1 CCA 1974) and the individual credit agreement (Section 60 Subsection 1 lit. (b) CCA 1974). Based on Section 20 Subsection 1 CCA 1974, regulations regarding the calculation of the total charge for credit and APR for consumer credit were introduced.[697] The calculation did not only include the interest rate but *all* relevant charges[698] arising under the credit agreement.[699] These rules were specifically intended by the Crowther Committee[700] and enhanced the comparability of credit offers for consumers. Rules

694 Now contained in FCA Handbook CONC 3.

695 Section 44 Subsection 1 CCA 1974.

696 For an overview, cf. Eva Lomnicka, Chapter 39: Credit and Security. in Hugh Beale (ed), *Chitty on Contracts* (Volume 2), recital 39-076.

697 Consumer Credit (Total Charge for Credit) Regulations 1980, SI 1980/51 (28 April 1980). Now repealed and replicated by FCA rules (CONC App 1.1 and 1.2).

698 As far as they were not excluded under Regulation 5 Consumer Credit (Total Charge for Credit) Regulations 1980.

699 Regulations 3 to 6 Consumer Credit (Total Charge for Credit) Regulations 1980.

700 Lomnicka, *supra* note 696, recital 39-060.

on information and calculation of the APR were later also adopted by the First Consumer Credit Directive.

Access to Credit

The original CCA 1974 did not include provisions on the assessment of consumers' creditworthiness. The reason behind this may lie in the 'Crowther Report' which suggested that access to credit should not be restricted.

Other Provisions

Section 60 CCA 1974 provides that the Secretary of State (now the Treasury) shall introduce regulations specifying the content and form of the actual credit agreement, i.e. especially including the rights and duties of the agreement, the amount and charges of credit and remedies available to the consumer. Part VIII introduced new provisions on pawnbroking. Similar to the Moneylenders Act 1927 the original CCA 1974 still included a right on behalf of the courts to reopen 'extortionate' credit agreements (Section 137 Subsection 1 CCA 1974).

Summary

The CCA 1974 was the first comprehensive legislative instrument on consumer credit in the world. It consolidated the existing patchwork of regulatory instruments to harmonise and clarify rules benefitting both the market and individual consumers. By granting the Secretary of State the power to introduce regulations on specific issues,[701] the legislator ensured that the CCA 1974 remained flexible in a volatile market environment. The information duties with respect to the APR, advertisement and pre-contractual information, furthermore, prove to be a modern and sustainable model, which was also adopted by the First Consumer Credit Directive more than a decade later. Generally, the CCA 1974 is clearly the product of the (market-oriented) 'Crowther Report' which advocated that rather than restricting credit access, consumers should be able to make free (and informed) decisions in a regulated (licensed) market place.

701 Cf. ibid. recital 39-008 (fn. 32).

II. Consumer Credit Legislation after 1986

The CCA 1974 was enacted shortly after the UK joined the EEC in 1973. The subsequent Consumer Credit Directives and other Directives affecting consumer credit, nevertheless, had a strong impact on the future developments of consumer credit in the UK. The following subsections depict the impact of the Consumer Credit and other Directives on consumer credit legislation in the UK.

1. Consumer Credit Directives and Consumer Credit Act 2006

The First Consumer Credit Directive was introduced in 1986 more than a decade after the CCA 1974 and one year after the CCA 1974 finally came into force in 1985[702]. The Directive's scope with respect to both the applicability and the material rights and duties of the parties to the contract was much narrower than the CCA 1974.[703] For example, Section 2 Consumer Credit (Agreements) Regulations 1983[704] already provided for more detailed provisions with respect to the form and content of the agreement than Art. 4 CCD 1986 and Sections 43 et seq. CCA 1974 already provided for the regulation of information in advertisement from the start. Thus, only minor amendments of the CCA 1974 were necessary.[705]

Before the Second Consumer Credit was introduced in 2008, the British legislator enacted several new Regulations and the Consumer Credit Act 2006 (CCA 2006) to adapt consumer credit legislation to the rapid changes in the consumer credit market.[706] The report preceding the introduction of the CCA 2006 identified a lack of pre-purchase information, 'undue surprises post-purchase', 'unfair practices', 'illegal money lenders' and 'over-indebtedness' as the key problems that would have to be addressed by reformed consumer credit legislation.[707] Beside these consumer protection issues, the UK Government also proposed improvements on the European

702 Lomnicka, *supra* note 696, recital 39-002 (fn. 3).

703 European Commission (1995), *supra* note 613, pages 73-74.

704 SI 1983/1553 (19 May 1985).

705 European Commission (1995), *supra* note 613, pages 73-74.

706 Compared to GBP 32 million in 1971, GBP 49 billion were owed in credit card debt, cf. UK Government (Department of Trade and Industry), Fair, Clear and Competitive: The Consumer Credit Market in the 21st Century (White Paper), December 2003, pages 4, 12 et seq.; Lomnicka, *supra* note 696, 39-010.

707 White Pater, ibid., pages 5, 19 et seq.

level to ensure 'a properly functioning single European marketplace for credit with the potential to boost competition, generate better deals and ensure consumers have enough protection to shop confidently across borders', including cross-border data access and reformed rules on information duties, APR calculation, unfair practices and debt recovery.[708] Beside the Regulations – among others the Consumer Credit (Advertisements) Regulations 2004[709] and the Consumer Credit (Disclosure of Information) Regulations 2004[710] – the CCA 2006 widened the scope of the CCA 1974 for consumer credit agreements by removing the maximum amount of credit (Section 2 CCA 2006), so consumer credit agreements are now simply defined as 'an agreement between an individual ("the debtor") and any other person ("the creditor") by which the creditor provides the debtor with credit of any amount (Section 8 Subsection 1 CCA 1974). The previous power of the courts to re-open 'extortionate' credit agreements (Section 137 Subsection 1 CCA 1974) was replaced with the power to amend, replace or issue orders relating to 'unfair relationships' (Sections 19 to 22 CCA 2006 and Sections 140A to 140D CCA 1974).[711]

The Second Consumer Credit Directive was enacted by way of several Regulations in 2010.[712] As the scope of the Second Consumer Credit Directive is still narrower than that of the CCA 1974, 'consumer credit agreements' according to the British understanding of the term are now regulated by two different regimes.[713] By way of the Consumer Credit (EU Directive) Regulations 2010[714] the CCA 1974 was amended to include respective provisions of the Directive, among others on pre-contractual explanations (Section 55A CCA 1974), the requirement of the assessment of creditworthiness (Section 55B CCA 1974) and data base access (amended Section 157 CCA 1974). Beside the newly introduced Section 55A CCA 1974 which essentially implements Art. 5 Section 6 CCD 2008, the Consumer Credit (Disclosure of Information) Regulations 2010[715] provide the detailed pre-contractual information duties included in Art. 5 Section 1 and Art. 6 CCD 2008 which must be provided by way of the Standard Euro-

708 Ibid. page 7.
709 SI 2004/1484 (31 October 2004).
710 SI 2004/1481 (31 May 2005).
711 For an overview of amendments, cf. also Lomnicka, *supra* note 696, recital 39-010.
712 For an overview, cf. ibid. recital 39-011.
713 Ibid.
714 SI 2010/1010 (30 March 2010).
715 SI 2010/1013 (30 April 2010).

pean Consumer Credit Information (Schedule 1 of the Consumer Credit (Disclosure of Information) Regulations 2010). Creditors whose credit agreements are not covered by the Second Consumer Credit can either 'opt in' or are subject to the previous Consumer Credit (Disclosure of Information) Regulations 2004.[716]

Due to its (partial) maximum harmonisation character and more detailed provisions, i.e. on pre-contractual information duties, the Second Consumer Credit Directive had a considerably stronger impact on the CCA 1974 than the First Consumer Credit Directive. The Directive's provisions were mostly implemented word-by-word to resemble the Directive as closely as possible.

2. Other Legislation

Legislative changes after the implementation of the Second Consumer Credit Directive had even greater impact on the CCA 1974. The most notable changes occurred following the introduction of the Financial Services Act 2012 (FSA 2012) which substantially amended the Financial Services and Markets Act 2000 (FSMA 2000).[717] The overall goal was to establish a new administrative financial regulator, the Financial Conduct Authority (FCA) (Part IA Sections 1A et seq. FSA 2012). In order to transfer competences relating to consumer credit from the former OFT to the new FCA, activities subject to licences under the CCA 1974 became 'regulated activities' under Section 22 FSMA 2000 (Section 107 FSA 2012).[718] Thus, since 2014 the FCA is responsible for the monitoring and supervision of the consumer credit market and issuing of respective licences under the FSMA 2000. Provisions on pre-contractual explanations and the assessment of creditworthiness (formerly Arts. 55A and 55B CCA 1974) have been repealed[719] and are now included in the FCA Handbook Section on Consumer Credit (Consumer Credit Sourcebook, "CONC") [720].

Since the law reform in 2014 consumer credit agreements are regulated under a dual system of the FSMA 2000 and the CCA 1974. A 'Review of

---

716 Lomnicka, *supra* note 696, recital 39-076.

717 The following overview is essentially based on Lomnicka, *supra* note 696, 39-002.

718 Cf. also The Financial Services and Markets Act 2000 (Regulated Activities) (Amendment) (No.2) Order 2013, SI 2013/1881 (25 July 2013).

719 Ibid. Art. 20 Sections 21, 22.

720 Cf. Part 9A FSMA 2012.

the retained provisions of the Consumer Credit Act' conducted by the FCA and published in March 2019 concludes that in order to retain a high standard of consumer protection the CCA 1974 should not be repealed. Such repeal would 'adversely affect' consumer rights as the FCA (currently) cannot 'replicate the same level of protection under [its] current rule-making powers'.[721] As of now, the provisions on consumer protection, information duties as well as sanctions could not all be replaced by FCA rules.[722]

In light of the departure from the EU, the Consumer Credit (Amendment) (EU Exit) Regulations 2018[723] and the Financial Services and Markets Act 2000 (Amendment) (EU Exit) Regulations 2019[724] provide for technical amendments to replace insufficient references to EU law.

The Financial Conduct Authority (FCA)

The FCA is authorised to monitor and supervise (Section 1L FSMA 2000) 'authorised persons', meaning those who have a licence under Part 4A FSMA 2000 to conduct financial business including consumer credit.[725] The FCA enacts rules (Section 137A FSMA 2000) and publishes guidance (Section 139A FSMA 2000) which are both published in the FCA Handbook that the authorised persons must and shall adhere by. The FCA has the power to ban and control products where necessary in light of consumer protection or ensuring functioning competition (Sections 137C, 137D FSMA 2000). The FCA can also impose financial penalties (Section 206 FSMA 2000), require restitution (Section 384 FSMA 2000), suspend (Section 206A FSMA 2000) or vary (Section 55J FSMA 2000) or apply for injunctions (Section 380 FSMA 2000). According to Section 138E FSMA 2000, however, none of these breaches constitutes an offence (Subsection 1) or makes the contract void or unenforceable (Subsection 2).

The FCA receives complaints from consumer organisations ('designated consumer bodies') to investigate 'a feature, or combination of features, of a market in the United Kingdom for financial services [that appears to be] significantly damaging the interests of consumers' (Section 234C FSMA

721 FCA, Review of retained provisions of the Consumer Credit Act: Final report (March 2019), recital 1.20.

722 Ibid. recitals 1.19, 1.25, 1.34 and 1.35.

723 SI 2018/1038 (28 September 2018).

724 SI 2019/632 (22 March 2019).

725 The following overview is essentially based on Lomnicka, *supra* note 696, recital 39-063.

2000) and references from scheme operators and regulated persons (Section 234D FSMA 2000). Claims by private individuals against regulated credit businesses are not dealt with by the FCA but the Financial Ombudsman Service (Part XVI FSMA 2000).[726]

Pre-Contractual Information (CONC 4)

Beside the Consumer Credit (Disclosure of Information) Regulations 2010 which implement the material pre-contractual information duties under the Second Consumer Credit Directive,[727] rules on pre-contractual requirements are now to be found under CONC 4. The rules and guidance on pre-contractual information requirements apply to consumer credit lending, meaning all regulated credit agreements (CONC 4.2.1 Section 1).

CONC 4.2.4, 4.2.5[728] and 4.2.7[729] resemble Art. 5 Section 6 CCD 2008 in that they require pre-contractual information to be disclosed in a personalised manner and demand that the consumer must be placed 'in a position to assess whether the agreement is adapted to the customer's needs' (CONC 4.2.5 Section 1 lit. (a)). In addition, CONC 4.2.6 advises that the customer should be enabled 'to make a reasonable assessment as to whether the customer can afford the credit and to understand the key associated risks'. In cases of 'high-cost-short-term credit' the customer should be warned that 'the agreement would be unsuitable to support sustained borrowing over long periods and would be expensive as a means of longer-term borrowing' (CONC 4.2.8). The creditor is, furthermore, required to assure him- or herself that the consumer understands the given information (see CONC 4.2.9, 4.2.11, 4.2.12, 4.2.14, 4.2.16).

The requirements under CONC 4.2 are more comprehensive than those under the Second Consumer Credit Directive and aim at enabling the consumer to make an informed decision. The provisions do not only lay down rules to be followed but also offer guidance on the adequacy of information disclosure (i.e. CONC 4.2.4 or 4.2.16). The rules emphasise the duty of the creditor to consider the customer's interests and require him or her to act accordingly (see i.e. CONC 4.2.9, 4.2.10). Thus, the provisions also contain a policy of responsible lending which is reflected by the fact that

726 For a detailed account, cf. below pages 165 et seq.

727 CONC 4.2.3 explicitly states that disclosure requirements under Section 55 CCA 1974 and possible (temporary) unenforceability remain in place.

728 CONC 4.2.5. replaced Section 55 CCA 1974.

729 Among other CONC rules formerly part of the OFT's 'Irresponsible Lending Guidance'.

many provisions stem from the former OFT's 'Irresponsible Lending Guidance'. This policy is emphasised by specific bans of unfair practices relating pre-contractual information (CONC 4.8.2 et seq.). Such rules mark a shift from the previous purely market-oriented approach.

Access to Credit (CONC 5.2A)

The provisions on the assessment of creditworthiness were revised in 2018. Now CONC 5.2A contains rules on the assessment of creditworthiness. The rules and guidance on the assessment of creditworthiness apply to consumer credit lending, meaning all regulated credit agreements (CONC 5.2A.1) except in certain cases of pawning where 'the customer's total financial liability [...] is not capable of exceeding the true market value of the article pawned by the customer and the effect of the passing of property in the pawned article to the firm [...] would, therefore, be (at the very least) to discharge the debt secured by the pawn and any other obligation [...] including any expenses of sale' (CONC 5.2A.2 Section 1), overdraft without a prior agreement (CONC 5.2A.2 Section 2 lit. (a)), non-commercial agreements (CONC 5.2A.2 Section 3) and 'small borrower-lender supply agreements' (CONC 5.2A.2 Section 4).

In accordance with Art. 8 CCD 2008, CONC 5.2A.4 provides for a mandatory assessment of the borrower's creditworthiness in case of entering into a regulated (consumer) credit agreement (Section 1) and increasing the amount of credit (Section 2) or credit limit (Section 3). An increase of the amount of credit or credit limit shall also include cumulative raises (CONC 5.2A.6). Resembling Art. 8 Section 1 CCD 2008, according to CONC 5.2A.7 the assessment can be based on information provided by the consumer or information obtained from a credit reference agency as long as a reasonable creditworthiness assessment can be ensured depending on the individual circumstances (CONC 5.2A.8).

Furthermore, CONC 5.2A.10 et seq. provide details on the substance of the creditworthiness assessment. According to CONC 5.2A.10 the assessment must include considerations regarding the possibility of partial and total default of the customer. Relevant elements of consideration include the potential borrower's income from savings and other financial assets and how these savings and assets would be used to repay the credit (CONC 5.2A.12 Section 2, 5.2A.13) as well as other contractual or statutory payment obligations (CONC 5.2A.12 Section 4). Possible additional loans (CONC 5.2A.12 Section 3) or personal guarantees or indemnities (CONC 5.2A.14) regarding repayments must not be considered. The creditor must take into account possible 'significant adverse impact[s] on the customer's financial situation' (CONC 5.2A.12 Section 5). Further considerations – depending on the individual circumstances of the case – are listed in rules CONC 5.2A.20. and 5.2A.21 and guidance CONC 5.2A.22, 5.2A.23, 5.2A.24 and 5.2A.25.

The creditor must not conclude a (consumer) credit agreement with the potential borrower without a prior assessment of creditworthiness (CONC 5.2A.4, 5.2A.5). In connection with the rules set out in CONC 5.2A (CONC 5.2A.5 Section 1) and having 'proper regard to the outcome of that assessment in respect of affordability risk' (CONC 5.2A.5 Section 2) this ban implies that credit should not be granted in case of a negative outcome of the assessment of creditworthiness. Creditors must, further, 'establish, implement and maintain clear and effective policies and procedures' of creditworthiness assessment (CONC 5.2A.33).

CONC 5.2A contains comprehensive and detailed rules and guidance on the execution and evaluation of a mandatory creditworthiness assessment – similarly to the Mortgage Credit Directive – taking into account not only the possibility of default on the credit but also the individual factors that determine whether the potential borrower can afford to take out consumer credit. The rules and guidance provisions emphasise that the creditor must consider the individual circumstances of each case as much as the (future) financial well-being of his or her customer. Thereby, the FCA encourages creditors to implement a policy of responsible lending that ensures a high level of consumer protection.

In addition, the FCA has launched a market study in 2019 'to examine how the credit information market operates and the impact it has on consumers' in order to gather information on

> the [accessibility], coverage and quality of credit information, the [market structure and] effectiveness of competition between credit reference agencies, and the extent of consumer engagement [and understanding of credit information and how it impacts their behaviour].[730]

The study shall also consider 'whether vulnerable customers are disproportionately affected by the way credit information is used, and whether any alternative approaches might deliver better outcomes for consumers'.[731] UK policy on consumer credit has, thus, shifted from a purely market-ori-

---

730 FCA, 'FCA launches review of the Credit Information Market' (Financial Conduct Authority, 27 June 2019) <https://www.fca.org.uk/news/press-releases/fca-launches-review-credit-information-market> accessed 19 September 2019.

731 Ibid.

ented to a more individual-focussed approach more recently. Nevertheless, such policy also aims at protecting the market as increasing over-indebtedness poses a danger to its stability (see also below).

3. Adjudication of Consumer Credit Legislation

Cases involving claims by private individuals against lenders relating consumer credit legislation are adjudicated by the courts as well as the Financial Ombudsman Services (FOS).

a. The Courts

According to Section 141 Subsection 1 CCA 1974 jurisdiction on consumer credit agreements lies solely with the county courts under English law. Beside having the power to enforce agreements upon action by the creditor (Section 141 Subsection 1 lit. (a) CCA 1974) the courts may also make an order with respect to unfair relationships (Sections 140A, 140B CCA 1974).

Enforcement Orders

In case the creditor does not comply with disclosure duties[732] under Section 55 Subsection 1 CCA 1974 the credit agreement will only be enforceable against the debtor by order of the court (Section 55 Subsection 2 CCA 1974). Such enforcement orders can be granted under Section 127 Subsection 1 CCA 1974. According to Section 127 Subsection 1 CCA 1974 such an order may only be refused if the court considers a rejection justified in light of (i) 'the prejudice caused to any person by the contravention in question, and the degree of culpability for it' and (ii) the power of the court to reduce or discharge a sum payable according to Section 127 Subsection 2 CCA 1974 or impose certain conditions or vary the agreement under Sections 135 and 136 CCA 1974[733].

---

732 Including duties under the Consumer Credit (Disclosure of Information) Regulations 2010.

733 For examples of such variations, cf. *Hurstanger Ltd v Wilson* [2007] 4 All ER 1118 and *London North Securities Ltd v Meadows* [2005] EWCQ Civ 956.

'Unfair Relationship'

Beside the power to grant (or reject) an enforcement order, the courts can also make an order under Section 140B CCA 1974 if the credit agreement constitutes an 'unfair relationship'. The power does not only relate to the current credit agreement itself but also related agreements[734] and credit agreements that have already ended[735].

According to Section 140A Subsection 1 CCA 1974 relationship is unfair if (a) any of the terms of the agreement or a related agreement are unfair, (b) because of 'the way in which the creditor has exercised or enforced any of his rights' and/or (c) 'any other thing done (or not done) by, or on behalf of, the creditor (either before or after the making of the agreement or any related agreement)'. The scope of discretion on behalf of the court is, thus, very broad (see also Section 140A Subsection 2 CCA 1974). The control of terms even goes further than envisaged under the Unfair Contract Terms Act as it does not only include terms at the time when the agreement was concluded.[736]

'Terms' under Section 140A Subsection 1 lit. (a) CCA 1974 most frequently include terms relating to credit charges and fees[737] as well as terms stemming from related agreements[738]. The courts must determine whether such charges are reasonable under the individual circumstances of each case.[739] In *Holyoake v Candy*[740] the court held that guidance could be sought from *Maple Leaf v Rouvroy*,[741] *Paragon Mortgages Ltd v McEwan-Peters*[742] and *Rahman v HSBC*[743], i.e. whether there exist 'sound commer-

734 Section 140C Subsection 4 CCA 1974.

735 Section 140A Subsection 4 CCA 1974.

736 Cf. also Lomnicka, *supra* note 696, recital 39-218.

737 Which fall outside the scope of the Unfair Contract Terms Directive under the core exclusion. Cf. i.e. *Mark Alan Holyoake and others v Nicholas Anthony Christopher Candy and others* [2017] EWHC 3397 (CH); *Chubb & Bruce v Dean & Anr* [2013] EWHC 1282 (CH); *Upendra Rasikdal Patel v Vithalbhai Bikabhai Patel* [2009] EWHC 3264 (QB); *Robert Shaw v Nine Regions Limited* [2009] EWHC 3514 (QB).

738 Lomnicka, *supra* note 696, recital 39-219. Cf. i.e. *Link Financial Limited v Mrs Teresa North Wilson* [2014] EWHC 252 (CH).

739 Cf. Lomnicka, ibid., recital 39-220.

740 [2017] EWHC 3397 (CH) at [346].

741 *Maple Leaf Macro Volatility Master Fund and others v Jacques Rouvroy, Krzystof Trylinski* [2009] EWHC 257 (Comm) at [274], [276], [288] and [289].

742 *Paragon Mortgages Limited v Robert McEwan-Peters, Rachel Frances McEwan-Peters* [2011] EWHC 2491 (Comm) at [54(b)].

743 *Shafik Rahman and others v HSBC Bank plc* [2012] EWHC 11 (Ch) at [274]-[278], [280]-[281].

cial reasons' for the term, whether the term was individually negotiated and the scale of lending[744].

'The way the creditor has exercised any of his rights' under Section 140A Subsection 1 lit. (b) CCA 1974 means that regarding 'unfairness' it does not only matter *that* the creditor could enforce his or her rights but also *in which way* he or she did so. It has been indicated that in order to determine the unfairness of behaviour it can be relevant whether the creditor applied pressure prior to the conclusion of the agreement, whether the creditor believed that the borrower had experience regarding the respective credit arrangement, whether the creditor could reasonably believe that the customer had (not) read the terms of the agreement and whether the debtor voiced doubts regarding the terms in question at the time of the conclusion of the agreement.[745] Thus, it matters whether the creditor took into account the debtor's interests at the time of the conclusion of the agreement.[746]

'Any other thing done (or not done) by, or on behalf of, the creditor' according to Section 140A Subsection 1 lit. (c) CCA 1974 is the most open-ended option of finding a relationship unfair. In light of the previous case-law on the Moneylenders Act 1927, it includes pre- as well as post-contractual behaviour.[747] Examples of cases where unfairness was found under this option are *Plevin v Paragon Finance Ltd*,[748] *Doran v Paragon Personal Finance Ltd*[749] and *Patel v Patel*[750]. In all cases a lack of information to be disclosed at the conclusion or during the agreement led to the finding of unfairness.

In case the court finds an unfair relationship, it may make an order according to Section 140B Subsection 1 CCA 1974. Among the seven different options, the court can choose from requiring repayments, requiring to carry out or abstain from certain activities, reducing or discharging sums payable under the agreement, requiring the return of securities, setting

744 Ibid. at [275], [278].

745 *Mark Alan Holyoake and others v Nicholas Anthony Christopher Candy and others* [2017] EWHC 3397 (CH) at [346]; *Maple Leaf Macro Volatility Master Fund and others v Jacques Rouvroy, Krzystof Trylinski* [2009] EWHC 257 (Comm) at [274].

746 For more examples, cf. Lomnicka, *supra* note 696, recital 39-221.

747 Ibid. recital 39-222.

748 [2014] UKSC 61 at [18]-[20]. See also *Pilgrim Rock Ltd v Mr. Iwaniuk* [2019] EWHC 203 (Ch).

749 *Christopher Doran, Joanne Doran v Paragon Personal Finance Limited* [2018] 6 WLUK 518 at [41] et seq.

750 [2009] EWHC 3264 (QB) at [73]-[78].

aside duties imposed on the debtor, altering terms of the agreement or directing accounts to be taken.

Sections 140A to 140D CCA 1974 offer the courts a broad array of power to intervene in unfair relationships. The provisions as well as the case-law show flexible solutions to rectify unfair relationships and a willingness on behalf of the courts to take measures accordingly. With respect to term control under the Unfair Contract Terms Directive, the measures, however, also bear the potential for conflict as they allow for more flexible measures than envisaged under Art. 6 Section 1 UCTD. In this regard, it has been clarified in *Greenlands Trading Ltd v Pontearso* that the test of unfairness under Section 140A CCA 1974 is not identical with the test under the Unfair Contract Terms Directive (Part 2 of the Consumer Rights Act 2015) which bears more restrictions on the court.[751]

b. The Financial Ombudsman Service

Beside the possibility of going to court to resolve a dispute, consumers can approach the FOS if their problem relates to a regulated agreement under the FSMA 2000 (Part XVI and Schedule 17 FSMA 2000). According to Section 225 Subsection 1 FSMA 2000 the FOS 'provides for a scheme under which certain disputes may be resolved quickly and with minimum formality by an independent person'. The FOS is funded by the 'authorised persons' (Section 234 FSMA 2000). It, nevertheless, emphasises its independence from the covered businesses.[752] The FOS offers services free of charge for consumers. According to Section 228 Subsection 2 FSMA 2000 the ombudsmen of the FOS must decide what is 'fair and reasonable in all the circumstances of the case'. Such decisions are based on the available facts of the case, the applicable laws, codes of good conduct and the rules

751 *Greenlands Trading Ltd & Anor v Girolama Pontearso* [2019] EWHC 278 (Ch) at [49]. Cf. also with respect to the distinction between basis and exclusion clauses, *Michael Carney, Roberta Carney and others v N M Rothschild & Sons Limited* [2018] EWHC 958 (Comm) at [73], [81] et seq.

752 FOS, 'How is the Financial Ombudsman Service funded?' (*The Financial Ombudsman Services*) <https://www.financial-ombudsman.org.uk/faqs/rules-powers-information-us/financial-ombudsman-service-funded> accessed 21 September 2019.

set out in the FCA Handbook.[753] In case the ombudsman rules in favour of the consumer, he or she may grant the consumer a 'money award' or direct the business to take certain steps to rectify the situation (Section 229 Subsection 2 FSMA 2000). If either party to the dispute is not satisfied with the result they may still initiate court proceedings on the matter.

The FOS has seen a constant rise of complaints regarding consumer credit since 2014.

Year	**Total number of complaints received**	**Complaints regarding consumer credit**	**Proportion**
2018/2019[754]	388,392	68,758	ca.17.7%
2017/2018[755]	339,967	36,349	ca. 10.6%
2016/2017[756]	321,283	25,984	ca. 8%
2015/2016[757]	340,899	13,382	ca. 3.9%
2014/2015[758]	329,509	9,572	ca. 2.9%
2013/2014[759]	512,167	7,630	ca. 1.4%

The FOS states that the rise in complaints regarding consumer credit relates to the stark rise of granted consumer credit and a general increase in UK household debt (also see below).[760] They also mention that more complaints by consumers were upheld in the area of 'high-cost credit, such as payday loans and instalment loans' in 2017/2018 (around six out of ten cases)[761] which could indicate practices of irresponsible lending. The FOS especially notes a rise in complaints on short-term lending in which credit businesses failed to assess the affordability of debt on behalf of the consumer.[762] Consequently, the FOS highlights that there exists an increased danger of vulnerability due to consumers' overindebtedness resulting, in

753 FOS, 'How we make decisions' (*The Financial Ombudsman Services*) <https://www.financial-ombudsman.org.uk/who-we-are/make-decisions> accessed 21 September 2019.

754 FOS, Data in more depth (May 2019), pages 5, 8.

755 FOS, Annual Review 2017/2018 (30 May 2018), pages 55, 57.

756 FOS, Annual Review 2016/2017 (June 2017), pages 51, 53.

757 FOS, Annual Review 2015/2016 (May 2016), pages 48, 50.

758 Ibid.

759 FOS, Annual Review 2014/2015 (May 2015), page 48.

760 Ibid. page 15.

761 Ibid.

762 FOS, 'Annual Review 2018/2019 (Banking and borrowing)' (*Financial Ombudsman Service*, May 2019) <https://annualreview.financial-ombudsman.org.uk> accessed 22 September 2019.

part, from irresponsible lending.[763] With respect to consumer credit, almost 50% of complaints had been upheld by ombudsmen in 2017/2018[764] and 41% in 2018/2019[765]. The reports also reveal that consumer credit issues most frequently arise with people aged under 34 rather than the age groups above.[766]

4. Practical Effects

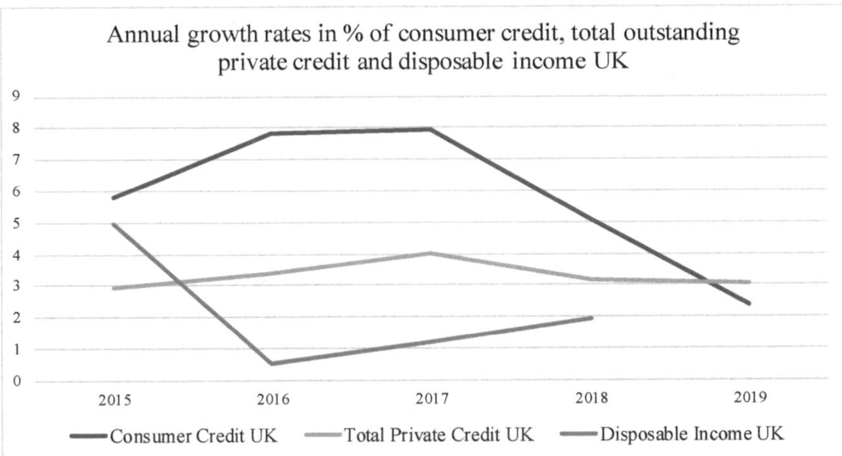

Reports of the Bank of England show that consumer credit has been growing again since 2011, reaching a peak by the end of 2016.[767] The table shows that consumer credit has out-grown overall private credit and both rates have been growing stronger than the disposable household income.[768] According to the Bank of England's quarterly Credit Conditions Survey, credit businesses loosened the availability of unsecured credit to

763 FOS (2017), *supra* note 756, pages 16 et seq.

764 FOS (2018), *supra* note 755, page 61.

765 FOS (2019), *supra* note 754, page 14.

766 Ibid. page 69; FOS (2018), *supra* note 756, page 65.

767 Cf. Bank of England, 'Household credit' (*Bank of England*, 11 January 2019) <https://www.bankofengland.co.uk/statistics/visual-summaries/household-credit> accessed 21 September 2019.

768 Data set out in Annex 2. Regarding lower growth rates of household income, cf. Bank of England, Financial Stability Report, June 2017, Issue No. 41, page 14.

consumers between 2012 and 2016.[769] The loosened availability increased competition which led to lower interest rates and a rapid growth in consumer credit.[770] It made up for 7% of the total outstanding domestic loans with UK banks in 2017.[771] The Bank of England considers the stark growth in consumer credit a risk to the country's financial stability because, unlike mortgages, the majority of consumer credit is unsecured in case of default.[772] Furthermore, the strong interlink of consumer credit debt and unemployment means an accumulation of risk factors in case of economic recession.[773] Therefore, the Bank of England's Financial Policy Committee announced a stronger focus on consumer credit in the course of the Bank of England's 2017 stress test and supported initiatives of the Prudential Regulation Authority and the FCA to improve the quality of lending, i.e. by reviewing rules and guidance on the assessment of creditworthiness.[774] The 2017 stress test revealed that while consumer credit only amounted to 7% of UK domestic loans, 'they contributed to nearly 40% of projected losses on these loans'.[775] As a consequence, 'regulatory capital buffers for individual firms' were set to ensure that losses resulting from consumer credit defaults could be absorbed.[776] Major UK banks proved to be resilient in 2018.[777] Furthermore, according to the quarterly Credit Conditions Survey credit businesses have tightened the credit scoring criteria for consumer credit since 2018.[778]

Growth rates of consumer credit have only slowed down since 2017. It is possible that the tightening of availability and related slowed growth of consumer credit have been influenced by the revised, stricter FCA rules the assessment of creditworthiness and other FCA measures in 2018. The Bank of England acknowledged that these regulatory instruments could have a further dampening effect in the future[779]. Growth in consumer credit has, thereby, slowed down to 5.6% in May 2019 compared to 11% in 2016 and household consumer credit debt relative to incomes has stabilised below

769 Bank of England, ibid. page 15.
770 Ibid.
771 Bank of England, Financial Stability Report, June 2018, Issue No. 43, page 33.
772 Bank of England (2017), *supra* note 768, page16.
773 Ibid.
774 Ibid.
775 Bank of England (2018), *supra* note 771.
776 Ibid. pages 7, 34.
777 Bank of England, Financial Stability Report, July 2019, Issue No. 45, page 16.
778 Ibid. page 34.
779 Ibid. page 16.

the 1997-2006 average.[780] At the same time, however, the default rate on unsecured loans has risen in the past years from 9.5% in 2017 to 22.1% in the second quarter of 2019 according to a survey among lenders[781] and the total number of write-offs on consumer loans has risen constantly from 1.0% in 2017 to 1.7% in 2019.[782] Similarly, the numbers of county court judgments for debt against consumers (CCJs)[783] and private insolvencies[784] have seen a rise since 2015.

III. Consumer Image

Since the Crowtherian view of a financial vehicle that must be accessible for all (rational consumers), the UK regulatory development has shifted toward a policy which is not merely focussed on informing a rational consumer on the conditions of consumer credit, but also on notions of responsible lending which is focussed on a holistic assessment of the individual consumer's financial needs. Especially, since the financial crisis in 2008 consumer credit is not just acknowledged as a motor for consumption and economic growth but also as a potential danger to financial stability. The continued efforts of review by public authorities shows that the notion of consumer protection rather than fostering of economic growth has moved to the centre of attention of the British legislator. However, while the regulatory focus has shifted toward responsible lending, rules on consumer credit are nevertheless still also targeted at the functioning of the market.

IV. Interim Conclusion: Consumer Credit Legislation

Since the introduction of the CCA 1974, UK consumer credit legislation underwent a lot of changes which were not only influenced by European legislation. The most severe change was not caused by the Second Consumer Credit Directive but the FSA 2012 and partial consolidation with the FSMA 2000. Since then rules on the assessment of creditworthiness

780 Ibid.

781 Bank of England, Credit Conditions Survey, Survey Results 2019 Q2 (21 June 2019), page 7.

782 Cf. Annex 2, Table 6.

783 694,627 (2015) compared to 1,080,944 (2019), cf. Annex 2, Table 7.

784 Cf. Annex 2, Table 9.

and provision of pre-contractual information have been part of the FCA rulebook. They provide a flexible and comprehensive framework consisting of both mandatory rules and guidance to enhance consumer protection. Furthermore, an elaborate framework of the broad judicial control mechanism under Sections 140A et seq. CCA 1974 and alternative dispute resolution provided by the FOS beside the monitoring and supervising authority of the FCA ensure that rules are enforced. The services offered by the FOS are free of charge and ensure that judicial enforcement remains accessible.

Most court cases relating to the creditor's duties prior to the contract will be decided under the broad control mechanism of Section 140A CCA 1974. Whether the court finds an unfair relationship heavily depends on the individual circumstances of the case. The discretion that comes with the norm goes beyond the scope of term control under the Unfair Contract Terms Directive. The case-law suggests that courts are willing to intervene on the basis of Sections 140A, 140B CCA 1974 to amend or discharge contractual obligations.

The current (newly) stable UK numbers on the relation between household income and consumer credit show that the tightened regulatory measures work effectively while the FOS' findings show that enforcement of such rules is equally important. This is especially true in light of rising default numbers regarding consumer credit and CCJs.

From an economic perspective the numbers indicate that the tightening of creditworthiness assessment measures has had a positive effect on consumer credit lending in the UK. While the numbers on default, FOS proceedings and CCJs indicate that looser lending led to financial difficulties on behalf of consumers, the stricter creditworthiness assessment requirements appear to lead to more responsible lending. The effect on default and CCJ numbers can only be assessed in the near future. The Covid-19 pandemic may affect such numbers negatively. These findings appear to confirm the above-made assumption of effectiveness, namely that a responsible and, thus, rather restrictive policy of consumer lending benefits both consumers and the economy most. In the UK such effect appears to have been achieved by the implementation of stricter rules on creditworthiness assessment rather than pre-contractual information duties.

Unfortunately, the maximum harmonisation character of the Second Consumer Directive led to the establishment of two separate regimes on consumer credit in the UK. The departure from the European Union opens the door for a unification of consumer credit regulation regimes and avoidance of further possible conflicts between the UCTD and Sections

140A et seq. CCA 1974. Under the Second Consumer Credit Directive, both the duty to provide pre-contractual information and the duty to assess the consumer's creditworthiness have been implemented by the UK accordingly. Both duties were later extended to kinds of consumer credit not covered by the Second Consumer Credit Directive. Especially the latter duty which had only been introduced by the Second Consumer Credit Directive, has been developed further with special regard for consumers' interests with respect to the affordability of credit. Meanwhile, the provisions on pre-contractual information contained in the CONC 4 and the Consumer Credit (Disclosure of Information) Regulations 2010 mostly resemble Art. 5 CCD 2008. Nevertheless, especially the provisions contained in the FCA Handbook reveal a much stronger focus on the interests of the consumer and responsible lending than on the principles envisaged by the Second Consumer Credit Directive. The tightening of creditworthiness provisions has shown the desired slowed down growth of consumer credit. The reform of European consumer credit legislation may lead in the same direction; in this case, similar to the legislation preceding the First Consumer Credit Directive, the UK would have set an example with respect to consumer credit legislation again.

Chapter 6: Consumer Credit in Germany

The following chapter depicts the developments around consumer credit regulation in Germany.

A. *History of Consumer Credit Legislation in Germany*

The history of modern German consumer credit legislation begins with the German Hire Purchase Act (*Abzahlungsgesetz*, hereinafter "AbzG") in 1894. In 1862 the mass sale of furniture and sewing machines as hire-purchase emerged on the German market. One prominent example was the purchase of sewing machines from the 'Singer' company. By 1888 they sold 2/3 of their 500,000 sewing machines by way of standardised forms and hire purchase.[785] With its business model 'Singer' also forced 80% of its competitors out of business.[786] Due to wide spread poverty and at the same time mass industrialisation which drew workers to the cities many women were dependent on the machines to make extra money and keep their families above the poverty line.[787] As wages remained low many were dependent on hire-purchase. An estimated 80% of the population were hire-purchase customers at that time.[788] The emergence of hire-purchase also led to usurious business practices as the dependence grew on behalf of workers, including the offer of defective goods for which there existed no legal recourse at the time.[789] The AbzG goes back to an initiative of chambers of commerce to protect other cash sale businesses from unfair competition practices.[790] Thereby, the AbzG was not primarily consumer focussed but aimed at providing a level playing field for businesses. One Parliamentarian at the time commented that workers served only as the 'deco-

785 Udo Reifner, Ewald Weitz and Rolf Uesseler, *Tatsachen zum Verbraucherschutz im Konsumentenkredit - Ergebnisse einer rechtswissenschaftlichen Lehrveranstaltung*, 65, 70. I thank Prof. Hans-W. Micklitz for his useful comments on this matter.

786 Ibid. 70. Udo Reifner, *Alternatives Wirtschaftsrecht am Beispiel der Verbraucherverschuldung - Realitätsverleugnung oder soziale Auslegung im Zivilrecht*, 117.

787 Reifner, ibid.

788 Reifner, Weitz and Uesseler, *supra* note 785, 70.

789 Ibid. 71; cf. also Reifner, *supra* note 786, 118-119.

790 Reifner, Weitz and Uesseler, ibid., 71; Reifner, ibid., 120-122.

rum' of the Act.[791] The AbzG did not contribute to increased consumer protection but 'unofficial enforcement' and threats to consumers remained common.[792] Modern hire-purchase for luxury goods such as cars only emerged from 1926 onward.[793]

This development shows a marked difference to the UK. In the UK several pieces of legislation were introduced at the turn and in the beginning of the 20th century to combat unfair practices. Unlike the AbzG the Moneylenders Acts specifically aimed at protecting customers from fraudulent behaviour and excessive interest rates. They even gave the courts the power to redraft harsh agreements. The AbzG did not include such specific provisions. In contrast German protection norms regarding credit businesses had been removed in 1867 which had the effect of an extreme liberalisation of the market.[794] Unlike in the UK, this development was not reconsidered in Germany despite an increasing number of court cases concerning forms of consumer credit[795].

In the following years and especially in the course of rapid economic growth after the end of Word War II the number of hire-purchase agreements grew even further.[796] Consequently, the law was amended in the following years, namely 1969, 1974 and 1976.[797] However, no new legislation was introduced and existing legislation only focussed on hire-purchase rather than including modern and emerging forms of consumer credit. In 1967 even maximum chargeable interest rates were lifted which led to an 'explosion' of consumer debt in Germany.[798]

§ 1 AbzG provided that in case of default the seller had a right of withdrawal and a right to repossession of the respective good only insofar as he

---

791 Reifner, ibid., 120.

792 Reifner, Weitz and Uesseler *supra* note 785, 72.

793 Ibid. 72; Reifner, *supra* note 786, 123 et seq. For a detailed analysis of consumer credit history in Germany, cf. Reifner, Weitz and Uesseler, ibid., 70-81 and Reifner, ibid., 116-140.

794 Reifner, Weitz and Uesseler, ibid. 65; Reifner, ibid., 117.

795 In 1890 the Local Court (*Amtsgericht*) Tiergarten recorded 14,000-17,000 cases regarding hire-purchase out of a total 118,000 proceedings, cf. Reifner, Weitz and Uesseler, ibid., 67.

796 Heinrich Kessler, Abzahlungsgesetz. in Werner Ballhaus, Wolfgang Gelhaar, Heinrich Kessler, Hans-Robert Metzger and Reinhold Weber (eds), *Das Bürgerliche Gesetzbuch mit besonderer Berücksichtigung der Rechtsprechung des Reichsgerichts und des Bundesgerichtshofs – Kommentar, Band II, 2. Teil*, recital 4.

797 Ibid. recital 1.

798 Udo Reifner, *Handbuch des Kreditrechts - Verbraucherkredit und Realkredit*, § 19 recitals 2, 3.

would return the paid instalments to the buyer. According to § 2 AbzG the buyer had to compensate the buyer for any reduction in value resulting from the use of the object. § 1a AbzG[799] included the formal requirement for the agreement to be in writing as well as for certain information to be provided to the buyer, including the total and instalment purchase prices, the amount, number and due dates of instalments and the APR. Furthermore, a copy of the agreement had to be handed to the customer. §§ 1b to 1d AbzG[800] provided for a withdrawal right within one week after the conclusion of the contract on behalf of the customer which the customer had to be expressly informed of.

Similar to the developments in the 19th century, the German legislator was also a late runner when it came to modern consumer credit legislation despite full industrialisation at that time. In the 1970s the calls for consolidated and broader consumer credit legislation became louder. In 1976 it was recommended that the new legislation should not merely include hire-purchase agreements but also other forms of credit as well as rules on credit intermediaries.[801] Again, in 1980, it was suggested to implement a broad consumer credit law covering the whole breadth of forms of consumer credit.[802] In light of increasing problems with permanent indebtedness formal legislative proceedings were initiated in 1984.[803]

In the meantime, the courts had developed jurisdiction to declare agreements with overburdening interest rates ineffective in light of the usury provision § 138 Section 2 BGB (individual usury).[804] In addition, the courts further developed the broader instrument of unfair credit relationships under § 138 Section 1 BGB at the beginning of the 1980s which clearly focussed on consumer protection rather than market competition (social usury).[805] This doctrine is mainly focussed on the imbalance of bargaining power between lenders and consumers. The lender shall be forced to reflect his or her behaviour in accordance with what constitutes reasonable

799 Inserted by way of the Gesetz zur Änderung des Abzahlungsgesetzes, BGBl. I 1541, No. 90 (4 September 1969).

800 Inserted by way of the Zweites Gesetz zur Änderung des Abzahlungsgesetzes, BGBl. I 1169, No. 52 (16 May 1974).

801 Eberhard Rebmann, Verbraucherkreditgesetz. in Harm Peter Westermann (ed), *Erman: Bürgerliches Gesetzbuch*, recital 3.

802 Ibid. recital 4.

803 Ibid. recital 5.

804 Cf. ibid. recital 6.

805 Reifner, *supra* note 798, § 19 recital 153.

market behaviour (toward consumers).[806] This development reflects a general shift of the use of § 242 BGB and general clauses by German courts. While it had been considered mainly a mean of correction and interpretation by the Imperial Court of Justice (*Reichsgericht*), decisions by the German Federal Supreme Court (*Bundesgerichtshof*) reveal that its status changed to a principle underlying the entire law of obligations.[807] Under this premise the courts may modify each norm in the law of obligations with reference to § 242 BGB.[808] The courts are thereby able to react to modern developments more flexibly. The shift also reflects the political and societal changes that Germany underwent in the 20th century. The development of § 242 BGB reflects an evolution from a liberal bourgeois society which is reflected in the original BGB to a social rule of law and social market economy. Rather than 19th century formalism we can now note a relativisation of private rights.[809] The development thereby reflects the introduction of the welfare state principle (Art. 20 Section 1 GG) after World War II.[810]

Thus, in Germany the courts assumed the role of developing an instrument of consumer protection in consumer credit relationships rather than the legislator. This marks a stark contrast to the UK where the legislator considered consumer protection rather than unfair competition practices from the beginning of the 20th century and shaped respective rules.

B. *Impact of European Consumer Credit Directives*

Eventually the German Consumer Credit Law (*Verbraucherkreditgesetz*, hereinafter "VKG") came into force in 1991 and basically constituted the German implementation of the First Consumer Credit Directive.[811] Furthermore, the new statutory instrument aimed at improving indebted con-

806 Ibid.
807 Wieacker, *supra* note 117, 527. I thank Prof. Hans-W. Micklitz for his useful comments on this matter.
808 Ibid. 527, 607.
809 Wieacker, *supra* note 117, 539.
810 Ibid. 540, 541, 543, 622.
811 Cf. also Deutscher Bundestag, Beschlußempfehlung und Bericht des Rechtsausschusses zum Entwurf eines Gesetzes über Verbraucherkredite, zur Änderung der Zivilprozeßordnung und anderer Gesetze, BT-Drs. 11/8274 (25 October 1990), page 19.

sumers' situations[812] and the AbzG was incorporated in the VKG in order to clarify the statutory provisions on hire-purchase which had become too complex after the law reforms in 1969, 1974 and 1976[813]. Therefore, the new VKG did not only fulfil the minimum harmonisation requirements of the Directive but also included further provisions, such as a withdrawal right (§ 7 VKG) as well as provisions on credit intermediaries (§§ 15 to 17 VKG). The VKG did not include a separate provision on pre-contractual information. § 4 VKG (in line with Art. 6 CCD 1986) provided for information duties at the conclusion of the contract. Beside the introduction of the VKG, the provisions on default action were eased for indebted consumers (§§ 688, 690 and 691 D-ZPO).

Before the Second Consumer Credit Directive was implemented, the VKG was integrated into the BGB in the course of the modernisation of the law of obligations. Since the further implementation of the Second Consumer Credit Directive[814] and the implementation of the Mortgage Credit Directive[815] the main provisions on consumer credit are now contained in §§ 356b, 491 to 505e BGB. Furthermore, as a consequence of the implementation of the Second Consumer Credit Directive Art. 247 §§ 3 to 12 Introductory Act to the German Civil Code (*Einführungsgesetz zum Bürgerlichen Gesetzbuch*, hereinafter "EGBGB") contain the Directive's detailed provisions on information duties and Art. 247 §§ 13 to 13b EGBGB contain provisions on credit intermediaries. Furthermore, Annexes 4 to 8 of the EGBGB norm contain standard forms, such as the Standard European Consumer Credit Information (Annexes 4 and 5).[816] The legislator included these provisions in the EGBGB to relieve the BGB from the complex provisions and to attribute statutory character to the European standard forms.[817]

812 Ibid. pages 19-20.

813 Ibid. page 20.

814 Gesetz zur Umsetzung der Verbraucherkreditrichtlinie, des zivilrechtlichen Teils der Zahlungsdiensterichtlinie sowie zur Neuordnung der Vorschriften über das Widerrufs- und Rückgaberecht), BGBl. I 2355, No. 49 (3 August 2009).

815 Gesetz zur Umsetzung der Wohnimmobilienkreditrichtlinie und zur Änderung handelsrechtlicher Vorschriften, BGBl. I 396, No. 12 (16 March 2016).

816 Gesetz zur Einführung einer Musterwiderrufsinformation für Verbraucherdarlehensverträge, zur Änderung der Vorschriften über das Widerrufsrecht bei Verbraucherdarlehensverträgen und zur Änderung des Darlehensvermittlungsrechts, BGBl. I 977, No. 39 (29 July 2010).

817 Deutscher Bundestag, Entwurf eines Gesetzes zur Umsetzung der Verbraucherkreditrichtlinie, des zivilrechtlichen Teils der Zahlungsdiensterichtlinie sowie

Scope

After the implementation of the Mortgage Credit Directive in 2016, § 491 BGB applies to 'general consumer credit agreements' and 'mortgage consumer credit agreements' (§ 491 Section 1 BGB). General consumer credit agreements are defined as 'nongratuitous loan contracts between an entrepreneur as lender and a consumer as borrower' (§ 491 Section 2 Sentence 1 BGB). According to § 13 BGB '[a] consumer means every natural person who enters into a legal transaction for purposes that are predominantly outside his trade, business or profession' and according to § 14 BGB '[an] entrepreneur means a natural or legal person or a partnership with legal personality who or which, when entering into a legal transaction, acts in exercise of his or its trade, business or profession'. § 491 Sections 2 to 4, § 506 Section 4, § 510 Section 3 and § 655a Section 1 BGB implement the exceptions contained in Art. 2 Section 2 CCD 2008 and define the scope of consumer credit regulation.[818] However, § 491 Section 2 No. 1 BGB merely mentions the minimum credit amount of EUR 200 but does not include a credit limit of EUR 75,000.[819] Thus, unlike under EU law, credit amounts exceeding EUR 75,000 are accepted as consumer credit under German law. Such credit is subject to the same German norms (derived from European law) as credit amounts between EUR 200 and EUR 75,000 but is not subject to European law.

Pre-contractual Information

The requirement for pre-contractual information was implemented in § 491a BGB. The content of such pre-contractual information required under the Second Consumer Credit Directive is contained in Art. 247 §§ 2 to 5, 8 to 13a EGBGB and includes the Standard European Consumer Credit Information form in Annexes 4 and 5 of Art. 247 EGBGB. § 491 Section 3 BGB implements Art. 5 Section 5 CCD 2008 literally. In the course of explaining the credit agreement to the consumer in order to put him or her in a position to be able to evaluate the (personal consequences) of the credit agreement Art. 247 § 3 Section 3 EGBGB requires the creditor to ex-

---

zur Neuordnung der Vorschriften über das Widerrufs- und Rückgaberecht, BT-Drs. 16/11643 (21 January 2009), page 66.

818 However, the German implementation does not exempt credit agreements according to Art. 2 Section 2 lit. (h).

819 The limit is only mentioned regarding the possibility to include securities on which information is missing in the credit agreement (§ 494 Section 6 Sentence 3 BGB). Such securities can, nevertheless, be demanded if the credit amout exceeds EUR 75,000.

plain the credit amount and APR by way of a representative example taking into account the consumer's individual preferences. According to Art. 247 § 4 Section 2 EGBGB requires any additional information not required under statutory law to be included separately to make sure the consumer realises that such information is conveyed to him on a voluntary basis.

Access to Credit

The duty to conduct a creditworthiness assessment prior to granting consumer credit is contained in §§ 505a, 505b and 505d BGB. These provisions were only inserted together with the implementation of the Mortgage Credit Directive. The original creditworthiness assessment required by the Second Consumer Credit Directive had been included in § 509 BGB. However, the legislator still mainly relied on § 18 Section 2 Banking Act (*Gesetz über das Kreditwesen*, hereinafter "KWG")[820] and § 2 Section 3 Law on the Supervision of Payment Service Providers (*Gesetz über die Beaufsichtigung von Zahlungsdiensten*, hereinafter "ZAG")[821] which had a supervisory public law rather than substantive private law character.[822] Since 2016 §§ 505a et seq. BGB contain a consolidated private law creditworthiness assessment duty which is not subsidiary to supervisory banking provisions anymore.[823] While the old § 509 BGB still allowed the creditor to grant the credit in case of a negative outcome of the creditworthiness assessment as long as he or she warned the debtor of the consequences of taking out credit in this case,[824] the new § 505a BGB provides that the creditor may only grant the consumer credit in case of a positive outcome of the creditworthiness assessment. The German legislator, thereby, specifically extended the requirements under the Mortgage Credit Directive to consumer credit especially considering the CJEU's judgment in *LCL Le Crédit Lyonnais SA v Fesih Kalhan.*[825] Such extension is permissible because the European legislator only provided for a duty to conduct a creditworthiness assessment but did not include concrete provisions on the consequences of a

820 Now § 18a KWG.

821 Now § 3 Section 4 Sentence 4 ZAG.

822 Cf. Jan Schürnbrand and Christoph Andreas Weber, § 505a. in Franz Jürgen Säcker and others (eds), *Münchener Kommentar zum Bürgerlichen Gesetzbuch (2019)*, recital 2.

823 Ibid.

824 Ibid. recital 8.

825 Cf. Deutscher Bundestag, Entwurf eines Gesetzes zur Umsetzung der Wohnimmobilienkreditrichtlinie, BT-Drs. 18/5922 (7 September 2015), pages 97-98.

breach of such duty.[826] The German implementation of the creditworthiness assessment duty under Art. 8 CCD 2008, therefore, appears to be both in line with the will of the European legislator and the case-law of the CJEU.

According to § 505b BGB and in line with the CJEU's judgment in *CA Consumer Finance SA v Ingrid Bakkaus and others* the creditor is free to rely on his or her own experience, information provided by the consumer him- or herself and/or information provided by a third party, i.e. commercial databases for the collection of data regarding a consumer's creditworthiness as long as the creditor's decision is reasonable.

§ 505d BGB provides for the consequences of a breach of the duty to conduct a (proper) creditworthiness assessment prior to granting consumer credit. Such consequences entail that the APR may be lowered (Section 1 Sentence 1), the debtor may terminate the consumer credit agreement at any point without being liable for prepayment penalties (Section 1 Sentence 3) and that the debtor is not liable for any breaches of contract, i.e. delayed payments (Section 2), insofar as the agreement had not been concluded if a proper assessment of creditworthiness had been conducted. § 505d BGB is not applicable if the consumer willingly or due to gross negligence provided the creditor with false information regarding his or her creditworthiness (Section 3).

C. *Consumer Credit Adjudication*

The following section will look at the adjudication of consumer credit measures in practice as well as practical effects that can be observed with respect to consumer lending.

I. Court Practice

As the norms in question (§§ 491, 491a and §§ 505a et seq. BGB and Art. 247 EGBGB) have only been implemented into German law quite recently in 2010 and 2016, there does not exist a lot of guiding court case-law on these consumer credit provisions under German law. There does exist a

826 Under Art. 23 CCD 2008 penalties must be 'effective, proportionate and dissuasive'. Cf. also ibid. page 97; Schürnbrand and Weber, *supra* note 822, recital 8.

body of case-law on the VKG.[827] However, the VKG did not include provisions on pre-contractual information and creditworthiness assessments. Under the VKG information only had to be provided in the actual contractual document at the conclusion of the contract.

With respect to pre-contractual information duties under § 491a BGB almost all cases that dealt with such duties substantively were heard at lower German courts. For example, the Higher Regional Court (*Oberlandesgericht*, hereinafter "OLG") Düsseldorf held that § 491a BGB in connection with Art. 247 EGBGB was only applicable to concrete credit offers rather than letters that invited consumers to make an appointment with their bank advisor.[828] Furthermore, § 491a BGB has often been mentioned where the T&Cs of a consumer credit agreement were disputed.[829] While pre-contractual information cannot in itself be classified as T&Cs, it may serve as an indicator for the assessment of T&Cs.[830] The German Federal Supreme Court has dealt with § 491a BGB substantively in one decision. The court decided that the creditor does not have to inform the consumer separately regarding credit intermediary fees that were included in the calculation of interest.[831] More recently, cases have concerned withdrawal rights under linked credit agreements for the purchase of cars, four of which the Regional Court (*Landgericht*, hereinafter "LG") Ravensburg has referred to the CJEU with questions regarding Arts. 10, 14 CCD 2008.[832]

No cases have been published with respect to the creditworthiness assessment duties according to §§ 505a et seq. BGB. With respect to the for-

---

827 A search on the German law data base www.juris.de on the 30 August 2020 found 995 decisions that mentioned the VKG and 265 decisions that considered § 4 VKG (search for NORM: "§ 4 VerbrKrG"). 49 out of those 265 judgments were given by the German Federal Supreme Court.

828 OLG Düsseldorf, judgment of the 22 September 2015, reference number: I-20 U 46/15, 20 U 46/15, juris, recital 19.

829 Cf. i.e. OLG Düsseldorf, judgment of the 28 April 2016, reference number: I-6 U 152/15, 6 U 152/15, WM 2017, 664.

830 OLG Düsseldorf, judgment of the 22 September 2015, reference number: I-20 U 46/15, 20 U 46/15, juris, recital 42.

831 German Federal Supreme Court, judgment of the 9 July 2019, reference number: XI ZR 53/18, NJW-RR 2020, 116.

832 CJEU cases C-187/20 *JL, DT v BMW Bank GmbH, Volkswagen Bank GmbH*, C-33/20 *UK v Volskwagen Bank GmbH*, C-155/20 *RT, SV, BC v Volkswagen Bank GmbH, Skoda Bank - Zweigniederlassung der Volkswagen Bank GmbH*; LG Ravensburg, decision of the 7 July 2020, reference number: 2 O 84/20, juris.

mer § 509 BGB the possibility of damages claims in case of a breach of the duty to conduct a creditworthiness assessment was discussed only once.[833]

II. Alternative Dispute Resolution

The low number of cases may be explained by the introduction of alternative dispute resolution mechanisms (see § 14 Law on injunctions in case of breaches of consumer law and other breaches, *Gesetz über Unterlassungsklagen bei Verbraucherrechts- und anderen Verstößen*, hereinafter "UKlaG") and supervision by the Federal Financial Supervisory Authority (*Bundesanstalt für Finanzdienstleistungsaufsicht*, hereinafter "BaFin") under the Law on the Federal Financial Supervisory Authority (*Gesetz über die Bundesanstalt für Finanzdienstleistungsaufsicht*, hereinafter "FinDAG").

§ 14 Section 1 Sentence 1 No. 2 UKlaG provides that disputes can be taken to arbitration bodies (mentioned above) beside the consumers' right for the dispute to be heard by the courts. As not all arbitration bodies are obliged to publish reports on cases or statistics it is difficult to assess the possibly relieving impact of alternative dispute resolution in the field of consumer credit. The arbitration body of the German Federal Bank (*Deutsche Bundesbank*) publishes annual activity reports according to § 34 Section 1 VSBG. They specify the complaints it receives each year regarding consumer credit since 2017. In this regard it received 126 complaints in 2017[834] and 66 complaints in 2018[835]. The activity report from 2016 indicates that the numbers have been even higher in 2016 (ca. 148 complaints) but have been falling since.[836] In 2016 most cases concerned credit processing fees and consumers' withdrawal rights.[837] In 2017 most cases concerned consumers' withdrawal rights.[838] In 2018 most cases concerned the

---

833 OLG Brandenburg, judgment of the 26 April 2017, reference number: 4 U 178/15, juris, recital 66.

834 Deutsche Bundesbank, Schlichtungsstelle bei der Deutschen Bundesbank Tätigkeitsbericht 2017 (3 January 2018), page 14.

835 Deutsche Bundesbank, Schlichtungsstelle bei der Deutschen Bundesbank Tätigkeitsbericht 2018 (3 January 2019), page 14.

836 Deutsche Bundesbank, Schlichtungsstelle bei der Deutschen Bundesbank Tätigkeitsbericht 2016 (11 January 2017), page 14.

837 Ibid. page 17.

838 Deutsche Bundesbank (2017), *supra* note 834, page 20.

withdrawal from or termination of consumer credit agreements but occasionally also the refusal of a credit institution to grant consumer credit.[839]

The numbers and issues mentioned in the activity report of the German Federal Bank's arbitration body can also be taken as an indicator that the rules on pre-contractual information and creditworthiness assessment are adhered by well.

D. *Practical Effects*

The consumer credit volume has been growing at a slow and stable rate while the average household debt in Germany is rather low compared to the other depicted legal systems in this work (see Annex 2, Table 5).

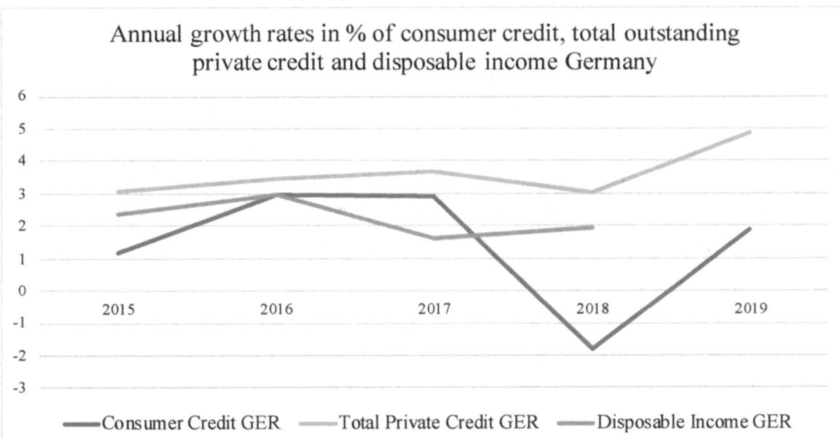

The table shows that the growth rate of consumer credit has been constantly lower than the growth rate of the total outstanding private credit.[840] Since 2017 the growth rate has, furthermore, been lower than the growth rate of the average disposable household income. In relation to the population the total outstanding private debt appears lower than in the UK while the total proportion of consumer credit amounts to ca. 19%. However, the

839 Deutsche Bundesbank (2018), *supra* note 835, page 20.
840 For detailed data, cf. Annex 2.

proportion of consumer credit in relation to the private credit volume has continuously decreased since 2014.[841]

On average private households in Germany pay EUR 8 per month to repay consumer loans.[842] Furthermore, the number of private insolvencies has been falling continuously since 2010.[843] These numbers indicate that most consumers can afford the consumer credit they take out and that the burden of repayment is (on average) reasonable compared to their household income. This finding is also supported by the fact that the overall repayment rate regarding instalment credit – meaning that the credit was repaid fully in accordance with the terms of the credit agreement and no default took place – is high in Germany (ca. 97.9 % in 2018).[844] With respect to creditworthiness assessments, it has been noted that since 2012 the number of requests at the SCHUFA, the largest German provider for creditworthiness data, by banks in relation to credit requests have been growing constantly.[845]

The positive numbers cannot, however, be solely explained by stricter consumer credit regulation. It must also be considered, that Germans tend to handle their finances conservatively, meaning that they rather rely on savings than credit.[846] Furthermore, the stable and growing German economy in the 2010s constitutes a contributing factor to better financial wellbeing of consumers. This will most likely change due to the Covid-19 pandemic and, thus, influence the numbers of credit default and private insolvencies negatively.

---

841 Cf. Annex 2, Table 1.

842 Statista Research Department, 'Monatliche Ausgaben privater Haushalte in Deutschland für die Tilgung und Verzinsung von Konsumentenkrediten von 2009 bis 2017 (in Euro)' (*statista*, 25 January 2019) <https://de.statista.com/statistik/daten/studie/538659/umfrage/monatliche-ausgaben-privater-haushalte-fuer-tilgung-und-verzinsung-von-konsumentenkrediten/> accessed 6 November 2019.

843 Cf. Annex 2, Table 9.

844 Cf. Annex 2, Table 6; SCHUFA, SCHUFA Kredit-Kompass 2019: Empirische Untersuchung der privaten Kreditaufnahme in Deutschland (Mai 2019), page 9, 11.

845 SCHUFA, SCHUFA Kredit-Kompass 2017: Empirische Untersuchung der privaten Kreditaufnahme in Deutschland (Mai 2017), page 9; SCHUFA (2019), *supra* note 844, page 11.

846 Cf. *supra* notes 171 and 172.

E. Consumer Image

The German consumer image revealed in consumer credit regulation mostly resembles that of the rational consumer of the European legislator. Since the implementation of the Second Consumer Credit Directive and Mortgage Credit Directive, the German consumer credit regulation is almost entirely based on EU law. The only deviation that can be noted are the strict consequences of a failed creditworthiness assessment. These consequences are, however, also based on EU law, namely the Mortgage Credit Directive, which appears to move in a direction of requiring more consumer protection rather than merely prescribing information duties.

F. Interim Conclusion

Although a Hire-Purchase Act had already been introduced in the 19th century, Germany was a late runner with respect to comprehensive consumer credit legislation. The AbzG was not an instrument targeting consumer protection but served the goal of combatting unfair competition practices. Specific consumer protection mechanisms were developed under the general clause of § 138 BGB by the courts at a late stage at the beginning of the 1980s. Germany thereby developed in stark contrast to the UK where the legislator rather than the courts introduced comprehensive legislation on forms of consumer credit. In Germany comprehensive consumer credit legislation was only introduced with the (gold-plated) implementation of the First Consumer Credit Directive in 1991. Furthermore, the German legislator saw the Mortgage Credit Directive as an opportunity to refine general consumer credit legislation as well as introducing strict consequences in case of a breach of the duty to conduct a proper assessment of creditworthiness prior to granting consumer credit. It can, thus, be said that German consumer credit legislation remains largely influenced, and in fact introduced, by European consumer credit legislation.

From an economic perspective the consumer credit regulatory system appears to work effectively in Germany. Unsecured consumer credit has been growing slower than the total (partially secured) private credit volume and consequently the proportion of consumer credit with respect to the total credit volume has decreased continuously. Furthermore, the numbers on repayment, default and insolvencies reveal that most households can afford the consumer credit they take out. In addition, the table indicates that the disposable household income has been growing steadily and stronger than consumer credit since 2017. This means that individual and macro-risks associated with consumer credit are low. The German legislator implements rules that are considered helpful by institutional and behavioural theorists, i.e. rules on pre-contractual information, including sample documents in the EGBGB, and creditworthiness assessments. As the pre-contractual information requirements are largely the same in the UK and Germany, the positive economic findings may be especially associated with the strict German rules on creditworthiness assessments and entailed consequences in case of failure to comply with the rules. From a behavioural perspective the German regulation appears especially effective because it only allows for lending if the consumer reasonably appears to be able to repay the loan. This regulatory tool is fit to prevent consumers from taking out a loan who overestimate their financial abilities.

G. Comparative Analysis

CCD 2008	**UK**	**Germany**
Art. 5	CONC 4, Consumer Credit (Disclosure of Information) Regulations 2010	§ 491a BGB in connection with Art. 247 §§ 2 to 5, 8 to 13a EGBGB
Art. 8	CONC 5.2A	§§ 505a, 505b BGB

It shall now be evaluated to which extent the German and UK consumer credit regulation regimes are comparable and whether German consumer credit regulation can serve as a future model for the UK. Both the UK and Germany underwent industrialisation in the 19th century and their respective societies have, thus, been subject to similar economic developments in this regard, however, with differing economic policies. As has been pointed out, consumer credit regulation developed quite differently in the UK and Germany. Both countries underwent industrialisation in the 19th century; however, at a different speed and different points in time. While UK regulation evolved gradually through several stages and kinds of predominant forms of consumer credit, the first modern form of regulation, the AbzG, was introduced in Germany in 1894 in the course of rapid modernisation and remained the only Act until the 1990s. The AbzG also was not intended as a consumer but rather a market protection instrument. Consumer protection rules were developed later by the courts. The first comprehensive piece of consumer credit legislation was the (gold-plated) implementation of the First Consumer Credit Directive in 1991. In contrast, consumer credit regulation was created by the UK legislator, continued to evolve gradually and resulted in the first comprehensive piece of consumer credit regulation in Europe in 1974. The approaches to consumer credit regulation also resemble the different effects of common law and civil law traditions. While in the UK the law derives from tradition and experience the civil law tradition is founded on ideas and principles. In the UK the law-maker adapted to the modern development of consumer credit quickly and benefited from long-standing experience with earlier forms of consumer credit. In contrast, the German legislator did not adapt to the development. At a rather late stage the courts intervened based on a modern and more legal activist approach to the use of general clauses.

It must, therefore, be concluded that the two consumer credit regulation regimes can only be compared to a limited extent. While the UK was the first country to introduce comprehensive consumer credit regulation and assumed the role of a 'legal pioneer' also with respect to the development of EU consumer regulation, Germany was a recipient of consumer credit regulation from the EU. While the UK legislator takes part actively in developing consumer credit legislation, Germany rather reacts to European legislative developments.[847] German consumer credit law is limited to the implementation of the European Consumer Credit Directives and, therefore, does not contain comparable provisions to Sections 140A CCA 1974. It has a more limited scope than the comprehensive UK consumer credit legislation. Unfair credit relationships can, however, be struck down by the courts applying the doctrines developed under § 138 Section 1 BGB.

The lower numbers of cases decided by alternative dispute resolution bodies in Germany compared to those of the FOS could indicate that consumer credit legislation is abided more diligently in Germany. However, alternative dispute resolution bodies are not well-established under German law and due to their relatively recent introduction may not be as well known among consumers. It is questionable whether these numbers can actually be compared. Most Germans pursue conservative strategies with respect to borrowing which is also exemplified by the steady and decreasing level of the volume of consumer credit compared to the total volume of private credit in Germany. In contrast, the UK has experienced a stark growth in consumer credit between 2011 and 2016 which indicates that British consumers are more inclined to take out credit. Such different atti-

847 Cf. also Micklitz, *supra* note 189, 279-280.

tudes may, thus, also serve as an explanation for consumer credit lending phenomena.

The European model consumer image followed by the German legislator and the UK consumer image are similar. Both are moving toward a more protective direction focussing on rules regarding consumers' creditworthiness. While the UK has started to implement stricter rules more recently and currently reviews even stricter rules based on behavioural insights, the German legislator has already implemented rules entailing strict consequences for the creditor in case of non-compliance. Bearing in mind the more conservative financial attitude of German consumers, the strict German rules may, nevertheless, provide insights for future UK legislation. As recent developments in the UK have shown, stricter consumer credit regulation with respect to the assessment of creditworthiness appears to have had the desired effect of slowed down growth of consumer credit. Regulating consequences could bear a further, complementing preventative effect when it comes to consumer lending and have positive effects from a behavioural standpoint, namely preventing individuals from overestimating their abilities and overburdening themselves financially.

Chapter 7: Consumer Credit in Norway

A. *History of Consumer Credit (Legislation) in Norway*

The concept of consumer credit can be traced back to the 19th century in Norway. The beginnings lie in the practical necessity for alternative payment methods due to unsteady income situations caused by seasonal labour. For such customers it was difficult – if not impossible – to receive a bank loan. Thus, local business owners would grant them a credit to enable the purchase of their goods.[848] The roots of consumer credit, thus, do not solely relate to the industrialisation but also societal conditions in Norway. In addition to these local credit practices, the pawnbroking business also grew and spread across the country and especially the urban area of Kristiania (today's Oslo). This led the government to pass the Interest Rates Act (*renteloven*) in 1888 which limited the maximum interest rates that could be charged as a first regulatory instrument.[849] The availability of instalment payments in the course of later industrialisation and modernisation triggered further regulation. As a first regulation, the local police had to consent to instalment purchases for certain goods to protect purchasers from paying instalments for goods that were suitable for instalment purchases.[850] In addition the Sale of Goods on Instalment Act (*avbetalingsloven*)[851] was introduced in 1916. The Norwegian law-maker specifically referred to the German AbzG as a source of inspiration.[852] Alternative payment methods were mostly used by people who could otherwise not have afforded certain consumption goods and were accordingly inexperienced with respect to such purchases. The aforementioned early regulatory in-

848 Christine Myrvang, 'På kreditt og avbetaling – en kulturhistorie om nye markedspraksiser' [2007] 86 (1) Historisk Tidsskrift 57 (62).

849 *Renteloven* (29 June 1888); Myrvang, ibid. (63).

850 For example, you could not use instalment payments for luxury articles in Oslo and Arendal, Myrvang, ibid., (68-69). The police's power was only reduced in the 1950s, cf. Myrvang, ibid., (79).

851 *Lov om kjøp på avbetaling (avbetalingsloven)* (21 July 1916).

852 Justis- og politidepartementet, Om utfærdigelse av en lov om kjøp paa avbetaling, Ot. prp. nr. 36 (1916), page 14.

struments as well as their preparatory works show awareness for weaker party protection in Norway.[853]

The Sale of Goods on Instalment Act underwent revision with the Act relating to the Sale of Goods on Credit (*kredittkjøploven*, hereinafter "Credit Purchase Act")[854] in 1985 to reflect developments in the credit market.[855] In the law-making process Norway considered developments in the USA and other European countries, among them especially the introduction of the CCA 1974 in the UK.[856] The legislative processes of both modern pieces of consumer credit legislation until this point, thus, reveal a tradition of looking toward foreign legislative instruments from countries that had undergone industrialisation and consumer movements earlier for inspiration. The later implementation of EU regulation on consumer credit, thus, does not appear as an entirely foreign concept to the Norwegian law-maker.

In 1992 the First Consumer Credit Directive was incorporated into the Credit Purchase Act[857] according to the original Annex XIX No. 4[858] to the EEA Agreement. The preparatory works reveal that the Credit Purchase Act had already satisfied most of the criteria demanded by the First Consumer Credit Directive and even provided broader consumer protection, i.e. with regard to its scope of applicability.[859] Nevertheless, the Norwegian law-maker considered the necessary changes an improvement of consumer protection especially with regard to broader pre-contractual information duties which would provide the consumer with a better oversight over the economic consequences of credit agreements.[860]

---

853 Ibid. pages 13 et seq.; Myrvang, *supra* note 848, (69-71). Cf. also for a general theme of weaker party protection and social dimension, Letto-Vanamo and Tamm, *supra* note 236, 8.

854 *Lov om kredittkjøp (kredittkjøploven)* (21 June 1985).

855 Justis- og politidepartementet, Om lov om kredittkjøp m.m., Ot. prp. nr. 38 (1984-1985), page 6.

856 Ibid.; Hans Fredrik Marthinussen and others, *Kredittkjøp m.v.*, 33-45 and especially 40-44 with respect to the CCA 1974.

857 *Lov om endringer i enkelte lover som følge av EØS-avtalen* (27 November 1992).

858 Now cf. Annex XIX Nr. 7h to the EEA Agreement.

859 Justis- og politidepartementet, Om lov om lovvalg i forsikring, lov om gjennomføring i norsk rett av EØS-avtalens vedlegg V punkt 2 om fri bevegelighet for arbeidstakere m.v innenfor EØS og lov om endringer i enkelte lover som følge av EØS-avtalen, Ot. prp. nr. 72 (1991-1992), page 37.

860 Ibid. page 42.

In 1999 the Financial Agreements and Financial Assignment Act (*finansavtaleloven*, hereinafter "Financial Agreements Act")[861] was introduced beside the Credit Purchase Act in the aftermath of a financial crisis in Norway in the 1980s.[862] The Financial Agreements Act aimed at regulating and standardising (not just consumer) contracts in the financial and insurance industry. In light of the obligation to implement the fully harmonising Second Consumer Credit Directive[863] another reform of credit regulation took place. This reform resulted in the incorporation of the Credit Purchase Act into the Financial Agreements Act and the eventual repeal of the Credit Purchase Act. Consumer credit legislation has thereby been fully incorporated in the Financial Agreements Act (Chapter 3 of the Act).

B. *Impact of the Consumer Credit Directive 2008/48/EC and Norwegian Consumer Credit Legislation Today*

The Second Consumer Credit Directive has led to several changes in the Financial Agreements Act. With respect to consumer credit, it can be said that due to the fully harmonising nature of the Second Consumer Credit Directive, Norwegian consumer credit legislation today is almost entirely based on EU consumer credit legislation. In the following, changes to rules on the scope of consumer credit legislation on mandatory information and access to credit are outlined.

Scope

The Financial Agreements Act does not solely apply to consumer credit agreements. With respect to the scope of applicability § 1 Section 5 Financial Agreements Act refers to rules on consumer credit in Chapter 3 of the Act. The scope of applicability of Chapter 3 (§ 44) refers to credit agreements in general and is not limited to agreements with consumers. The scope of Chapter 3, thus, does not exclude all agreements mentioned in

---

861 *Lov om finansavtaler og finansoppdrag (finansavtaleloven)* (25 June 1999).

862 Justiskomiteen, Innstilling fra justiskomiteen om lov om finansavtaler og finansoppdrag (finansavtaleloven), Innst. O. Nr. 84 (1998-1999), Ot.prp. nr. 41 (1998-99) page 5.

863 Cf. Annex XIX Nr. 7h to the EEA Agreement; Justis- og politidepartementet, Endringer i finansavtaleloven mv. (gjennomføring av direktiv 2008/48/EF om kredittavtaler for forbrukere mv.), Prop.65 L (2009-2010), page 9. The integration of the Credit Purchase Act into the Financial Agreements Act had already been suggested in 1999, cf. Justiskomiteen, ibid., page 15.

Art. 2 of the Directive but only agreements according to Art. 2 lit. d), f), g), i) and j) CCD 2008 (cf. § 44 Sections 2, 7 Financial Agreements Act).[864] While the term consumer (§ 2 Section 1 sentence 2 Financial Agreements Act) remained unchanged and slightly deviates from the Directive's definition[865] the other definitions listed in Art. 3 have been incorporated in § 44a Financial Agreements Act.

Pre-Contractual Information

Regarding pre-contractual information, §§ 4, 5 Credit Purchase Act and § 47 Financial Agreements Act previously stated which pre-contractual information had to be provided. However, the provisions were not considered as comprehensive as the Directive's list of mandatory pre-contractual information.[866] In light of the fully harmonising effect of the Directive, the existing provisions were, therefore, replaced with § 46a Financial Agreements Act which incorporated Arts. 5-7 CCD 2008.[867] The duty to provide adequate explanation with regard to the credit agreement (Art. 5 Section 6) was implemented in the separate § 46c Financial Agreements Act.

Access to Credit

Neither the Credit Purchase Act, nor the Financial Agreements Act had previously contained provisions on the assessment of creditworthiness of potential loan takers. It was assumed that it was the loan giver's inevitable interest to conduct such an assessment before handing out a loan.[868] While the existing Norwegian provisions already contained the so called 'duty to dissuade' (*frarådningsplinkt*), there existed no explicit provisions that would have satisfied the Directive's requirements. In order to implement Arts. 8 and 9 CCD 2008, the new § 46b Financial Agreements Act was, therefore, introduced.

---

864 Justis- og politidepartementet, ibid. page 31 with reference to Recital 10 of Directive 2008/48/EC.

865 'not mainly related to business activities' in § 2 compared to 'acting for purposes which are outside his trade, business or profession' in Art. 3 a) the Directive.

866 Rune Sæbø and others, *Kredittavtaler – Gjennomføring i norsk rett av forbrukerkredittdirektivet (2008/48/EF) m.m.*, 55.

867 Justis- og politidepartementet, *supra* note 863, page 75.

868 Sæbø and others, *supra* note 866, 58.

Further Norwegian Regulation of Consumer Credit: The Duty to Dissuade

During the drafting process of the Financial Agreements Act in the 1990s different possibilities were discussed to prevent consumers' overindebtedness in Norway.[869] Eventually, the 'duty to dissuade (*frarådningsplikt*) was introduced in § 47 Financial Agreements Act (and later also § 9a Credit Purchase Act) as an instrument to ensure that the consumer was able to make an informed decision with regard to his or her individual circumstances.[870] Under the *frarådningsplikt* the loan giver is obliged to inform the loan taker about his or her individual financial situation and possible difficulties that may therefore arise with respect to the re-payment of the loan, thus, *dissuading* the prospective loan taker from overburdening him- or herself. It is, thereby, a codified version of the duty of loyalty (*lojalitetsplikt*) under Norwegian law under which the stronger party to a contract shall take into account the weaker party's interests.[871] It is, thereby, also a feature that uniquely fits in the Norwegian legal system. As the analysis of sociological factors revealed, OECD studies have shown high interpersonal trust rates in a homogenous societal setting. Interpersonal trust is a necessary condition for a successful dissuasion under the *frarådningsplikt*. If the borrower does not trust the lender, he or she may not believe that the dissuasion serves him or her best. The sociological prerequisites, thereby, play a critical role in understanding this legal instrument. It, thereby, also differs from the former German § 509 BGB which simply provided for a duty to warn the creditor of negative consequences of the conclusion of a credit agreement and was placed in completely different sociological setting.

Inter alia, it was intended to dissuade banks from giving out loans to customers who would not be able to re-pay them.[872] While this duty does not prohibit consumers to take out loans, it shall contribute to more informed decisions and, eventually, a lower rate of people taking out loans who actu-

869 Erling Selvig and others, *Finansavtaler og finansoppdrag – Utredning nr. 1 fra Banklovkommisjonen*, 59-63.

870 Justiskomiteen, *supra* note 862, pages 16-17. NB: The *frarådningsplikt* is not only applicable in 'classic' consumer credit relationships but in any credit relationship that involves a consumer.

871 Erling Selvig and others, *Frarådningsplikt i kredittkjøp – Utredning nr. 17 fra Banklovkommisjonen*, 36. See also below, note 1327. Compared to the general clause (§ 36, cf. below) § 47 Financial Agreements Act can be considered *lex specialis*, cf. Ståle René Matre, *Forbrukerkredittdirektivet (2008/48/EF) – Forholdet til kredittgivers frarådingsplikt etter finansavtaleloven § 47*, 29.

872 Selvig and others, ibid., 24.

ally cannot afford to do so.[873] In addition to the expected positive economic effect of lower rates of overindebtedness, loan givers face the possibility that the loan agreement may be found invalid and, thus, becomes subject to change as a sanction for omitting their *frarådningsplikt*.[874] The *frarådningsplikt* can be considered a mixture of the duty to explain the credit agreement to the consumer (Art. 5 Section 6 CCD 2008) and the duty to assess the consumer's creditworthiness (Art. 8 CCD 2008).

In the course of the implementation of the Second Consumer Credit Directive, the *frarådningsplikt* incurred changes as well. The first version of § 47 Financial Agreements Act stated that if the applicant's economic situation did not allow for the taking and re-payment of a loan the loan giver had to inform him or her about this in writing. Otherwise the loan giver faced the risk of invalidity of and, thus, amendments to the loan agreement. After the reform of the Financial Agreements Act in 2010, § 47 does not only require that the respective consumer must be informed in writing (Section 1 Sentences 1 and 2) but also, as far as possible, orally (Section 1 Sentence 3). If the consumer proceeds despite being warned, he or she must confirm by signature that the loan giver fulfilled the requirements of the *frarådningsplikt* orally and in writing (Section 1 Sentence 4). These changes are considered enhancements of the dissuading effect and shall clarify to the consumer the risks he or she enters into.[875]

C. Consumer Credit Adjudication

The majority of cases concerning the Financial Agreements Act are not adjudged by the courts but consumer tribunals and most prominently the Financial Appeals Tribunal for Banks (*finansklagenemnda bank*, FINKNB). As of the 28 November 2018, 23 cases had been decided by the Norwegian Supreme Court, 246 cases had been decided by Courts of Appeal and 70 cases had been decided by District Courts.[876] The Norwegian Supreme Court has not dealt with the Second Consumer Credit Directive at all. The

873 Ibid. 25, 61; Justis- og politidepartementet, *supra* note 863, page 84; Sæbø and others, *supra* note 866, 63.

874 Sæbø and others, ibid.

875 Justis- og politidepartementet, *supra* note 863, page 91.

876 Only considering civil law matters.

frarådningsplikt was mentioned in three cases, but has not been successfully invoked in any of them.[877]

In comparison, 1384 cases had been decided by the Financial Appeals Tribunal for banks. The high number of cases raised in front of the Tribunal, rather than in front of regular courts can be explained with the easy access and cost-saving procedure readily available to consumers.

The following table indicates that §§ 46-46c Financial Agreements Act are not raised and mentioned often compared to § 47 Financial Agreements Act which, although with a different wording, had been part of the Financial Agreements Act before.[878] For the table I only considered cases that were admissible and finally decided by the Financial Appeals Tribunal for banks. Furthermore, some cases dealt with more than one of the researched norms. Thus, some cases were counted in more than one row of the table. The cases regarding § 47 Financial Agreements Act did not only consider classic consumer credit cases because § 47 Financial Agreements Act applies to all credit agreements that involve consumers.

Provision	Total number of cases	Successful	Unsuccessful
§ 46	5	0	5
§ 46a	4	1	3
§ 46b	13	1	12
§ 46c	2	0	2
§ 47	123	12	111

877 Norwegian Supreme Court cases *A v Gjensidige NOR Sparebank ASA* [2004] Rt. 2004, 156; *Halvor Lognvik, Harald Lognvik v Storebrand Bank ASA (Lognvik)* [2012] Rt. 2012, 355 and *Ivar Petter Røeggen v DNB Bank ASA (Røeggen)* [2013] Rt. 2013, 388.

878 I gathered the relevant data from the Norwegian legal database 'Lovdata' (www.lovdata.no). On the 28th November 2018 I logged in on 'Lovdata' and started my case research. I used the advanced search tool and chose the Financial Appeals Tribunal for Banks (finansklagenemnda – bank) as the adjudicating body. I, furthermore, used the repective parameters "finansavtaleloven § 46", "finansavtaleloven § 46a", "finansavtaleloven § 46b", "finansavtaleloven § 46c" and "finansavtaleloven § 47" and looked for decisions between 2010 until 2018.

It must be noted positively that many cases mentioned the EU legislative sources[879] and even CJEU case-law[880] regarding the provisions in question. Furthermore, the low number of (successful) cases possibly indicates that loan givers adhere by the rules regarding the provision of information and explanation prior to the conclusion of the credit agreement.

D. Practical Effects

The relatively low numbers of disputes concerning consumer protection norms deriving from the Second Consumer Credit Directive indicate that the respective provisions have been implemented well in everyday practice.

However, one must acknowledge that indebtedness among Norwegian consumers is very common. The intended positive effects of the assessment of creditworthiness (§ 46b Financial Agreements Act), full explanation of the credit agreement (§ 46c Financial Agreements Act) and the *frarådningsplikt* (§ 47 Financial Agreements Act) may, thus, be questioned.

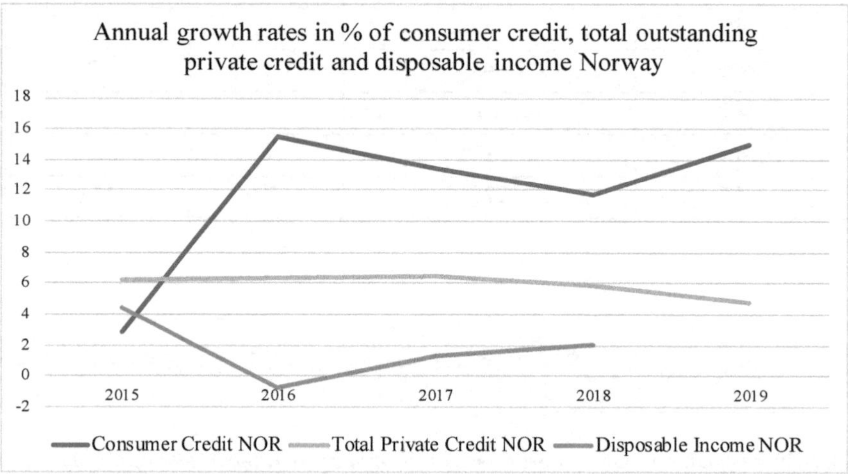

Household debt in Norway is generally high (cf. Annex 2, Table 5). The table shows that the amount of consumer credit has risen in the past years,

879 i.e. decisions FinKN-2014-439 and FinKN-2013-443.

880 i.e. decision FinKN-2015-72 discussing CJEU judgment C-449/13, *CA Consumer Finance SA v Ingrid Bakhaus and others* [2014].

especially in comparison to general household debt.[881] In 2018 consumer credit rose by 11.73% compared to 2017 while general household debt only rose by 5.91%.[882] In 2019 the total sum of consumer credit taken out amounted to NOK 178.3 billion[883] (ca. GBP 15 billion and ca. EUR 17 billion). While this only amounts to 3-4% of the total Norwegian household debt, the Financial Supervisory Authority of Norway and the Norwegian Central Bank have voiced their concerns with respect to a steady rise in consumer credit especially because of the risks that the typically high interest rates entail for consumers.[884] At the same time the numbers on consumer default rates[885] and debt collection proceedings[886] have been rising continuously since 2014. In addition, the debt registry data shows that consumer debt is unevenly distributed. Most consumer loans are small but a small minority has accumulated large consumer debt.[887]

This apparent weakness in consumer protection led to criticism regarding the practice of creditworthiness assessment, explanation duty and especially the *frarådningsplikt*, which can be regarded as a combination of the former two requirements.[888] First, the low number of successful cases in front of the Financial Appeals Tribunal for banks also indicates that it seldomly serves as an effective protection mechanism in consumer protection

881 For detailed data, cf. Annex 2. In 2019 the Norwegian Debt Registry published new numbers on consumer credit in Norway which are considerably higher than the numbers published on consumer credit by the *finanstlisynet* before. As the Debt Registry was founded to achieve an overview of consumer debt in Norway, the new numbers appear more realistic than prior statistics. According to numbers of the *finanstlisynet* consumer credit growth actually slowed down.

882 Cf. Annex 2, Table 2.

883 Cf. Annex 2, Table 1.

884 The Financial Supervisory Authority of Norway, Retningslinjer for forsvarlig utlånspraksis for forbrukslån - oppsummering av undersøkelse om finansforetakenes gjennomføring, Saksnr. 18/568 (12 June 2018) page 1; Marius Hagen, Lars-Tore Turtveit and Bjørn Helge Vatne, Norges Bank Aktuell Kommentar: Sterk vekst i forbrukslån, Nr. 1/2017, page 2; Norges Bank, Financial Stability Report 2019 – Vulnerabilities and Risks (2019), pages 11-12.

885 Cf. Annex 2, Table 6.

886 Cf. Annex 2, Table 7.

887 Norges Bank, *supra* note 884, page 20.

888 Cf. i.e. Dag Jørgen Hveem and Ellen Katrine Nyhus, 'Frarådingsplikten: Til bankens eller forbrukerens beste?' [2013] 30 (4) Praktisk økonomi & finans 53-65; Tanja Jørgensen, *Forbrugerkredit: retligt og retspolitisk*, 472; Piia Kalamees, Kåre Lilleholt and Karin Sein, 'Responsible Lending in Estonian and Norwegian Law' [2015] (1-2) EuCML 29 (34); Lena Strand and Mia Sveen, *Utlånspraksis for forbrukslån - En kvalitativ studie av finansinstitusjoners utlånspraksis*, 123.

cases. This may be explained by the fact that it must only be abided by the banks if their customers already seem to be obviously ineligible to take out a loan. If the bank has reason to think that their prospective customer will be able to re-pay the loan, they are not obliged to follow the *frarådningsplikt*'s strict requirements. Many tribunal cases show that the *frarådningsplikt* is often unsuccessfully invoked because the banks could argue that they believed that their customers were financially well off.[889] It should, thus, be considered to apply the *frarådningsplikt* to every customer bearing any risk with respect to the consumer credit in question. However, second, it is questionable whether this will actually increase the *frarådningsplikt*'s effectiveness. Even if the loan giver tries to dissuade the customer, he or she is still free to take out the loan anyway. Thus, the protection mechanism does not necessarily work to the benefit of the consumer but the loan giver. By fulfilling their legal duties loan givers cannot be held liable for problems that they warned the consumer about and tried to dissuade him or her from.[890]

Third, the *frarådningsplikt*'s practice reveals further problems. The dissuasion effect is often severely mitigated because the loan giver offers the respective consumer an alternative loan. Furthermore, the *frarådningsplikt* comes into play at a late stage of the loan taking process and is labelled as a formality,[891] so that the consumer has already made his or her decision and as a result cannot be convinced to change his or her mind. This is shown by a field study conducted by *Hveem and Nyhus*, in which 100% of participants ended up taking out the loan after having been 'dissuaded'.[892] A study conducted in 2017 even showed that the majority loan givers do not make use of the *frarådningsplikt* with respect to consumer credit at all.[893]

The Norwegian government has reacted to the stark rise in consumer credit. In 2017 the Ministry of Finance suggested several changes to consumer credit legislation.[894] Among other things, the Ministry suggests a reform of pre-contractual information duties and the explanation duty

---

889 Cf. i.e. decisions FinKN-2013-334, FinKN-2011-635, FinKN-2011-642 and FinKN-2011-477. Cf. also Hveem and Nyhus, ibid., (62) with similar results.

890 Jørgensen, *supra* note 888.

891 Hveem and Nyhus, *supra* note 889, (63); cf. also Kalamees, Lilleholt and Sein, *supra* note 888.

892 Cf. Hveem and Nyhus, ibid., (59-61).

893 Strand and Sveen, *supra* note 888, 119.

894 Finansdepartement, Finansmarkedsmeldingen 2016–2017, Meld. St. 34 (2016-2017), pages 49-53.

(§§ 46a, 46c Financial Agreements Act),[895] the possibility to prohibit loan giving if the assessment of credit worthiness indicates that the customer in question is not eligible for the loan (§ 47 Financial Agreements Act),[896] a reform of the assessment of creditworthiness (§ 46b Financial Agreements Act)[897], a stricter regulation of consumer credit advertising (§ 46 Financial Agreements Act)[898] as well as the introduction of a mandatory consideration time period[899]. As a first consequence, the Debt Information Act was passed in 2017 which aims at the establishment of new and more comprehensive private debt registries that can provide an overview of the loan takers' existing credit engagements in order to improve the assessment of creditworthiness.[900] Since the implementation, three companies have been granted a concession to open a private debt registry.[901] On the 1 July 2019, the Law on debt information for the creditworthiness assessment of private persons[902] was introduced. It aims at improving the accessibility of credit information for both banks and consumers to consequently allow for a better creditworthiness assessment. Furthermore, the Norwegian legislator plans to introduce a duty on behalf of the creditor to reject a credit application in case of a negative outcome of a creditworthiness assessment.[903] The political activism regarding consumer credit and increased societal interest and discourse in this respect possibly led to the slowed growth of consumer credit since 2018.[904]

895 Ibid. 50.
896 Ibid.
897 Ibid.
898 Ibid. 51-52.
899 Ibid. 52.
900 *Lov om gjeldsinformasjon ved kredittvurdering av privatpersoner (gjeldsinformasjonsloven)* (16 June 2017); Barne- og likestillingsdepartementet, Lov om gjeldsinformasjon ved kredittvurdering av privatpersoner (gjeldsinformasjonsloven), Prop. 87 L (2016-2017).
901 Barne- og likestillingsdepartement, 'Saksgang: Gjeldsinformasjonsloven' (*Regjeringen*, 18 October 2018) <https://www.regjeringen.no/no/dokument/dep/bld/sak/saksgang-gjeldsinformasjonsloven/id2608025/> accessed 17 November 2019.
902 *Lov om gjeldsinformasjon ved kredittvurdering av privatpersoner (gjeldsinformasjonsloven)* (1 July 2019).
903 Barne- og likestillingsdepartement, 'Gjeldsinformasjonsloven' (*Regjeringen*, 5 July 2019) <https://www.regjeringen.no/no/tema/forbruker/gjeldsinformasjonsloven/id2510537/> accessed 17 November 2019.
904 Norges Bank, *supra* note 884, page 12.

E. Consumer Image

Norwegian consumer credit regulation is traditionally based on a vulnerable consumer image. Consumer credit regulatory measures that originally derive from Norwegian law aim to protect the weaker party. One example for such protective regulation is the *frarådningsplikt* which embodies the Norwegian duty of loyalty and compels the stronger party to take into account the interests of the weaker party while at the same time empowering the weaker party to make an informed decision (even if in practice the measure does not appear to dissuade effectively). The recent legislative initiatives also reveal concerns for the financial well-being of consumers. At the same time, most Norwegian consumer credit regulation nowadays derives from EU law which is based on a rather rational consumer image. The two approaches to consumer protection, thus, conflict. It remains to be seen whether a possible reform of (fully harmonising) EU consumer credit regulation moves closer to the image of a vulnerable consumer and the apparent conflict can, thus, be solved.

F. Interim Conclusion

Norwegian legislation on consumer credit exists since the beginning of the 20th century. The Norwegian legislator has pursued a tradition of looking toward other countries that had already implemented consumer credit legislation. While the first Sale of Goods on Instalment Act 1916 was inspired by the then relatively modern German AbzG further legislation was especially inspired by UK consumer credit legislation. As a country that was industrialised at a later stage it made sense that Norway would look toward successful foreign legislative projects. Considering this background, the implementation of EU Directives later did not pose problems for the Norwegian law-maker. The current rules on information and explanation duties resemble the Second Consumer Credit Directive. The Financial Appeals Tribunal for banks as the main adjudicating body can be said to take into account European legal developments in its decision making. It can, therefore, be concluded that the EEA state Norway abides by European legislation well.

However, in practice consumer credit legislation has not unfolded its desired effect. Consumer credit debt has become a problem. It appears that information, creditworthiness assessment and explanation duties are merely seen as formalities. Although Norway aims at a higher protection standard with the *frarådningsplikt*, it appears that this additional protection mechanism has not led to the desired dissuasion from entering into overburdening consumer credit agreements.

From an economic perspective the Norwegian model of consumer credit regulation does not work effectively. While, institutionally, the *frarådningsplikt* mirrors local social norms and factors, it does not work efficiently as it appears to be easily circumvented. In that respect it appears inefficient in light of behavioural theory. Economic numbers indicate that consumers are left more vulnerable in light of rising numbers of default and debt collection proceedings. From a behavioural standpoint it appears adequate and necessary that the Norwegian government plans to implement stricter rules on creditworthiness assessment. The first measure of introducing a transparent debt register appears useful from an institutional as well as a behavioural perspective. Institutionally, the register fits in with the societal values of trust and fairness as it allows both parties to evaluate the basis of the contractual relationship and grants the consumer an opportunity to openly reflect his or her decisions. It, thereby, strengthens the *frarådningsplikt*. At the same time the openness appears useful from a behavioural standpoint. The register compiles information that the consumer may not have an overview of. Thereby, it becomes easier for the consumer to reflect on the consequences of his or her decision. However, the register does not prevent the consumer from overestimating his or her abilities. Therefore, stricter consequential regulation, i.e. prohibiting lending to overindebted individuals, also appears necessary.

G. Comparative Analysis

CCD 2008	UK	Germany	Norway
Art. 5	CONC 4, Consumer Credit (Disclosure of Information) Regulations 2010	§ 491a BGB in connection with Art. 247 §§ 2 to 5, 8 to 13a EGBGB	§§ 46a, 46c Financial Agreements Act
Art. 8	CONC 5.2A	§§ 505a, 505b BGB	§ 46b, 47 Financial Agreements Act

If the UK was to join the EEA it would still be bound by existing and most likely future EU legislation on consumer credit. It shall now be evaluated if the UK and Norwegian – as well as to a lesser extent German – consumer credit regulatory regimes are comparable and whether the Norwegian model serves as an inspiration for future UK consumer credit regulation.

The analysis has revealed that with respect to consumer credit legislation Norway traditionally took inspiration from other jurisdictions and finally adopted EU regulation on consumer credit. It, thereby, strongly differs from the UK which has been a fore runner when it comes to consumer credit. The differences may be explained by the fact that mass industrialisation took place later in Norway. Until the beginning of the 20th century Norway's economy had been dominated by the primary sector. Mass (luxury) consumption only evolved at a later stage. It makes sense that the Norwegian legislator looked at jurisdictions which had already undergone mass industrialisation entailing the phenomenon of mass consumption. This evolution of consumer credit law also made Norwegian consumer credit regulation perceptive for 'outside' regulation, i.e. (mandatory) EU rules on consumer credit.

Similar to the UK and unlike Germany, alternative bodies are the main mean of dispute resolution and well-established in Norway. As has been pointed out above the UK and Norway generally reveal similarities in this sector considering, however, that Norwegian alternative institutions are also based on a sociological rather than purely economic rationale. They appear to provide an effective mean of dispute resolution.

The only 'Norwegian specialty' left is the *frarådningsplikt*. However, the duty to dissuade a potential borrower from taking out credit that he or she cannot afford has missed its target and appears ineffective. Despite the *frarådningsplikt* consumer credit has been growing at record levels until 2017. It can, thus, be derived from the Norwegian consumer credit regulatory model that a mere warning regarding the possible overburdening associated with consumer credit will oftentimes not prove an effective mean to prevent vulnerable consumers from taking out credit. Furthermore, it is questionable whether the *frarådningsplikt* would fit in the English regulatory framework. As Norwegian law is applied in a rather homogenous society with similar underlying values it appears as an embodiment of the duty of loyalty for and cooperation with one another. Such a duty does not exist as a principle under English law and the societal prerequisites differ from Norway. Lastly, the *frarådningsplikt* also does not appear to have the desired positive economic effect as economic indicators reveal. While institutionally the *frarådningsplikt* appears fit for purpose, it remains ineffective from a behavioural perspective as circumvention appears easily possible. The current system of Norwegian consumer credit regulation, thus, does not serve as an example for future consumer credit regulation.

Chapter 8: Consumer Credit in Switzerland

A. *History of Consumer Credit (Legislation) in Switzerland*

Compared to the United Kingdom, Germany and Norway the areas of hire-purchase agreements and small loans were regulated at a late stage in Switzerland despite industrialisation in the 19th century. The first measures were introduced in several cantons around and after World War I.[905] This federalist implementation reflects the historic autonomy of cantons and relative weakness of the federal government at the beginning of the 20th century. Arts. 226-228 OR were introduced in 1911 and provided 'rudimentary protection' for the buyer under hire-purchase agreements.[906] In the 1940s the Federal Council began drafting comprehensive federal legislation on hire-purchase agreements that would apply to the whole Confederation.[907] The Federal Council found in 1946 that a growing indebtedness deepened social problems especially for those in need.[908] However, they, furthermore, repeatedly pointed out that many problems relating to small loans were not related to social disadvantages but to the inability of people to restrain their consumption.[909] The Federal Council saw the solution for many of the problems caused by the small loan business in subjecting borrowers to custodial measures to educate them on more 'vir-

---

905 Swiss Federal Council, Botschaft des Bundesrates an die Bundesversammlung betreffend den Entwurf zu einem Bundesgesetz über den Abzahlungs- und den Vorauszahlungsvertrag, 26 January 1960, Bundesblatt 1960 I 523 (528 et seq.), i.e. Schweizer Gesetz über die Ausübung der Handelsgewerbe in the canton of Schwyz (21 April 1902); Loi du 18 novembre 1935 sur la police du commerce of the canton of Vaud. Cantons could introduce such legislation under their competence for policing and local trade regulation.

906 Swiss Federal Council, Botschaft über ein Konsumkreditgesetz, 12 June 1978, Bundesblatt 1978 II 485 (493-494).

907 Swiss Federal Council (1960), *supra* note 905, (523-524).

908 Swiss Federal Council, Bericht des Bundesrates an die Bundesversammlung zum Postulat betreffend Bekämpfung des Wuchers im Kleinkreditwesen, 6 September 1946, Bundesblatt 1946 III 85 (106).

909 Ibid. (95-96).

tuous' dealings with money.[910] In the aftermath, the first initiative to regulate hire-purchase-agreements and small loans at the federal level failed.[911]

A new legislative initiative with respect to hire-purchase agreements and advance payment agreements was launched in 1954.[912] The preparatory documents, *inter alia*, specifically refer to the German, English and Norwegian regulations on hire-purchase agreements.[913] It was the legislator's aim to increase social security by protecting the buyer from abuse and to ensure proper contractual provisions to create a level playing field between seller and buyer; thereby, protecting the principle of freedom of contract.[914] Thus, the new measures were based on, both, principles of social justice and market considerations. The Federal Act regarding the hire-purchase and advance payment agreement (*Bundesgesetz über den Abzahlungs- und Vorauszahlungsvertrag*) came into force in 1963 by way of amendment of the existing Arts. 226-228 OR.

In practice, however, the new provisions lacked clarity. Academia as well as the courts found them unsatisfactory.[915] It was further found that lenders could easily circumvent the existing provisions; thus, unfair practices continued[916] although the industry had implemented further self-regulatory preventative measures in this regard[917]. Therefore, legislative procedures for the revision of the existing norms and introduction of new regulation regarding small loans commenced in the 1970s.[918] Beside the aim of increased social security that already underlied the existing provisions, the new legislation especially aimed at preventing consumers' overindebtedness.[919] In order to determine new, more effective means of protection in the area of hire-purchase agreements and small loans, *inter alia*, existing legislation in Germany, Norway and the United Kingdom as

910 Ibid. (97).

911 Swiss Federal Council (1960), *supra* note 905, (524).

912 Ibid. (525).

913 Ibid. (531-532).

914 Ibid. (538).

915 Hans Giger, Teil I: Vorbemerkungen zum Verbraucherschutz. in Heinz Hausheer and Hans Peter Walter (eds), *Berner Kommentar zum schweizerischen Privatrecht, Band VI: Obligationenrecht – Der Konsumkredit*, recitals 51, 52; cf. also Swiss Federal Council (1978), *supra* note 906, (494-498).

916 Swiss Federal Council (1978), ibid., (515).

917 Ibid. (515).

918 Ibid. (508 et seq., 527 et seq.).

919 For example, by prohibiting the accumulation of loans, ibid. (575 et seq.); cf. also Bernd Stauder, Konsumkreditrecht. in Ernst A. Kramer (ed), *Schweizerisches Privatrecht, Band 10: Konsumentenschutz im Privatrecht*, 225.

well as proposals for the First Consumer Credit Directive under EEC Law were considered and specifically used as a source of inspiration.[920] The emerging modern forms of consumer credit remained unregulated.[921]

In the aftermath of the failed attempt to introduce federal legislation on consumer credit, some cantons introduced regulatory measures based on public law (cf. Art. 73 Section 2 OR, Art. 6 ZGB).[922] Federal legislation was only introduced in 1993. If Switzerland had joined the EEA it would have had to implement the First Consumer Credit Directive (cf. original Annex XIX No. 4 to the EEA Agreement[923]). After the Swiss accession to the EEA failed, the content of the First Consumer Credit Directive was nevertheless implemented into Swiss law as the Swiss Consumer Credit Act 1993 (KKG 1993) as part of the 'Swisslex' package. However, rather than solving problems, the introduction of the new federal legislation caused more of them. The Act was introduced *beside* the existing OR-provisions *as well as* existing cantonal provisions. This led to an unprecedented fragmentation of different norms that would sometimes even apply to the same cause of action leading to varying consumer protection standards.[924]

Therefore, a revision aimed at unifying the law on consumer credit and protecting vulnerable consumers from the risks relating to consumer credit.[925] Thereby, the KKG 1993 was amended and the OR-provisions were repealed to create a complete and overriding federal body of consumer credit law.[926] The new Swiss Consumer Credit Act was passed in 2001 and came into force in 2003 (hereinafter "KKG 2001"). While the basic structure of the new legislation still resembles and some norms remained unchanged from the KKG 1993, additional provisions are 'Swiss-made'.[927] Thus, the KKG 2001 combines legislation derived from European law requiring euro compatible interpretation and Swiss norms that explicitly de-

920 Swiss Federal Council (1978), *supra* note 906, (519-527). Cf. also Giger, *supra* note 915, recital 53; Stauder, ibid.

921 Stauder, ibid.

922 Swiss Federal Council, Botschaft betreffend die Änderung des Bundesgesetzes über den Konsumkredit, 14 December 1998, Bundesblatt 1999 III 3155 (3162 et seq.); Stauder, *supra* note 919, 226; critical Giger, *supra* note 915, recitals 55, 57.

923 Now Annex XIX Nr. 7h to the EEA Agreement.

924 Swiss Federal Council (1998), *supra* note 922, (3164); Giger, *supra* note 915, recital 56; Stauder, *supra* note 919, 226.

925 Swiss Federal Council (1998), ibid., (3165-3166).

926 Ibid. (3166).

927 Michael Barnikol, *Die Schutzinstrumente des schweizerischen Konsumkreditrechts*, 15 et seq.

viate from European law and are, thereby, exempted from the principle of euro compatibility.[928]

The new legislation's main aim was to prevent overindebtedness. Unlike the European attempts to regulate consumer credit rather than prescribing information duties, the KKG 2001 focusses on the assessment of creditworthiness to protect the consumer from the risks borne by consumer credit. The outcome in comparison to the European Consumer Credit Directives is outlined below.

B. Impact of European Consumer Credit Directives

The following section depicts selected areas of the KKG 2001 and compares them with the corresponding provisions of the Consumer Credit Directives. It, furthermore, includes provisions of the KKG 2001 that do not correspond with provisions of the Consumer Credit Directives.

Scope (Arts. 1-8 KKG 2001)

The definitions on the credit agreement, the creditor, the consumer, the credit intermediary, the total cost of credit and the annual percentage rate of charge included in Arts. 1-6 KKG 2001 largely correspond with the Consumer Credit Directives. However, unlike the Consumer Credit Directives Art. 1 Section 2 KKG 2001 explicitly includes leasing contracts (lit. a) as well as (customer) credit cards (lit. b).[929] Furthermore, Art. 2 lit. a KKG 2001 defines the creditor as someone '[granting] credit in the course of his trade, business or profession' but as someone '[granting] credit commercially'[930] to exclude craftsmen who allow for deferred payments.[931] Since 2019 Art. 2 lit. b KKG 2001 includes a 'natural or legal person who grants credit non-commercially with the help of a crowdlending intermediary'[932]

928 Ibid. 40 et seq.; Stauder, *supra* note 919, 231.

929 However, not all provisions apply to these contracts, cf. Arts. 8, 11, 12, 29, 30 KKG 2001.

930 Als Kreditgeberin gilt jede natürliche oder juristische Person, die gewerbsmässig Konsumkredite gewährt. (Translation by author).

931 Stauder, *supra* note 919, 232.

932 Als Kreditgeberin gilt jede natürliche oder juristische Person, die unter Mitwirkung einer Schwarmkredit-Vermittlerin nicht gewerbsmässig Konsumkredite gewährt. (Translation by author).

which is defined under Art. 4 Section 2 KKG 2001.[933] Art. 7 KKG 2001 largely corresponds with Art. 2 CCD 2008.

The comparison of the scope of the respective legislative instruments shows the differentiated approach of the Swiss KKG 2001 with respect to European law. On the one hand, the norm structure basically remains the same, while on the other hand, the content varies, ranging from virtually identical provisions to modified European provisions and newly introduced Swiss provisions. This leads to different degrees of intensity when it comes to a possible euro compatible interpretation of norms.

Pre-Contractual Information (Art. 3 S-UWG)

The KKG 2001 does not provide for pre-contractual information duties corresponding to Art. 5 CCD 2008. It only includes provisions on the information that must be included in the credit agreement itself (Art. 9 KKG 2001).[934]

Access to Credit (Arts. 22-32a KKG 2001)

Preventative measures regarding overindebtedness of consumers lie at the heart of Swiss consumer credit legislation (cf. Art. 22 KKG 2001).[935] In this light, Arts. 22-32a KKG 2001 provide requirements regarding the assessment of the borrower's creditworthiness. The responsibility for the assessment, thereby, completely shifts to the creditor. This reflects a changed image of the consumer compared to the KKG 1993. While the KKG 1993 resembled the First Consumer Credit Directive and, thus, the image of a rational consumer, the shift toward a focus on preventative measures reflects an image of a vulnerable consumer in need of protection.[936] By aiming at the prevention of overindebtedness, thus, protecting consumers from financial ruin, the respective provisions of the KKG 2001 can be interpreted

---

933 Cf. Swiss Federal Council, Botschaft zum Finanzdienstleistungsgesetz (FIDLEG) und zum Finanzinstitutsgesetz (FINIG), 4 November 2015, Bundesblatt Nr. 50, 8901 (8945) for explanatory notes.

934 Cf. Arts. 10-12 KKG 2001 for the mandatory content of hire purchase, leasing and (customer) credit card agreements.

935 Swiss Federal Council (1998), *supra* note 922, (3156); Stauder, *supra* note 919, 248.

936 Barnikol, *supra* note 927, 39-40, 47; Stauder, ibid., 249; Swiss Federal Council (1998), ibid., (3165). The cantonal legislation preceding the KKG 2001 already mirrored such an image, Barnikol, ibid., 108.

as deriving from the state's duty to ensure a minimum subsistence level (cf. Art. 12 Swiss Constitution).[937]

Arts. 27a and 28 KKG 2001 require an assessment of the borrower's creditworthiness before consumer credit is granted.[938] According to Art. 28 Section 2 KKG 2001 a consumer 'is regarded as creditworthy if he or she can pay back the loan without having to use the non-seizable part of his or her income according to Art. 93 Section 1 Federal Act on Debt Collection and Insolvency (*Bundesgesetz über Schuldbetreibung und Konkurs*)'[939]. The seizable part is calculated according to cantonal guidelines. These must include the actual rent payable by the consumer, taxes to be paid by the consumer and obligations recorded by the official information agency (see below) (Art. 28 Section 3 KKG 2001). The assessment must be based on an assumed amortisation within three years even if the agreement provides for a longer period (Art. 28 Section 4 KKG 2001). The credit assessment criteria must be included in the credit agreement (Art. 9 Section 2 lit. j KKG 2001).

According to Art. 25 KKG 2001 the creditor (or crowdlending intermediary) must report the granted (or mediated) credit as well as outstanding payments that constitute at least 10% of the net credit sum to the information agency for consumer credit (*Informationsstelle für Konsumkredit*, hereinafter "IKO"[940]) which is established by all commercially active creditors (Art. 23 Section 1 KKG 2001).[941] The IKO collects all relevant data and makes it available to creditors and crowdlending intermediaries (Art. 24 KKG 2001).

---

937 Barnikol, ibid., 112 et seq.

938 Cf. Arts. 27a, 28 Section 5 KKG 2001 for crowdlending situations, Art. 29 KKG 2001 for leasing agreements and Art. 30 KKG 2001 for (customer) credit card agreements.

939 Die Konsumentin oder der Konsument gilt dann als kreditfähig, wenn sie oder er den Konsumkredit zurückzahlen kann, ohne den nicht pfändbaren Teil des Einkommens nach Artikel 93 Absatz 1 des Bundesgesetzes vom 11. April 1889 über Schuldbetreibung und Konkurs beanspruchen zu müssen. (Translation by author).

940 Cf. Art. 23 KKG 2001; formerly the central agency for credit information (*Zentralstelle für Kreditinformation, ZEK*) which continues to exist. Loans that are not recorded at the IKO but at the ZEK must also be considered by creditors if they have access to the data, Stauder, *supra* note 919, 254. Regarding the issue of consumers' access to data and data protection in this regard, cf. a full analysis in Barnikol, *supra* note 927, 116-125.

941 Cf. Art. 26 KKG 2001 for leasing agreements and Art. 27 KKG 2001 for (customer) credit card agreements.

Art. 31 Section 1 KKG 2001 allows creditors and crowdlending intermediaries to rely on the consumer's statements regarding their financial situation. However, the consumer's statements must not constitute the only evidence for his or her creditworthiness.[942] If the provided information appears 'obviously incorrect' (Art. 31 Section 2 KKG 2001), i.e. if the information provided by the consumer and the IKO do not match,[943] or the creditor or crowdlending intermediary is in doubt regarding the consumer's statements (Art. 31 Section 3 KKG 2001) the provided information must be examined.

Art. 32 KKG 2001[944] provides for sanctions in case the creditor does not abide by his or her duties. If the creditor seriously violates his or her credit assessment duties (Arts. 27a-31 KKG 2001) he or she will lose the whole credit sum, interest and additional costs (Art. 32 Section 1 KKG 2001). This means that the credit agreement remains valid; thus, the creditor continues to be under a duty to provide the consumer with the agreed credit but the consumer is no longer obliged to pay it back and is eligible to claim back the money already paid. In case of a less severe violation of credit assessment duties or a violation of the duty to report to the IKO (Arts. 25-27 KKG 2001) the creditor merely loses the credit's interest and costs (Art. 32 Section 2 KKG 2001). This harsh sanction mechanism shall contribute to the preventative nature of the Act. The provision does not (only) sanction the violation of a legal duty but shall ensure an effective prevention of overindebtedness.[945]

The provisions relating to the assessment of the borrower's creditworthiness clearly deviate from the original KKG 1993 and reveal a different image of consumer protection compared to the preceding legislation. They do not implement European norms and, thus, do not require euro compatible interpretation.

942 Stauder, *supra* note 919, 258.

943 Ibid.

944 Cf. Art. 32a KKG 2001 for crowdlending intermediaries. For a detailed discussion of the sanction mechanism under the KKG 2001, cf. Barnikol, *supra* note 927, 153-239.

945 Stauder, *supra* note 919, 259.

C. Consumer Credit Adjudication

Not a lot of case-law exists on the KKG 2001. One explanation for this may be provided by the availability of the Swiss Banking Ombudsman where consumers can proceed against the creditor free of charge. Regarding court case-law on (the discussed provisions on) consumer credit by cantonal courts and the Swiss Federal Court, a search resulted in a total of 79 cases discussing or mentioning the KKG 2001 since 2004.[946] In 53 cases the KKG 2001 was either not applicable or mentioned in the course of criminal or administrative proceedings. 18 cases dealt with leasing and credit card agreements or licensing issues (cf. Art. 39, 40 KKG 2001). Of the remaining eight cases, five were decided in favour and three against the consumer.

With respect to the cases decided in favour of the consumer one concerned the inclusion of documents relating to the assessment of creditworthiness in the credit agreement (Art. 9 Section 2 lit. j KKG 2001),[947] one concerned the requirements regarding the termination of a credit agreement under Art. 18 KKG 2001,[948] one concerned the minimum requirements regarding the content of the credit agreement (Art. 9 KKG 2001)[949] and two concerned violations of provisions relating to the material assessment of creditworthiness (Arts. 28, 31 KKG 2001) and sanctioning under Art. 32 KKG 2001[950]. With respect to the cases that were not decided in favour of the consumer, one related to the assessment of creditworthiness and sanctioning[951] while two others concerned the same proceeding relating to the classification of a student loan as consumer credit (Art. 3 KKG 2001).[952]

946 Using the database www.swisslex.ch (using the search terms "Konsumkreditgesetz" and "Erlass: 221.214.1 - KKG / LCC" separately) on the 26 April 2019.

947 Supreme Court of Bern (*Obergericht des Kantons Bern*), *A AG v B* [2013] ZK 13 320.

948 Supreme Court of Thurgau (*Obergericht des Kantons Thurgau*) [2010] Rechenschaftsbericht des Obergerichts des Kantons Thurgau an den Grossen Rat, RBOG 2010, 108-111.

949 Cantonal Court of Fribourg (*Tribunal cantonal du Canton de Fribourg*) [2008] Freiburger Zeitschrift für Rechtsprechung, RFJ 2008, 78-82.

950 Swiss Federal Court, *X v Y AG* [2014] 5A_114/2014; Supreme Court of Bern, *A v B* [2016] ZK 16 148.

951 Cantonal Court of Vaud (*Tribunal cantonal du Canton de Vaud*) [2016] Journal des tribunaux (Droit Cantonal), JdT 2016 III, 184-187.

952 Swiss Federal Court, *X v Bank Y* [2013] BGE 139 III 201; Supreme Court of Bern, *Student X v Bank Y* [2012] ZK 12 269.

A search of selected cases decided by the Swiss Banking Ombudsman[953] resulted in seven cases concerning consumer credit and leasing between 2004 and 2012. Of those cases only one concerned alleged violations of creditworthiness assessment rules and was not decided in favour of the consumer.[954] It is not possible to analyse the decision because it lacks a judicial reasoning. The annual report 2017, furthermore, includes a case report with respect to a dispute regarding an improper assessment of creditworthiness. The ombudsman stated that he could not solve the conflict due to a lack of court case-law.[955] Apart from the selected case reports, the Swiss Banking Ombudsman also publishes statistics regarding the number of cases arising regarding consumer credit. These numbers have remained relatively low.[956]

The low number of cases may indicate that the KKG 2001's preventative measures work. Furthermore, the total number of Swiss court cases indicates that the courts are aware of the provisions of the KKG 2001. However, due to the low number of cases where the KKG 2001 was actually applicable, no conclusion can be reached on the effect of the introduction of the KKG 2001 on the adjudication of consumer credit cases.

D. *Practical Effects*

Swiss household debt is the fourth highest among OECD countries (cf. Annex 2, Table 5). However, consumer credit only makes up a small portion of the total debt.[957]

According to a study conducted in 2017, 9% of Swiss people lived in a household with at least one small/consumer credit.[958] The most common reasons for taking out a loan – including both secured and unsecured con-

953 Conducted using the German version of the website www.bankingombudsman.ch on the 26 April 2019.

954 Swiss Banking Ombudsman, Jahresbericht 2004, 'Volljährig und damit eigenverantwortlich', page 21.

955 Swiss Banking Ombudsman, Jahresbericht 2017, pages 40-41.

956 37 cases in 2017, cf. ibid., page 51. 47 cases in 2018, cf. Swiss Banking Ombudsman, *supra* note 470, page 55.

957 Cf. Annex 2, Table 1.

958 Anonymous, 'Verschuldung (Art und Kumulierung von Schulden)' (*Bundesamt für Statistik*) <https://www.bfs.admin.ch/bfs/de/home/statistiken/wirtschaftliche-soziale-situation-bevoelkerung/einkommen-verbrauch-vermoegen/verschuldung.html> accessed 19 June 2020.

sumer loans – were the purchase of a car (23.3%) and the purchase of a second home or home interior for the primary residence (15.7%). Only 5.9% of credit was taken because of financial difficulties and 1.9% of borrowers used credit to pay for other loans.[959] In addition, only 5.9% of participants agreed to the statement that they would sometimes buy something knowing that they actually cannot afford it. In a study conducted in 2013, 92.2% of participants showed a conservative attitude toward their financials, stating that they would first earn the money before they would spend it, while 87.4% said they felt uncomfortable with indebtedness.[960]

The proportion of consumer credit in the whole credit market had continuously decreased until 2016 as the following graph illustrates.[961]

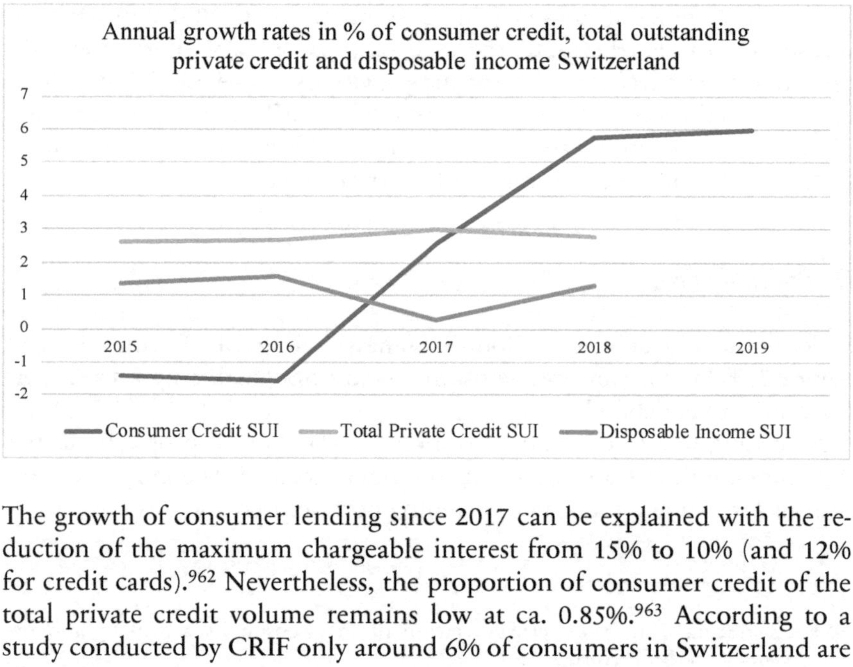

The growth of consumer lending since 2017 can be explained with the reduction of the maximum chargeable interest from 15% to 10% (and 12% for credit cards).[962] Nevertheless, the proportion of consumer credit of the total private credit volume remains low at ca. 0.85%.[963] According to a study conducted by CRIF only around 6% of consumers in Switzerland are

959 Ibid. (Wichtigster Grund für Konsumkredite).

960 Ibid. (Subjektive Beurteilung der Einstellung zu Geld with respective Excel-chart).

961 Data set out in Annex 2.

962 Verordnung zum Konsumkreditgesetz (VKKG), changed on 10 December 2015 (effective on 1 July 2016).

963 Cf. Annex 2, Table 1.

overindebted.[964] Only 2.5% of consumer credit agreements involved payment arrears in 2017.[965] Numbers on default regarding consumer credit are not available. The existing numbers, however, indicate that the KKG 2001 provides an effective mean to maintain the volume of unsecured outstanding consumer credit at a low level compared to the overall volume of outstanding credit and prevent overindebtedness as the legislator envisaged. Furthermore, the conservative financial attitude of Swiss people may also contribute to the decreasing numbers of consumer credit.

E. Consumer Image

While the Swiss legislator first acted according to the image of a rational consumer, the image has changed since the introduction of the KKG 2001. The KKG 2001 clearly envisages a vulnerable consumer in need of protection. Therefore, the emphasis clearly lies on the assessment of creditworthiness in connection with harsh penalties in case of non-compliance rather than pre-contractual information duties which are not included in the KKG 2001 anymore.

F. Interim Conclusion

Historically, Swiss consumer credit legislation did not follow a straight path. Compared to other European countries legislative measures were implemented relatively late or not at all because they turned out too controversial in Parliament. Rather separate measures were introduced at cantonal level. However, in the 1990s this regulatory area saw a change with the introduction of the KKG 1993. Subsequently, after decades of hesitant and fragmented regulation the comprehensive and ambitious KKG 2001 was introduced. While the preceding legislation had merely implemented an EU Directive, this piece of consumer credit legislation can be called 'Swiss-made'. Compared to the current Second Consumer Credit Directive, the KKG 2001 is more ambitious, mainly due to a different image of the consumer. Instead of relying on the rational consumer's ability to understand complicated financial transactions, the Swiss legislator takes a restrictive approach which does not just protect the consumer from overindebtedness

964 Cf. Annex 2, Table 8.
965 Cf. Annex 2, Table 6.

but also society as a whole as it prevents the accumulation of unsecured debt that could pose a risk to the stability of the whole financial system. Thereby, the market is stabilised not just because of the lower accumulation of unsecured credit but also because dubious lenders are kept out of the market by the threat of drastic sanctions. In this light, some Swiss commentators have concluded that the implemented Second Consumer Credit Directive is comparatively unambitious and, thus, should not serve as a role model for further autonomous adaptation in the area of consumer credit law.[966] Although court as well as alternative dispute resolution caselaw and comprehensive economic data are rare, the existing material indicates that the Swiss approach has worked. Beside a low number of cases that had to be adjudicated, the economic data shows a low proportion of unsecured debt deriving from consumer credit with respect to the total Swiss credit volume and a low degree of overindebtedness among the Swiss population.

G. Comparative Analysis

CCD 2008	UK	Germany	Norway	Switzerland
Art. 5	CONC 4, Consumer Credit (Disclosure of Information) Regulations 2010	§ 491a BGB in connection with Art. 247 §§ 2 to 5, 8 to 13a EGBGB	§§ 46a, 46c Financial Agreements Act	-
Art. 8	CONC 5.2A	§§ 505a, 505b BGB	§ 46b, 47 Financial Agreements Act	Arts. 22-32a KKG 2001

Under the bilateral Swiss model, the UK would not be bound by European consumer credit legislation. It shall now be determined whether the Swiss, UK – and to a lesser extent Norwegian and German – approaches to consumer credit regulation are comparable and whether the Swiss approach may serve as a source of inspiration for UK consumer credit regulation.

Unlike in the UK, Germany and Norway the development of consumer credit legislation started relatively late in Switzerland. One reason for this draws back to the historical findings depicted above namely that due to law-making powers lying with the cantons a very fragmented system of

966 Marlis Koller-Tumler, Konsumkredite - eine kleine Tour d'Horizon mit Blick auf die EU. in Susan Emmenegger (ed), *Kreditrecht SBT 2010*, 45; Felix Schöbi, 'Die neue Verbraucherkreditrichtlinie und das Konsumkreditgesetz' [1 September 2008] Jusletter recital 37.

rules on consumer credit emerged. As many rules are sourced locally (cf. also the analysis of sociological factors in Switzerland) it made sense at first to let the cantons develop individual administrative rules.

Later the three other depicted countries served as inspiration for early unified Swiss consumer credit legislation. Similar to Norway it made sense to look at foreign more developed consumer credit regulation. At first Switzerland may, thus, be characterised as a recipient of consumer credit legislation. The late start may be explained by the federalist structure, i.e. cantons introduced their own rules and a reluctance to interfere too much with the freedom of contract. However, this position has changed as the Swiss legislator realised that strict rules on creditworthiness assessment not only protect consumers but also the stability of the market. From being a late runner Switzerland, thereby, turned into a fore runner of consumer credit regulation. The UK and Swiss positions are therefore nowadays similar. Swiss and UK consumer policy are also comparable based on the evaluation of societal factors. While historically and sociologically the assessment of comparability has revealed differences, most importantly Switzerland's and the UK's economic premises are similarly based on a liberal policy refraining from intervention where possible. It is, therefore, likely that both legislators will only interfere where necessary with respect to consumer credit policy.

Since 2001 Swiss consumer credit law has developed independently from EU law and, thus, differs from the other depicted systems. Nowadays, Swiss consumer credit regulation comes closest to the German form of regulation. Both systems provide for strict rules of creditworthiness assessments including penalty provisions in case of non-compliance. In addition, Swiss legislation also covers the modern lending form of 'crowdlending'.

Systematically, Switzerland can be classified as a civil law country close to the German civil law system. However, this does not prevent a comparative analysis with UK consumer credit legislation. Especially Swiss and UK consumer images appear similar even though a vulnerable consumer image may appear to conflict with a liberal economic policy. While the UK is moving toward legislation which is rather targeted at vulnerable consumers, the Swiss legislator already drafted the KKG 2001 according to the image of vulnerable consumers when it comes to consumer credit. The view that such regulation becomes necessary shall ensure sustainable consumption which can likewise contribute to economic growth and does not necessarily conflict with liberal policy.

Instead of an informational approach – that underlies Norwegian consumer credit policy – Swiss consumer credit regulation relies on a strict assessment of creditworthiness based on a central and accessible database and harsh penalties in case of non-compliance. The Swiss approach has resulted in a low number of disputes and a very low volume of consumer credit compared to the total private Swiss credit volume. The risk of defaulting borrowers of unsecured loans for the financial system is low. The low volume indicates a restrictive policy of lending consumer credit in line with the intention of the Swiss legislator. Similarly, to Germany, however, the low volume of consumer credit may also be attributed to a conservative attitude of Swiss consumers toward borrowing.

A too restricted consumer credit policy can also bear harmful effects on the economy. However, Switzerland's GDP has been rising constantly since the early 2000s which indicates that the economy is not affected negatively by such restrictions. Under the parameters of this dissertation Switzerland has, therefore, introduced the most effective system of consumer credit regulation. Consumer loans are readily available but lending is handled restrictively to prevent the overburdening of consumers. It can, therefore, serve as an inspiration for the UK. Swiss consumer credit legislation offers a comprehensive example of restrictive regulation that aims at responsible lending. Elements of a centralised administrative credit information agency, a thorough and documented creditworthiness assessment and harsh penalties in case of non-compliance with strict requirements regarding the creditworthiness assessment could prove as valuable input for a stricter consumer credit regulation which, nevertheless, does not prohibit lending consumer credit but demands an informed and responsible decision of the creditor. Rather than intervening with the individual decision of the creditor the legislator sets out the legal framework for lending. This system shifts risks away from the vulnerable consumer in a protective manner which does not prevent or stigmatise consumer lending in general. The threat of harsh financial consequences for creditors likely ensures compliance while vulnerable consumers are prevented from creditors who disregard the possible detrimental overburdening effects of consumer credit they cannot afford. The effective and modern Swiss consumer credit regulation can, therefore, serve as an example for future UK – as well as European, German and Norwegian – legislation on consumer credit.

Part III: Unfair Terms in Consumer Contracts Status Quo

Chapter 9: European Legislation on Unfair Terms in Consumer Contracts

The Unfair Contract Terms Directive was introduced in 1993 as one of the first and still most notable and legislative consumer protection mechanisms. Although, the Unfair Contract Terms Directive has been in place for more than 25 years and remains largely untouched until today, the large amount of CJEU case-law indicates its immense relevance to European consumer protection today.

A. *Rationale behind the European Regulation of Unfair Terms in Consumer Contracts*

As has been explained above (cf. pages 44 et seq.) unfair terms have emerged as a problem of mass production and consumption. A perfect contract scenario would presume that both parties evaluate all terms and negotiate a fair outcome. However, with lengthy T&Cs provided by the supplier in small print, consumers oftentimes do not read or consider T&Cs; thus, do not make entirely informed decisions. Unregulated T&Cs also pose a risk to fair competition as traders who offer goods at much lower prices may only be able to do so if they include terms detrimental to the consumer. The EEC's Member States had started to implement legislation on unfair terms from the 1970s onward.[967] By the 1990s a fragmented system of unfair term control had evolved in Europe and the EEC felt the necessity to enact a European measure regarding unfair terms.[968] However, despite the fact that Member States had enacted legislation on unfair terms, the instruments differed significantly. This was reflected in a Green Paper in 1984 which laid out proposals for either a strict Community-wide prohibition of clauses (German model) or an option which preferred sector specific negotiations between consumer organisations and the industry

967 Kommission der Europäischen Gemeinschaften, Vorschlag für eine Richtlinie des Rates über mißbräuchliche Klauseln in Verbraucherverträgen, KOM(90) 322 endg. – SYN 285 (3 September 1990), pages 6 et seq. (Technische Beilage). The comparative analysis is only available in German.

968 Micklitz, *supra* note 89.

(UK/Nordic model).[969] The options, thereby, reflect the general options laid out above, the latter one being favoured in this work. However, in the end, after several amendments, the German approach succeeded with some exemptions from the scope of term control:[970] The fairness test under Art. 3 Sections 1 and 2 only applies to terms that have not been negotiated individually, 'contractual terms which reflect mandatory statutory or regulatory provisions and the provisions or principles of international conventions to which the Member States or the Community are party' are exempted from term control under the UCTD (Art. 1 Section 2), the main subject matter of the contract and the adequacy of price are exempted from the fairness test as long as they are in 'plain intelligible language' (Art. 4 Section 2, 'core exclusion'), statutory warranty provisions are not included, the UCTD's appendix contains an indicative grey list of terms that may be deemed unfair instead of a prohibitive black list of terms and the UCTD is only drafted as a minimum harmonisation Directive. Thus, Member States can gold-plate it (see also Art. 8).[971]

The original aim of setting minimum standards for drafting T&Cs was not achieved.[972] The UCTD was introduced in 1993 and based on Art. 114 TFEU (then Art. 100a Treaty of Rome). On the one hand, the choice of formal legal basis reveals that it is the Directive's goal to harmonise the internal market. On the other hand, the Directive's preamble reveals that the UCTD also aims to enhance consumer protection across the EU (then EEC).[973] It, thus, establishes a link between the EU's goal of a harmonised and closer growing internal market and the goal of consumer protection.[974]

The CJEU has held that the underlying principle of the Directive is the combat of 'inequality of bargaining power' between a knowledgeable seller and a consumer who cannot influence the terms of the agreement.[975] Following the CJEU's argument, the UCTD, thus, offers an instrument to improve the consumer's bargaining power in a scenario where he or she

---

969 Ibid. with reference to COM(1984) 55 (9 February 1984).
970 The list is similar to that in Micklitz, ibid., recital 3.4.
971 Ibid. recital 3.5.
972 Ibid. recital 3.4.
973 Cf. Recitals 5-10 UCTD.
974 Nebbia, *supra* note 567, 3.
975 Cf. i.e. ECJ judgment C-240-C-244/98, *Océano Grupo Editorial SA v Murciano Quinter and Salvat Editores SA v Sánchez Alcón Prades* (*Océano*) [2000]; ECJ judgment C-168/05, *Mostaza Claro v Centro Móvil Milenium SL* (*Mostaza Claro*) [2006].

would otherwise be exposed to a power imbalance in favour of the seller. Furthermore, it has been mentioned that the Directive shall also serve to eventually contribute to removing the unfair terms from the market.[976]

It can, thus, be summarised that the UCTD aims at both, the functioning of the (internal) market and consumer protection by ensuring fairness in standard form contracts.

B. Legislative Developments

The main European legislative measure in the area of unfair terms is the Unfair Contract Terms Directive.

I. The Unfair Contract Terms Directive

Scope of Applicability

The UCTD only applies to contracts between sellers or suppliers and consumers (Art. 1 Section 1 UCTD). Sellers and suppliers include publicly as well as privately owned entities (Art. 2 lit (c) UCTD). A consumer is 'any natural person who [...] is acting for purposes which are outside his trade, business or profession' (Art. 2 lit (b) UCTD). Unlike in the Second Consumer Credit Directive, the consumer is considered not only as the weaker party of the contract but also as one who is not as knowledgeable;[977] thus, not circumspect as the *Gut Springenheide* definition suggests.[978]

The UCTD, furthermore, only applies to non-individually negotiated terms (Art. 3 Section 1 UCTD), thus, mostly standard contracts. According to Art. 3 Section 2 UCTD a 'term shall always be regarded as not individually negotiated where it has been drafted in advance and the consumer has therefore not been able to influence the substance of the term'. Apart from this limitation, the Directive does not formally exclude certain types of contract.[979]

976 Opinion of Advocate General Tizzano, ECJ judgment C-473/00, *Cofidis SA v Jean-Louis Fredout* [2002] Recital 63.

977 Cf. i.e. ECJ judgment C-240-C-244/98, *Océano* [2000] recital 25.

978 Peter Rott, Unfair contract terms. in Christian Twigg-Flesner (ed), *Research Handbook on EU Consumer and Contract Law*, 290.

979 Recital 10 of the UCTD mentions 'contracts relating to employment, contracts relating to succession rights, contracts relating to rights under family law and contracts relating to the incorporation and organization of companies or part-

Exemptions and limitations have already been listed above. First, the term control mechanisms in the UCTD only apply to not-individually negotiated contracts (Art. 2 lit (a), Art. 3 Section 1 UCTD). According to Art. 3 Section 2 UCTD '[a] term shall always be regarded as not individually negotiated where it has been drafted in advance and the consumer has therefore not been able to influence the substance of the term, particularly in the context of a pre-formulated standard contract'. The limitation originates from the German approach to dealing with unfair terms (see § 305 BGB, more below).[980] Second, Art. 1 Section 2 UCTD exempts mandatory, statutory or regulatory provisions and terms based on international conventions from both the transparency as well as the unfairness test. The exemption applies to provisions 'that apply between the contracting parties provided that no other arrangements have been established'[981] meaning 'independently of [the parties'] choice or [...] by default'[982]. Third, Art. 4 Section 2 UCTD exempts from the unfairness test under Art. 3 Section 1 UCTD terms relating to the definition of the subject matter of the contract and/or the adequacy of the price and remuneration if they are drafted in plain intelligible language.[983] These exceptions must be interpreted in a strict and uniform manner across the EU because of their exceptional character.[984]

With respect to the main subject matter of the contract the CJEU states that it includes the terms

---

nership agreements' as exemptions. However, these contracts will usually be excluded anyways because they do not involve suppliers and consumers, ibid., 291; Micklitz, *supra* note 89, recital 3.12. The supposed 'exemption' of insurance contracts in Recital 19 of the UCTD only refers to the certain elements of the contract, Micklitz, ibid., recital 3.13.

980 Nebbia, *supra* note 567, 119-120.

981 Recital 13 UCTD.

982 CJEU judgment C-266/18, *Aqua Med sp. z o.o.v Irena Skóra* [2019] recital 33; CJEU judgment C-186/16, *Ruxandra Paula Andriciuc and Others v Banca Românească SA* (*Andriciuc*) [2017] recital 29; CJEU-judgment C-92/11, *RWE Vertrieb AG v Verbraucherzentrale Nordrhein-Westfalen eV* (*RWE*) [2013] recital 26.

983 The exemption does not apply to the transparency control under Art. 5 UCTD, cf. CJEU judgment C-470/12, *Pohotovosť s. r. o. v Miroslav Vašuta* (*Pohotovost*) [2014]. It, furthermore, does not apply to terms included in the UCTD's Annex (grey list), cf. CJEU judgment C-143/13, *Bogdan Matei and Ioana Ofelia Matei v SC Volksbank România SA* (*Matei*) [2015] recital 60.

984 CJEU judgment C-143/13, *Matei* [2015] recital 50; CJEU judgment C-26/13, *Árpád Kásler and Hajnalka Káslerné Rábai v OTP Jelzálogbank Zrt* (*Kásler*) [2014] recital 42.

> [...] that lay down the essential obligations of the contract and, as such, characterise it. By contrast, terms ancillary to those that define the very essence of the contractual relationship cannot fall within the notion of the 'main subject-matter of the contract'.[985]

Terms that lay down such 'essential obligations' must be determined by taking into account 'the nature, general scheme and the stipulations of the [...] agreement, and its legal and factual context [...]'[986]; thus, suggesting an individual assessment of the term and its contractual environment.

With respect to terms relating to the 'adequacy of the price and remuneration, on the one hand, as against the services or goods supplies in exchange, on the other' the CJEU emphasises that as opposed to terms relating to the main subject matter of the contract, price terms are not generally excluded from judicial review but merely limited to everything but the quality/price ratio because 'no legal scale or criterion exists that can provide a framework for, and guide, such a review'.[987] A 'price term' is, furthermore, not merely classified as such because it relates in some way to the price or remuneration to be paid (i.e. the calculation of repayment instalments) but must also determine the service that will be provided in exchange.[988] Thus, the 'price adequacy limitation' is interpreted rather narrowly.

Scope of Term Control

In *Commission v Spain*[989] the ECJ distinguished the *in concreto*, meaning individual, term control under Art. 3 Section 1 and Art. 5 UCTD and the *in abstracto* term control, meaning control in the course of administrative or collective proceedings, under Art. 7 UCTD in connection with Art. 3 Section 1 UCTD or Art. 5 UCTD. The proceedings have different purposes and must, thus, be viewed procedurally distinct from each other while still

---

985 CJEU judgment C-143/13, *Matei* [2015] recital 54. Cf. also CJEU judgment C-186/16, *Andriciuc* [2017] recital 35; CJEU judgment C-96/14, *Jean-Claude Van Hove v CNP Assurances SA* (*Van Hove*) [2015] recitals 33-35; CJEU judgment C-26/13, *Kásler* [2014] recital 49.

986 CJEU judgment C-26/13, *Kásler* [2014] recital 51.

987 Ibid. recital 55.

988 Ibid. recital 59.

989 ECJ judgment C-70/03, *Commission of the European Communities v Kingdom of Spain* [2004] recital 16 (only referring to Art. 5 UCTD explicitly).

complementing each other to achieve a high consumer protection standard.[990]

1. in concreto

The Unfair Contract Terms Directive provides two mechanisms of term control: one regards the (formal) transparency and the other the (substantive) fairness of the term.

Transparency

Art. 5 and Recital 20 of the UCTD provide for the principle of transparency in *written* not individually negotiated consumer contracts. This means that terms must be drafted in 'plain, intelligible language'. In case this principle is not adhered by, 'the interpretation most favourable to the consumer shall prevail' in individual proceedings according to Art. 5 UCTD (*contra preferentem* rule). The requirement of plain, intelligible language must be interpreted broadly according to CJEU case-law.[991] 'The requirement of transparency of contractual terms [...] cannot [...] be reduced merely to their being formally and grammatically intelligible'.[992]

> Therefore, the requirement that a contractual term must be drafted in plain intelligible language is to be understood as requiring also that the contract should set out transparently the specific functioning of the mechanism to which the relevant term relates and the relationship between that mechanism and that provided for by other contractual terms, so that that consumer is in a position to evaluate, on the basis of clear, intelligible criteria, the economic consequences for him which derive from it.[993]

---

990 CJEU Joined Cases C-381/14 and C-385/14, *Jorge Sales Sinués and Youssouf Drame Ba v Caixabank SA and Catalunya Caixa SA (Catalunya Banc S.A.)* (*Sales Sinués and Drame Ba*) [2016] recital 30.

991 Cf. CJEU judgment C-186/16, *Andriciuc* [2017] recital 44; CJEU judgment C-26/13, *Kásler* [2014] recital 72.

992 CJEU judgment C-26/13, *Kásler* [2014] recital 71.

993 CJEU judgment C-186/16, *Andriciuc* [2017] recital 45; CJEU judgment C-154/15, *Francisco Gutiérrez Naranjo v Cajasur Banco SAU, Ana María Palacios Martínez v Banco Bilbao Vizcaya Argentaria SA (BBVA), Banco Popular Español SA v Emilio Irles López and Teresa Torres Andreu* (*Gutiérrez*) [2016] recital 50.

This definition reveals that the transparency requirement mainly serves the rational consumer to enable him or her to make an informed decision. Art. 5 UCTD does not only require the contractual term to be drafted in a clear manner (contractual transparency) but also refers to pre-contractual information duties to put the consumer in a position from which he or she can make an informed decision (institutional transparency).[994] In this regard the way in which the information is presented must take into account the individual position of the consumer.[995] Pre-contractual information in this sense includes all the material that the consumer receives before concluding the contract[996] which brings the UCTD close to the Unfair Commercial Practices Directive as well as other EU legislative acts which provide information duties. A term's lack of transparency does not automatically lead to it also being unfair.[997] Such assessment has to be conducted according Art. 3 Section 1 UCTD under which the lack of transparency can constitute a contributing factor[998].

Unfairness

The 'unfairness rule' under Art. 3 Section 1 UCTD provides that

> [a] contractual term which has not been individually negotiated shall be regarded as unfair if, contrary to the requirement of good faith, it causes a significant imbalance in the parties' rights and obligations arising under the contract, to the detriment of the consumer.

The unfairness test, thus, contains two components: a breach of 'good faith' and a 'significant imbalance'. Both elements must be read together and are interconnected. This follows from Recital 16 of the UCTD which provides that

> [...] the assessment, according to the general criteria chosen, of the unfair character of terms [...] must be supplemented by a means of making an overall evaluation of the different interests involved; [...] this

---

994 CJEU judgment C-186/16, *Andriciuc* [2017] recitals 47-48. For the distinction between contractual and institutional transparency, cf. Micklitz, *supra* note 89, recital 3.18.

995 CJEU judgment C-96/14, *Van Hove* [2015] recital 48.

996 Cf. CJEU judgment C-186/16, *Andriciuc* [2017] recital 46.

997 CJEU judgment C-421/14, *Banco Primus SA v Jesús Gutiérrez García* (*Banco Primus*) [2017] recital 64.

998 Cf. i.e. CJEU judgment C-472/10, *Nemzeti Fogyasztóvédelmi Hatóság v Invitel Távközlési Zrt* (*Invitel*) [2012] recital 28.

> constitutes the requirement of good faith; [...] in making an assessment of good faith, particular regard shall be had to the strength of the bargaining positions of the parties, whether the consumer had an inducement to agree to the term and whether the goods or services were sold or supplied to the special order of the consumer; [...] the requirement of good faith may be satisfied by the seller or supplier where he deals fairly and equitably with the other party whose legitimate interests he has to take into account.

In this regard, the CJEU emphasises the lack of individual negotiations under which the consumer could have engaged with the terms of the contract more intensely. Thus, a term can be considered to be contrary to good faith if the consumer would not have reasonably agreed to the term(s) in question after individual negotiations.[999]

With respect to the '(significant) imbalance in the parties' rights and obligations arising under the contract' a comparison between the respective term and substitute provisions under the applicable national law in absence of that term marks the assessment's starting point.[1000] Such comparison allows the court to evaluate to what extent the term(s) deviate from statutory law to the detriment of the consumer. If no relevant statutory provisions exist, Art. 4 Section 1 UCTD provides that 'the nature of the goods or services for which the contract was concluded and by referring, at the time of conclusion of the contract, to all the circumstances attending the conclusion of the contract and to all the other terms of the contract or of another contract on which it is dependent' should be considered. In addition, a grey list list of terms (see below) offers guidance for the assessment. If an imbalance is found it can be considered 'significant' if it results in

> [...] a sufficiently serious impairment of the legal situation in which the consumer, as a party to the contract in question, is placed by reason of the relevant national provisions, whether this be in the form of a restriction of the rights which, in accordance with those provisions, he enjoys under the contract, or a constraint on the exercise of those

---

999 CJEU judgment C-415/11, *Mohamed Aziz v Caixa d'Estalvis de Catalunya, Tarragona i Manresa (Catalunyacaixa)* (*Aziz*) [2013] recital 69. Confirmed in CJEU judgment C-421/14, *Banco Primus* [2017] recital 60; CJEU judgment C-186/16, *Andriciuc* [2017] recital 57.

1000 CJEU judgment C-421/14, *Banco Primus* [2017] recital 59; CJEU judgment C-415/11, *Aziz* [2013] recital 68.

> rights, or the imposition on him of an additional obligation not envisaged by the national rules.[1001]

It, thus,

> [...] cannot be limited to a quantitative economic evaluation based on a comparison between the total value of the transaction which is the subject of the contract and the costs charged to the consumer under that clause.[1002]

The assessment must consider all the circumstances of the individual case, both economically and legally. It is, furthermore, possible that the 'cumulative effect' of several provisions of the respective contract lead to the unfairness of all the terms that contribute to it.[1003]

In addition, according to Art. 3 Section 3 the UCTD's Annex contains 'an indicative and non-exhaustive list of [...] terms that may be regarded as unfair'. In *Commission v Sweden* the CJEU stated that the list itself does not have to be reproduced in the respective national legislation as long as the list's content is accessible for consumers.[1004] While some had argued that the list should be granted presumptive effect as to the unfairness of a term,[1005] the CJEU emphasised that the list only serves as indication and illustration[1006] and stated that 'a term appearing in the list need not necessarily be considered unfair and, conversely, a term that does not appear in the list may none the less be regarded as unfair';[1007] thus, denying presumptive effect. However, subsequent case-law indicates that the CJEU now makes substantive use of the list as an interpretative mean in assessing a term's unfairness while still referring to it as guidance.[1008]

1001 CJEU judgment, C-226/12, *Constructora Principado SA v José Ignacio Menéndez Álvarez (Álvarez)* [2014] recital 23.

1002 Ibid. recital 22.

1003 CJEU judgment C-377/14, *Ernst Georg Radlinger and Helena Radlingerová v Finway a.s.* [2016] recitals 95, 101.

1004 ECJ judgment C-478/99, *Commission of the European Communities v Kingdom of Sweden* [2002] recitals 22, 23. Sweden had included the list in the *travaux préparatoires*. As these are consulted regularly under Nordic legal tradition the mention sufficed.

1005 Micklitz, *supra* note 89, recital 3.24 with more references.

1006 ECJ judgment C-478/99, *Commission of the European Communities v Kingdom of Sweden* [2002] recital 22.

1007 Ibid. recital 20.

1008 Cf. CJEU judgment C-415/11, *Aziz* [2013] recitals 74-75 (referring to No. 1 lit. (e), (q) of the UCTD's Annex); CJEU judgment C-92/11, *RWE* [2013] recitals 40 et seq. (referring to No. 2 lit. (b), (d) of the UCTD's Annex); CJEU

More generally, the CJEU holds that they only provide guidance with respect to the UCTD's term control measures but refrains from assessing the individual circumstances of the case. Such assessment lies with the national courts.[1009] However, similarly to the substantive use of the UCTD's Annex, more recently the CJEU has tended to give the national courts substantive 'guidance' on how to interpret the term(s) in front of them.[1010]

If a contract contains an unfair term this term will not bind the consumer. However, the rest of the contract shall continue to be binding if possible (Art. 6 Section 1 UCTD). Art. 6 Section 2 UCTD provides that Member States must ensure adequate consumer protection even if the respective contract is dealt with under the laws of a non-Member State. According to the CJEU, Art. 6 Section 1 UCTD is a mandatory rule which the Member States and respective courts and administrative authorities shall not deviate from.[1011] Courts shall not amend the term(s) in question in order for them to remain applicable[1012] because such revision would undermine the deterrent effect of the UCTD[1013]. This principle is only limited by Art. 6 Section 1 UCTD in that the contract shall 'be capable of continuing in existence without the unfair terms'. If the continued applicability of the contract itself constitutes a detriment to the consumer, the contract may be nullified altogether.[1014] In case a term has been found unfair and,

---

judgment C-472/10, *Invitel* [2012] recitals 79, 84, 86, 87 (referring to No. 1 lit. (j) of the UCTD's Annex); ECJ judgment C-240-C-244/98, *Océano* [2000] recital 22 (referring to No. 1 lit. (q) of the UCTD's Annex), confirmed in CJEU judgment C-137/08, *VB Pénzügyi Lízing Zrt. v Ferenc Schneider* (*Pénzügyi*) [2010] recital 54; Micklitz, *supra* note 89, recitals 3.24a, 3.26; Rott, *supra* note 978, 298.

1009 ECJ judgment C-237/02, *Freiburger Kommunalbauten GmbH Baugesellschaft & Co. KG v Ludger Hofstetter and Ulrike Hofstetter* [2004] recital 18, 22; CJEU judgment C-243/08, *Pannon GSM Zrt. v Erzsébet Sustikné Győrfi* (*Pannon*) [2009] recital 43.

1010 Cf. CJEU judgment, C-226/12, *Álvarez* [2014] recital 23; CJEU judgment C-415/11, *Aziz* [2013] recitals 66 et seq.; CJEU Case C-453/10, *Jana Pereničová and Vladislav Perenič v SOS financ spol. s r. o.* (*Pereničová*) [2012] recitals 43, 44.

1011 CJEU judgment C-421/14, *Banco Primus* [2017] recital 41; CJEU judgment C-488/11, *Dirk Frederik Asbeek Brusse und Katarina de Man Garabito gegen Jahani BV* (*Asbeek*) [2013] recital 38.

1012 CJEU judgment C-421/14, *Banco Primus* [2017] recital 71 with further references.

1013 CJEU judgment C-154/15, *Gutiérrez* [2016] recital 60; CJEU judgment C-488/11, *Asbeek* [2013] recitals 57, 58.

1014 CJEU judgment C-118/17, *Zsuzsanna Dunai v ERSTE Bank Hungary Zrt* (*Dunai*) [2019] recital 55.

therefore, not binding, the consumer may also be entitled to restitutionary damages for payments that have already occurred due to the unfair term.[1015]

The principle of effectiveness in Art. 7 Section 1 UCTD is closely related to Art. 6 Section 1 UCTD. While Art. 6 Section 1 UCTD alone provides for an effective remedy if a term is found unfair, Art. 7 Section 1 UCTD more generally speaks of 'effective means' which cover both the remedial as well as the procedural side of term control.[1016] In this context the CJEU states that the national courts not only have the power[1017] but are under an *ex officio* duty to assess unfair terms even if such a claim is not raised by the consumer[1018]. Not only shall the courts, thereby, ensure that consumers are protected from the unfair term(s) in question but also achieve a deterrent effect to prevent the use of unfair terms in light of Art. 7 Section 1 UCTD.[1019] The duty to assess unfair terms without respective claims ends where it would have to 'make up fully for the total inertia on the part of the consumer'.[1020] Art. 7 Section 1 UCTD also aims to ensure that consumers have access to justice. Thus, the CJEU states that beside the *ex officio* duty within proceedings, access to such proceedings must not be limited by procedural provisions or a lack of information on the rights of the consumer.[1021] This approach reflects the CJEU's conflicted policy on national procedural law which, on the one hand, emphasises the Member States' procedural autonomy due to a lack of harmonising EU law in this area,[1022] while, on the other hand, insisting on the effective implementation of European legislative measures,[1023] thus, nevertheless interfering with the Member States' procedural law.

1015 CJEU judgment C-154/15, *Gutiérrez* [2016] recital 62, 63.

1016 CJEU judgment C-176/17, *Profi Credit Polska S.A. w Bielsku Białej v Mariusz Wawrzosek* (*Profi Credit*) [2018] recitals 44, 59, 62, 63.

1017 ECJ judgment C-240-C-244/98, *Océano* [2000] recital 29.

1018 ECJ judgment C-168/05, *Mostaza Claro* [2006] recital 38. Confirmed in CJEU judgment C-243/08, *Pannon* [2009] recital 35; CJEU judgment C-415/11, *Aziz* [2013] recitals 41, 46; CJEU judgment C-421/14, *Banco Primus* [2017] recital 43.

1019 ECJ judgment C-240-C-244/98, *Océano* [2000] recital 28.

1020 CJEU judgment C-40/08, *Asturcom Telecomunicaciones SL v Cristina Rodríguez Nogueira* (*Asturcom Telecomunicaciones*) [2009] recital 47.

1021 Cf. CJEU judgment C-176/17, *Profi Credit* [2018] recital 69.

1022 Cf. CJEU judgment C-40/08, *Asturcom Telecomunicaciones* [2009] recital 38; ECJ judgment C-168/05, *Mostaza Claro* [2006] recital 24.

1023 Cf. ECJ judgment C-240-C-244/98, *Océano* [2000] recital 26.

2. in abstracto

While the *in concreto* control of terms considers the individual circumstances affecting the consumer in each case, the *in abstracto* term control shall serve to prevent the use of unfair terms for all consumers on a more general level. While Arts. 3 and 5 UCTD determine the material scope of judicial control, Art. 7 UCTD demands collective procedural and administrative measures. They shall ensure a preventative and effective control of unfair terms.[1024] In this regard Art. 7 Section 1 UCTD provides that

> Member States shall ensure that, in the interests of consumers and of competitors, adequate and effective means exist to prevent the continued use of unfair terms in contracts concluded with consumers by sellers or suppliers.

According to Art. 7 Section 2 UCTD such 'means' include that

> [...] persons or organizations, having a legitimate interest under national law in protecting consumers, may take action according to the national law concerned before the courts or before competent administrative bodies for a decision as to whether contractual terms drawn up for general use are unfair, so that they can apply appropriate and effective means to prevent the continued use of such terms.

Consumer organisations or respective public authorities can apply for injunctions against the continued use of the unfair term(s).[1025] However, Art. 7 Section 1 UCTD does not entail that consumer organisations have a right to intervene in individual proceedings.[1026] As for the effect of a judgment in collective proceedings on individual proceedings the CJEU stated in *Invitel* that the Directive's effectiveness criterion requires that the injunction applies to all consumers who have been subject to the unfair terms in question.[1027] However, the decision is silent on the effect on other suppliers who have used the same or similar standard terms. In the later case *Biuro Podróży 'Partner'* the CJEU clarified that another user of a term that has been found unfair in a previous court decision can be liable for such use based on the previous decision as a long as minimal procedural standards according to Art. 47 of the Charter of Fundamental Rights of the

---

1024 Also cf. Unfair Contract Terms Directive, Recitals 23, 24.

1025 Cf. Rott, *supra* note 978, 309 critical of the effectiveness of the mean.

1026 CJEU Case C-470/12, *Pohotovost* [2014] recital 56.

1027 CJEU judgment C-472/10, *Invitel* [2012] recital 38.

European Union (right to an effective remedy and to a fair trial) for the accused are met.[1028] Thus, decisions in collective proceedings do not automatically unfold *but bear the potential* for *erga omnes* effect.[1029] Especially in light of the courts' *ex officio* duty to assess unfair terms (see above), the findings of collective proceedings can unfold effect with respect to other (similar) contracts and proceedings, however, still bearing in mind the distinction between individual and collective proceedings[1030]. This includes that individual and abstract procedures must have an 'equal procedural standing', meaning that 'every consumer must be able to dissociate himself from collective action and bring an individual action'[1031] because the consumer may 'find himself constrained by the approach which the consumer protection association has taken to the case and will be unable to alter its substance or include other claims [and he] will also be affected by any delay which [may pose] an obstacle to his protection as a consumer'[1032]. Art. 7 Section 2 UCTD, thereby, supplements the principle of (procedural) effectiveness as outlined above.[1033]

II. Further Directives which affect the Regulation of Unfair Terms in Consumer Contracts

The Unfair Contract Terms Directive is related to several other consumer Directives.

The Unfair Commercial Practices Directive aims at tackling unfair commercial practices to ensure 'the proper functioning of the internal market and achieve a high level of consumer protection' (Art. 1 Unfair Commercial Practices Directive). In *Pereničová* the CJEU held that an unfair com-

1028 CJEU judgment C-119/15 *Biuro podróży 'Partner' Sp. z o.o, Sp. komandytowa w Dąbrowie Górniczej v Prezes Urzędu Ochrony Konkurencji i Konsumentów* (*Biuro podróży 'Partner'*) [2016] recital 47. Cf. also CJEU judgment C-169/14, *Juan Carlos Sánchez Morcillo and María del Carmen Abril García v Banco Bilbao Vizcaya Argentaria SA* [2014] recitals 48 et seq.

1029 Cf. also Fabrizio Cafaggi, Re-Jus Casebook: Effective Justice in Consumer Protection (2018) 95-96.

1030 Opinion of Advocate General Szpunar in CJEU Joined Cases C-381/14 and C-385/14, *Sales Sinués and Drame Ba* [2016] recitals 69-73.

1031 Ibid. recital 71.

1032 Ibid. recital 73.

1033 Cf. also CJEU judgment C-472/10, *Invitel* [2012] recital 35; CJEU Joined Cases C-381/14 and C-385/14, *Sales Sinués and Drame Ba* [2016] recital 30.

mercial practice has no direct effect on the validity of a term[1034] but can be considered as 'one element among others on which the competent court may base its assessment of the unfairness of contractual terms under [Art. 4 Section 1] of [the UCTD]'.[1035] The unfair practice must be evaluated in light of all the circumstances of the individual case.[1036] The Unfair Commercial Practices Directive can, thus, serve as guidance to assess the (un-) fairness of a term. Furthermore, as the scope of the Unfair Commercial Practices Directive is broader than that of the UCTD (see i.e. Art. 2 lit. (d) Unfair Commercial Practices Directive), it is likely that an unfair term under the UCTD may also constitute an unfair commercial practice under the Unfair Commercial Practices Directive.[1037]

It was originally intended that the Consumer Rights Directive[1038] should have included provisions on unfair terms to replace the Unfair Contract Terms Directive.[1039] In the end Art. 32 Consumer Rights Directive only amends the UCTD (Art. 8a) to include a duty on behalf of the Member States to inform the Commission of any changes they make under Art. 8 UCTD and, thereby, ensure the uniform application of the Directive.[1040]

Furthermore, the UCTD is interrelated with several (sector-)specific EU legislative instruments such as the already depicted Second Consumer Credit Directive and other measures which provide for consumer rights and/or information duties or more generally on the jurisdiction of claims

---

1034 CJEU Case C-453/10, *Pereničová* [2012] recital 46.

1035 Ibid. recital 43.

1036 Ibid. recital 44.

1037 Ibid. recitals 38, 45, 47.

1038 Directive 2011/83/EU of the European Parliament and of the Council of 25 October 2011 on consumer rights, amending Council Directive 93/13/EEC and Directive 1999/44/EC of the European Parliament and of the Council and repealing Council Directive 85/577/EEC and Directive 97/7/EC of the European Parliament and of the Council.

1039 Howells, *supra* note 595, 439.

1040 For such a list, cf. European Commission, Guidance on the interpretation and application of Council Directive 93/13/EEC of 5 April 1993 on unfair contract terms in consumer contracts, COM(2019) 5325 (22 July 2019) Annex 2.

in cross-border disputes[1041] which can become relevant in the assessment of the (un-) fairness and/or (in-) transparency of a term.[1042]

III. 'A New Deal for Consumers'

In 2018 the European Commission introduced its 'New Deal for Consumers', a legislative package to update and improve European consumer protection measures.[1043] The 'New Deal' aims at

> [modernising] existing rules and fill the gaps in the current the consumer *acquis*, [providing] better redress opportunities for consumers, support effective enforcement and greater cooperation of public authorities in a fair and safe Single market, [increasing] cooperation with partner countries outside the EU, [ensuring] equal treatment of consumers in the Single market and guarantee that national competent authorities are empowered to tackle any problems with 'dual quality' of consumer products, [improving] communication and capacity-building to make consumers better aware of their rights and help traders, especially small and medium-sized enterprises, to comply more easily with their obligations [and] [looking] at future challenges for consumer policy in a fast evolving economic and technological environment.[1044]

The 'New Deal' relates to a Directive amending Council Directive 93/13/ EEC, Directive 98/6/EC, Directive 2005/29/ and Directive 2011/83/EU as

1041 Regulation (EU) No 1215/2012 of the European Parliament and of the Council of 12 December 2012 on jurisdiction and the recognition and enforcement of judgments in civil and commercial matters (Brussels I), Convention on jurisdiction and the recognition and enforcement of judgments in civil and commercial matters (30 October 2007) (Lugano Convention), Regulation (EC) No 593/2008 of the European Parliament and of the Council of 17 June 2008 on the law applicable to contractual obligations (Rome I), Regulation (EC) No 864/2007 of the European Parliament and of the Council of 11 July 2007 on the law applicable to non-contractual obligations (Rome II).

1042 For an extensive list, cf. European Commission (2019), *supra* note 1040, pages 13-15.

1043 European Commission (2018), *supra* note 571.

1044 Ibid. pages 3-4.

regards better enforcement and modernisation of EU consumer protection rules[1045] as well as a Directive to repeal the Injunctions Directive[1046].

For the UCTD this means that under Art. 1 of Directive (EU) 2019/2161 a new Art. 8b is inserted which requires Member States to lay down rules regarding penalties for infringements with respect to unfair terms in consumer contracts.[1047] These penalties must be 'effective, proportionate and dissuasive' (Art. 8b Section 1). The penalty shall be imposed by the competent administrative authority or a court (Art. 8b Section 4). The Directive aims at harmonising national penalty provisions which currently differ across the EU.[1048]

1045 Directive (EU) 2019/2161 of the European Parliament and of the Council of 27 November 2019 amending Council Directive 93/13/EEC and Directives 98/6/EC, 2005/29/EC and 2011/83/EU of the European Parliament and of the Council as regards the better enforcement and modernisation of Union consumer protection rules (27 November 2019).

1046 Directive (EU) 2020/1828 of the European Parliament and of the Council of 25 November 2020 on representative actions for the protection of the collective interests of consumers and repealing Directive 2009/22/EC (25 November 2020), also applying to proceedings relating to the UCTD, cf. Art. 2 Section 1, Annex I Section 2 of Directive (EU) 2020/1828.

1047 The transposition period ends on the 28 November 2021 (rules must be applied from the 28 May 2022 onward).

1048 Directive (EU) 2019/2161, Recital 5.

Chapter 10: Unfair Terms in Consumer Contracts in the United Kingdom

The following chapter depicts the development of consumer protection law with respect to unfair terms (in consumer contracts) under English law. Again, the analysis is divided into developments prior to the UK's Membership in the EEC/EC, and EU respectively, and developments as a Member State. As it is difficult to determine a change of developments along periodic timelines, the criteria for allocating legal developments within the former or the latter time period shall constitute of material legislative developments. This means that the Unfair Contract Terms Act 1977 (UCTA 1977) will be discussed under developments prior to joining the EEC despite the UK having already joined the EEC in 1972 because the UCTA 1977 goes back to national legislative efforts dating before the UK became an EEC Member State.

A. *Unfair Contract Terms before 1993*

Drawing back to the original common law position, the area of unfair terms may at first appear as an unlikely target for legislative regulation of private legal relationships.[1049] As has been pointed out above (pages 55 et seq.) English law is underlied by liberal theory which emphasises the freedom of parties to contract rather than allowing outside intervention. Under classic common law theory equitable and statutory intervention should remain exceptional. Nevertheless, the UK legislator put in place regulatory measures in the second half of the 20th century. The following section depicts English legal developments in the area of interpretation of contract terms leading to the introduction legislation that restricted and regulated the interpretation of certain types of clauses.

1049 Cf. for a critical account of such regulation, Patrick S. Atiyah, *Essays on Contract*, 364 et seq.

I. Common Law Contract Term Construction

The common law rules on contract law can be divided into two broad categories: incorporation of terms in the contract and the construction (or interpretation) of contract terms. Both legs of term control consider the element of fairness.[1050] Under the rules on the incorporation of contract terms, certain terms may not be incorporated in case of a lack of understanding without proper explanation,[1051] inducement through misrepresentation[1052] or if a document does not purport contractual effect[1053] even if the parties signed the contract.[1054] Incorporations by notice are subject to the conditions that notice was given before the contract,[1055] contained in a document that should have contractual effect[1056] and was sufficiently brought to the intention[1057] of the contractual party.[1058]

If a term can be considered to be incorporated in the contract the courts will apply various principles of contract term construction to determine the meaning of the term in question.[1059] Such principles must be understood as sources of guidance rather than a strict pattern of rules; they are applied flexibly depending on the matter before the court.[1060] Generally, contract term construction is based on objective principles. As Lord Hoffmann stated in *Investors Compensation Scheme Ltd v West Bromwich Building Society*

1050 Nebbia, *supra* note 567, 28-29.

1051 Cf. i.e. *Saunders v Anglia Building Society* [1971] AC 1004 at 1016 per Lord Reid.

1052 Cf. i.e. *Curtis v Chemical Cleaning and Dyeing Co. Ltd* [1951] 1 KB 805 at 808-809 per Denning LJ (as he then was).

1053 Cf. i.e. *Grogan v Robin Meredith Plant Hire & Anor* [1996] CLC 1127 at 1130-1131 per Auld LJ.

1054 Ewan Mckendrick, *Contract Law: Text, Cases and Materials*, 317-318.

1055 Cf. i.e. *Olley v Marlborough Court Ltd.* [1949] 1 KB 532 at 548 per Denning LJ (as he then was).

1056 Cf. i.e. *Chapelton v Barry Urban DC* [1940] 1 KB 532 at 538 per Slesser LJ. With reference to *Parker v South Eastern Railway* [1877] 2 CPD 416 at 422 per Mellish LJ (and at 424 per Baggalay LJ).

1057 Cf. *Interfoto Picture Library Ltd v Stiletto Visual Programmes Ltd* [1989] QB 433 at 438 per Dillon LJ and at 439 per Bingham LJ (as he then was). See also *O'Brien v MGN Ltd* [2002] CLC 33 at [20] – [21] per Hale LJ (as she then was) and at [28] per Sir Anthony Evans.

1058 McKendrick, *supra* note 1054, 322-331.

1059 Ewan McKendrick, Chapter 13: Express Terms. in Hugh Beale (ed), *Chitty on Contracts* (Volume 1), recital 13-041.

1060 Ibid. recital 13-042.

> Interpretation is the ascertainment of the meaning which the document would convey to a reasonable person having all the background knowledge which would reasonably have been available to the parties in the situation in which they were at the time of the contract.[1061]

Thus, the purpose of contract term construction is not the determination of the parties' subjective intentions;[1062] what matters is only the contract in front of the court.

To ascertain such objective meaning the courts consider all facts that are relevant to the case and were known to both parties at the conclusion of the contract.[1063] The contract must be considered as a whole to ascertain the meaning of contractual provisions.[1064] In this sense, the interpretation of contracts constitutes a 'unitary exercise'.[1065] It is, furthermore, 'iterative' meaning that 'each suggested interpretation is checked against the provisions of the contract and its commercial consequences are investigated'.[1066]

Beside these general principles of construction, the common law also follows principles which bear a more 'rule-like' character.[1067] They include the *contra preferentem* rule which provides that in case of an ambiguity that

1061 *Investors Compensation Scheme Ltd v West Bromwich Building Society & Ors.* [1997] CLC 1243 at 1257. See also *Arnold v Britton and others* [2015] AC 1619 at [15] per Lord Neuberger, *Wood v Capita Insurance Services Ltd* [2017] AC 1173 at [10] per Lord Hodge.

1062 Cf. also *Lukoil Asia Pacific Pte Ltd v Ocean Tankers (Pte) Ltd* [2018] 1 CLC 94 at [8] per Popplewell J and *BP Gas Marketing Ltd v La Société Sonatrach, Sonatrach Gas Marketing UK Limited* [2016] EWHC 2461 (Comm) at [37].

1063 *Arnold v Britton and others* [2015] AC 1619 at [21] per Lord Neuberger; *Prenn v Simmonds* [1971] 1 WLR 1381 at 1385 per Lord Wilberforce; *Arnold v Britton and others* [2015] AC 1619 at [17]. Cf. also *Savills (UK) Ltd v Blacker* [2017] EWCA Civ 68 at [33] per Patten LJ (on the importance of the contract's context); *Fomento de Construcciones y Contratas SA v Black Diamond Offshore Ltd* [2016] EWCA Civ 1141 at [12] per Clarke LJ (on the difference between the ordinary and the literal meaning of a word).

1064 Cf. *Wood v Capita Insurance Services Ltd* [2017] AC 1173 at [10] per Lord Hodge.

1065 *Rainy Sky SA & Ors v Kookmin Bank* [2011] 2 CLC 923 at [21] per Lord Clarke; *Wood v Capita Insurance Services Ltd* [2017] AC 1173 at [11] per Lord Hodge; [2015] AC 1619 at [76] per Lord Hodge.

1066 *Wood v Capita Insurance Services Ltd* [2017] AC 1173 at [12] and [15] per Lord Hodge; *Arnold v Britton and others* [2015] AC 1619 at [77] per Lord Hodge.

1067 McKendrick, *supra* note 1059, recitals 13-042 and 13-095 et seq.

cannot otherwise be resolved by principles of construction a term shall be interpreted against the grantor.[1068]

The depicted common law rules on incorporation and construction reveal a focus on procedural fairness rather than a review of terms in light of substantive fairness considerations.[1069]

II. Exemption Clauses and Introduction of the Unfair Contract Terms Act 1977

The following section depicts the development of rules on exemption clauses before and after the introduction of the UCTA 1977.

1. Before the Unfair Contract Terms Act 1977

The control of exemption – including exclusion and limitation – clauses holds a somewhat special place in the area of common law term control.[1070] Generally, the same principles of term construction apply to exemption clauses as to all other kinds of contract clauses.[1071] However, in the past the courts had adopted a particularly strict approach with respect to exclusion and – to a lesser extent[1072] – limitation clauses.

Essentially, exclusion clauses must be drafted clearly and unambiguously.[1073] In case of (inherent) ambiguity the clause will be found ineffective under the *contra preferentem* rule. In the past, the courts would use the

1068 Ibid. recital 13-095. For an example, cf. *John Lee & Son (Grantham) Ltd v Railway Executive* [1949] 2 All ER 581 at 583 per Evershed MR.

1069 Cf. also Geraint Howells, 'The European Union's Influence on English Consumer Contract Law' [2017] 85 The George Washington Law Review 1904 (1910).

1070 Beside the common law the Sale of Goods Act 1893 included certain rules to prevent the restriction of liabilities (Sections 12 to 15) in relation to the sale of goods. Cf. today Sections 12 to 15 Sale of Goods Act 1979 and the Supply of Goods (Implied Terms) Act 1973.

1071 Simon Whittaker, Chapter 15: Exemption Clauses. in Hugh Beale (ed), *Chitty on Contracts* (Volume 1) recital 15-007; *Whitecap Leisure Ltd v John H. Rundle Ltd* [2008] EWCA Civ 429 at [20] per Moore-Bick LJ; *Air Transworld Limited v Bombardier Inc* [2012] EWHC 243 (Comm) at [25] per Cooke J.

1072 Cf. *Ailsa Craig Fishing Co Ltd v Malvern Fishing Co Ltd and Another* [1983] 1 WLR 964 at 970 per Lord Fraser.

1073 Whittaker, *supra* note 1071, recital 15-008.

principle extensively reflecting a strict approach with respect to exclusion clauses.[1074] More recent case-law, however, suggests a much more restricted use of the *contra preferentem* rule, namely only as a 'last resort' after the application of the general principles of contract term construction.[1075] Before the introduction of the UCTA 1977 the 'doctrine' of fundamental breach had been developed. Under this 'rule' the proferens could not rely on an exclusion clause if he was guilty of a 'fundamental breach of the contract'; [1076] thus, extending the principle of construction that a fundamental breach has to be underlied by sufficient clarity to be a rule of law[1077]. In *Photo Production v Securior Transport* the House of Lords held that especially in light of the introduction of the UCTA (and the possibility of an assessment of reasonableness) there was no need for a doctrine of fundamental breach[1078] and that the validity of an exclusion clause depended on its construction rather than a fundamental breach of a party[1079].

2. The Unfair Contract Terms Act 1977

While sector-specific legislation had been introduced on terms in certain contracts since the 19th century,[1080] the UCTA 1977 constituted the first specific legislative instrument for the control of unfair – exemption – contract clauses (as well as non-contractual notices). The UCTA 1977 imple-

---

1074 Cf. *Wallis, Son & Wells v Pratt & Haynes* [1911] AC 394 at 396-398 per Lord Alverston CJ; *Andrew Brothers (Bournemouth), Limited v Singer and Company, Limited* [1934] 1 KB 17 at 21-23 per Scrutton LJ.

1075 Cf. *Persimmon Homes Limited and others v Ove Arup & Partners Limited, Ove Arup & Partners International Limited* [2017] EWCA Civ 373 at [52] per Jackson LJ with reference to *K/S Victoria Street (a Danish Partnership) v House of Fraser (Stores Management) Limited and others* [2011] EWCA Civ 904 at [68] per Thomas LJ (as he then was).

1076 Cf. i.e. *Karsales (Harrow) Ltd v Wallis* [1956] 1 WLR 936 at 940 per Denning LJ (as he then was); *Charterhouse Credit Co Ltd v Tolly* [1963] 2 QB 683 at 710 per Donovan LH; *Harbutt's "Plasticine" Ltd v Wayne Tank and Pump Co Ltd* [1970] QB 447 at 467 per Lord Denning MR (misleadingly citing *Suisse Atlantique Société d'Armement Maritime SA v NV Rotterdamsche Kolen Centrale* [1967] 1 AC 361, cf. McKendrick, *supra* note 1054, 415.

1077 McKendrick, ibid.

1078 *Photo Production Ltd v Securior Transport Ltd* [1980] AC 827 at 843 per Lord Wilberforce.

1079 Ibid. at 850-851 per Lord Diplock.

1080 Cf. Howells, *supra* note 1069, (1911).

mented the proposal set forth by the Law Commission in 1975.[1081] The need for term control was summarised by the Law Commission as follows:

> We are in no doubt that **in many cases they operate against the public interest** and that the prevailing judicial attitude of suspicion, or indeed of hostility, to such clauses is well founded. All too often they are introduced in ways which result in **the party affected by them remaining ignorant of their presence or import until it is too late.** That party, even if he knows of the exemption clause, will **often be unable to appreciate what he may lose by accepting it.** In any case, he **may not have sufficient bargaining strength** to refuse to accept it. The result is that the risk of carelessness or of failure to achieve satisfactory standards of performance is thrown on to the party who is not responsible for it or who is unable to guard against it. Moreover, by excluding liability for such carelessness or failure, the **economic pressures to maintain high standards of performance are reduced.** There is no doubt that the misuse of these clauses is objectionable.[1082]

Specific case-law on exemption and limitation clauses had evolved before so the introduction of a statute can be seen as a continuation of common law rules. As will be shown below the UCTA 1977 had a clearly defined scope (as opposed to a general test of terms' fairness).

Scope of the UCTA 1977

Only Parts I and III of the UCTA apply to English law, while Part II applies exclusively to Scottish law. The UCTA 1977 mainly applies to clauses that aim to limit or exclude business liability (Section 1 Subsection 3 UCTA 1977). According to Section 14 UCTA a 'business includes a profession and the activities of any government department or local or public authority'.[1083]

The first control mechanism under the UCTA 1977 relates to clauses that aim to exclude or limit liability for negligence (Sections 2, 5 Subsection 1 lit. (a) UCTA 1977).[1084] 'Negligence' is defined under Section 1 Subsection 1 UCTA 1977 as a breach of (a) a contractual obligation 'to take

1081 The Law Commission and the Scottish Law Commission, Exemption Clauses Second Report, Law Com. No. 69, Scot. Law Com No. 39 (5 August 1975).

1082 Ibid. Recital 11 (emphasis added).

1083 For further details, cf. Whittaker, *supra* note 1071, 15-072.

1084 Section 4 UCTA, furthermore, included a provision on unreasonable indemnity clauses relating to negligence in consumer contracts.

reasonable care or exercise reasonable skill in the performance of the contract, (b) a common law duty to take reasonable care or (c) the duty of care under the Occupiers' Liability Act 1957. 'Negligence' under the UCTA 1977, therefore, does not cover strict liability (as it arises without fault).[1085] The courts have, furthermore, not accepted arguments that a clause defining the parties' obligations under the contract[1086] or a clause that negated the duty of care[1087] were out of scope with reference to Section 13 Subsection 1 UCTA 1977 which provides that clauses that fall under Section 2 UCTA 1977 also include those 'which exclude or restrict the relevant obligation or duty'[1088]. According to Section 1 Subsection 4 UCTA 1977 it does not matter whether 'the breach was inadvertent or intentional, or whether liability for it arises directly or vicariously'. Furthermore, according to Section 2 Subsection 3 UCTA 1977 a 'person's agreement to or awareness of' a term does not automatically lead to the acceptance of the risk involved.

The second control mechanism in the UCTA 1977 only applied to contracts 'where one [of the parties] deals as a consumer or on the other's written standard terms of business' (Section 3 Subsection 1 UCTA 1977). According to (the original) Section 12 UCTA 1977 a person

> [dealt] as a consumer' if (a) he neither [made] the contract in the course of a business nor holds himself out as doing so and (b) the other party [did] make the contract in the course of a business and in the case of a contract governed by the law of the sale of goods or hire-purchase, or by section 7 of [the UCTA], the goods passing under or in pursuance of the contract are of a type ordinarily supplied for private use or consumption.

'Dealing in the course of a business' meant that the transaction had to constitute an integral part of it; thus, in certain cases companies could act as a

1085 McKendrick, *supra* note 1054, 421.

1086 *Phillips Products Ltd v Hyland* [1987] WLR 659 at 664-666 per Slade LJ.

1087 *Smith v Eric S. Bush* [1990] AC 831 at 857 per Lord Griffiths (introducing a 'but for' test regarding the duty to take reasonable care) and at 873 per Lord Jauncey.

1088 Cf. *Titan Steel Wheels Limited v The Royal Bank of Scotland plc* [2010] EWHC 211 (Comm) at [104] per Steel J and *Avrora Fine Arts Investment Limited v Christie, Manson & Woods Limited* [2012] EWHC 2198 (Ch) at [144] per Newey J (as he then was) on the extent of Section 13 UCTA 1977; McKendrick, *supra* note 1054, 448.

consumer as well.[1089] To fall under the requirement of 'standard terms of business' a term must (i) be written, (ii) be a term of business and (iii) be part of the other party's standard terms of business and (iv) the other party must deal on those written standard terms of business.[1090] Furthermore, the other party must use the terms habitually rather than occasionally.[1091] 'Standard terms of business' do not exclude prior individual negotiation.[1092] However, such negotiation should not have added 'more than insubstantial variations to the terms which may otherwise have been habitually used by the other party' as they will likely otherwise not be considered 'standard terms of business' of the other party anymore.[1093] According to (the original) Section 3 Subsection 2 UCTA 1977 the term user could not (a) 'when himself in breach of contract, exclude or restrict any liability of his in respect of the breach' or (b) 'claim to be entitled to render a contractual performance substantially from that which was reasonably expected of him or [...] render no performance at all'.

The third control mechanism under the UCTA 1977 relates to clauses that aim to limit or exclude statutory or common law obligations in contracts for the sale of goods and under hire-purchase-agreements (Sections 6, 7 UCTA 1977).

Unfair Term Control

Two types of term control must be distinguished. Section 2 Subsection 1, Section 6 Subsections 1, 2 and Section 7 Subsection 2 of the original UCTA[1094] provided for the absolute ineffectiveness of terms. Absolute ineffectiveness is the consequence of essential and severe breaches, such as the exclusion or limitation of liability for death or personal injury resulting from negligence (Section 2 Subsection 1 UCTA 1977).

1089 *R. & B. Customs Brokers Co Ltd v United Dominions Trust Ltd v Saunders Abbott (1980) Ltd* [1988] 1 WLR 321 at 330 per Dillon LJ.

1090 *African Export-Import Bank and others v Shebah Exploration and Production Co Ltd and others* [2018] 1 WLR 487 at [18] per Longmore LJ.

1091 Ibid. at [20]; *British Fermentation Products Ltd v Compair Reavell Ltd* [1999] 2 All ER (Comm) 389 at [46] per Bowsher J; *Chester Grosvenor Hotel Co Ltd v Alfred McAlpine Management Ltd* [1991] 56 BLR 115 at 131 per Stannard J.

1092 *St Albans City and District Council v International Computers Ltd* [1997] FSR 251 at 262-263 per Nourse LJ.

1093 *African Export-Import Bank and others v Shebah Exploration and Production Co Ltd and others* [2018] 1 WLR 487 at 487.

1094 Now Section 2 Subsection 1, Section 6 Subsection 1 and Section 7 Subsection 3A UCTA 1977.

Breaches under Section 2 Subsection 2, Section 3 Subsection 2, Section 4 Subsection 1, Section 6 Subsection 3 and Section 7 Subsections 3, 4 of the original UCTA 1977 result only in the relative ineffectiveness of a term, namely only insofar the term is considered unreasonable.[1095]

Test of Reasonableness

Section 11 Subsection 1 UCTA 1977 sets out the test of reasonableness. It provides

> that the term shall have been a fair and reasonable one to be included having regard to the circumstances which were, or ought reasonably to have been, known to or in the contemplation of the parties when the contract was made.

In cases where liability shall be restricted to 'a specified sum of money' Section 11 Subsection 4 UCTA 1977 requires that the court must have special regard to 'the resources which he could expect to be available to him for the purpose of meeting the liability should it arise' and 'how far it was open to him to cover himself by insurance'. Furthermore, Schedule 2 of the UCTA 1977 sets out guidelines for the application of the reasonableness test which unlike the wording of Section 11 Subsection 2 suggests, is can be considered in all instances of determining the unreasonableness of a term.[1096] The guidelines in Schedule 2 are not exhaustive.[1097] The following guidelines shall be considered by the courts in determining the reasonableness of a term:[1098]

(a) the strength of the bargaining positions of the parties relative to each other, taking into account (among other things) alternative means by which the customer's requirements could have been met;
(b) whether the customer received an inducement to agree to the term, or in accepting it had an opportunity of entering into a similar contract with other persons, but without having a similar term;
(c) whether the customer knew or ought reasonably to have known of the existence and the extent of the term (having regard, among other

1095 Now Section 2 Subsection 2, Section 3 Subsection 2, Section 6 Subsection 1A and Section 7 Subsections 1A, 4 UCTA 1977.

1096 McKendrick, *supra* note 1054, 428; Whittaker, *supra* note 1071, 15-097.

1097 Cf. *Overseas Medical Supplies Ltd v Orient Transport Services Ltd* [1999] CLC 1243 at [9]-[10] per Potter LJ.

1098 For case-examples regarding the listed guidelines, cf. Whittaker, *supra* note 1071, 15-097 (fn. 550-554).

things, to any custom of the trade and any previous course of dealing between the parties);

(d) where the term excludes or restricts any relevant liability if some condition was not complied with, whether it was reasonable at the time of the contract to expect that compliance with that condition would be practicable;

(e) whether the goods were manufactured, processed or adapted to the special order of the customer.

The considerations mainly reveal concern for circumstantial, procedural fairness, i.e. in the process of bargaining, and thereby fall in line with previous common law case-law. Generally, the courts are equipped with a broad discretion when it comes to weighing the factors to determine the (un-)reasonableness of a term.[1099] *McKendrick* lists several factors which the courts frequently consider such as the meaning of the clause, equality of bargaining power, the clause as a whole and circumstances at the time of conclusion of the contract, 'dangers of relaxation of the clause in practice' and the potential conversion of an exclusion into a limitation clause.[1100]

If a court considers a term unreasonable, they can only declare the term to be unreasonable but are not allowed to amend or re-write the term.[1101]

Summary

This section has shown the move of term control by means of the assessment of incorporation and construction to the interpretation under the UCTA 1977 which introduced a substantive assessment of terms' reasonableness (mainly) in the area of exclusion and limitation clauses. The UCTA 1977 reflects the general approach of English common law to treat exemption clauses as a defence rather than to conduct a holistic assessment of the contract and the embedded term.[1102] The UCTA 1977 thereby falls in line with previous case-law and marks a continuation of rules on term control. Such continuation also fits with the historic evolution of the UK

1099 Roger Brownsword and John N. Adams, 'The Unfair Contract Terms Act: a decade of discretion' [1988] 104 LQR 94 (104 et seq., 113-114); McKendrick, *supra* note 1054, 429. For orientation cf. also the requirement of reasonableness under the Sale of Goods Acts 1893/1979 (i.e. Section 14, 'reasonably fit for purpose').

1100 McKendrick, ibid., 429-434 with several references.

1101 Whittaker, *supra* note 1071, 15-113.

1102 Ibid. 15-003.

and the common law. While this approach has been criticised in the past,[1103] the UCTA 1977 and respective case-law show that the defence-approach is still prevalent in English law[1104]. The limited scope of the UCTA 1977, furthermore, shows a reluctance by the legislator to impose a broad mean of term control that could beat the potential of conflict with existing common law rules. The UCTA 1977, on the contrary, despite introducing substantive term control, was received well by the judiciary as it unified principles that had been developed under common law before and essentially manifested them under a legislative instrument.

B. Unfair Terms Legislation after 1993

The Unfair Contract Terms Directive broadened the available term control mechanisms under the existing common law and UCTA 1977 regimes. Today provisions deriving from the Unfair Contract Terms Directive are implemented in Part 2 of the Consumer Rights Act 2015 (CRA 2015) which replaced the UTCCRs 1999.

I. Impact of European Legislation on English Legislation on Unfair Terms

The following section depicts the implementation of the Unfair Contract Terms Directive into and subsequent problems arising under English law.

1. Unfair Terms in Consumer Contracts Regulations

The UCTD was first implemented in the UTCCRs 1994[1105] which apply to all covered contracts concluded on or after the 1 July 1995 (Regulation 1 UTCCRs 1994). However, they were soon replaced by the UTCCRs 1999[1106] which apply to all covered contracts concluded on or after the 1 October 1999 (Regulation 1 UTCCRs 1999). Unlike the UTC-

1103 McKendrick, *supra* note 1054, 450-452 with reference to Brian Coote, *Exception Clauses*, 9-11, 17-18.

1104 Cf. i.e. *Phillips Products Ltd v Hyland* [1987] WLR 659 at 662, 664 per Slade LJ; Whittaker, *supra* note 1071, 15-003 with further references.

1105 SI 1994/3159 (1 July 1995).

1106 SI 1999/2083 (1 October 1999).

CRs 1994, the UTCCRs 1999 copied most of the UCTD's provisions and, thus, followed the UCTD more closely.[1107]

Scope

The scope of applicability under the UTCCRs 1999 is the same as under the UCTD (see Regulations 4 to 6 UTCCRs 1999).

in concreto

Regulation 7 UTCCRs 1999 implements the transparency test while Regulation 5 UTCCRs 1999 implements the fairness test provided by the UCTD. The wordings do not deviate from Arts. 3 and 5 UCTD significantly. The UCTD's Annex's indicative list is contained in Schedule 2 UTCCRs 1999. Regulation 8 UTCCRs 1999 resembles Art. 6 UCTD.

in abstracto

In Regulations 10 to 15 UTCCRs 1999 the Office of Fair Trading (OFT) was set up as the main administrative authority to deal with unfair terms in consumer contracts. Under Regulation 10 UTCCRs 1999 it was responsible for complaints on unfair terms by individuals as well as especially – under Regulation 11 UTCCRs 1999 – by qualifying bodies set out in Schedule 1 of the UTCCRs 1999 (among others the Data Protection Registrar and the Rail Regulator). The OFT as well as the qualifying bodies were able to apply for injunctions under Regulation 12. They were, furthermore, equipped with investigatory rights to obtain relevant information on alleged infringements. According Regulation 15 the OFT was also responsible for publishing information on undertakings as well as more generally on the functioning of the UTCCRs 1999. Thereby, the UK implemented abstract measures of collective consumer protection required by Art. 7 UCTD.

Overlap with the UCTA 1977

When the UTCCRs 1999 were introduced in 1999 the UCTA 1977 had already been in place for more than 20 years. The two legislative regimes both overlap and differ from each other.[1108] While the UCTA 1977 at the time applied to both consumer and non-consumer contracts, the UTC-

1107 McKendrick, *supra* note 1054, 455; Whittaker, *supra* note 645, 38-213.

1108 For an overview, see The Law Commission and the Scottish Law Commission, Unfair Terms in Contracts, Law Com No. 292, Scot Law Com No. 199 (February 2005), recitals 2.4-2.7.

CRs 1999 specifically focus on contracts between sellers or suppliers and consumers only. While the UCTA 1977 applies both to contracts and non-contractual notices, the UTCCRs 1999 only apply to consumer contracts. However, when it comes to consumer contracts the UTCCRs 1999 cover a broader range than the UCTA 1977 (*inter alia*, insurance contracts[1109]).

With respect to the actual term control, the UCTA 1977 restricts such (mostly) to exclusion and limitation clauses while both the transparency and the fairness test cover all kinds of clauses. However, the fairness test at the time only concerned terms in not individually negotiated contracts. Under the UCTA 1977 the courts have stated that negotiations can precede the use of standard business terms as long as they do not substantially change the terms proposed by one party.[1110]

Thus, not individually negotiated exemption and exclusion clauses in consumer contracts could be subject to both the fairness test under the UTCCRs 1999 and the test of reasonableness under the UCTA 1977. The two tests are also very similar: both equip the courts with a broad margin of discretion, both specifically take into account an inequality of bargaining power and under both tests various circumstances of the case must be considered in the course of the assessment. Nevertheless, because the fairness test under the UTCCRs 1999 applies to more than merely exclusion and limitation clauses considerations under the fairness test can differ from those under the test of reasonableness which is, in this sense, restricted. Thus, while appearing similar the tests could also lead to different results depending on the individual circumstances.[1111] The introduction of the UTCCRs 1999 also marked a disruption of the apparent continuous development of term control under English law as it did not merely apply to exemption and limitation clauses which control had been well-established under common law already but rather a previously undefined area of general non-negotiated terms.

Lastly, the consequences of finding a term unreasonable or unfair are the same. According to Regulation 8 Section 1 UTCCRs 1999 the courts could only declare the unfairness and that, consequently, the respective term does not bind the consumer. Similarly, under the UCTA 1977 the courts can only declare a term unreasonable and, thus, ineffective. The courts could not amend or re-write the terms under either regime.

1109 Excluded from the UCTA 1977 according to Section 1 Subsection 2 in connection with Schedule 1 Subsection 1 lit. (a) UCTA 1977).

1110 Cf. footnotes 1092 and 1093.

1111 For an overview, cf. also Whittaker, *supra* note 645, 38-297.

In 2005 the Law Commission recommended a unified measure of term control in consumer contracts[1112], while provisions in the (amended) UCTA 1977 should continue to apply to business contracts[1113]. The Law Commission also proposed that the new regime for consumers should be 'clearer and more accessible to the reader rather than being based on UCTA or the UTCCRs'. Negotiated terms 'should [also] be required to satisfy a "fair and reasonable" test' and consumer protection should generally not be reduced[1114] with the exception that 'consumers' should only cover natural persons under the new regime[1115]. They also recommended to keep (a reformulated version of[1116]) the UCTD's Annex's indicative list as part of the new regime including the possibility of public authorities to add further terms.[1117]

2. Good Faith in English Contract Law?

In their report the Law Commission also noted that 'good faith is a concept which is unfamiliar to English and Scots lawyers in this area of law'[1118] and should not be referenced in the 'fair and reasonable' test under the new regime as '[it would] be easier for UK lawyers to apply than a more "European" test which makes express reference to good faith'[1119]. Unlike the reasonableness test which had evolved under common law over time, the concept of good faith appeared much broader and unknown to English lawyers who are used to continuous development of the law rather than the sudden introduction of presumedly foreign concepts.

They, thereby, point to a more substantive issue related to the implementation of the Unfair Contract Terms Directive in English law. Under English law there does not exist a general doctrine of good faith.[1120] The

1112 Law Commission (2005), *supra* note 1108, recital 3.3.
1113 Ibid. summary of findings in paras 4.1 -4.7.
1114 Ibid. recital 3.3.
1115 Ibid. recitals 3.23-3.24.
1116 Ibid. recital 3.116.
1117 Ibid. recital 3.112.
1118 Ibid. recital 3.86.
1119 Ibid. recital 3.89.
1120 *Walford v Miles* [1992] 2 AC 128 at 138 per Lord Ackner; McKendrick, *supra* note 1054, 483; Gunther Teubner, 'Legal Irritants: Good Faith in British Law or How Unifying Law Ends Up in New Divergences' [1998] 61 MLR 11 (11); Whittaker, *supra* note 119, recital 1-044; Reinhard Zimmermann and Simon Whittaker, Good faith in European contract law: surveying the legal landscape.

reasons for this were summarised by Leggatt J (as he then was) in *Yam Seng Pte Ltd v International Trade Corporation Ltd* as follows:

> The first is [...] that the preferred method of English law is to proceed incrementally by fashioning particular solutions in response to particular problems rather than by enforcing broad overarching principles. A second reason is that English law is said to embody an ethos of individualism, whereby the parties are free to pursue their own self-interest not only in negotiating but also in performing contracts provided they do not act in breach of a term of the contract. The third main reason given is a fear that recognising a general requirement of good faith in the performance of contracts would create too much uncertainty. There is concern that the content of the obligation would be vague and subjective and that its adoption would undermine the goal of contractual certainty to which English law has always attached great weight.[1121]

The apparent non-existence of a general doctrine of good faith – in the sense of those in continental European civil law systems, such as Germany (see below) – does not, however, mean that the concept of good faith in the sense of fairness in contractual relationships is entirely foreign to English law. First, historically notions of good faith have existed under English law.[1122] Most famously in 1766 Lord Mansfield held that

> [good] faith forbids either party by concealing what he privately knows, to draw the other into a bargain, from his ignorance of that fact, and his believing the contrary. But either party may be innocently silent, as to grounds open to both, to exercise their judgment upon. [...] This definition of concealment, restrained to the efficient motives and precise subject of any contract, will generally hold to make it void, in favour of the party misled by this ignorance of the thing concealed.[1123]

Second, it has already been shown (see pages 145 et seq. above) that principles of fairness are not foreign to English law but have been developed in a

---

in Reinhard Zimmermann and Simon Whittaker (eds), *Good faith in European contract law*, 39-40.

1121 [2013] EWHC 111 (QB) at [123]; see also McKendrick, ibid., 490-492 with reference to Roger Brownsword, *Contract Law: Themes for the Twenty-First Century*, 114-120.

1122 Cf. Zimmermann and Whittaker, *supra* note 1120, 41-44.

1123 *Carter v Boehm* [1766] 2 Burrow 1905 at 1910.

fragmented manner rather than under a general doctrine. Similarly, Bingham LJ (as he then was) stated in *Interfoto Picture Library Ltd v Stilletto Visual Programmes Ltd* that

> English law has, characteristically, committed itself to no such overriding principle but has developed piecemeal solutions in response to demonstrated problems of unfairness. [...] Thus equity has intervened to strike down unconscionable bargains. Parliament has stepped in to regulate the imposition of exemption clauses and the form of certain hire-purchase agreements. The common law also has made its contribution, by holding that certain classes of contract require the utmost good faith, by treating as irrevocable what purport to be agreed estimates of damage but are in truth disguised penalty for breach, and in many other ways.[1124]

The several instances that Bingham LJ (as he then was) lists exemplify that English contract law has developed fairness principles. However, such developments are restricted to instances of apparent individual or collective vulnerability of contracting parties[1125] with respect to basic contract theory, which is underlied by freedom of contract and the binding force of contract. In this light, the English approach is flexible in its own way, intervening with concepts of fairness only where it appears necessary; in contrast to civil law systems in which flexibility is presumed under broad and general good faith provisions.

More recently, English courts have appeared friendlier toward a general principle of good faith especially with respect to 'good faith' clauses with a narrow scope[1126] and where such a principle derived from 'the clear intention of the legislator expressed in [a] statute[1127]. Most prominently, Leggatt J (as he then was) suggested – with reference to other common law jurisdictions[1128] as well as general principles such as honesty[1129] – in an *obiter dictum* in *Yam Seng Pte Ltd v International Trade Corporation Ltd* that there

---

1124 [1989] QB 433 at 439.

1125 Cf. also *ING Bank NV v Ros Roca SA* [2011] EWCA Civ 353 at [92] per Rix LJ (pointing out the sector specific legislative and common law interventions); Whittaker, *supra* note 119, recitals 1-049 et seq. for more examples.

1126 *Petromec Inc v Petroleo Brasileiro SA Petrobas and others (No. 3)* [2005] EWCA Civ 891 at [117]-[121] per Longmore LJ.

1127 *Timeload Ltd v British Telecommunication plc* [1995] EMLR 459 at 468 per Lord Bingham MR (as he then was).

1128 [2013] EWHC 111 (QB) at [125]-[129].

1129 Ibid. at [135] and [138].

exists an implied duty of good faith.[1130] Subsequent judgments, however, have not adopted such a broad view of a general principle of good faith underlying all contracts but again rather referred to specific categories where an intervention on the grounds of good faith was appropriate.[1131]

Coming back to the notion of good faith under the Unfair Contract Terms Directive, the question remains whether the explicit mention of the principle in Regulation 5 Section 1 UTCCRs 1999 introduced a foreign – namely German[1132] – concept of good faith to English law. On this point, I agree with *Whittaker* who rejects the notion of the imposition of a German concept of good faith and states that 'the Directive requires an autonomous interpretation of good faith'.[1133] He draws this conclusion both from the Directive itself and recent CJEU case-law. Recital 16 of the UCTD explains what the concept of good faith aims at (see above pages 224 et seq.). The explanation states that 'good faith' in the sense of the UCTD basically requires a holistic assessment of circumstances in each individual case and, thereby, comes close to the reasonableness test under the UCTA 1977 (as already stated above). This guidance helps to narrow the concept[1134] and shows that the notion of 'good faith' and the broad concept that English courts reject are not exactly the same. It is a flexible tool of contract interpretation which is limited to unfair terms in consumer contracts which had already been identified under the UCTA 1977 as in need of intervention.

Thus, while the Law Commission may have been right to point out that the phrase 'good faith' can appear irritating to English lawyers, it is not an entirely foreign concept. In light of English common law as well as legislative developments, one cannot reject that the notion of good faith has entered the arena at least in some categories of contract. As courts discuss the concept, they also narrow it down to fit into the common law tradition. Consumer contracts are one area where especially legislative developments indicate that notions of fairness should be considered in the assessment of

---

1130 Ibid. at [145].

1131 Cf. *Greenclose Ltd v National Westminster Bank plc* [2014] EWHC 1156 (Ch) at [150] per Andrews J; *Mid Essex Hospital Services NHS Trust v Compass Group UK and Ireland Ltd* [2013] EWCA Civ 200 at [105] per Jackson LJ. Also received negatively by the UK Supreme Court in *Marks & Spencer plc v BNP Paribas Securities Services Trust Co (Jersey) Ltd* [2015] UKSC 72 at [21] per Lord Neuberger.

1132 Whittaker, *supra* note 645, recital 38-266.

1133 Ibid. recitals 38-269-38-271.

1134 Ibid. recital 38-268.

a contract term. Furthermore, while the term 'good faith' may sound foreign to a common lawyer, its content with regard to the Unfair Contract Terms Directive is not entirely dissimilar from the test of reasonableness under the UCTA 1977 and the reasonableness requirements under the Sale of Goods Acts 1893/1979. It can, therefore, be concluded that the notion of good faith may add new elements to the assessment of terms in consumer contracts. However, it is not an alien that should or has to be removed from the English implementation of the Unfair Terms Directive.[1135]

3. Consumer Rights Act 2015

The Law Commission's recommendation in 2005 eventually was not adopted in the replacement of the UTCCRs 1999. Instead of drafting a new single Act that would combine consumer protection mechanisms of the UCTA 1977 and the UTCCRs 1999, the UTCCRs 1999 and parts of the UCTA 1977[1136] were replaced by Part 2 of the CRA 2015 on the 1st October 2015.

Scope

According to Section 61 Subsection 1 CRA 2015 provisions under Part 2 CRA 2015 only apply to 'contracts between a trader and a consumer'. A trader 'means a person acting for the purposes relating to that person's trade, business, craft or profession [...]' (Section 2 Subsection 2 CRA 2015). A consumer 'means an individual acting for purposes that are wholly or mainly outside the individual's trade, business, craft or profession' (Section 2 Subsection 3 CRA 2015). Compared to the UCTD the word 'mainly' was inserted to broaden the consumer definition to ensure instances of occasional private use of goods were also covered.[1137] As the definition refers to an 'individual', companies who could have been considered consumers under the UCTA 1977 are now excluded from the scope of protection under the CRA 2015.

1135 Disagreeing with Teubner, *supra* note 1120.

1136 The necessary amendments are contained in Schedule 4 CRA 2015. Furthermore, the Section 3 Misrepresentation Act 1967 does not cover consumer contracts within the meaning of Part 2 CRA 2015 anymore (cf. Schedule 4 Section 1 CRA 2015).

1137 Whittaker, *supra* note 645, recital 38-384.

'Consumer contracts' (Section 61 Subsection 3 CRA 2015) do not include contracts for employment or apprenticeship (Section 61 Subsection 2 CRA 2015). However, Part 2 CRA 2015 does include term control with respect to 'consumer notices' (Section 61 Subsection 7 CRA 2015) meaning notices relating 'to rights and obligations as between a trader and a consumer' or notices that '[purport] to exclude or restrict a trader's liability to a consumer (Section 61 Subsection 4 CRA 2015) and excluding notices relating to employment or apprenticeship (Section 61 Subsection 5 CRA 2015). Notices also include 'announcements [...] and any other communication or purported communication' (Section 61 Subsection 8 CRA 2015).

Reflecting the UCTD, terms (or notices) that reflect mandatory statutory or regulatory provisions or provisions or principles of an international convention are excluded from the scope of Part 2 CRA 2015 (Section 73 Subsection 1 CRA 2015). According to the Directive and CJEU case-law, mandatory statutory or regulatory provisions '[include] rules which, according to law, apply between the parties on the basis that no other arrangements have been established' (Section 73 Subsection 2 CRA 2015).[1138]

With respect to the fairness test under Section 62 Subsections 1, 4 CRA 2015, 'individually negotiated' terms are no longer excluded from the assessment.[1139] The new regime under Part 2 CRA 2015, thereby, adopts the broader approach of the UCTA 1977 rather than the more restrictive approach under the UTCCRs 1999.[1140] Section 64 CRA 2015 still contains the core exclusions provided under the UCTD (referring to transparent and prominent terms relating to the subject matter of the contract or the adequacy of price or remuneration). However, with respect to price terms, Section 64 Subsection 1 lit. (b) CRA 2015 has been substantially reformulated[1141] in light of the controversial decision in *Office of Fair Trading v Abbey National plc* [1142] and in order to align it more closely with CJEU case-law. It now reads that terms

---

1138 Cf. footnotes 981 and 982.

1139 Regarding the difficulties to reconcile the widening with the CJEU's case-law in *Aziz*, cf. Whittaker, *supra* note 645, recitals 38-277, 38-390.

1140 Cf. also The Law Commission and the Scottish Law Commission, Unfair Terms in Consumer Contracts: Advice to the Department for Business, Innovation and Skills (March 2013), recital 7.65.

1141 For the Law Commission's advice on this matter, cf. ibid. recitals 3.80-3.109.

1142 [2009] UKSC 6 (see more below).

> may not be assessed for fairness under Section 62 to the extent that the assessment is of the appropriateness of the price payable under the contract by comparison with the goods, digital content or services supplied under it.

With respect to former provisions from the UCTA 1977 which are now incorporated in Section 65 CRA 2015, Section 66 Subsection 1 CRA 2015 excludes insurance contracts including contracts 'to pay an annuity on human life' and contracts 'so far as they relate to the creation or transfer on an interest in land' from the scope of applicability. Furthermore, Section 66 Subsection 3 CRA 2015 excludes from the scope terms in relation to liability which is excluded or discharged under Section 4 Subsection 2 and Section 5 Damages (Scotland) Act 2011. According to Section 66 Subsection 4 CRA 2015 Section 65 also does not apply to certain liability of an 'occupier of premises to a person who obtains access to the premises for recreational purposes'.

Section 72 Subsection 2 CRA 2015, furthermore, extends the term control to terms included in secondary contracts that purport to '[reduce] the rights or remedies or [increase] the obligations of a person under another contract [...]'. The secondary contract does not have to be concluded by the same parties as the other contract and does not have to be a consumer contract covered under Part 2 CRA 2015 (Section 72 Subsection 3 CRA 2015) unless the contract is the settlement of a claim arising under the other contract (Section 72 Subsection 4 CRA 2015).

in concreto

The transparency test is now contained in Section 68 CRA 2015 which requires that a written term (Subsection 1) or consumer notice (Subsection 2) must be transparent, meaning that it must be expressed in plain and intelligible language and legible (Section 64 Subsection 3 CRA 2015). Section 69 Subsection 1 CRA 2015 implements Art. 5 UCTD in that it prescribes the *contra preferentem* rule as a consequence of failing to match the requirement of transparency.

The fairness test is implemented in Section 62 CRA 2015. As stated above it applies to all kinds of terms and does not exclude individually negotiated terms from the assessment. The rest of the provision remains the same. Furthermore, the UCTD's Annex's indicative list is implemented in Schedule 2 of the CRA 2015 (Section 63 CRA 2015). Three more terms have been added to the indicative list (Schedule 2 Part 1 Sections 5[1143], 12[1144] and 14[1145]). Further examples can be added by the Secretary of State (Section 63 Subsection 3 CRA 2015).

Section 65 CRA 2015 provides for the former UCTA 1977 control mechanisms relating terms in consumer contracts. Section 65 Subsection 1 provides for the absolute ineffectiveness of terms aiming to exclude or limit liability for death or personal injury. Section 65 Subsection 2 CRA 2015 emphasises that agreement to or knowledge of a term or notice excluding or limiting liability for negligence does not amount to acceptance of such.

According to Section 71 Subsection 2 CRA 2015 and in accordance with CJEU case-law depicted above, courts are under a duty to consider 'whether the term is fair even if none of the parties to the proceedings has raised that issue or indicated that it intends to raise it' as long as 'the court considers that it has before it sufficient legal and factual material to enable it to consider the fairness of the term' (Section 71 Subsection 3 CRA 2015).[1146]

Section 67 CRA 2015 resembles Art. 6 UCTD and provides that an unfair term is not binding on the consumer while the rest of the contract remains enforceable.

in abstracto

Section 70 in connection with Schedules 3 and 5 of the CRA 2015 confers powers to the CMA with respect to the enforcement of Part 2 CRA 2015. Schedule 3 sets out the powers to initiate proceedings for injunctions on behalf of regulators, including the CMA and other regulators (see Section 8 Schedule 3 of the CRA 2015), formerly known as qualifying bodies un-

---

1143 A term which has the object or effect of requiring that, where the consumer decides not to conclude or perform the contract, the consumer must pay the trader a disproportionately high sum in compensation or for services which have not been supplied.

1144 A term which has the object or effect of permitting the trader to determine the characteristics of the subject matter of the contract after the consumer has become bound by it. This Section is subject to limitation by Schedule 2 Part 2 Section 23.

1145 A term which has the object or effect of giving the trader the discretion to decide the price payable under the contract after the consumer has become bound by it, where no price or method of determining the price is agreed when the consumer becomes bound. This Section is subject to limitation by Schedule 2 Part 2 Sections 23-25.

1146 For a critical account of the legislative implementation of this duty, cf. Whittaker, *supra* note 645, recital 38-392.

der the UTCCRs 1999. Both the CMA and other regulators can initiate such proceedings (Section 3 Schedule 3 of the CRA 2015) upon complaints (Section 2 Schedule 3 of the CRA 2015). If a regulator other than the CMA considers a complaint or undertaking by an individual relevant to pursue proceedings upon it, the regulator must notify the CMA (Section 2 Subsection 2 and Section 6 Subsection 3 Schedule 3 of the CRA 2015). A regulator may apply for an injunction if a term or notice is unfair, it excludes liability for goods, digital content or services contracts, it excludes 'business liability for death or personal injury resulting from negligence' or if the term is untransparent (Section 3 Subsections 2 to 5 Schedule 3 of the CRA 2015). The regulator may also apply for an injunction if it has not received a complaint on the particular issue (Section 3 Subsection 6 Schedule 3 of the CRA 2015).

Furthermore, similar to the UTCCRs 1999 the CMA is still under a duty to publish information on proceedings and may publish general guidelines on unfair terms according to Section 7 Schedule 3 of the CRA 2015. In addition to Schedule 3 of the CRA 2015, Schedule 5 of the CRA 2015 sets out the investigatory powers by enforcers. Unfair contract term enforcers include the regulators under Schedule 3 (see Section 6 Schedule 5 of the CRA 2015).

Beside the power to apply for an injunction, enforcers, including the regulators under Schedule 3 of the CRA 2015, may initiate enforcement measure proceedings under Part 8 Enterprise Act 2002. As a specified law implementing an EU Directive Part 2 CRA 2015 falls under Section 212 Enterprise Act 2002[1147] a breach of any provision of Part 2 CRA can constitute a domestic infringement under Section 211 Enterprise Act 2002. According to Schedule 7 CRA 2015, a newly inserted Section 219A Enterprise Act will include enhanced consumer measures available in case of domestic infringements, such as 'measures offering compensation or other redress to consumers who have suffered a loss as a result of the conduct which has given rise to the enforcement order or undertaking' (Section 219A Subsection 2 lit. (a) Enterprise Act 2002). Section 219C Enterprise Act 2002 would also create a limited power on behalf of private enforcers to issue enhanced consumer measures.

With respect to the widened powers of enforcers *Whittaker* has noted that these could lack compatibility with EU law. He explains his doubts with the maximum harmonisation character of the Unfair Commercial

1147 Cf. Art. 2 Section 2 Enterprise Act 2002 (Part 8 Community Infringements and Specified UK Laws) (Amendment) Order 2015, SI 2015/1628 (1 October 2015).

Practices Directive.[1148] The gold-plating of the minimum harmonisation Unfair Contract Terms Directive must not collide with the maximum harmonisation Unfair Commercial Practices Directive. As it is possible that the use of unfair terms also constitutes an unfair commercial practice, courts must, thus, first evaluate if the use of unfair terms constitutes an unfair commercial practice before resorting to the measures under the CRA 2015. This may prove to be an especially difficult task with respect to the provisions deriving from the UCTA 1977.[1149] I agree with *Whittaker* on this point. However, the situation may have changed in light of the planned EU expansion of the courts' power to impose penalties in case of infringements of the UCTD under the newly envisaged Art. 8b UCTD (see pages 233 et seq. above) and the newly proposed Art. 11a Unfair Commercial Practices Directive which provides that

> Member States shall ensure that contractual and non-contractual remedies are also available for consumers harmed by unfair commercial practices in order to eliminate all the effects of those unfair commercial practices in accordance with their national law [and that] [...] [contractual] remedies shall include, as a minimum, the possibility for the consumer to unilaterally terminate the contract.[1150]

This would resemble the enhanced consumer measures in Section 219A Enterprise Act 2002. Thereby, the envisioned UK enforcement measures could fit in with the Unfair Commercial Practices Directive. It is, however, questionable whether the private enforcement of such measures breaches EU law, especially in light of the CJEU case-law in *Biuro podróży 'Partner'*.[1151] In any case, if the UK leaves the EU and is not bound by the Unfair Commercial Practices Directive anymore it would be free to implement the original enhanced consumer measures envisaged under Schedule 7 of the CRA 2015.

1148 Whittaker, *supra* note 645, recital 38-422.

1149 Ibid. recital 38-426.

1150 Art. 1 Proposal for a Directive of the European Parliament and the Council amending Council Directive 93/13/EEC of 5 April 1993, Directive 98/6/EC of the European Parliament and of the Council, Directive 2005/29/EC of the European Parliament and of the Council and Directive 2011/83/EU of the European Parliament and of the Council as regards better enforcement and modernisation of EU consumer protection rules, COM(2018) 185 final (11 April 2018).

1151 Cf. *supra* note 1028.

II. Adjudication of Unfair Terms (in Consumer Contracts) Legislation

The following section looks at the court case-law as well as measures taken by the CMA (formerly OFT) with respect to the UTCCRs 1999 and the CRA 2015.

1. The Courts

A comparatively low number of cases regarding the interpretation of the UTCCRs 1999 (and the CRA 2015) has made it up to the UK Supreme Court (formerly House of Lords). This may be explained by the easy availability of the CMA (formerly OFT) to launch complaints and the high costs involved in court proceedings in the UK.[1152] Thus, two of the three cases under which the Supreme Court (formerly House of Lords) discussed the UTCCRs 1999 in detail were brought by the Director General of Fair Trading and the OFT. While the establishment of a powerful public authority to administer complaints, launch investigations and apply for collective injunctions can constitute as a powerful tool to enforce the UCTD, it also appears necessary in light of high costs for (oftentimes) relatively small individual claims with respect to infringements related to the UTCCRs 1999 and CRA 2015. This first section depicts the three cases dealt with by the Supreme Court (formerly House of Lords) and provides a list of cases in which clauses have been found unfair while the next section takes a look at the actions taken by the CMA (formerly OFT).

Director General of Fair Trading v First National Bank plc (2001)[1153]
This was the first case in which the House of Lords discussed the UTCCRs. The House of Lords specifically dealt with the fairness test and the core exclusion from such. The Director General of Fair Trading challenged the following term contained in consumer credit agreements:

> Interest on the amount which becomes payable [upon default] shall be charged in accordance with [the contractual rates under Condition 4]

1152 Cf. Report prepared for the European Commission, 'Study on the Transparency of Costs of Civil Judicial Proceedings in the European Union', Annex 50: Country Report United Kingdom (30 December 2007).

1153 [2001] UKHL 52.

> [...] until payment after as well as before any judgment (such obligation to be independent of and not to merge with the judgment).[1154]

The court rejected a possible exclusion because of a relation to the bank's remuneration and stated that the core exclusion was to be interpreted narrowly. In this regard, Lord Bingham argued that a broad interpretation would contravene the objective of the Directive to provide protection against unfair terms in consumer contracts. A provision that prescribes an increased interest payable in case the creditor achieves a judgment against the borrower upon default, therefore, would not fall within it.[1155]

Lord Bingham went on to consider whether the term was fair and first evaluated the concept of fairness and good faith under the UCTD as follows:

> The requirement of good faith in this context is one of fair and open dealing. Openness requires that the terms should be expressed fully, clearly and legibly, containing no concealed pitfalls or traps. Appropriate prominence should be given to terms which might operate disadvantageously to the customer. Fair dealing requires that a supplier should not, whether deliberately or unconsciously, take advantage of the consumer's necessity, indigence, lack of experience, unfamiliarity with the subject matter of the contract, weak bargaining position or any other factor listed in or analogous to those listed in [Recital 16 of the UCTD]. Good faith in this context is not an artificial or technical concept [...]. It looks to good standards of commercial morality and practice. Regulation 4(1) lays down a composite test, covering both the making and the substance of the contract, and must be applied bearing clearly in mind the objective which the regulations are designed to promote.

Lord Bingham's interpretation reflects the English approach to 'good faith' as a holistic measure of contractual interpretation. While the Court of Appeal had held that the clause in question was unfair, the House of Lords reversed this decision unanimously. Lord Bingham stated that the term was fair because charging interest was included in the 'essential bargain' of the contract. He argued that the provisions on interest balanced the obliga-

1154 Ibid. at [2] per Lord Bingham.
1155 Ibid. at [12].

tions rather than causing a detrimental imbalance.[1156] Sufficient safeguards for consumers upon default were included in the CCA 1974.[1157]

Office of Fair Trading v Abbey National plc and others (2009)[1158]

The second case in front of the Supreme Court was decided in 2009. The OFT claimed that certain 'relevant charges'[1159] for current account customers were unfair. The question arose whether terms relating to such charges fell under the core exclusion relating to the adequacy of remuneration. Unlike the Court of Appeal that had relied on the perspective of the rational consumer when assessing whether a term can be considered part of the remuneration and, thus, held that the charges did not form part of the remuneration of the bank,[1160] the Supreme Court, nevertheless, held that the charges fell under the exclusion because the charges constituted a considerable part of the bank's revenue stream and formed 'an important part of the bank's charging structure'.[1161] It was, furthermore, argued that the bank's remuneration included the 'customer's potential liability' under a 'package of services offered by the banks' rather than the charges that are actually incurred.[1162] Thus, even if the charges were not excluded they could only be assessed as part of the whole packages of services, rather than singled out measures.[1163] The Supreme Court did not refer the matter to the CJEU regarding it as an *acte clair*.[1164]

The precedent set in *Abbey National* has been followed by subsequent English case-law.[1165] However, it is in clear conflict with the narrow inter-

1156 Ibid. at [20].

1157 Ibid. at [23].

1158 [2009] UKSC 6.

1159 Including unpaid item charges, paid item charges, overdraft excess charges and guaranteed paid item charges. For more details, cf. EWCA Civ 116 at [4] per Clarke MR.

1160 Ibid. at [91], [112] per Clarke MR.

1161 [2010] 1 AC 696 at [47] per Lord Walker.

1162 Ibid. at [98] per Lord Mance.

1163 Ibid. at [99] per Lord Mance.

1164 Ibid. at [49] per Lord Walker, at [91] per Baroness Hale and at [115] per Lord Mance. Dissenting on the issue at [91] per Lord Phillips and at [120] per Lord Neuberger.

1165 Cf. *Office of Fair Trading v Ashbourne Management Services Ltd* [2011] EWHC 1237 (Ch) (termination and penalty clause under contract for gym membership held unfair); *Foxtons Ltd v O'Reardon* [2011] EWHC 2946 (QB) at [56] per Seymour J (payment of agent's fee upon exchange of contracts excluded from review).

pretation under CJEU case-law depicted above.[1166] Nevertheless, it appears that English courts still follow the precedent set by *Abbey National* despite the conflict with European case-law.[1167] The continued application of the Supreme Court's case-law preceding the CJEU's, nowadays, settled case-law on the narrow interpretation of the core exclusions constitutes a clear breach of European law.

ParkingEye Limited v Beavis (2015)[1168]

While following the decision in *First National Bank* the courts had basically followed Lord Bingham's approach to the interpretation of a 'significant imbalance' and 'good faith',[1169] the Supreme Court expressly considered the CJEU's application of the fairness test in *Aziz* in its decision in *ParkingEye Ltd v Beavis*.[1170] The case concerned a car park where customers could park for free for up to two hours under conditions listed on a sign but would have to pay GBP 85 for staying any longer or not complying with the conditions listed on the sign. In this regard, ParkingEye Ltd had set up 20 large and legible signs to draw the customers' attention to the parking conditions.[1171] As a customer, Mr. Beavis, overstayed for more than an hour and ParkingEye Ltd sued him for the charges owed under the parking conditions. The Supreme Court held that the imposition of the penalty charge was fair in accordance with the UCTD and especially in light of the CJEU case-law in *Aziz*.[1172] With reference to Advocate General Kokott's opinion in *Aziz* who had pointed out that the evaluation of a 'significant imbalance' must consider the legitimate interests of both parties[1173] the Supreme Court found that there was an imbalance in the parties rights and obligations but that this imbalance was justified by the legitimate interest of the car park operator and land owner to ensure an efficient use of the car park.[1174] In contrast, Lord Toulson dissented with reference to the hy-

1166 Cf. CJEU judgment C-26/13, *Kásler* [2014] recital 59.

1167 *Casehub Ltd v Wolf Cola Ltd* [2017] EWHC 1169 (Ch) at [53]-[54] per Isaacs QC (cancellation fee in case of early termination excluded under Section 64 CRA 2015). For a critical view, cf. Whittaker, *supra* note 645, recital 38-426.

1168 [2015] UKSC 67.

1169 Cf. *Stephen West and Carol West v Ian Finlay Associates* [2014] EWCA Civ 316 at [51], [55] and [60] per Vos LJ (as he then was).

1170 [2015] UKSC 67 at [105] per Lord Neuberger and Lord Sumption.

1171 Ibid. at [90]-[91] per Lord Neuberger and Lord Sumption.

1172 Ibid. at [106]-[107] per Lord Neuberger and Lord Sumption.

1173 Ibid. at [106] per Lord Neuberger and Lord Sumption.

1174 Ibid. at [107] per Lord Neuberger and Lord Sumption.

pothetical test of whether the consumer would have agreed to the term in individual negotiations.[1175] Lord Mance avoided a conclusion under the hypothetical test and instead resorted to the factual circumstances of the case, such as the clear notice and the proportionate charge, to evaluate the term as fair.[1176]

Further Unfair Clauses

The following list provides examples for terms that have been held unfair by courts under the UTCCRs 1999:[1177]

- A clause under which builders excluded their liability under contracts for sale for new homes to carry out the design works with the necessary skill and care despite legal advice on behalf of the purchasers[1178]
- An arbitration clause which entailed that the consumer would have to initiate separate proceedings for defects under the National House Builders Council "Build Mark" Agreement and for other defects[1179]
- An untransparent arbitration clause under which the proceedings were disproportionately expensive in relation to the sums involved[1180]
- A term which provided that the customer would have to indemnify the trader for legal and other costs in all actions or proceedings[1181]
- A term under which an estate agent charged commission in case of renewal of a lease or the purchase of the property by the tenant[1182]

It can be concluded from the examples that the UTCCRs 1999 have been applied in various cases and circumstances and, thus, as intended, provide a broad consumer protection mechanism with respect to unfair terms.

1175 Ibid. at [308], [314] per Lord Toulson.

1176 Ibid. at [212] per Lord Mance. Cf. also Whittaker, *supra* note 645, recital 38-277.

1177 For more examples, cf. Whittaker, ibid., recitals 38-299-38-323.

1178 *Harrison v Shepherd Homes Ltd* [2011] EWHC 1811 (TCC) at [114] per Ramsey J.

1179 *Zealander & Zealander v Laing Homes Ltd* (2000) 2 TCLR 724 at 730 per Havery J.

1180 *Mylcrist Builders Ltd v Buck* [2008] EWHC 2172 (TCC) at [54]-[59] per Ramsey J.

1181 *Munkenbeck & Marshall v Harold* [2005] EWHC 356 (TCC) at [15] per Havery J.

1182 *Office of Fair Trading v Foxtons Ltd* [2009] EWHC 1681 (Ch) at [91]-[95], [107] per Mann J.

2. The CMA (formerly OFT)

The CMA (formerly OFT) is the main enforcement authority when it comes to unfair terms in consumer contracts. As explained above, the CMA is responsible both for publishing general guidance material on unfair terms as well as investigating cases involving the use of unfair terms including possibly the application for an injunction.

Guidance

The latest guidance document on unfair terms was released by the CMA in 2015.[1183] In the main part the guidance explains the functioning of Part 2 CRA 2015 while Annex A includes examples of unfair terms that had already been published by the OFT. With respect to the fairness test the CMA refers to already depicted English case-law.[1184] The terms listed in the Annex constitute examples of terms that have once actually been used by businesses and were investigated by the OFT and eventually deleted or amended afterwards.

Investigations and subsequent guidance of the OFT have focussed on various sectors specifically. Such sectors include care home contracts,[1185] tenancy agreements,[1186] terms in home improvements,[1187] health and fitness club contracts,[1188] holiday caravan agreements,[1189] consumer entertainment[1190] and package holiday contracts[1191].

More recently, the CMA started a campaign 'Check in on your terms' to promote the rules on unfair terms and encourage businesses to review

---

1183 CMA, Unfair contract terms guidance: Guidance on the unfair terms provisions in the Consumer Rights Act 2015, CMA37 (31 July 2015).

1184 Ibid. recitals 2.1-2.41.

1185 OFT, Guidance on unfair terms in care home contracts: A guide for professional advisers, OFT635 (1 October 2003).

1186 OFT, Guidance on unfair terms in tenancy agreements, OFT356 (1 September 2005).

1187 OFT, Guidance on unfair terms in home improvements contracts, OFT737 (1 March 2005).

1188 OFT, Guidance on unfair terms in health and fitness club agreements OFT373 (1 April 2002).

1189 OFT, Guidance on unfair terms in holiday caravan agreements, OFT734 (1 September 2005).

1190 OFT, Guidance on unfair terms in consumer entertainment contracts, OFT667 (1 December 2003).

1191 OFT, Guidance on unfair terms in package holiday contracts, OFT668 (1 March 2004).

their terms.[1192] Furthermore, the CMA has recently begun an investigation regarding cancellation policies in connection with the Covid-19 pandemic relating especially to weddings and private events, holiday accommodation and nurseries and childcare providers.[1193]

Investigations

The Annex indicates successful investigations on behalf of the OFT. While legislation on unfair terms has been amended since, the Annex can still serve as guidance as to which terms are considered fair or not under English law. The Annex only includes a summary of such terms because the number of successfully challenged terms 'runs into thousands'.[1194] The large number of cases pursued by the OFT is also reflected in the Unfair Contract Terms Bulletins which were frequently published between 1997 and 2004.[1195]

The work of the OFT (now CMA) has generally received favourable reviews. The National Audit Office (NAO) noted in 1999 that the OFT had 'settled [all but one case] through advice and undertakings'[1196] indicating the OFT had been successful at removing unfair terms from the market through negotiation. Thereby, the OFT had 'secured substantial financial benefits for consumers by acting under the Unfair Terms in Consumer Contracts Regulations'.[1197] Businesses told the NAO 'that the OFT's intervention had led to revised contracts that are easier for consumers to read

1192 CMA, 'Unfair terms won't protect your business' (*Competition and Markets Authority*) <https://fairterms.campaign.gov.uk> accessed 30 September 2019.

1193 CMA, 'COVID-19: CMA to investigate cancellation policy concerns' (*Competition and Markets Authority*, 30 April 2020) < https://www.gov.uk/government/news/covid-19-cma-to-investigate-cancellation-policy-concerns> accessed 28 August 2020; CMA 'Statement on coronavirus (COVID-19), consumer contracts, cancellation and refunds (Updated 28 August 2020)' (*Competition and Markets Authority*, 30 April 2020) <https://www.gov.uk/government/publications/cma-to-investigate-concerns-about-cancellation-policies-during-the-coronavirus-covid-19-pandemic/the-coronavirus-covid-19-pandemic-consumer-contracts-cancellation-and-refunds> accessed 28 August 2020.

1194 CMA, Unfair contract terms guidance: Guidance on the unfair terms provisions in the Consumer Rights Act 2015, CMA37, Annex A (31 July 2015) recital A9.

1195 For examples, cf. Iain Ramsay, *Consumer Law and Policy: Text and Materials on Regulating Consumer Markets*, 320 et seq.

1196 NAO, Report by the Comptroller and Auditor General: The Office of Fair Trading: Protecting the Consumer from Unfair Trading Practices (2 December 1999), recital 3.37.

1197 Ibid. recital 3.39.

and understand'.[1198] The NAO's report in 2003 indicated that the number of complaints regarding unfair terms in consumer contracts constantly increased even causing delays in the administration of complaints.[1199] The Law Commission also acknowledged that

> [...] the work of the OFT's Unfair Contract Terms Unit has had a major impact on the market. The OFT has secured the removal of many unfair terms which were almost certainly invalid under UCTA; and this shows that allowing parties to challenge terms in their individual contracts, while invaluable for them, has a limited impact on contracting practice generally.[1200]

Even the European Commission noted in its evaluative report on the implementation of the UCTD in 2000 that

> [the OFT has] encouraged direct negotiations between individual professionals and professional associations, with considerable success. At the level of individual negotiation the case of the United Kingdom is particularly interesting, since the Office of Fair Trading plays a pivotal role in eliminating unfair terms.[1201]

And while some commentators have voiced doubts on the effectiveness of administrative collective control of unfair terms for *all* consumers,[1202] *Susan Bright* has endorsed the work of the OFT.[1203] She contends that the enforcement against unfair terms by the OFT proves to be 'a much more effective way of preventing the continuing use of unfair terms and changing contracting practice'.[1204] The interpretation of terms by the OFT turns out

---

1198 Ibid. recital 3.40.

1199 NAO, Report by the Comptroller and Auditor General: The Office of Fair Trading Progress in Protecting Consumers' Interests (6 March 2003), recitals 4, 10.

1200 The Law Commission and the Scottish Law Commission, Unfair Terms in Contracts: A Joint Consultation Paper, Law Com. Consultation Paper No. 166, Scot. Law Com Consultation Paper No. 119 (3 July 2002) recital 5.99.

1201 European Commission, Report from the Commission on the implementation of Council Directive 93/13/EEC of 5 April 1993 on unfair terms in consumer contracts, COM(2000) 248 final (27 April 2000) page 24.

1202 Cf. Victor Goldberg, 'Institutional Change and the Quasi-Invisible Hand' [1974] 17 (2) The Journal of Law & Economics 461 (489).

1203 Susan Bright, 'Winning the battle against unfair contract terms' [2000] 20 (3) Legal Studies 331-352.

1204 Ibid. (333).

to be 'overtly [pro-consumer]'.[1205] She argues that the traders fear 'bad publicity' and, therefore, usually agree to amend or delete unfair terms. For traders such negotiations also bear the advantage that they can rest assured that their terms are fair as well as enforceable against customers.[1206] She concludes that the enforcement by a public body is the most effective way to enforce unfair terms legislation compared to the enforcement by private bodies or private claims due to a lack of 'resources and motivation'.[1207]

In addition to the negotiating approach, *Ramsay* emphasises that the OFT from the mid-2000s onward started to rely on high-impact cases to affect the use of (un-)fair terms.[1208] For example, following the *Abbey National* case, many banks consequently revised their terms and conditions.[1209] He summarises the OFT as a 'bargaining agent for consumers'.[1210] The OFT does not only represent consumer interests but also encourages the introduction of industry-wide codes of practice.[1211]

I agree with both *Bright* and *Ramsay*. The administrative enforcement appears as a very effective way to combat unfair terms broadly. Singular court proceedings by individuals or private organisations only tackle specific terms on a limited scale,[1212] while the CMA (formerly OFT) has built a reputation as a reasonable negotiator as well as strong enforcer across industries. The numbers of amended and deleted terms that 'run into thousands' indicate the effectiveness of the CMA's (formerly OFT's) approach with respect to the removal of unfair terms from the market. They remove or amend terms collectively and, thereby, ensure consumer protection on a broad scale. However, it must also be acknowledged that the collective proceedings in the UK are necessary due to a lack of affordability for most consumers to pursue unfair term infringements individually. It may, thus, be questioned whether an (effective) equal procedural standing of collective and individual proceedings as required under European law is ensured in the UK.[1213]

1205 Ibid. (342).
1206 Ibid. (335).
1207 Ibid. (352).
1208 Ramsay, *supra* note 1195, 330 et seq.
1209 Ibid. 344-345, 358.
1210 Ibid. 357.
1211 Ibid. 358.
1212 Cf. also Leff, *supra* note 96.
1213 Cf. Opinion of Advocate General Szpunar in CJEU Joined Cases C-381/14 and C-385/14, *Sales Sinués and Drame Ba* [2016] recitals 71, 73.

C. Consumer Image

With respect to unfair terms a shift in consumer images can be noted. Before the introduction of the UCTA 1977 the control of terms was limited to the principles of common law contract construction. The courts only intervened in rare cases with the exception of exemption and limitation clauses which were subject to a more rigorous review. The more interventionist case-law with respect to exemption and limitation clauses finally led to the introduction of the UCTA 1977 which preparatory works reveal concerns for vulnerable parties to the contract. Thus, especially with respect to consumers the legislator noted the need for a protective and interventionist measure. The test of reasonableness, thereby, allowed for a holistic assessment taking into account the interests and bargaining positions of the parties. Such picture of a rather vulnerable consumer is also reflected in the implementation of the UCTD. The concerns for consumer well-being encapsulated in the concept of good faith had not been a foreign concept to English law upon its introduction. Beside the exceptional regulation regarding unfair terms, English law is, however, still underlied by a rather liberal notion of the rational consumer.

D. Interim Conclusion

The previous sections have depicted the development of unfair term regulation before and after the introduction of the Unfair Contract Terms Directive.

First, it has been shown that traditionally the fairness of contract terms was not assessed under English common law contract construction. Principles of fairness, such as the doctrine of unconscionability exist but are only considered in a limited manner. With respect to exclusion and limitation clauses, however, courts had already adopted a strict approach using the *contra preferentem* rule.

Second, the special treatment of exclusion and exemption clauses was ultimately reflected in the introduction of the UCTA 1977 which provided for absolute and relative ineffectiveness of certain exclusion and limitation clauses relating to negligence and breaches of contract. The UCTA 1977 introduced the reasonableness test which gives courts the opportunity to conduct a holistic assessment of a term taking into account all the circumstances of the individual case.

Third, the UTCCRs were first introduced in 1994 and then revised in 1999. They provided an alternate regime of term control implementing the European Unfair Contract Terms Directive. While the two legislative instruments differed in scope, they also overlapped with respect to consumer contracts. The fairness test and the reasonableness test, despite their different wordings, also appear similar in that they offer the courts a measure to assess a term holistically. The UTCCRs 1999 and the provisions on consumer contracts under the UCTA 1977 were eventually replaced by Part 2 CRA 2015 which combined the two regimes.

Fourth, to many English common lawyers the fairness test first appeared (and may still appear) foreign due to its mention of 'good faith'. However, it has been shown that the UCTD has not introduced a general principle of good faith to English law, but rather refers to a limited concept which is distinctly European under the Directive. Lord Bingham's judgment in *First National Bank* as well as the guidance within the Directive itself and by the CJEU offer guidelines regarding the interpretation of the requirement. It has been shown that such a *specific* principle of good faith is not alien to English law but has rather been developed by English courts to fit into the common law tradition. Thus, the requirement of good faith under the UCTD is not as foreign as it may have appeared at first.

Fifth, a look at the case-law had revealed that meanwhile the UTCCRs 1994 and 1999 and the CRA 2015 have been applied frequently and to various kinds of clauses by the courts. However, with respect to the core exclusions *Abbey National* as well as subsequent case-law reveal deviations from the principles laid down by the CJEU. In case the UK will not be bound by the UCTD in the future, this could constitute a reason to amend legislation accordingly. The low number of cases in front of the Supreme Court does not, however, generally indicate a problematic adoption of the Directive; because sixth, the administrative enforcement of unfair term legislation plays a key role under the UK term control regime.

From the beginning the OFT has played a key role in enforcing unfair term legislation and has been very successful with a negotiating strategy as well as bringing high-impact cases to the courts. While the positive impact of the OFT's and CMA's work must be acknowledged, it may, however, be questioned whether consumers have equally easy access to collective and individual proceedings in the UK. In terms of effectiveness under EU law consumers should be free to decide whether to pursue a claim individually or collectively. In light of the high costs associated with court proceedings in the UK, the adherence with this European requirement may be questioned. Since the departure from the EU the UK is free to put more emphasis on the collective measures led by the CMA.

The expanded enhanced consumer measures (Schedule 7 of the CRA 2015) reflect the important role of the CMA (formerly OFT) and the UK legislator's willingness to provide for effective collective measures to combat the use of unfair terms on a broad scale. However, it has also been shown that the planned enhanced measures currently conflict with European unfair commercial practices law. The departure from the European Union offers an opportunity to introduce the enhanced consumer measures without conflicting with the principle of maximum harmonisation under the Unfair Commercial Practices Directive.

Finally, UK regulation of unfair terms appears effective under the economic parameters set out above. The CMA procedures offer a quick way to make businesses aware of their use of unfair terms. This potentially bears a positive effect on transaction costs as, on the one hand, businesses can follow the CMA's guidance on drafting (preventative effect) and, on the other hand, are quickly made aware by the CMA if their use of unfair terms is apparent (administrative intervention). For consumers this bears the positive effect that they can rely on the terms used in the market. Confident consumption bears as positive effect on demand and, thus, economic growth. Furthermore, the CMA offers consumers an efficient institution to seek relief. Rather than initiating long and costly court proceedings, the administrative body takes care of approaching businesses and initiating court proceedings if necessary. The enhanced consumer measures will strengthen the CMA's position and contribute to the preventative effect of administrative intervention in case of an alleged use of unfair terms.

Chapter 11: Unfair Terms in Consumer Contracts in Germany

The following chapter depicts the developments with respect to unfair terms in (consumer) contracts in Germany.

A. *History of Unfair Terms (in Consumer Contracts) in Germany*

Contractual term control has long formed an integral part of German private law. First, as an interpretative measure developed by German courts and later manifested in the Act dealing with the Law of General Terms and Conditions (*Gesetz zur Regelung des Rechts der Allgemeinen Geschäftsbedingungen*, hereinafter "AGBG") which served as an inspiration for the UCTD.

General terms and conditions first appeared in Germany in the 17th century[1214] and have been on the rise especially since the 19th century. The insurance industry, the transportation sector and banks were the first business sectors to use T&Cs as a mass phenomenon.[1215] First fragmented regulatory attempts can be traced back to laws in the former German small states[1216] but regulatory provisions applicable across the German Confederation were only introduced with the General German Commercial Code (*Allgemeines Deutsches Handelsgesetzbuch*) in 1861[1217]. The codification reflects the German civil law tradition. T&Cs were, however, treated like any other contractual clauses which reflects a traditional liberal view on term control in this area.[1218] The *contra preferentem* rule was applied to ambiguous terms.[1219] Furthermore, T&Cs were interpreted objectively, meaning

1214 Phillip Hellwege, *Allgemeine Geschäftsbedingungen, einseitig gestellte Vertragsbedingungen und die allgemeine Rechtsgeschäftslehre*, 3.

1215 Markus Stoffels, *AGB-Recht*, recital 15. For a detailed overview of developments beginning with Roman law, cf. Hellwege, ibid., 19 et seq.

1216 Cf. i.e. with respect to insurance contracts in Hamburg (1731), Lübeck (1757) and Prussia (1766), cf. Hellwege, ibid., 63-64, 76-77.

1217 Ibid. 42, 64.

1218 Ibid. 122, 126 et seq. However, *Hellwege* argues that even in the 19th century the normative character of T&Cs was acknowledged, cf. ibid. 122 et seq.

1219 Ibid. 132.

without regard for the parties' actual intentions unless they were clearly indicated.[1220]

The depicted liberal tendencies were typical for the first half of the 19th century when freedom of contract was a predominant theme and the market was liberalised, i.e. by the introduction of commercial freedom (*Gewerbefreiheit*) and the abolition of interest barriers.[1221] In the second half, however, more regulatory and judicial intervention is noticeable in light of the necessity to protect economically weaker contractual parties.[1222] This is also reflected in the case-law of the Imperial Court of Justice. Three approaches can be identified regarding the treatment of unfair terms in T&Cs.[1223] First, the courts interpreted clauses restrictively and applied the *contra preferentem* rule in cases of ambiguity (*Unklarheitenregel*). They did so especially with respect to clauses that shifted the risks of the contract to the customer, such as disclaimers of warranty and liability.[1224] However, thereby the courts often interfered with the contract itself rather than constructing it which amounted to a hidden review of content (*verdeckte Inhaltskontrolle*).[1225] Second, the courts reviewed the applicability of terms between the parties.[1226] Third, terms could be considered ineffective because of a breach of public policy (*Verstoß gegen die guten Sitten*) according to § 138 BGB if the trader exploited customers on the ground of a monopoly position.[1227] The Imperial Court of Justice classified such clauses by monopolists as ineffective due to an 'unlawful exercise of rights' ac-

1220 Ibid. 133. Cf. i.e. Imperial Court of Justice, judgment of the 13 December 1912, reference number: VII 228/12, RGZ 81, 117 at 119.

1221 Horst Locher, *Das Recht der Allgemeinen Geschäftsbedingungen*, 2.

1222 Ibid.

1223 Stoffels, *supra* note 1215, recital 22.

1224 Ibid. recital 23; Locher, *supra* note 1221, 8; Cf. i.e. Imperial Court of Justice, judgment of the 11 October 1918, reference number: VII 114/18, RGZ 94, 29 at 30.

1225 Stoffels, ibid., recital 23. Especially with respect to insurance contracts while terms in transportation contracts were reviewed openly, cf. Hellwege, *supra* note 1214, 197.

1226 Stoffels, ibid., recital 24; Locher, *supra* note 1221, 5.

1227 Stoffels, *supra* note 1215, recital 25. Cf. i.e. Imperial Court of Justice, judgment of the 15 December 1933, reference number: VII 292/33, RGZ 143, 24 at 28; Imperial Court of Justice, judgment of the 15 May 1920, reference number: I 25/20, RGZ 99, 107 at 109.

cording to the doctrine of good faith under § 242 BGB.[1228] However, the developed doctrines were criticised as too narrow.[1229]

The German Federal Supreme Court broadened the control measure regarding unfair terms in 1956.[1230] The Court developed the doctrine of 'unlawful exercise of rights' according to § 242 BGB further and held that in light of the 'modern multi-layered business world' it was impossible to introduce principles. On the basis of § 242 BGB the individual contractual relationship would have to be assessed and, if necessary, distinguished from other contractual relationships, i.e. business-to-business contracts from business-to-consumer contracts.[1231] The future case-law of the German Federal Supreme Court was, thus, based on the principle of 'abuse of contractual power' in light of § 242 BGB.[1232] In this regard the German Federal Supreme Court stated in 1965 that

> general terms and conditions can be considered ineffective if they contain unreasonable, surprising terms that embody the abusive pursuit of one-sided interests to the detriment of the business partner and after a balancing of interests contravene the usually required fairness in such transactions.[1233]

The Court, furthermore, emphasised the guiding character of existing statutory norms as follows:

> As far as the statutory dispositive provisions do not just result from considerations of expediency, but from the very nature of principles of justice, there must exist reasons for deviating from [these] provisions that justify a compatibility of the deviating term and the principles of law and fairness. […] The more [the respective dispositive provision is

1228 Imperial Court of Justice, judgment of the 14 August 1941, reference number: II 49/41, RGZ 168, 321 at 329-331.

1229 Cf. Ludwig Raiser, *Das Recht der allgemeinen Geschäftsbedingungen*, 280 et seq.

1230 German Federal Supreme Court, judgment of the 29 October 1956, reference number: II ZR 79/55, NJW 1957, 17 at 18-19.

1231 Ibid. at 18.

1232 Cf. German Federal Supreme Court, judgment of the 4 November 1964, reference number: VIII ZR 46/63, NJW 1965, 246 at 246.

1233 Ibid. at 246. 'Allgemeine Geschäftsbedingungen können danach der Rechtswirksamkeit entbehren, soweit sie unangemessene, überraschende Klauseln enthalten, in denen sich die Verfolgung einseitiger Interessen auf Kosten des Geschäftspartners verkörpert und die daher bei Abwägung der Interessen der normalerweise an solchen Geschäften beteiligten Kreise der Billigkeit widersprechen.' (Translation by author).

> based on considerations of justice], the higher is the standard for compatibility of deviation in general terms and conditions and the principle of good faith.[1234]

As has been pointed out with respect to consumer credit, this development exemplifies the modern use of § 242 BGB by the Federal Supreme Court. The general clause is not seen as a last resort but a general underlying theme of the law of obligations. Again – and much earlier than in the field of consumer credit – the courts assumed the leading role in developing the law. The theme of 'abuse of contractual power' reflects weaker party protection which had not previously been a general legal doctrine in the BGB. As has already been explained, § 242 BGB thereby also serves as a mean of introducing the welfare state principle to private law which had been foreign to BGB principles founded on the views of the 19th century liberal bourgeois population.[1235] The Federal Supreme Court's case-law on unfair terms reflects a willingness to make principled and normative decisions as guidelines for lower courts. Thereby new judicial doctrines are developed from 'top down' in contrast to traditional common law under which case-law and doctrines develop more gradually.[1236]

This concept of unfair term control pursuant to § 242 BGB contrasts with the approach under English law. Rather than a continuous development the Federal Supreme Court chose a principled approach introducing moral considerations rather than basing their decisions on classic contract law principles. The German approach thereby rather resembles equitable intervention under English law which, however, does not form the general base of term control under English law.

1234 Cf. German Federal Supreme Court, judgment of the 17 February 1964, reference number: II ZR 98/62, NJW 1964, 1123 at 1123. 'Soweit die Vorschriften des dispositiven Rechts ihre Entstehung nicht nur Zweckmäßigkeitserwägungen, sondern einem aus der Natur der Sache sich ergebenden Gerechtigkeitsgebot verdanken, müssen bei einer abweichenden Regelung durch Allgemeine Geschäftsbedingungen Gründe vorliegen, die für die von ihnen zu regelnden Fälle das dem dispositiven Recht zugrunde liegende Gerechtigkeitsgebot in Frage stellen und eine abweichende Regelung als mit Recht und Billigkeit vereinbar erscheinen lassen. [...] Je stärker [der Gerechtigkeitsgehalt der Norm] ist, ein desto strengerer Maßstab muß an die Vereinbarkeit von Abweichungen in Allgemeinen Geschäftsbedingungen mit dem Grundsatz von Treu und Glauben angelegt werden.' (Translation by author).

1235 Cf. Wieacker, *supra* note 117, 539-541, 543, 607, 622-623.

1236 Ibid. 607-608.

Beside the case-law, the issue of unfair terms in T&Cs was much discussed in academia from the 1930s onward.[1237] The most prominent author on unfair terms, *Ludwig Raiser*, laid the cornerstone with his monograph *Das Recht der allgemeinen Geschäftsbedingungen* in 1935. While he argued that T&Cs actually served a valuable purpose in a mass production and consumption society, he advocated rules to enable administrative authorities and courts to ensure that such T&Cs are used in a fair manner to prevent detrimental effects for both the individual consumer and society as a whole.[1238] He also inspired the German Federal Supreme Court to use dispositive statutory provisions as a guideline to assess the fairness of a term.[1239]

In the following years, a rich body of case-law on unfair terms and conditions emerged.[1240] The cases concerned, terms that excluded warranties and liability, limitation clauses, terms providing for limitation periods for customers' claims, lump-sum damages, penalty clauses, supplier's discretion clauses, the exclusion of customers' termination rights, terms of exclusivity, non-assignment clauses, the exclusion or limitation of set-offs, clauses regarding the burden of proof, shortened limitation periods, jurisdiction and arbitration clauses and clauses concerning interest rates.[1241]

The case-law as well as academic writing encouraged the legislator to develop statutory rules regarding the interpretation of T&Cs. Beside the wish to establish a solid legal framework to provide the courts with statutory orientation, the initiative was also and mainly motivated by the emerging consumer protection movement.[1242] The explanatory notes for the AGBG reveal that the legislator closely followed *Raiser's* suggestions:[1243] on the one hand, it emphasised the usefulness of T&Cs with respect to the rationalisation of mass transactions. On the other hand, it referred to the risks

1237 For an overview of literature published on T&Cs from 1935 onward, cf. Bundesminister der Justiz, Vorschläge zur Verbesserung des Schutzes der Verbraucher gegenüber Allgemeinen Geschäftsbedingungen, Erster Teilbericht der Arbeitsgruppe beim Bundesminister für Justiz (March 1974), pages 123 et seq.

1238 Raiser, *supra* note 1229, 98 et seq.

1239 Ibid. 293 et seq.

1240 Stoffels, *supra* note 1215, recital 32.

1241 Manfred Rehbinder, *Allgemeine Geschäftsbedingungen und die Kontrolle ihres Inhalts*, 24-25.

1242 Stoffels, *supra* note 1215, recital 34. Bundesminister der Justiz (1974), *supra* note 1237, page 19.

1243 Deutscher Bundestag, Entwurf eines Gesetzes zur Regelung des Rechts der Allgemeinen Geschäftsbedingungen (AGB-Gesetz), BT-Drs. 7/3919 (6 August 1975), page 10 with specific reference.

associated with the one-sided shift of risks to the detriment of the consumer. The legislator identified the powerful position of the term user as a danger to the principle of freedom of contract which 'cannot be accepted under a social market economy governed by the rule of law' especially in light of personal freedoms enshrined in Art. 2 Section 1 GG.[1244] The predominant aim of the AGBG was to balance the interests of the contractual parties and, thereby, legitimise T&Cs on the basis of the values embodied in the BGB. This aim is underlied by the assumption of an inequality of bargaining power in favour of the term user. The legislator, therefore, aimed to rebalance the parties' positions by introducing consumer protection provisions.[1245]

The AGBG was finally introduced in 1976 and came into force in 1977. With respect to procedural provisions the AGBG neither included provisions on a consumer protection authority nor on preventative model proceedings.[1246] However, under § 13 AGBGB it included the option for qualified entities (such as consumer protection organisations), business associations and the chambers of commerce and crafts to apply for injunctions (*Unterlassungsverfügung*). Furthermore, the court had to hand decisions to the Federal Cartel Office (*Bundeskartellamt*) which had to keep a register of all proceedings under §§ 13, 19 AGBG (§ 20 AGBG). The AGBG did not apply to contracts in the areas of employment, succession, family and company law (§ 23 Section 1 AGBG) as well as certain contracts in the transportation, telecommunication, postal, gas and electricity, building and insurance sectors (§ 23 Section 2 AGBG). It, furthermore, excluded the applicability in contracts with public entities and craftsmen (§ 24 AGBG). The AGBG did not solely apply to consumers.

Materially, the AGBG began by defining T&Cs under § 1 ABGB as

> all contract terms pre-formulated for more than two contracts which one party to the contract (the user) presents to the other party upon the entering into of the contract [...] It is irrelevant whether the provisions take the form of a physically separate part of a contract or are made part of the contractual document itself, what their volume is, what typeface or font is used for them and what form the contract

1244 Ibid. page 9. Cf. also Bundesminister der Justiz (1974), *supra* note 1237, 13-14.

1245 Deutscher Bundestag (1975), ibid., page 13.

1246 As had been previously suggested, cf. Bundesminister der Justiz, Vorschläge zur Verbesserung des Schutzes der Verbraucher gegenüber Allgemeinen Geschäftsbedingungen, Zweiter Teilbericht der Arbeitsgruppe beim Bundesminister für Justiz (March 1975), pages 16-19.

> takes. Contract terms do not become standard business terms to the extent that they have been negotiated in detail between the parties.

According to § 4 AGBG individually negotiated terms prevailed T&Cs (*Vorrang der Individualabrede*). Beside the definition of T&Cs, § 2 AGBG laid out under which circumstances such terms become part of the contract including the requirements for a clearly visible reference, the opportunity for the other party to take notice of the terms and the other parties' approval.

Formally, § 3 AGBG provided that clauses that surprised the other party, especially regarding the outward appearance of the contract, did not become part of the contract. In addition, § 5 AGBG codified the *contra preferentem* rule in case of ambiguity.

Substantively, § 9 AGBG included a general clause with respect to clauses that deviated from statutory law which stated that

> [provisions] in standard business terms are ineffective if, contrary to the requirement of good faith, they unreasonably disadvantage the other party to the contract with the user [and that an] unreasonable disadvantage is, in case of doubt, to be assumed to exist if a provision (1) is not compatible with essential principles of the statutory provision from which it deviates, or (2) limits essential rights or duties inherent in the nature of the contract to such an extent that attainment of the purpose of the contract is jeopardised.

In addition, § 10 AGBG included a grey list regarding, *inter alia*, variation and jurisdiction clauses. § 11 AGBG contained a black list regarding, *inter alia*, the exclusion of set-offs, lump sum damages clauses, liability for gross negligence and penalty clauses. The lists, thus, reflected previous case-law on unfair terms.

§ 6 Section 1 AGBG provided that in case a term was found unfair it became ineffective while the rest of the contract remained valid. In case, the term did not become part of the contract, statutory provisions replaced the respective term (Section 2). The whole contract became ineffective if the replacement according to Section 2 caused the other party of the contract unbearable hardship (Section 3).

The AGBG bore a striking resemblance with the Unfair Contract Terms Directive which was introduced later and clearly inspired by the German statute. It, thus, did not take much for the German legislator to implement the UCTD in 1996.[1247] § 24a AGBG amended the AGBG according to the Directive, namely broadening the scope of applicability for consumer contracts.

B. Legal Framework Today

In 2002 the provisions of the AGBG were incorporated in the BGB as part of the modernisation of the law of obligations.[1248] The material norms regarding T&Cs are now included in §§ 305 to 310 BGB while the procedural norms can be found in the UKlaG.

Generally, the norms on T&Cs contained in §§ 305 to 309 BGB apply to all, not just contracts between businesses (§ 14 BGB) and consumers (§ 13 BGB). Materially, the norms regulating T&Cs have not changed much compared to the preceding norms contained in the AGBG. § 305 BGB (formerly §§ 1 and 2 AGBG) defines T&Cs and together with §§ 305a (new) and 305b BGB (formerly § 4 AGBG) their incorporation into the contract. § 305c BGB and § 307 Section 1 Sentence 2 BGB (formerly §§ 3 and 5 AGBG) regulate surprising and ambiguous clauses and § 305c Section 2 BGB provides for the *contra preferentem* rule. § 306 BGB (formerly § 6 AGBG) provides for the legal consequences of non-incorporation or invalidity of a term. § 307 BGB (formerly § 9 AGBG) provides for the unfairness test adding in Section 1 Sentence 2 that a lack of clarity of the term can also lead to its invalidity. §§ 308 and 309 BGB (formerly §§ 10 and 11 AGBG) contain a grey list (§ 308 BGB) and a black list (§ 309 BGB) of terms.

§ 310 BGB contains exemptions formerly contained in §§ 23 and 24 AGBG with respect to certain provisions contained in §§ 305 to 309 BGB (§ 310 Sections 1, 2 and 4 BGB) as well as the additional provisions formerly contained in § 24a AGBG as a result of the implementation of the UCTD (§ 310 Section 3 BGB).

Beside the term control under §§ 307 to 309 BGB, the use of unfair terms can also constitute an unfair commercial practice under German law

1247 Gesetz zur Änderung des AGB-Gesetzes und der Insolvenzordnung, BGBl. I 1013, No. 36 (19 July 1996).

1248 Gesetz zur Modernisierung des Schuldrechts, BGBl. I 3138, No. 61 (29 November 2001).

under § 3 Act Against Unfair Competition (*Gesetz gegen den unlauteren Wettbewerb*, hereinafter "D-UWG").[1249]

C. *Abstract Control Mechanisms relating to Unfair Terms in Consumer Contracts*

Under German law there exist two possibilities of abstract term control: collective court proceedings initiated by qualified entities, especially consumer organisations and to a lesser extent term control by public administrative and supervisory authorities.

I. Consumer Organisations

Injunctions

According to § 1 in connection with § 3 UKlaG qualified entities, business associations and the chambers of commerce and crafts can initiate proceedings to obtain an injunction against the user of unfair terms. Qualified entities are such that include the representation of consumer interests by way of information and advice in their articles of incorporation and are of a certain size, durability and reliability who have successfully applied to be included on a list (§ 4 Section 2 Sentence 1 UKlaG) which is published by the Federal Office of Justice (*Bundesamt für Justiz*) each year according to § 4 Section 1 UKlaG.[1250] Furthermore, it is presumed that consumer organisations (*Verbraucherzentralen und andere Verbraucherverbände*) that are funded with public funds can be considered qualified bodies (§ 4 Section 2 Sentence 2 UKlaG). In case the claim concerns terms in insurance or capital investment contracts or contracts with building societies the BaFin must be heard by the court (§ 8 Section 2 UKlaG, also see below). If the court finds the term(s) in question unfair, they are regarded invalid insofar affected consumers refer to the injunction judgment (*Unterlassungsurteil*) (§ 11 Sentence 1 UKlaG) as long as the term user cannot submit that a subsequent decision of the Federal Supreme Court or the Joint Senate of the

1249 German Federal Supreme Court, judgment of the 31 May 2012, reference number: I ZR 45/11, NJW 2012, 3577 at [46], [47].

1250 Cf. Bundesamt für Justiz, Liste qualifizierter Einrichtungen gemäß § 4 des Unterlassungsklagengesetzes (UKlaG) (11 May 2021), currently listing 76 qualified bodies.

Highest Federal Courts (*Gemeinsamer Senat der Obersten Gerichtshöfe des Bundes*) has declared the term(s) regarding the transaction in question valid (§ 11 Sentence 2 in connection with § 10 UKlaG). The provisions of the UKlaG do not apply to labour law (§ 15 UKlaG) because the adjudication of labour disputes shall not take place in front of ordinary but specific labour courts.[1251] Before consumer organisations take a matter to the court they shall issue a warning (*Abmahnung*) against the user of alleged unfair terms.[1252] In case the warning proceedings are successful the user of unfair terms must compensate the issuer of the warning the necessary expenses (in analogy to § 12 Section 1 Sentence 2 D-UWG).[1253]

The German approach to assign collective term control measures to private actors was celebrated as progressive – especially compared to administrative measures – at first.[1254] However, it now receives criticism for being ineffective due to structural deficits.[1255] *Micklitz and Rott* point out that the *locus standi* of consumer organisations is limited by the requirements of § 4 Section 2 UKlaG (unlike that of business associations) and, thereby, unduly complicates proceedings for consumer organisations. While the Federal Ministry of Justice and Consumer Protection (*Bundesministerium für Justiz und Verbraucherschutz*) received suggestions for an additional administrative control mechanism positively,[1256] such further control mechanisms have not yet been implemented. For example, the German legislator waived the opportunity to introduce administrative competences in the course of the implementation of the Regulation on consumer protection cooperation (CPC) but rather still relied on private enforcement[1257]. However, in this regard the implementation of the revised CPC may shift more

---

1251 Stoffels, *supra* note 1215, recital 1217.

1252 Cf. Hans-W. Micklitz and Peter Rott, § 5 UKlaG. in Wolfgang Krüger and Thomas Rauscher (eds), *Münchener Kommentar zur ZPO (2017)*, recitals 9, 10; see also § 12 Section 1 D-UWG.

1253 Ibid. recitals 11 et seq.

1254 Cf. Hans-W. Micklitz and Peter Rott, Vorbemerkung zu § 1 UKlaG. in Wolfgang Krüger and Thomas Rauscher (eds), *Münchener Kommentar zur ZPO (2017)*, recital 16; Stoffels, *supra* note 1215, recital 1221 with further references.

1255 Micklitz and Rott, ibid., recitals 24, 49.

1256 Bundesministerium für Justiz und Verbraucherschutz, 'Verbraucherrechtstage 2016: Neue Wege in der Durchsetzung des Verbraucherrechts' (*Bundesministerium für Justiz und Verbraucherschutz*, 15 April 2016) <https://www.bmjv.de/SharedDocs/Artikel/DE/2016/04152016_Verbraucherrechtstage. html> accessed 16 October 2019.

1257 Cf. § 7 Law on the Enforcement of EC Consumer Protection (*EG-Verbraucherschutzdurchsetzungsgesetz*).

responsibility toward the administration.[1258] They also criticise that the information and registration system formerly contained in § 20 AGBG never really unfolded sufficient effect and was not implemented in the UKlaG.[1259] Furthermore, they claim that specific procedural norms regarding collective proceedings (*Verbandsverfahren*) should have been adopted instead of referring to the standard civil law procedural norms under the D-ZPO (see § 5 UKlaG), for example regarding the burden of proof.[1260]

In addition, consumer organisations tasked with the enforcement of unfair term control through collective proceedings are not equipped well enough financially to ensure broad and effective control that can also unfold preventative effect with respect to the introduction of unfair terms to the market.[1261] Furthermore, Germany lacks an institutional framework that would allow consumer organisations to negotiate unfair terms with (leading) business associations similar to examples of the CMA in the UK and the Consumer Authority in Norway (see below).[1262]

A study of proceedings initiated by consumer organisations between 2006 and 2010 revealed that the number of proceedings had been rising over the years.[1263] Consumer organisations had been successful in stopping the use of unfair terms by issuing warnings against the users of such terms.[1264] Similar results can be observed for proceedings between 2015

1258 Cf. Bundesministerium für Justiz und Verbraucherschutz, Referentenentwurf für den Entwurf eines Gesetzes zur Änderung des EG-Verbraucherschutzdurchsetzungsgesetzes (27 May 2019), page 24, which states that consumer organisations will no longer be able to assume some of the investigation and enforcement competences included in the Regulation (EC) No 2006/2004 of the European Parliament and of the Council of 12 December 2017 on cooperation between national authorities responsible for the enforcement of consumer protection laws and repealing Regulation (EC) No 2006/2004.

1259 Micklitz and Rott, *supra* note 1254, recital 20.

1260 Ibid. recitals 21-23. Unlike Caroline Meller-Hannich and Armin Höland, *Evaluierung der Effektivität kollektiver Rechtsschutzinstrumente für Verbraucher im nationalen Recht und rechtliche Bewertung ausgewählter Ansätze zu ihrer Fortentwicklung*, 139-140.

1261 Cf. Meller-Hannich and Höland, ibid., 14, 140; Micklitz and Rott, ibid., recital 37; Alexander Witt, Vor § 1 UKlaG. in Peter Ulmer, Hans Erich Brandner and Horst-Diether Hensen (eds), *AGB-Recht Kommentar*, recital 10.

1262 Micklitz and Rott, ibid., recital 49.

1263 Hans-W. Micklitz, Vorbemerkung zu § 1 UKlaG. in Wolfgang Krüger and Thomas Rauscher (eds), *Münchener Kommentar zur ZPO (2013)*, recital 33.

1264 Ibid. recitals 31, 33.

and 2018.[1265] Only a low number of cases enter court proceedings. In 2018 consumer organisations (*Verbraucherzentralen*) issued a total of 351 warnings regarding 2,476 unfair terms. 259 of such warnings (regarding 1,944 terms) resulted in declarations of discontinuance (DoDs). 69 warnings (regarding 401 terms) resulted in first instance court cases and seven such cases (regarding 20 terms) went up to a court of second instance. The following table illustrates further data for the years 2015 to 2017:

Year	Warnings (terms)	DoDs (terms)	1st Instance (terms)	2nd Instance (terms)	3rd Instance (terms)
2017	264 (1,398)	182 (953)	70 (445)	25 (90)	5 (14)
2016	229 (1,172)	137 (794)	62 (335)	23 (66)	4 (6)
2015	271 (1,201)	203 (949)	53 (210)	19 (43)	4 (15)

However, the study of numbers between 2006 and 2010 also observed that most (especially but not only court) proceedings were initiated by a few consumer organisations.[1266] *Micklitz*, therefore, criticised that it appeared as if the smaller consumer organisations funded by state governments (*Landesverbraucherzentralen*) were not as active due to the activity of larger publicly funded consumer organisations.[1267] Despite the high success rates of the analysed proceedings (ca. 90%) the overall system of abstract unfair term control remains ineffective due to the relatively low number of overall proceedings[1268] and lack of systematic control[1269]. Compared to the overall assumed numbers of unfair terms in use, the (successful) proceedings led by consumer organisations appear as 'a drop in the ocean' (*Tropfen auf den heißen Stein*).[1270] In practice, thus, an ambivalence of 'institutional effectiveness and the systematic deficiencies'[1271] can be observed.

Consumer organisations have also initiated 'high profile' court proceedings with respect to unfair terms in consumer contracts[1272] that receive a

1265 The data has been kindly provided by a representative of *Verbraucherzentrale Bundesverband e.V.*, a German publicly funded private consumer organisation, by way of e-mail (22 November 2019).

1266 Micklitz, ibid., recital 33.

1267 Ibid. recital 35; Micklitz and Rott, *supra* note 1254, recital 35.

1268 Micklitz and Rott, ibid., recitals 31, 37.

1269 Ibid. recital 36. For example, the state consumer organisations cannot make use of the titles acquired by the federal consumer organisations.

1270 Ibid. recital 31.

1271 Ibid.

1272 Cf. ibid. (fn 65); Witt, *supra* note 1261, recital 8.

lot of attention in the media[1273] and, therefore, bear a potential preventative effect in that they make businesses and consumers aware of unfair terms and cause businesses to change their T&Cs or prevent them from using such terms at all. Such cases included, *inter alia*, terms that provided for advance payment in package holiday[1274] and air travel contracts,[1275] processing charges in consumer credit contracts,[1276] terms providing for price increases in gas supply contracts,[1277] untransparent clauses in pension insurance contracts,[1278] terms regarding the repurchase value of life insurance contracts[1279] as well as several unfair clauses in contracts for the repair of motor vehicles[1280].

Removal of Terms

Because the use of unfair terms can be classified as an unfair commercial practice, consumer organisations can also claim for the unfair terms to be removed (*Beseitigungsanspruch*) and possibly for the consequential loss to be reimbursed (*Folgenbeseitigungsanspruch*)[1281] under § 8 Section 1 D-UWG and (in rare cases) for the profits accumulated based on the use of the res-

---

1273 Witt, ibid.

1274 German Federal Supreme Court, judgment of the 9 December 2014, reference number: X ZR 85/12, VuR 2015, 350.

1275 German Federal Supreme Court, judgment of the 16 February 2016, reference number: X ZR 97/14, NJW 2016, 2404.

1276 German Federal Supreme Court, judgment of the 13 May 2014, reference number: XI ZR 405/12, NJW 2014, 2420.

1277 German Federal Supreme Court, judgment of the 31 July 2013, reference number: VIII ZR 162/09, NJW 2013, 3647.

1278 German Federal Supreme Court, judgment of the 13 January 2016, reference number: IV ZR 38/14, VuR 2016, 145.

1279 German Federal Supreme Court, judgment of the 25 July 2012, reference number: IV ZR 201/10, NJW 2012, 3023.

1280 German Federal Supreme Court, judgment of the 14 July 1987, reference number: X ZR 38/86, NJW 1987, 2818.

1281 Cf. granting a claim for the reimbursement of consequential loss OLG Dresden, judgment of the 10 April 2018, reference number: 14 U 82/16, WM 2018, 1304 (currently heard at the German Federal Supreme Court, reference number: XI ZR 252/18); however, critically Bianca Baldus and Rainer Siedler, 'Kompensation von „Streuschäden“ im Bankgeschäft nach § 8 UWG?' [2018] 18 (10) BKR 412-420; Herrmann-Josef Bunte, 'Folgenbeseitigungsanspruch nach dem UWG bei unzulässigen AGB-Klauseln?' [2016] (20) ZIP 956-961; Tilman Schultheiß, 'Der Folgenbeseitigungsanspruch bei unwirksamen AGB' [2019] (1) WM 9-16.

pective unfair terms to be handed over and transferred to the Federal Budget (*Bundeshaushalt*) according to § 10 Section 1 D-UWG.

Musterfeststellungsklage

In 2018 the German legislator introduced a model declaratory action (*Musterfeststellungsklage*) as a mean of collective redress pursuant to §§ 606 et seq. D-ZPO.[1282] The new legal action aims at easing access to justice for consumers as well as relieving courts which would otherwise have to deal with claims regarding similar or the same matters separately.[1283] § 606 Section 1 D-ZPO provides that qualified entities according to the UKlaG which have at least 350 natural persons or ten further entities active in the same field as members (No. 1), have been included in the list of qualified entities according to § 4 UKlaG for at least four years (No. 2), mostly perform tasks of consumer education and advice according to their articles of association (No. 3), do not initiate the model declaratory action to obtain profits (No. 4) and only receive a maximum of 5% of their financial resources from businesses (No. 5). If such a qualified entity plans to initiate a model declaratory action it publishes the envisaged action in a special litigation register (*Klageregister*) at the Federal Office of Justice pursuant to § 607 D-ZPO in which consumers can subsequently register their claims according to § 608 D-ZPO. If the model declaratory action succeeds the consumer who previously registered his or her claim must then again to court to claim individual damages based on the model declaratory judgment (see §§ 611 to 613 D-ZPO).

As of the 31 August 2020, nine model declaratory actions had been registered with the Federal Office of Justice. Three proceedings have been successful in the first instance regarding the increase of rents due to modernisation measures,[1284] the variable calculation of interest for savings contracts[1285] and claims for subscription bonuses against an insolvent energy

1282 This mechanism still appears to be in line with the Injunctions Directive (EU) 2020/1828, Arts. 4 and 7. However, it may become necessary to expand the collective action to include measures of direct redress and injuctive measures, cf. Arts. 7-9.

1283 Cf. Deutscher Bundestag, Entwurf eines Gesetzes zur Einführung einer zivilprozessualen Musterfeststellungsklage, BT-Drs. 19/2439 (4 June 2018), page 16.

1284 OLG Munich, judgment of the 15 October 2019, reference number: MK 1/19, BeckRS 2019, 24323.

1285 OLG Dresden, judgment of the 17 June 2020, reference number: 5 MK 1/20, juris; OLG Dresden, judgment of the 22 April 2020, reference number: 5 MK 1/19, VuR 2020, 306.

provider[1286]. Two claims were discarded by courts due to a lack of standing on behalf of the respective consumer organisations.[1287] Three proceedings have been opened for registration but not decided by the respective courts.[1288] Lastly, a model declaratory action against Volkswagen AG with respect to the diesel emissions scandal had been heard by the OLG Brunswick;[1289] however, the parties concluded a settlement and the claimants withdrew their claims on the 4 May 2020. It is yet to be seen whether the model declaratory action provides an effective mean to combat consumer law infringements.[1290]

II. Public Administration

Public administrative bodies only have limited authority to control unfair terms (in consumer contracts) and none which derives from powers under the UCTD or its implementation. Such administrative term control (guided by §§ 307 to 309 BGB) is limited to a few (highly regulated) areas. For example, T&Cs used by building societies (*Bausparkassen*) are subject to a preventative term control by the BaFin according to § 9 Section 1 Law on Building Societies (*Gesetz über Bausparkassen*). Similarly, investment contract terms (*Anlagebedingungen*) are subject to preventative term control by the BaFin according to §§ 163, 267 Law on Capital Investment (*Kapitalanlagegesetzbuch*). Such preventative term control, however, does not unfold prejudicial effect. Thus, even authorised terms can be subject to judicial review.[1291] In addition, the BaFin is entitled to conduct subsequent term control where it appears necessary regarding insurance contracts to avoid and eliminate 'maladministration' (*Missstände*) according to § 298 Sec-

1286 OLG Munich, judgment of the 21 July 2020, reference number: MK 2/19, BeckRS 2020, 19794.

1287 OLG Stuttgart, judgment of the 20 March 2019, reference number: 6 MK 1/18, BKR 2019, 298; OLG Brunswick, judgment of the 12 December 2018, reference number: 4 MK 2/18, BKR 2019, 294.

1288 OLG Dresden, reference number: 5 MK 2/20; OLG Dresden, reference number: 5 MK 2/19; OLG Frankfurt (Main), reference number: 24 MK 1/18.

1289 OLG Brunswick, reference number: 4 MK 1/18.

1290 Cf. also Martin Beckmann and Guido Waßmuth, 'Die Musterfeststellungsklage (Teil II)' [2019] (3) WM 89 (96); Sabine Riesner, 'Sisyphusaufgabe: Vereinbarkeit von effektivem kollektivem Verbraucherschutz mit der Vermeidung einer kommerziellen Klageindustrie?' [2019] (32) ZIP 1507 (1515).

1291 Cf. Andreas Fuchs, Vor § 307 BGB. in Peter Ulmer, Hans Erich Brandner and Horst-Diether Hensen (eds), *AGB-Recht Kommentar*, recital 96.

tion 2 Law on the Supervision of Insurance Companies (*Gesetz über die Beaufsichtigung der Versicherungsunternehmen*).[1292] Furthermore, there used to exist approval procedures for T&Cs under competition law involving the Federal Cartel Office which have, however, been removed in 2007.[1293]

The BaFin is equipped with investigatory powers under the FinDAG. Pursuant to § 4 Section 1a Sentence 2 FinDAG the BaFin can take measures that are adequate and necessary to prevent or remove consumer rights' abuses with respect to businesses that fall under the supervision of the BaFin (i.e. mainly banks and insurers) if clarification is deemed necessary in light of consumer protection principles. Such measures include claims for injunctions as well as repayment claims if it is unlikely that individual consumers will initiate such claims themselves.[1294] The abuse of consumer rights includes infringements of § 307 Section 1 BGB.[1295]

D. Unfair Terms in Consumer Contracts in Court Practice

The rules on T&Cs have not only been developed by the courts until the introduction of the AGBG, but also applied frequently thereafter. Since the introduction of the AGBG the courts have produced over 15,000 decisions in relation to T&Cs.[1296] With respect to unfair terms in consumer contracts (involving § 310 Section 3 BGB and § 24a AGBG), there exist approximately 184 decisions by the German Federal Supreme Court alone.[1297] This number, also has to be seen in light of the fact that § 310 Section 3 BGB and § 24a AGBG as such have not unfolded large effect by themselves but only served to complement the existing norm structure of term control already contained in the AGBG.[1298] This means that, first, the number of cases dealing with unfair terms in consumer contracts not cit-

1292 Cf. ibid. recital 97.

1293 Cf. ibid. recitals 78, 82.

1294 Peter Rott, 'Thesen zur Durchsetzung des Verbraucherschutzrechts durch die BaFin' [2019] (26) WM 1189 (1192-1194).

1295 Ibid. (1192).

1296 Micklitz, *supra* note 189.

1297 The number is a result of a search of court cases involving "§ 310 Abs. 3 BGB" (111) and "§ 24a AGBG" (70) separately on the German law data base www.beck-online.de on the 27 October 2019. With respect to a search regarding cases that dealt only with "§ 307 BGB" the search found over 2,000 cases for the German Federal Supreme Court alone.

1298 Peter Ulmer and Carsten Schäfer, § 310 BGB. in Peter Ulmer, Hans Erich Brandner and Horst-Diether Hensen (eds), *AGB-Recht Kommentar*, recital 48.

ing § 310 Section 3 BGB (or § 24a AGBG) but diving right into the existing term control pursuant to §§ 305 et seq. BGB is presumably far higher and that, second, the impact of the UCTD can, therefore, said to be minimal.

It is, in this light, not possible for this analysis to portray all unfair terms that have been dealt with by the courts in the course of term control according to §§ 305 et seq. BGB. Instead, the analysis will shortly depict some areas which have been focus points of term control by the courts to depict the area-specific relevance of term control under German law and allow for a comparison with the other depicted legal systems. The following cases do not necessarily only relate to consumer cases but shall serve to illustrate some of the German Federal Supreme Court's case-law on unfair terms.

Banking and Consumer Credit

Many cases regarding the control of unfair terms have arisen in the banking sector. Most cases concerned the validity of banking fees,[1299] for example regarding a fee for the deposit of money at the bank counter (held unfair),[1300] arrangement fees for a building loan agreement (held fair)[1301] or a fee for the transfer of a securities account (held unfair)[1302]. The German Federal Supreme Court has, thereby, developed case-law under which it evaluates the fairness of term by assessing whether the activity charged is included in the duties legally required of a bank. Such costs must not be charged separately but included in the main price catalogue, i.e. part of the

1299 For an overview of invalid remuneration clauses, cf. Andreas Fuchs, (8) Banken (Kreditinstitute). in Peter Ulmer, Hans Erich Brandner and Horst-Diether Hensen (eds), *AGB-Recht Kommentar*, recitals 48 et seq.; Wolfgang Wurmnest, § 307 BGB. in Franz Jürgen Säcker and others (eds), *Münchener Kommentar zum Bürgerlichen Gesetzbuch (2019)*, recitals 195 et seq. However, under the revised law on payment services (under EU Directive 2015/2366, cf *supra* note 630) many such fees may now constitute the main subject matter of the contract and, thus, cannot be assessed under the UCTD anymore (but see unfavourable Federal Supreme Court, judgment of the 12 September 2017, reference number: XI ZR 590/15, NJW 2017, 3649).

1300 German Federal Supreme Court, judgment of the 30 November 1993, reference number: XI ZR 80/93, NJW 1994, 318., cf. for a deviating opinion in light of the new payment services Directive, OLG Munich, judgment of the 12 October 2017, reference number: 29 U 4903/16, ZIP 2018, 213.

1301 German Federal Supreme Court, judgment of the 7 December 2010, reference number: XI ZR 3/10, NJW 2011, 1801 (*Schwäbisch Hall*).

1302 German Federal Supreme Court, judgment of the 30 November 2004, reference number: XI ZR 200/03, NJW 2005, 1275.

interest rates or for account management fees.[1303] A lot of cases have arisen specifically regarding (consumer) credit agreements. Rather than referring to specific (consumer) credit regulatory norms, most cases concerned (unfair) terms in such agreements.[1304] Such cases especially concerned handling fees[1305] and default interest[1306].

Insurance Contracts

Another important area of term control are insurance contracts.[1307] Beside specific term control norms in the German Insurance Contract Act (*Versicherungsvertragsgesetz*), §§ 305 et seq. BGB apply to terms in insurance contracts. Examples for invalid terms in insurance contracts include an unfair term in a travel health insurance agreement which excluded the insurer's liability in case the sickness or injury could or should have been treated before travelling,[1308] unfair limitation clauses regarding psychological treatments contained in private health insurance policies,[1309] an unfair ten-year-prolongation clause included in an accident insurance policy,[1310] an untransparent exclusion clause contained in a credit instalment insurance (*Ratenschutzversicherung*) relating to 'serious illness'[1311] and untransparent

1303 Stoffels, *supra* note 1215, recitals 521a, 521b. Cf. also German Federal Supreme Court, judgment of the 30 November 1993, reference number: XI ZR 80/93, NJW 1994, 318 (319) and German Federal Supreme Court, judgment of the 13 November 2012, reference number: XI ZR 500/11, NJW 2013, 995.

1304 For an overview, cf, Andreas Fuchs, (16) Darlehensverträge. in Peter Ulmer, Hans Erich Brandner and Horst-Diether Hensen (eds), *AGB-Recht Kommentar*, recitals 1 et seq.; Wurmnest, *supra* note 1299, recitals 208 et seq.

1305 Cf. i.e. German Federal Supreme Court, judgment of the 13 May 2014, reference number: XI ZR 170/13, WM 2014, 1325.

1306 Cf. Fuchs, *supra* note 1304, recitals 21-24.

1307 For an overview, cf. Harry Schmidt, (54) Versicherungsbedingungen. in Peter Ulmer, Hans Erich Brandner and Horst-Diether Hensen (eds), *AGB-Recht Kommentar*, recitals 1 et seq.

1308 German Federal Supreme Court, judgment of the 2 March 1994, reference number: IV ZR 109/93, NJW 1994, 1534.

1309 Cf. i.e. German Federal Supreme Court, judgment of the 16 June 2014, reference number: IV ZR 257/03, VuR 2005, 22; German Federal Supreme Court, judgment of the 17 March 1999, reference number: IV ZR 137/98, NJW 1999, 3411.

1310 German Federal Supreme Court, judgment of the 13 July 1994, reference number: IV ZR 107/93, NJW 1994, 2693.

1311 German Federal Supreme Court, judgment of the 10 December 2014, reference number: IV ZR 289/13, WM 2015, 223.

clauses relating to the repurchase value and calculation of costs included in life insurance policies[1312].

Telecommunication Contracts

The courts have also heard several cases regarding telecommunication contracts.[1313] Beside the specific norms contained in the German Telecommunication Act (*Telekommunikationsgesetz*), §§ 305 et seq. BGB determine the term control of clauses included in agreements of telecommunication services. Unfair clauses included a term that provided for 'non-usage',[1314] fees for changing the payment method,[1315] clauses for the provider's discretion regarding remuneration without providing the concrete purpose or amount of such price increases[1316] and a limitation clause regarding liability for damages that occur due to the use of a mobile phone abroad[1317].

Gym Contracts

The courts have also heard several cases regarding gym contracts.[1318] A minimum contractual period of 24 months is permissible[1319] as long as the consumer had a reasonable chance to try out the available facilities and choose between different contractual models[1320]. Meanwhile, a limitation of the customer's termination right in case of serious illness or pregnancy has been held unfair.[1321] A gym provider can neither limit his or her

1312 Cf. *supra* note 1279.

1313 Wurmnest, *supra* note 1299, recitals 179 et seq.

1314 OLG Schleswig, judgment of the 3 July 2012, reference number: 2 U 12/11, BeckRS 2012, 15906.

1315 OLG Düsseldorf, judgment of the 18 July 2002, reference number: 6 U 218/01, BeckRS 2002, 6241.

1316 Ibid.

1317 OLG Düsseldorf, judgment of the 31 October 1996, reference number: 6 U 206/9, BeckRS 9998, 15202.

1318 Wurmnest, *supra* note 1299, recitals 135 et seq.

1319 German Federal Supreme Court, judgment of the 8 February 2012, reference number: XII ZR 42/10, NJW 2012, 1431.

1320 LG Essen, judgment of the 26 February 2009, reference number: 10 S 356/08, BeckRS 2009, 9904.

1321 Cf. *supra* note 1319.

liability to intent and gross negligence or exclude liability for subsequent damage[1322] nor exclude the customers' right to bring their own drinks[1323].

The examples show that §§ 305 et seq. BGB are applied by the courts frequently in various areas. Many cases have arisen in typical consumer-related areas which shows the importance of term control mechanisms as part of German consumer protection law.

E. Consumer Image

German unfair terms in consumer contracts regulation aims at protecting the weaker party of the contract, thus, reflecting the image of a vulnerable consumer. The clear intention of the legislator has been the correction of an imbalance of bargaining power, albeit not necessarily involving consumers. At the same time the German legislator aimed at legitimising T&Cs so they can be used effectively in the market and easing decision-making for rational consumers.

F. Interim Conclusion

The unfair term control mechanisms have a long-standing history under German law and are an example for case-law that was finally codified by the legislator. Technically, the development, thereby, bears striking similarities with the common law of contract. However, the German evolution of contract term control is based on the German concept of good faith which comes closer to equitable intervention rather than specific contract law doctrines. While materially, there exists a rich body of case-law regarding concrete term control and the respective §§ 305 et seq. BGB are applied frequently by the courts, the German model lacks institutional complexity and accessibility for consumers. Comprehensive administrative term control mechanisms do not exist in Germany. Abstract control mechanisms are rather left with private consumer organisations which are equipped with standing to pursue legal claims on behalf of consumers. However, instead of one comprehensive system, the German model of del-

1322 OLG Munich, judgment of the 30 March 1995, reference number: 29 U 4222/94, NJW-RR 1995, 1467.

1323 OLG Brandenburg, judgment of the 25 June 2003, reference number: 7 U 36/03, BeckRS 2003, 30321643.

egation has developed in a fragmented way, equipping consumer organisations with more competences, such as the newly introduced model declaratory action, rather than evaluating the existing system. Within the existing system, it must be positively acknowledged that consumer organisations have fought several court battles and raised awareness for consumer issues with respect to unfair terms. However, the impact of collective claims and enforcement could be greater if consumer organisations were equipped with more (financial) resources and the whole system was revised rather than adding new elements to it. Such a revised system, relying on administrative rather than pure judicial term control could also relieve the courts which, as has been shown, have to deal with (consumer) claims relating to unfair terms frequently.

The German regulatory system, therefore, appears ineffective under the parameters of this work. The mere reference to principles of good faith does not offer businesses a concrete guideline and, thus, does not help to reduce transaction costs. Guidance can only be derived from the grey and black lists in §§ 308, 309 BGB and court case-law. It is, thus, difficult to assess the impact on transaction costs. At the same time the institutional system does not offer consumers a quick and easy way to obtain clarification regarding the fairness of a term. Consumer organisations can only issue warnings and ultimately initiate court proceedings. Such powers do not appear as compelling as an administrative procedure. The preventative effect of the German collective system, therefore, appears weak. The chances of unfair terms entering the market consequently becomes more likely. Such likeliness bears the danger of lower consumer confidence regarding the fairness of T&Cs. The Covid-19 pandemic may serve as a further catalyst for this development as many consumers have been and will be confronted with presumably unfair cancellation policies, i.e. by airlines or event organisers. In many cases consumers could only resort to consumer organisations which could effectively only appeal to the term users to reimburse their customers or ultimately initiate long court proceedings. An administrative agency or administrative powers granted to the consumer organisations would have served as a more effective mean of enforcement.

The fact that many collective as well as individual cases still end up at the courts, furthermore, indicates that transaction costs on the secondary level are higher than in the UK where not as many cases appear to require adjudication by the courts. The differences may well be explained by the differing institutional framework in Germany where means of alternative dispute resolution are not as common as in the UK and, therefore, the parties are often more likely to resort to the courts. Furthermore, modern German unfair term regulation has been institutionalised from the 1950s onward, first in the form of court case-law and later by way of the AGBG. Unlike the UK, the unfair term regulation largely remained unamended so that rather than developing a new legislative regime the institutionalised norms have continued to exist as have the associated procedures.

However, lastly, it must be acknowledged that the German balance of individual and collective actions is rather effective in light of EU law. Under German law, it is relatively easy to dissociate oneself from collective actions and individual actions are easily available. Both 'legs of term control' are, thereby, accessible, albeit not equally effective under the parameters of this dissertation.

G. Comparative Analysis

UCTD	UK	Germany
Transparency Test	Section 61 CRA 2015	§§ 305c, 307 BGB
Fairness Test	Section 68 CRA 2015	§ 307 BGB
List of Terms	Schedule 2 CRA 2015	§§ 308, 309 BGB
Abstract Control	Section 70, Schedules 3 and 5 CRA 2015	§§ 1, 3 UKlaG

The unfair term regulatory mechanisms in Germany and the UK must now be compared and evaluated especially in light of their effectiveness under EU parameters as well as the parameters set out in this work.

The analysis of societal factors has shown differences and similarities. As has been pointed out above, both countries underwent industrialisation in the 19th century and, thus, experienced similar societal developments in this regard. With respect to economic policy Germany has proven more interventionist, albeit as the consumer credit analysis has shown, not necessarily with respect to modern consumer-related legislation.

An English lawyer will first note that the German law on unfair terms is based on the principle of good faith which is disputed by some under English common law. The fact alone that German law is based on a principle that sounds foreign to English common lawyers does not, however, exclude comparability of the regulatory measures in the UK and Germany. It has been shown that German law regarding unfair terms historically developed in quite a similar way to the English common law of contract. It can especially be noted that both systems have applied the *contra preferentem* rule. In the 19th century liberal notions of freedom of contract had still been predominant and T&Cs were not treated as a distinct group of contract terms. T&Cs and, thereby, unfair terms had been a mass phenomenon not least since the Industrial Revolution in the 19th century. Furthermore, it must be noted that the codification of unfair term regulation was initiated by court case-law both in the UK and Germany. Until today, much of German law on unfair terms is shaped by court case-law.

The two systems differ, however, regarding the scope and system of legislation. The UK has pursued a restricted approach, i.e. by restricting the applicability of the UCTA 1977, *inter alia*, to limitation and exemption clauses and the unfair term legislation under the CRA 2015 to consumer contracts while for other contracts the English common law principles of contract remain applicable. The German legislator introduced a broad control mechanism which does not only apply to consumer contracts, is not limited to certain types of terms and embedded in the statutory system of the BGB. Unlike the English concept the approach of German courts – which later inspired the introduction of the AGBG – was based on a principled interpretation of § 242 BGB. The German approach to term control is therefore a normative one and more comparable to equitable intervention than English contract law principles. This provides an explanation for the starkly differing scopes and approaches to term control legislation and decisions in the UK and Germany.

The UCTD had less of an impact on the German system of term control than on English legislation, as the German AGBG essentially served as inspiration for the UCTD. With respect to regulation implemented according to the UCTD the two legal systems now use similar consumer definitions and the scope of such regulation is largely the same except for the fact that the UK does not exempt individually negotiated agreements from the scope of applicability.

Regulations on unfair terms before and after the introduction both in the UK and Germany have targeted weaker party protection. However, it must be noted that the English common law is still rather underlied by the notion of the rational consumer.

Materially, with respect to unfair terms in consumer contracts, courts in both jurisdictions have heard cases regarding various types of terms and various legal and economic areas, especially those concerning consumer issues. It can, furthermore, be seen that in both legal systems cases regarding bank and credit fees have arisen which appear to be areas that are typically subject to term control proceedings. With respect to the UK Supreme

Court's decision in *Abbey National* it is likely that German courts would have come to a different conclusion as German courts distinguish between bank charges that form essential obligations of the bank and collateral fees more clearly. Thus, the fact that certain fees form a considerable part of a bank's revenue stream would not prevent a German court from subjecting the respective clause to term control. The clear distinction appears in line with EU law and could – if the UK remains bound by EU law in this area – serve as a comparative example for the future. Similarly, with respect to the UK House of Lords decision in *Director General of Fair Trading v First National Bank plc* it is likely that a clause regarding increased default interest would have been subject to term control under German law. The fairness assessment conducted by Lord Bingham, on the other hand, is similar to a fairness assessment under German law which would likely also consider terms regarded unfair and included in §§ 308, 309 BGB (i.e. the UCTD's Annex).

The UK and German case-law also reveals similarities with respect to gym contracts. However, the outcomes of cases have been different. In *Office of Fair Trading v Ashbourne Management Services Ltd* it was found that a minimum contractual period of 24 months was unfair.[1324] In contrast such a minimum period has been held fair by the German Federal Supreme Court. Similarly, it had been found under both jurisdictions, however, that a suspension or cancellation of the contract must be possible in case of serious illness.

Unlike in Germany, not a lot of court cases regarding insurance terms have arisen under English law. This may be explained by the non-applicability of the UCTA 1977 regarding insurance contracts (now Section 66 Subsection 1 CRA 2015).

Systematically, great differences can be noted between the provisions of administrative control and collective proceedings in the UK and Germany. The UK attributes a strong role in the enforcement of laws on unfair terms in consumer contracts to the CMA. The OFT and CMA respectively have, thereby, dealt with thousands of cases in the past decades. Beside bringing collective cases to the courts, the CMA also publishes guidelines and reaches out to businesses to ensure that terms are removed from the market effectively for all consumers. As a public authority, the CMA can rely on public funding for proceedings. The UK approach, thereby, reflects a focus on enforcing law on unfair terms for all market participants which also

---

1324 *Office of Fair Trading v Ashbourne Management Services Ltd* [2011] EWHC 1237 (Ch) at [174] per Kitchin J.

reflects the UK's rather liberal economic approach. The greatest effectiveness is achieved for everyone if the market is free from unfair terms and consumers can make free decisions.

On the contrary, Germany has not established an administrative authority for the control of unfair terms in consumer contracts. The focus still lies on traditional term control based on equitable notions. The difference to the UK may result from a different market approach as depicted in the comparative analysis of economic factors. Instead, private consumer organisations are tasked with enforcing law on unfair terms and lead collective court proceedings. However, it cannot be ensured that these organisations are funded adequately to fulfil their tasks effectively. Administrative powers only play a peripheral role. Thus, the thousands of cases that have been dealt with by the OFT and CMA respectively in the UK, have been heard by German courts, mostly in the course of individual proceedings. It has been shown that rather than establishing a coherent framework for collective enforcement, the German system consists of a fragmented patchwork of mechanisms for collective term control. Compared to the UK, the German approach appears ineffective regarding collective claims. In terms of the parameters of this dissertation, the UK system, therefore, appears more effective. However, under EU parameters which emphasise equal accessibility, the German system appears more effective.

In comparison it has, thus, been shown that the material control mechanisms have more in common than it may appear from looking at the differing legal approaches. However, the German approach is an unlikely candidate for inspiring legal changes regarding post-Brexit regulation on unfair terms in consumer contracts. The UK has long pursued an approach that focussed on the systematic effectiveness of term control for the benefit of the many (market participants). In contrast the German system focusses on intense individual material term control and relies on private organisations and individual proceedings. Therefore, the German approach will not serve as a role model regarding the law on unfair terms in consumer contracts in the UK after Brexit.

Chapter 12: Unfair Terms in Consumer Contracts in Norway

A. *History of Unfair Terms (in Consumer Contracts) in Norway*

Legislation prior to the Incorporation of the Directive

The Scandinavian countries had realised the importance of regulating unfair terms in the 1970s and 1980s.[1325] In 1983 Norway together with the other Scandinavian countries, thus, introduced § 36 Contracts Act (hereinafter "§ 36") that says that

> [a]n agreement can completely or partially be set aside or changed in so far as it would seem unreasonable or against good business practice to assert the claim. This also applies to unilateral dispositions.
> The decision does not only consider the agreement's content, the parties' positions or the conditions at the time of the contract's conclusion but also conditions that arise later and other circumstances.
> The rules in the first and second paragraphs apply accordingly when it would seem unfair to assert a claim under current commercial practice or other contractual custom.[1326]

The clause is drafted in a very general manner and accordingly is referred to as the 'General Clause'. An underlying Nordic concept of § 36 is that of loyalty (*lojalitet*) and means that each contracting party – especially the stronger one – must take into account the other's interests. This duty of loyalty has long been an important principle underlying Nordic legal doctrine.[1327] It can also be linked to the sociological findings of high interper-

---

1325 Kåre Lilleholt, 'Application of General Principles in Private Law in the Nordic Countries' [2013] 20 Juridica International 12 (14).

1326 'En avtale kan helt eller delvis settes til side eller endres for så vidt det ville virke urimelig eller være i strid med god forretningsskikk å gjøre den gjeldende. Det samme gjelder ensidig bindende disposisjoner.
Ved avgjørelsen tas hensyn ikke bare til avtalens innhold, partenes stilling og forholdene ved avtalens inngåelse, men også til senere inntrådte forhold og omstendighetene for øvrig.
Reglene i første og annet ledd gjelder tilsvarende når det ville virke urimelig å gjøre gjeldende handelsbruk eller annen kontraktrettslig sedvane.' (Translation by author).

1327 Lilleholt, *supra* note 1325, (15).

sonal trust rates and a homogenous society. The link to the duty of loyalty is also reflected in the preparatory works leading to the General Clause according to which the main motivation was to protect the weaker contractual party from the abuse of the stronger contractual party's position especially in standard contracts.[1328] The goals pursued with § 36, thus, closely resemble the ambitions underlying the UCTD.[1329]

Due to its general nature, the courts' case-law plays an important role when it comes to the clause's interpretation. The first Norwegian Supreme Court decision on § 36 dates back to 1988.[1330] In the *Røstad*-case the majority stated that § 36

> according to its wording granted the courts a general and discretionary power to consider whether the contract should be set aside or changed. The legal review shall not only consider whether the agreement was unreasonable at the time it was entered into but also if it became so due to changed conditions. From the wording one cannot derive any limitations with respect to the nature of the conditions which can be relevant – it is crucial whether the agreement became unreasonable.
>
> According to our legal tradition a norm like this also bears a dynamic element: the perception as to what is unreasonable cannot be bound to an ascertained point in time.[1331]

The minority held that

> one has to put considerable weight on the preparatory works when determining the scope of § 36. The norm shall be a safety valve and catch

1328 Justis- og politidepartementet, Om lov om endringer i avtaleloven 31 mai 1983 nr. 4 m.m. (generell formuerettslig lempingsregel), Ot. prp. nr. 5 (1982-1983), page 3.

1329 Cf. *supra* note 975.

1330 Norwegian Supreme Court, *Staten v/Forsvarsdepartementet v Andreas Røstad (Røstad)* [1988] Rt. 1988, 276.

1331 Ibid. (284) per Judge Skåre: 'Bestemmelsen gir etter sin ordlyd domstolene en generell og skjønnsmessig myndighet til å vurdere om en avtale skal settes til side eller endres. Ved vurderingen skal det ikke bare legges vekt på om avtalen var urimelig da den ble inngått, men også om den er blitt det på grunn av endrede forhold. Det kan av ordlyden ikke utledes noen begrensing med hensyn til arten av de forhold som kan være relevante - avgjørende er om avtalen er blitt urimelig.
Etter vår rettstradisjon må det i en bestemmelse som dette også legges inn et dynamisk element: Oppfatningen av hva som er urimelig, kan ikke bindes til noe bestemt tidspunkt.' (Translation by author).

different kinds of unreasonableness in all areas of contract within restitution law.[1332]

The preparatory works of the norm state that the criteria for finding a contract term to be unreasonable or unfair (*urimelig*) are strict.[1333] While the majority opinion reflects a wide interpretation of the norm, the minority opinion handles the norm much stricter. The cases that followed *Røstad* were decided in accordance with the minority opinion, thus, setting the threshold for a successful invocation of § 36 high.[1334] It affords a 'qualified unreasonableness'.[1335] As a consequence of this development, the number of cases in which the General Clause has been decisive in Norwegian Supreme Court cases is rather low.[1336]

B. Legal Framework Today

Norway was obliged to implement the UCTD under Art. 72 EEAA in connection with No. 7a of Annex XIX to the EEA Agreement.

As the UCTD is a minimum level harmonisation Directive,[1337] the states that were obliged to implement the UCTD were left with some leeway. This led to several proceedings led by the then EC Commission against then EC Member States claiming that the national implementation was insufficient.[1338]

1332 Ibid. (289-290) per Judge Endresen: 'Etter mitt syn må det legges betydelig vekt på forarbeidene når virkeområdet for § 36 skal fastlegges. Bestemmelsen skal være en sikkerhetsventil og fange opp urimelighet av forskjellig slag på alle kontraktsområder innen formueretten.' (Translation by author).

1333 Justis- og politidepartementet, *supra* note 1328, page 30.

1334 Cf. Norwegian Supreme Court cases *Heidi Gilde and others v Olav Moksnes and others (Selsbak)* [1990] Rt. 1990, 284 (295-296) and *Røeggen* [2013] Rt. 2013, 388 (referring to the *Selsbak*-case at recital 53).

1335 Cf. Norwegian Supreme Court Cases *Smestad Nye Handelshus AS v Anne Juvet* [2012] Rt. 2012, 1537, recital 46 and *HelgelandsKraft AS v Sigurd Einar and others* [2014] Rt. 2014, 351, recital 39.

1336 Lilleholt, *supra* note 1325, (16); the low number of cases may partly derive from the importance of the aforementioned tribunals which are often chosen as an easier way to settle consumer cases, cf. also Marie Natland Wabakken, *Om standardiseringen av en rettslig standard – En analyse av forbrukeravtaledirektivet og forholdet til avtaleloven § 36*, 18.

1337 Nebbia, *supra* note 974, 14.

1338 ECJ judgments C-144/99, *Commission of the European Communities v The Netherlands* [2001]; C-372/99, *Commission of the European Communities v Italy*

Norway – like the other Scandinavian states[1339] – decided that § 36 sufficed as an implementation of the Directive and that § 36 offered consumers an even broader protection than the Directive which only applies to non-individually negotiated contract terms.[1340]

The only Norwegian legal change that occurred was the introduction of § 37 Contracts Act (hereinafter "§ 37") which reads as follows:

> For terms that have not been individually negotiated and that concern an agreement between a consumer and a trader, the following applies:
>
> 1. When applying § 36 attention shall be paid to the circumstances mentioned in § 36 Section 2. Subsequent circumstances shall, however, not be considered significant to the detriment of the consumer with the effect that a contractual term which would otherwise be considered unreasonable, will be considered reasonable.
> 2. If one or more terms bear a significant bias to the detriment of the consumer with regard to the parties' rights and duties under the agreement, the consumer can, by applying § 36, claim that the remaining agreement shall be binding for the parties, if it can remain in place with unchanged content.
> 3. In case of doubt about the interpretation of the contractual term, the term shall be interpreted in favour of the consumer.
> 4. A trader who claims that the contractual term is individually negotiated bears the burden of proof in this regard.[1341]

[2002]; C-478/99, *Commission of the European Communities v Kingdom of Sweden* [2002]; C-70/03 *Commission of the European Communities v Kingdom of Spain* [2004].

1339 Cf. *supra* note 251.

1340 Justis- og politidepartementet, Om lov om endring i avtaleloven, Ot. prp. nr. 89 (1993-1994), page 3, cf. also Art. 8 UCTD, which explicitly allows for the retainer of existing provisions that offer broader consumer protection.

1341 'For vilkår som ikke er individuelt forhandlet, og som inngår i en avtale mellom en forbruker og en næringsdrivende, gjelder følgende:

1. Ved anvendelse av § 36 skal det tas hensyn til forhold som nevnt i § 36 annet ledd. Senere inntrådte forhold skal likevel ikke tillegges betydning til skade for forbrukeren med den virkning at et avtalevilkår som ellers ville anses som urimelig, blir ansett som rimelig.
2. Hvis ett eller flere avtalevilkår medfører en betydelig skjevhet til skade for forbrukeren i de rettigheter og plikter partene har etter avtalen, kan forbrukeren ved anvendelse av § 36 kreve at avtalen for øvrig skal være bindende for partene, dersom den kan bestå med uforandret innhold.

The Norwegian implementation of the UCTD adds the possibility declaring a term unfair without setting the whole contract aside to § 36, an interpretative rule in favour of the consumer and a burden of proof reversal against the trader in consumer cases. § 36 remains the norm under which a term may be considered unfair with respect to material law. § 36 goes further than the Directive in that it includes terms that have been individually negotiated, terms that define the contract's subject matter and price terms. However, § 37 and § 36 lack two traits that the Directive mentions. First, the list of terms that may be regarded as unfair has not been implemented into Norwegian law (Art. 3 Section 3 in connection with the Annex of the UCTD).[1342] And second, § 37 does not refer to the requirement of the terms' 'plain and intelligible' wording but connects the legal consequence of an interpretation in favour of the consumer (Art. 5 UCTD) to the *interpretation* of the term (§ 37 No. 3).[1343] The preparatory works provide an explanation for the way the Directive was implemented in Norway.

As to the implementation of the list of terms that may be regarded as unfair, the Norwegian Department of Justice argued that such a list does not constitute a sufficient mean to prevent the use of unfair terms.[1344] According to the Department, the list's wording was not clear enough but too general and many of the listed terms would already fall under § 36.[1345] Moreover, the Department brought forward that the list set a lower consumer protection standard than already existent under Norwegian law and would, thus, bear the risk that the overall consumer protection standard would be adjusted to a lower level if the list was to be included in the im-

---

3. Ved tvil om tolkningen av et avtalevilkår, skal vilkåret tolkes til fordel for forbrukeren.
4. En næringsdrivende som hevder at et avtalevilkår er individuelt forhandlet, må godtgjøre dette.' (Translation by author)

Furthermore, § 37 contains a definition of the term 'consumer' (cf. Art. 2 (b) UCTD) and the application on contracts connected to a Member State but dealt with under a non-Member State's law (cf. Art. 6 (2) UCTD).

1342 According to the ECJ judgment C-478/99, *Commission of the European Communities v Kingdom of Sweden* [2002] recital 22 does not have to be implemented but has to be made available to be considered in relevant decisions.

1343 The ECJ held in the similar case C-144/99, *Commission of the European Communities v The Netherlands* [2001] that the respective Dutch implementation was not sufficient.

1344 Justis- og politidepartementet, *supra* note 1340, page 10.

1345 Ibid.

plementation.[1346] Overall, the arguments brought forward against the implementation of the list reflected a fear of loss of § 36's flexibility and fairness standard.

As to the inclusion of the requirement of 'plain and intelligible' language, the Department brought forward that such a standard already existed under Norwegian law.[1347] According to the Department, the 'clarity rule' (*uklarhetsregelen*) is a well-established unwritten principle of Norwegian law. Thus, it was held unnecessary to implement a provision under Art. 5 UCTD.[1348] Furthermore, they included concerns about the conformity with Norwegian legal tradition, under which most interpretative rules with respect to contract law are unwritten. A codification would pose questions as to the rank and status of other, unwritten legal principles.[1349]

However, under the impression of the other Nordic countries' implementation of the UCTD – thus, to ensure legal homogeneity in the Nordic realm – and due to concerns voiced by the Norwegian Bar Association (*Den Norske Advokatforening*) and the Consumer Authority, the Department nevertheless decided to include a provision.[1350] The wording ('interpretation' instead of 'plain and intelligible' wording) was considered to be more open and, thus, consumer friendly.[1351]

C. *Abstract Control Mechanisms relating to Unfair Terms in Consumer Contracts*

Beside § 37, § 9a Marketing Control Act (*markedsføringsloven*) (now § 22 Marketing Control Act)[1352] provides that

> [t]erms that are used or intended to be used in the business with consumers can be prohibited if they are found to be unreasonable against

1346 Ibid.
1347 Ibid.
1348 Ibid.
1349 Ibid.
1350 Ibid.
1351 Ibid. 11.
1352 *Lov om kontroll med markedsføring og avtalevilkår mv. (markedsføringsloven)* (1 June 2009).

> the consumer and it is found that the prohibition is necessary for public reasons [...].[1353]

Under §§ 39, 40 Marketing Control Act the Consumer Authority and the Market Council have the power to prohibit such clauses. They also offer advice and keep a dialogue with different branches of industry on the use of standard terms.[1354] The unfair term control under the Marketing Control Act, thereby, also offers a preventative consumer protection measure in that the Consumer Authority negotiates standard contract terms with traders' associations under the threat of prohibition of certain clauses. Furthermore, the Consumer Authority has the power to impose sanctions on traders who do not comply (§§ 42, 43 Marketing Control Act).

D. Unfair Terms in Consumer Contracts in Court Practice

The following sections depict which kind of implications have followed from the UCTD's Norwegian implementation.

I. Administration

The Consumer Authority aims to maintain a positive relationship with businesses and encourages them to contact the Consumer Authority in case they have any questions regarding fair terms in contracts. In this regard, the Consumer Authority also produces guidelines which contain specific advice of 'industry-specific pitfalls'. The Consumer Authority does not produce any statistics on unfair terms in consumer contracts specifically and partly because the main focus of their work lies with unfair marketing practices and not unfair terms. This is also reflected in the low number of cases that go up to the Market Council for dispute resolution relating to

---

1353 'Vilkår som nyttes eller tilsiktes nyttet i næringsvirksomhet overfor forbrukere kan forbys når de finnes urimelige overfor forbrukerne, og det finnes at forbud tilsies av allmenne hensyn.' (Translation by author).

1354 Cf. i.e. advice on standard terms for digital services, Forbrukertilsynet, 'Forbrukertilsynets veiledning om avtalevilkår for digitale tjenester' <https://www.forbrukertilsynet.no/lov-og-rett/veiledninger-og-retningslinjer/forbrukertilsynets-veiledning-om-avtalevilkar-digitale-tjenester> accessed 17 November 2019.

unfair terms, the last one appearing in 2017[1355] (before the Consumer Authority was equipped with sanctioning powers in 2018). The Consumer Authority acts upon consumers' complaints, their own research and also based on media revelations. In assessing whether to launch investigations, they consider the seriousness of the breach as well as the extent to which the case is symptomatic of a pressing consumer issue.[1356]

The low number of investigatory cases and disputes that have to be resolved by the Market Council indicates that the dialogue with businesses works very well as a mean to prevent unfair terms from entering the market.

II. Adjudication

As described above, tribunals play a very important role in the application of laws in Norway. Thus, I first look at the relevance of § 37 and the UCTD in front of the courts and then examine its application in front of tribunals separately.

1. The Courts

§ 37 was first mentioned but eventually not considered by the Norwegian Supreme Court in 2006[1357] and again in 2011[1358].

The latter case *Nye Major* depicts how § 37 and the Directive could have led to a positive outcome for the consumer. The case dealt with a term in a contract that concerned that the purchase of real property. The contract term in question stated that the 'seller aims at completion of the property

1355 Markedsrådet, MR-2017-658: Klarna AB (29 June 2017) (decision not based on provisions on unfair terms but § 48 Financial Agreements Act).

1356 All information contained in this paragraph has been kindly provided by a representative of the Consumer Authority by way of e-mail (17 October 2019).

1357 Norwegian Supreme Court, *Tønnevoldsgate 30 AS v Are Groheim Berntsen and others* [2006] Rt. 2006, 1715.

1358 Norwegian Supreme Court, *Kristin Amalia Ellingsen and others v Sørkedalsveien 9 AS (Nye Major)* [2011] Rt. 2011, 670. Also cf. Norwegian Supreme Court, *Naturbetong AS v Erik O. Jacobsen (Krusesgate)* [2011] Rt. 2011, 679 in which § 37 was not mentioned but referred to the *Nye Major*-case.

in the second half of 2007'.[1359] The building works were not completed by then and the buyers consequently claimed damages. The buyers brought forward that the clause was to be interpreted as the actual completion date and that due to unclear wording that clause had to be interpreted in favour of the consumer (see § 37 No. 3) as the actual completion date.[1360] § 37 was not considered by the Norwegian Supreme Court judges. Instead, the claim was rejected based on an interpretation of the wording and circumstances of the contract.[1361]

First, it seems rather obscure that the Norwegian Supreme Court outrightly rejected the possible applicability of § 37 No. 3 without comprehensive reasoning.[1362]

Second, the consideration of the indicative list of terms that may be regarded as unfair could have led to a different outcome.[1363] While there is no term on the list that matches the term in question exactly, one could have arrived at the conclusion that the respective contract clause was unfair by looking at the list as a whole and extracting its underlying principles. Many of the list's terms deal with situations where the seller or trader is granted a position from which he can unilaterally change the terms of the contract.[1364] One can, thus, extract that terms that are drafted in a manner that gives the seller or trader disproportionate unilateral powers to the detriment of consumers may be regarded as unfair even though they are not mentioned in the *non-exhaustive indicative* list. Even if the term in question was found to be drafted in clear and intelligible language, it could have nevertheless fallen into the aforementioned category. As 'aiming' does not mean the same as actually 'completing' this term leaves the seller with a lot of leeway as to the completion date of the building, thus, leaving him with disproportionate powers as to the fulfilment of the contract to the detriment of the consumer who does not know when fulfilment will eventually take place. Consideration of the UCTD could, therefore, have made a difference.

The first time § 37 and the UCTD were discussed was the landmark *Røeggen*-case in 2013.[1365] There it was held that the Directive and conse-

1359 'Selger tar sikte på ferdigstillelse av Boligen 2. halvår 2007.' (Translation by author).

1360 Norwegian Supreme Court, *Nye Major* [2011] Rt. 2011, 670, recitals 14 and 15.

1361 Ibid. recitals 37 et seq.

1362 Ibid. recital 41.

1363 Cf. also Lilleholt, *supra* note 1325, (17).

1364 Examples in the Annex can be found in Nr. 1 (c), (j), (k), (m) and (p).

1365 Norwegian Supreme Court, *Røeggen* [2013] Rt. 2013, 388.

quently § 37 do not bear independent significance as the threshold for finding unfairness under the Directive was higher than under § 36. According to the Norwegian Supreme Court the Directive was directed at countries with weaker consumer protection to raise the consumer protection level there, while Norway had already introduced § 36 as a protection mechanism.[1366] Furthermore, the Court argued that there did not exist enough case-law by the CJEU to define the meaning of the Directive.[1367] They then referred to the Department of Justice's preparatory works regarding § 37 and found that their arguments reflected the intention of the law-maker and that the standard of consumer protection under § 37 did not differ from the one set in § 36.[1368] The Court argued that the Directive appeared as an expression of the importance of consumer protection that had to be reflected in the general interpretation of § 36.[1369] The claimant eventually succeeded in *Røeggen* because of a breach of information rights prior to the conclusion of the contract under § 36.

Beside the 'side-lining' of § 37, the interpretation of § 36 in this case is not in line with CJEU case-law systematically. While the CJEU acknowledges that a lack of pre-contractual information can lead to the lack of transparency of a term,[1370] it does not automatically make it unfair but requires an additional assessment of fairness in light of Art. 3 UCTD[1371]. In *Røeggen* the Norwegian Supreme Court solely based its decision on a breach of information duties which could have led to a different outcome under the UCTD.

The fact that a breach of information rights was decisive in *Røeggen* also stands for a shift in the Norwegian Supreme Court's use and view of § 36. The case explicitly refers to the *Fokus Bank*-decision[1372] which was based on the *Lognvik*-decision[1373]. Both decisions concerned investments and the respective advice the banks gave consumers.

1366 Ibid. recital 46.

1367 Ibid. recital 57.

1368 Ibid. recital 58-60.

1369 Ibid. recital 61.

1370 Cf. CJEU judgment C-186/16, *Andriciuc* [2017] recitals 47-48; CJEU judgment C-96/14, *Van Hove* [2015] recital 48.

1371 Cf. i.e. CJEU judgment C-472/10, *Invitel* [2012] recital 28.

1372 Norwegian Supreme Court, *Aronsen Holding AS and others v Fokus Bank, filial av Danske Bank A/S (Fokus Bank)* [2012] Rt. 2012, 1926.

1373 Norwegian Supreme Court, *Lognvik* [2012] Rt. 2012, 355.

In *Lognvik* the majority held that '§ 36 covered the unreasonable agreements, not the irrational ones'[1374]. In the respective case this meant that the judges did not focus on the specific content, but to which degree the bank (objectively) provided the necessary information to understand the consequences of the agreement.[1375] Unreasonableness could only be established in case of a 'qualified lack' of information that was causal for the consumer's decision.[1376] Meanwhile, Judge Endresen – who gave the minority opinion – emphasised the consumer's actual (subjective) perception of the information[1377] and the relationship of the parties, especially the bank's advisory position[1378]. The Norwegian Supreme Court in *Fokus Bank* and *Røeggen* again focussed on the information (objectively) provided in the course of the bargaining process preceding the conclusion of the contract. This shows a shift away from a 'content oriented' to a 'process oriented' control of unfair terms under § 36. § 37 and the UCTD, however, (also) require a 'content oriented' control of terms. The practical development of the use of § 36, thereby, deviates from the term control mechanism under EU and EEA law. As a consequence, it is possible that the control of unfair terms under § 36 does in fact not cover the scope of the Directive as the preparatory works originally indicated. Moreover, the decision is a typical example of the Norwegian Supreme Court's loyalty towards the Norwegian Parliamentary law-maker. It must be questioned whether it is enough to refer to the preparatory works of the implementing authority or the preparatory works on the European level should rather also be included.[1379]

After *Røeggen* § 37 has only been mentioned once[1380] but never been discussed in light of the Directive again by the Norwegian Supreme Court. Meanwhile, *Johan Giertsen* found twelve Norwegian Supreme Court cases, in which § 37 and the UCTD would have been applicable. Out of these

1374 Ibid. recital 82 per Judge Arnesen.

1375 Ibid. recitals 60, 67, 70 et seq. per Judge Arnesen.

1376 Ibid. recital 68 per Judge Arnesen.

1377 Ibid. recital 123-124 per Judge Endresen.

1378 Ibid. recitals 86, 145 et seq. per Judge Endresen.

1379 The Norwegian Supreme Court case *Gerd Eriksen and others v Løten kommune* [1997] Rt. 1997, 1965 (1968) provides an example for a decision that disagreed with the Norwegian Parliament's preparatory works due to their 'misunderstanding' of the intention of the European Directive in question, thus, proving that the Norwegian Supreme Court attributes special weight to considerations behind European legislation.

1380 Norwegian Supreme Court, *A v Danica Pensjonsforsikring AS* [2014] Rt. 2014, 379.

twelve, § 37 and the UCTD were only discussed in *Røeggen*.[1381] The number of cases in which § 37 was mentioned by Courts of Appeal (18 cases) and District Courts (10 cases) is slightly higher. Most of these cases, however, do not discuss the Directive in detail. Only one Court of Appeal judgment mentions the Directive's grey list.[1382] By not discussing the UCTD in detail – thereby, setting a strong precedent – but granting § 37 and the UCTD no independent significance, the Norwegian Supreme Court's interpretation in *Røeggen* has contributed to a diminished relevance of the implications of the UCTD and a stronger emphasis on the pre-existing norm of § 36[1383].

The UCTD's implementation and respective case-law has sparked criticism. First, the implementation of Art. 5 UCTD is criticised. Instead of including the important requirement of 'plain and intelligible' wording, that also bears relevance as to whether a term is considered unreasonable or not (cf. Art. 4 UCTD), § 37 No. 3 is drafted in a manner that does not sufficiently reflect the UCTD's intention.[1384]

Second, the court in *Røeggen* is wrong to point out that the ECJ/CJEU at that point had not provided details on material unfairness of a term but left it to the national courts. The court refers to the ECJ decision in *Freiburger Kommunalbauten v Hofstetter*[1385]. However, eight days before the decision in *Røeggen*, on the 14 March 2013, the CJEU assumed competence to interpret the unfairness of a term.[1386] The court, thus, should have gone beyond national laws, also considering EEA/EU legal sources.[1387] A lack of consideration endangers the EEA principles of efficiency and homogeneity. This leads to an *ex officio* duty on behalf of lawyers and judges to consider EEA law.[1388]

Third, a study of Norwegian Supreme Court cases shows that § 37 and the UCTD are not frequently mentioned. Some cases could have been de-

1381 Johan Giertsen, *Avtaler*, 216-217.

1382 Borgarting Court of Appeal, *Christian Corneliussen v Norwegian Air Shuttle ASA* [2016] LB-2015-37187.

1383 Cf. regarding the 'revitalisation' of the general clause, Kåre Lilleholt, 'Revitalisering av generalklausulen?' [2013] 126 (4-5) Tidsskrift for rettsvitenskap 550-566.

1384 Giertsen, *supra* note 1381, 211-212; Wabakken, *supra* note 1336, 34.

1385 ECJ judgment C-237/02, *Freiburger Kommunalbauten v Hofstetter* [2004].

1386 CJEU judgment C-415/11, *Aziz* [2013] recitals 65-76.

1387 Cf. also Giertsen, *supra* note 1381, 215.

1388 For a general as well as consumer law specific *ex officio* duty on behalf of the courts, cf. Lisa-Mari Moen Jünge, *EØS-rettens tjenere – Om norske domstolers plikt til å anvende EØS-rett ex officio*.

cided in favour rather than against the consumer if § 37 and the UCTD had been considered.[1389] This especially includes the list of terms that may be regarded as unfair that is rarely mentioned by courts and tribunals.[1390] The list could provide a preventative measure for unfair terms as it would give businesses and consumers a guideline as to what is and is not allowed.[1391]

Fourth, the legal consequence of keeping the contract in place while declaring only the unfair term invalid (Art. 6 (1) UCTD) has not been correctly implemented into Norwegian law.[1392] Under § 37 No. 2 in connection with § 36 the consumer can *claim* to keep the contract in place without the unfair term. Under § 36 a court could even change the term in question instead of declaring it not binding on the consumer. In this respect the UCTD provides a stricter, more preventative measure which is emphasised by CJEU case-law.[1393] If the trader must expect that the legal consequence of finding a term to be unfair, will be to keep in place that contract without the onerous term used to the advantage of the trader, he or she will think twice about including it in the first place.[1394]

2. The Tribunals

The following part comprises an analysis of the use of § 37 and the UCTD in front of alternative dispute resolution tribunals. These cases are considered to provide an overview of *actual* consumer protection with respect to the UCTD in Norway as consumer cases are mostly raised at alternative dispute resolution institutions rather than the courts. This approach is in-

---

1389 Giertsen, *supra* note 1381, 243; Marte Eidsand Kjørven, 'Anvendelse av avtaleloven § 36 ved salg av finansielle instrumenter til forbruker; kommentar til Rt 2012, s. 355 (Lognvik)' [2012] 51 (7) Lov og Rett 387 (401, 405-406); Lilleholt, *supra* note 1325, (17); Wabakken, *supra* note 1336, 56-57; this applies especially to the Norwegian Supreme Court cases *Fokus Bank* [2012] Rt. 2012, 1926 and *Lognvik* [2012] Rt. 2012, 355.

1390 Lilleholt, *supra* note 1325, (17), referring to Norwegian Supreme Court cases *Nye Major* [2011] Rt. 2011, 670 and *Krusesgate* [2011] Rt. 2011, 679.

1391 Giertsen, *supra* note 1381, 250.

1392 cf. for a full analysis Finn Arnesen, Valget mellom endring og ugyldighet i forbrukerkontrakter. in Erling Hjelmeng and Viggo Hagstrøm (eds), *Ugyldighet i privatretten: minnebok for Viggo Hagstrøm*, 49-62.

1393 Cf. i.e. CJEU judgment C-421/14, *Banco Primus* [2017] recitals 41, 71.

1394 Cf. also CJEU judgment C-618/10, *Banco Español de Crédito SA v Joaquín Calderón Camino* [2012] recital 69.

spired by the works of *Carsten Smith*, a representative of Legal Realism in Norway. He argued that decisions by inferior courts should be attributed more weight in legal analysis as they provide a more comprehensive picture of the *de facto* application of legal norms.[1395] As there exist no comprehensive statistics on tribunals' decisions regarding unfair terms in consumer contracts, I conducted a study of the tribunals' use of § 37 in April and May 2018.[1396]

Out of 500 cases 127 cases considered § 37. In 25 cases § 36 was successful and § 37 was not considered, in 79 cases § 36 was not successful and § 37 was not considered. In 269 cases § 37 was inapplicable, inadmissible or subject to a statute of limitations. Not including non-applicable cases, this means that in 55% of cases § 37 was considered, in 11% of cases a claim under § 36 was successful without considering § 37 and in 34% of cases a claim under § 36 was unsuccessful without considering § 37. Most of the cases that considered § 37 were decided in 2013 and 2014 (ca. 63.7%). The majority of cases that considered § 37 were decided by the FINKNB (ca. 66.9%) and the Financial Appeals Tribunal for insurance companies (FINKNF, ca. 26%). The Electricity Appeals Tribunal (ELKN, ca. 2.4%), FKU (ca. 2.4%) and Market Council (ca. 0.8%) accounted for the least number and the House Rental Appeals Tribunal for none of the cases that considered § 37. 55% of cases that related to § 37 mainly considered the reasoning of the *Røeggen*-judgment.[1397] Only one tribunal decision considered the UCTD's grey list. This case turned out successful for the claimant. Only ca. 4% of cases considered the Directive's content.

108 cases in front of the Financial Appeals Tribunal for banks and the Financial Appeals Tribunal for insurance companies concerned an alleged

1395 Slagstad, *supra* note 254, (227-228); Carsten Smith, *Statsliv og rettsteori*, 347-351.

1396 I especially thank Stian Øby Johansen (University of Oslo) for the help and input regarding this research. I gathered the relevant data from the Norwegian legal database 'Lovdata' (www.lovdata.no). On the 16th April 2018 I logged in on 'Lovdata' and started my case research. I used the advanced search tool and chose the Electricity Appeals Tribunal (elklagenemnda), the Financial Appeals Tribunal (finansklagenemnda), the Consumer Appeals Tribunal (forbrukerklagenemnda), the House Rental Appeals Tribunal (husleietvistutvalget) and the Market Council (Markedsrådet) as tribunals for the study. I used the parameters "avtaleloven § 36" and "avtaleloven § 37" and looked for decisions from 1995 until 2018. I received 760 search results. I then exported the 500 results that 'Lovdata' qualified as relevant to an Excel-sheet and looked at the reasoning in each case.

1397 Claimants were successful in ca. 37% and unsuccessful in ca. 63% of such cases.

breach of information duties with respect to investment contracts; thus, a similar constellation as that in *Røeggen*.

Most other cases arose in relation to insurance contracts and most cases that mentioned § 37 did so with respect to the *uklarhetsregel* pursuant to § 37 No. 3. The following clauses are examples for decisions considering § 37 or the Directive and finding the term invalid: a penalty clause imposing an excessive withdrawal fee on the consumer,[1398] a variation clause as to the monthly leasing rate because of changes in the money lending market (grey list mentioned),[1399] a variation clause providing for a unilateral reduction of the degree of invalidity under an insurance contract[1400] and a supplier's discretion clause providing that the seller could decide how festival tickets would be despatched so that consumers were required to pick them up at a given location (Directive discussed)[1401]. In contrast, a variation clause providing for the power to unilaterally lower the bonus of a car insurance[1402] and a penalty clause relating to the calculation of premiums[1403] were held valid while § 37 was mentioned.

The following examples are clauses that were held invalid according to § 36 without mentioning § 37: a variation clause regarding a unilateral price increase,[1404] a limitation clause providing that only mobile phones were covered that could be proven to have been used directly before damage took place by showing 'net traffic',[1405] a travel insurance policy's limitation clause with respect to coverage of 'co-habitants'[1406] and a clause limiting coverage to damage caused by 'external accidental means'[1407]. And the following exemplary clauses were held valid in light of § 36: variation clauses with respect to the calculation of electricity prices,[1408] a supplier's discretion clause relating to the use and calculation of exchange rates,[1409] a life insurance policy's limitation clause with respect to coverage of 'co-

1398 ELKN-2015-288.
1399 FinKN-2017-204.
1400 FinKN-2016-203.
1401 FKU-2010-1147; FKU-2010-1251.
1402 FSN-7055; FSN-6925.
1403 FSN-6526.
1404 ELKN-2016-259 (furthermore, the contractual conditions were only published on the electricity provider's website but not the website which the customer used to conclude the contract).
1405 FinKN-2014-264.
1406 FinKN-2011-100 (must have lived together for two years).
1407 FSN-7156.
1408 ELKN-2015-62; ELKN-2014-183.
1409 FinKN-2016-285.

habitants',[1410] a limitation clause providing for 25% less coverage in case of recklessness,[1411] a limitation clause providing that only mobile phones were covered that could be proven to have been used directly before damage took place by showing 'net traffic',[1412] a clause that transferred the risk of faulty craftsmen's work to the insured[1413] and a travel insurance policy's limitation clause allowing only for coverage in case of cancellation of travel due to death in the family if that death occurred 'in the North'[1414].

Similar clauses could lead to different outcomes under different circumstances which speaks for an individualistic and interpretative approach – similar to the Swiss one (see below) – rather than a general prohibitive one. For example, a clause limiting liability to the insured only if the 'cohabitant' has not resided with him or her for more than two years was held to be unfair in case of a travel insurance and fair in case of life insurances.

It must be positively acknowledged that in the majority of applicable cases § 37 was considered and, thus, even if the claim failed the available means of consumer protection mechanisms had been applied. The majority of cases that considered § 37 were decided in 2013 and 2014. This development must be seen in light of the *Røeggen*-judgment of 2013. Under the impression of *Røeggen*, more cases considered § 37 but especially the reasoning of the Norwegian Supreme Court decision. A majority of cases that considered § 37 was decided under the impression of *Røeggen*. Out of these cases only ca. 37% were successful on the claimant's side. It is likely that *Røeggen* led to a trend and motivated consumers to assert claims against similar contracts. Thus, the number of cases similar to *Røeggen* increased. The increased numbers due to the publicity of *Røeggen* also led to an increased number of cases in which arguments were unfounded. The *Røeggen*-judgment has been frequently quoted especially by the Financial Appeals Tribunal. However, this does not appear to have raised attention with respect to the UCTD itself.

Most cases that mentioned § 37 or the Directive – including those referring to *Røeggen* – did so with regard to the ambiguity rule (Art. 5 UCTD, § 37 No. 3) likely because such a rule had existed under Norwegian law before the introduction of the UCTD. Art. 5 UCTD and § 37 No. 3 seem to

---

1410 FinKN-2016-230; FinKN-2013-525; FinKN-2013-524; FinKN-2011-246; FSN-7141; FSN-6491 (must have lived together for two years).

1411 FinKN-2016-404.

1412 FinKN-2014-263 (in this case the phone had not been used for four days based on which the majority decided against the consumer).

1413 FinKN-2011-250.

1414 FinKN-2011-163; FSN-6754.

have had a positive and clarifying impact on the use of the *uklarhetsregel*. As a further specialty of Norwegian law, price clauses (and those relating to the main subject matter of the contract) can be subjected to control under § 37. The results show that terms are controlled on a case-by-case basis, meaning that the declaration of unfairness in one case does not entail a general declaration of unfairness. This individual mean of term control contrasts starkly with the general term control under the Marketing Control Act. It, furthermore, reflects the individual justice approach in § 36 which provides a general mean of term control but affords an individual evaluation in each case. This individualistic approach regarding *in concreto* proceedings[1415] as well as the different approach regarding collective term control[1416] are both in line with EU law. However, the UCTD's Annex could be used as guidance more often.[1417]

Of course, both the quantitative and qualitative results must be treated cautiously as each individual case has its own evidentiary and factual basis. The results must not be used as a sole mean to evaluate the implementation of consumer protection regarding unfair terms in Norway.[1418]

E. Consumer Image

Originally § 36 (and consequently § 37) was underlied by a vulnerable consumer image requiring a material term control to re-establish a balance of bargaining power between the parties (see the *Røstad* case) and providing a broad protection mechanism. However, the paradigm appears to have shifted since. In following decisions such as *Lognvik*, *Fokus Bank* and *Røeggen* the Norwegian Supreme Court focussed much more on the circumstances of the case, i.e. information duties which would reflect more of a

1415 Cf. CJEU judgment C-377/14, *Ernst Georg Radlinger and Helena Radlingerová v Finway a.s.* [2016] recital 95.

1416 Cf. Opinion of Advocate General Szpunar in CJEU Joined Cases C-381/14 and C-385/14, *Sales Sinués and Drame Ba* [2016] recitals 69-73.

1417 Cf. i.e. CJEU judgment C-415/11, *Aziz* [2013] recitals 74-75.

1418 Cf. Slagstad, *supra* note 254, (224): '[...] it is highly uncertain how much empirical investigations can tell us – they must be considered "more as illustrations of problems that are posed than as answers to the general question of whether and under what conditions laws are respected and work according to their purpose" [...].', quoting Vilhelm Aubert, *Rettens sosiale funksjon*, 164: 'må ses mer som illustrasjoner av problemstillinger enn som svar på det generelle spørsmålet om, og under hvilke betingelser, lover blir etterlevet og virker etter sin hensikt.'

rational consumer image. At the same time, the broad abstract term control mechanism embodied by the Consumer Authority reveals a concern for the fairness in the market and aims at broad consumer protection and enabling consumers to become confident market actors. A clear consumer image either based on the vulnerable or the rational consumer can, thus, not be identified but lies somewhere in between.

F. Interim Conclusion

The preventative administrative control of terms by the Consumer Authority under § 22 Marketing Control Act appears to function well. Under the economic parameters set out for this dissertation the Norwegian regulatory approach appears effective. The collective term control is underlied by cooperation and trust which are key institutional elements of Norwegian society. Through this cooperation transaction costs are kept low. If cases require adjudication there exists the cost-saving alternative of tribunals which require less transaction costs than court proceedings. It can, thus, be said that with special regard to Norwegian institutional factors the Norwegian model of term control appears especially adequate in its specific institutional setting.

However, the implementation of §§ 36, 37 seems more problematic. Due to the implementation's nature, the UCTD is not considered by courts, tribunals and lawyers frequently but only seen as an add-on for the pre-existing § 36. While at the outset the legislator presumed that the realm of § 36 would cover the UCTD and the introduction of the additional § 37 would, thus, suffice as an implementing measure, subsequent case law has proven otherwise. While the UCTD requires a content-oriented control of terms, the application of § 36 leads in the direction of a merely process-oriented control with respect to the circumstances of the conclusion of the contract. This development means that the UCTD is not in fact covered by § 36 and accordingly bears the risk that consumer protection under the UCTD is not fully realised. Moreover, it has been shown that the lack of consideration of § 37 and the UCTD has led to unfavourable outcomes in court cases where the consumer could have otherwise been successful. More generally, this lack of consideration, furthermore, reflects a breach of the courts' *ex officio* duty to consider EEA law.

Norway provides a positive example with respect to procedural effectiveness in light of EU law, as both collective and individual proceedings are easily accessible. On the one hand, the Consumer Authority offers a broad collective term control, while consumers can access individual proceedings – especially in front of tribunals but also court proceedings – easily. It is, however, hereby suggested that actual consumer protection in front of consumer tribunals could be improved if the indicative list of unfair terms in the UCTD was provided under a national legal act or administrative order and not just in the preparatory works. Its indicative character could provide orientation as to when a term should be considered unfair especially in light of the broad scope of the wording of § 36. This orientation measure would be helpful especially for non-lawyers who are not as well acquainted with (European) law and could ensure that decisions are made in accordance with EEA law, thus, preserving legal homogeneity and a European consumer protection standard even at the lowest level of adjudication.

G. Comparative Analysis

UCTD	**UK**	**Germany**	**Norway**
Transparency Test	Section 61 CRA 2015	§§ 305c, 307 BGB	§ 37 No. 3 Contracts Act
Fairness Test	Section 68 CRA 2015	§ 307 BGB	§§ 36, 37 Contracts Act
List of Terms	Schedule 2 CRA 2015	§§ 308, 309 BGB	Preparatory Works
Abstract Control	Section 70, Schedules 3 and 5 of the CRA 2015	§§ 1, 3 UKlaG	§ 22 Marketing Control Act

If the UK was to join the EEA it would still be by the Unfair Contract Terms Directive. It must now be evaluated whether the Norwegian, UK – and to a lesser extent German – implementations of the UCTD are comparable and whether the Norwegian approach could serve as future inspiration for the UK after leaving the EU.

The consumer definition and scope of applicability is similar in all three jurisdictions. In Norway, however, price clauses and clauses relating to the subject matter of the contract are not excluded from the scope of applicability. Unlike under UK legislation and similar to German legislation, § 37 only covers non-individually negotiated agreements. Furthermore, cases regarding banking and credit agreements have been the subject of major court proceedings. The *Røeggen* case concerned information duties with respect to consumer credit agreements and is, thus, hardly comparable with the portrayed English case-law.

There exists a comprehensive and easily accessible alternative dispute resolution tribunal system in Norway which can be linked to the sociological factors of high interpersonal trust rates and a homogenous society.

Most tribunal cases have arisen with respect to insurance contracts. In this regard, the Norwegian case-law resembles that of Germany rather than the UK where cases regarding insurance contracts have not arisen as frequently. Interestingly, Norwegian tribunal case-law reveals similar cases to German court case-law especially regarding exclusion and limitation clauses in (travel) health insurance contracts. However, the similar subject matters do not mean that the Norwegian and German approaches are systematically similar and, thus, closer to each other. The depicted tribunal case-law reveals a rather individualistic approach to unfair terms even if they are included in T&Cs, meaning that each case is decided in light of the individual circumstances rather than with effect to other agreements. This approach reflects the underlying legal realist theory of § 36 and Norwegian law in general. In contrast, Germany introduced a 'special law' on T&Cs dealing specifically with the problems associated with the mass use of contract terms rather than continuing to base the entire body of rules on T&Cs solely on § 242 BGB. The differences especially with respect to the more individualistic approach under Norwegian law may also be related to differing sociological factors, i.e. Norway being characterised as a rather homogenous society while German society is rather heterogenous. Judgments based on individual circumstances may be better accepted where both parties are likely to found their beliefs on the same value set (see also below).

While in Norway the task of a broad kind of term control is left with the Consumer Authority, it is an essential feature of judicial term review under §§ 305 et seq. BGB and the UCTD in Germany. There does not exist a separate system of administrative control under German law. Thus, the Norwegian and German approaches differ considerably even though they are underlied by similar notions of fairness and good faith and in practice address similar legal areas. While they are both relatively effective under EU parameters, the Norwegian approach – offering administrative collective term control – appears more effective than the German one. In this regard, the Norwegian and UK approaches are very similar and the discursive practice by the Consumer Authority may prove informative for the CMA.

It is, however, questionable whether the Norwegian and UK approaches to material term control are comparable. Under Norwegian law, § 36 provides for a general clause that aims at covering a broad range of areas in a flexible manner as well as a rather less significant addition to implement the UCTD (§ 37). However, the underlying principle of fairness is not clearly defined. § 36 fits in with the principles of Scandinavian Legal Realism under which courts shall be equipped with a broad discretion to decide according to the individual circumstances of the case. It is, furthermore, based on the duty of loyalty – a broad concept similar to the duty of good faith under German law. These principles are foreign concepts under the English common law of contract. While fairness may be considered, the elements of consideration must be clearly defined. A broad concept of undefined 'fairness' or 'good faith' remains foreign to English law. The concepts underlying § 36 are, furthermore, rooted in the rather homogenous and compromise oriented Norwegian society. Considerations under such a broad norm will normally be value-based. For such considerations to be accepted by the parties to the dispute, their values must be founded on a similar basis. In this regard Norwegian sociological factors differ from those of the UK.

It must, therefore, be concluded that the Norwegian and UK approaches are hardly comparable and that due to these differences the Norwegian material term control does not serve as a future model for the UK. Regarding the approach to collective term control, however, the discursive approach by the Consumer Authority may prove informative for the similarly structured CMA.

Chapter 13: Unfair Terms in Consumer Contracts in Switzerland

Switzerland was not obliged and did not decide to autonomously adapt the UCTD. Instead over the years a fragmented system of different provisions and case-law was established which shall be portrayed in the following sections.

A. *History and Overview of Unfair Terms (in Consumer Contracts) in Switzerland*

While the first attempts to regulate unfair terms date back to the beginning of the 20th century,[1419] the general as well as the consumer specific law on unfair terms remains fragmented until today.[1420] The Swiss legislator's reluctance to introduce comprehensive legislation on unfair terms may be explained by a will to 'protect' the liberal orientation of existing bodies private law. Such an attitude is revealed in the preparatory documents for respective legislation.[1421] In the following, the legal areas containing regulation with respect to unfair terms are portrayed separately in order to ensure a concise depiction of regulatory measures.

1419 Alexander Brunner, Entwicklung des schweizerischen Rechts der Allgemeinen Geschäftsbedingungen. in Alexander Brunner, Anton K. Schnyder and Andrea Eisner-Kiefer (eds), *Allgemeine Geschäftsbedingungen nach neuem Schweizer Recht*, 19; Alexander Brunner, Allgemeine Geschäftsbedingungen. in Ernst A. Kramer (ed), *Schweizerisches Privatrecht, Band 10: Konsumentenschutz im Privatrecht*, 124.

1420 Thomas Koller, 'Einmal mehr: Das Bundesgericht und seine verdeckte AGB-Inhaltskontrolle' [2008] 17 (8) AJP 943 (943); Esther Widmer, *Missbräuchliche Geschäftsbedingungen nach Art 8 UWG: Unter besonderer Berücksichtigung der Allgemeinen Geschäftsbedingungen von Banken*, recital 28.

1421 Cf. Parliamentary discussions preceding the S-UWG revision, i.e. Parliamentarians Schwander and Gadient, National Council, Protocol of Parliamentary Session on the 8 March 2011, AmtlBull. NR 2011, 1 (222-223) or Council of States, Protocol of Parliamentary Session on the 17 March 2011, AmtlBull. StR 2011, 1 (304).

I. Law of Obligations

In contrast to Germany, there does not exist a clear dogmatic distinction between the interpretation of individually negotiated contracts and T&Cs.[1422] Accordingly, no separate (normative) body of norms has been developed to regulate such T&Cs in mass contracts but the traditional interpretative canon of contract law applies equally to individually negotiated contracts and T&Cs.[1423] The interpretation of all general terms and conditions regardless of the involvement of consumers follows a three-step-scheme:[1424]

1. Test of Applicability (*Geltungskontrolle*) relating to the effective incorporation of the general terms and conditions,[1425]
2. Interpretative Review (*Auslegungskontrolle*) according to the general interpretative canons of Swiss contract law (cf. Art. 18 OR)[1426] and
3. Review of Content (*Inhaltskontrolle*) relating to the limits set by the general legal framework[1427].

Before the introduction of a specific norm with respect to consumer contracts (see below), consumer related issues were discussed as part of the *Geltungskontrolle* and *Auslegungskontrolle*.

As part of the *Geltungskontrolle*, it is questioned whether and how the general terms and conditions have been incorporated into the contract

1422 Wolfgang Wiegand, Die Auslegung Allgemeiner Geschäftsbedingungen. in Heinrich Honsell and others (eds), *Privatrecht und Methode: Festschrift für Ernst A. Kramer*, 334.

1423 Ibid. 331 et seq.; Claire Huguenin, *Obligationenrecht - Allgemeiner und Besonderer Teil*, recital 609.

1424 Peter Gauch and others, *Schweizerisches Obligationenrecht*, recital 1127; Helmut Heiss, Art 8. in Reto Heizmann and Leander D. Loacker (eds), *UWG Kommentar*, recital 80; Huguenin, ibid., recitals 613 et seq.; Anton K. Schnyder, Einführung in die Dogmatik der AGB nach schweizerischem und europäischem Recht. in Alexander Brunner, Anton K. Schnyder and Andrea Eisner-Kiefer (eds), *Allgemeine Geschäftsbedingungen nach neuem Schweizer Recht*, 48; Nadia Walker, *Kontrolle von Konsumenten-AGB unter besonderer Berücksichtigung der Inhaltskontrolle nach Art 8 UWG*, 30-31; Widmer, *supra* note 1420, recital 67. For a critical view and, thus, different categorisation, cf. Thomas Probst, Art 8. in Peter Jung and Philippe Spitz (eds), *Stämpflis Handkommentar UWG*, recital 155 (fn. 199) who distinguishes (1) a review of consensus (*Konsenskontrolle*), (2) test of validity (*Gültigkeitskontrolle*) and (3) the interpretative review (*Auslegungskontrolle*).

1425 Huguenin, ibid., recital 613 et seq.; Schnyder, ibid.

1426 Huguenin, ibid., recital 627 et seq.; Schnyder, ibid., 50.

1427 Huguenin, ibid., recital 631; Schnyder, ibid., 51.

(*Einbeziehungskontrolle*).[1428] They can either be incorporated by way of complete incorporation (*Vollübernahme*), meaning that the party receiving the general terms and conditions has fully read and understood the provisions, or by way of global incorporation (*Globalübernahme*), meaning that the receiving party has agreed to the general terms and conditions but not read them explicitly.[1429] It is presumed that T&Cs are usually incorporated by way of global incorporation.[1430] It must then be examined whether any terms would have appeared unusual to the receiving party if they had read and fully understood the general terms and conditions (*Ungewöhnlichkeitsregel*).[1431] In case a term is found to be unusual and the receiving party did not know about the term, the respective provision does not bear any legal effect due to a lack of consensus.[1432]

As part of the *Auslegungskontrolle*, it is examined whether any term entails an inherent ambiguity that cannot be resolved by any of the interpretative canons in light or Art. 18 Section OR (see below) (*Unklarheitenregel*).[1433] If an ambiguous term cannot be clarified it will be interpreted against the party relying on it (*contra preferentem* rule).[1434] Thereby, the Swiss system of term control still resembles basic (former) term control mechanisms in the UK and Germany (cf. above).

This approach to the interpretation of general terms and conditions has been criticised heavily for a systematically incorrect review of content as part of the *Geltungskontrolle* and *Auslegungskontrolle*, thus, introducing a *hidden* review of content (*verdeckte Inhaltskontrolle*).[1435] Furthermore, the existing system under the Swiss Code of Obligations does not provide sufficient protection of the weaker party to the contract.[1436] As a consequence, calls for an *open* content review (*offene Inhaltskontrolle*) have been voiced.[1437]

1428 For a more detailed overview, cf. Widmer, *supra* note 1420, recitals 71 et seq.

1429 Huguenin, *supra* note 1423, recitals 614, 618; Probst, *supra* note 1424, recital 156 (as part of the *Konsenskontrolle*).

1430 Huguenin, ibid., recital 618; Widmer, *supra* note 1420, recital 81.

1431 Huguenin, ibid., recital 619 et seq.; Probst, *supra* note 1424, recitals 167 et seq. For a detailed depiction see below ('Legal Framework Today').

1432 Probst, ibid., recital 181; Walker, *supra* note 1424, 57.

1433 Huguenin, *supra* note 1423, recital 629; Probst, ibid., recital 207.

1434 Huguenin, ibid.

1435 For an overview, cf. Walker, *supra* note 1424, 59-61, 71-73. Similar to the criticism in Germany before the introduction of the AGBG, cf. *supra* note 1225.

1436 Probst, *supra* note 1424, recital 209.

1437 Cf. Huguenin, *supra* note 1423, recital 633; Koller, *supra* note 1420, (951-953); Probst, ibid., recital 210; Wiegand, *supra* note 1422, 343.

II. Law on Unfair Trading Practices

In 1986, the legislator responded to calls for an open content review with the introduction of Art. 8 S-UWG 1986.[1438] Art. 8 S-UWG 1986 provided that

> [A person] especially acts unfairly who uses pre-formulated general terms and conditions that misleadingly cause a disadvantage to a contractual party:
> a. by severely deviating from the legal order directly or by analogy or
> b. by providing an allocation of rights and obligations that severely deviates from the nature of the contract.[1439]

Unfortunately, Art. 8 S-UWG 1986 did not entirely resolve the problems relating to the interpretation of T&Cs but rather caused more uncertainty. First, the provision was inserted in the Law on Unfair Trading Practices instead of the Code of Obligations. This appears problematic because the nature of the norm cannot be fully ascertained as belonging to competition law and the law on unfair trading practices or contract law.[1440] Second, Art. 8 S-UWG 1986 was not drafted in a clear and intelligible manner. Especially the phrase 'misleadingly' (*in irreführender Weise*) caused great confusion and in practice led to a heavily restricted use of Art. 8 S-UWG 1986.[1441] The courts were confronted with a wording that required 'misleading unfairness' while 'obvious unfairness' did not suffice.[1442] Although

---

1438 Swiss Federal Council, Botschaft zu einem Bundesgesetz gegen den unlauteren Wettbewerb, 18 May 1983, Bundesblatt 1983 II 1009 (1051-1053).

1439 Unlauter handelt insbesondere, wer vorformulierte allgemeine Geschäftsbedingungen verwendet, die in irreführender Weise zum Nachteil einer Vertragspartei:
a. von der unmittelbar oder sinngemäss anwendbaren gesetzlichen Ordnung erheblich abweichen oder
b. eine der Vertragsnatur erheblich widersprechende Verteilung von Rechten und Pflichten vorsehen. (Translation by author). Refining the definition of unfair commercial dealings contained in Art. 2 S-UWG 1986/2011.

1440 Heiss, *supra* note 1424, recitals 36, 43 et seq.; Peter Jung, Die systematische Stellung der offenen AGB-Inhaltskontrolle im UWG – Vertrags- und wettbewerbsrechtliche Folgeprobleme. in Alexander Brunner, Anton K. Schnyder and Andrea Eisner-Kiefer (eds), *Allgemeine Geschäftsbedingungen nach neuem Schweizer Recht*, 130 et seq.; Probst, *supra* note 1424, recital 1; Walker, *supra* note 1424, 113-114. See also below 'Nature of Art. 8 UWG 2011'.

1441 Probst, ibid., recital 214.

1442 Heiss, *supra* note 1424, recital 32.

the Swiss legislator had previously expressed the intention to create a content-oriented norm[1443] the requirement of misleadingness was inserted to emphasise its nature as a norm relating to unfair commercial dealings[1444]. The wording led to a restrictive use of Art. 8 S-UWG 1986[1445] and did not improve the regulatory position on unfair terms that had existed prior to the introduction of Art. 8 S-UWG 1986. Thus, despite the good intentions behind the norm, it remained without considerable effect.[1446]

The Swiss legislator realised the shortcomings of the legislation on unfair terms and accordingly revised Art. 8 S-UWG 1986 in 2011.[1447] Art. 8 S-UWG 2011 which is still in force today reads as follows:

> [A person] especially acts unfairly who uses general terms and conditions that contrary to good faith provide for a significant and unjustified imbalance between the contractual rights and contractual obligations to the disadvantage of consumers.[1448]

While many had called for an integration into the Code of Obligations to achieve more clarity with respect to the interpretation of unfair terms,[1449] the legislator decided to maintain the unclear interpretative dichotomy under the Code of Obligations and the Law on Unfair Trading Practices and, thus, a mixed individual (contract law) and abstract (competition law) control measure.[1450] Unlike Art. 8 S-UWG 1986, Art. 8 S-UWG 2011 only applies to contracts with consumers. Furthermore, the requirement of 'misleadingness' has been replaced with a violation of the principle of good faith (*Treuwidrigkeit*) and the requirement of severe deviation from the le-

---

1443 Swiss Federal Council (1983), *supra* note 1438, (1072).

1444 Probst, *supra* note 1424, recital 213.

1445 It was only applied in 14 cases of which 9 did not find a violation of Art. 8 S-UWG 1986, cf. Probst, ibid., recital 214 (fn. 321).

1446 Ibid.; Walker, *supra* note 1424, 99-100.

1447 Swiss Federal Council, Botschaft zur Änderungn des Bundesgesetzes gegen den unlauteren Wettbewerb, 2 September 2009, Bundesblatt 2009 Nr. 38 6151 (6152). For a detailed analysis of the legislating process leading to the revised Art. 8 S-UWG, cf. Brunner (2014), *supra* note 1419, 25 et seq.; Widmer, *supra* note 1420, recitals 174 et seq.

1448 Unlauter handelt insbesondere, wer allgemeine Geschäftsbedingungen verwendet, die in Treu und Glauben verletzender Weise zum Nachteil der Konsumentinnen und Konsumenten ein erhebliches und ungerechtfertigtes Missverhältnis zwischen den vertraglichen Rechten und den vertraglichen Pflichten vorsehen. (Translation by author).

1449 Probst, *supra* note 1424, recital 214.

1450 Jung, *supra* note 1440, 162-163. See more below 'Nature of Art. 8 S-UWG 2011'.

gal order or the nature of the contract has been replaced with the requirement of a 'significant and unjustified imbalance'. These changes reveal a strong influence of European law, namely the UCTD, which also served as inspiration in the course of the legislative reform procedure.[1451] As Switzerland is not legally obliged to implement the UCTD, Art. 8 S-UWG 2011 thereby provides an example for partial autonomous adaptation of European law.[1452] Consequently, Swiss courts shall consider the UCTD and related CJEU case-law without being legally bound by it.[1453]

B. Legal Framework Today

The following section depicts the Swiss legal framework of interpretation of unfair terms in consumer contracts as of today. The individual examination combines the Law of Obligation's three-step-scheme and the special protection mechanism under Art. 8 S-UWG 2011. While the first two steps apply to the individual review of all general terms and conditions, the review of content in light of Art. 8 S-UWG 2011 only applies to consumer contracts. In addition to the individual term control mechanism there also exists the possibility of an abstract term control which shall be depicted at the end of this section.

I. Geltungskontrolle

As mentioned above the three-step-control-scheme starts with the test of applicability which concerns the question whether the general terms and conditions have been effectively included in the respective contract. The inclusion does not require actual acknowledgement of the general terms

---

1451 Swiss Federal Council (2009), *supra* note 1447, (6171, 6173, 6179), which explicitly refers to the UCTD including its Annex; Probst, ibid., recital 11; Florent Thouvenin, 'Art 8 UWG: Zur Strukturierung eines strukturlosen Tatbestandes' [29 October 2012] Jusletter recital 2; Widmer, *supra* note 1420, recitals 222 et seq.

1452 Cf. Probst, *supra* note 1424, recital 153; Schnyder, *supra* note 1424, 71. Unlike *Widmer* who finds that Art. 8 S-UWG 2011 does not embody autonomous adaptation of European law at all, cf. Widmer, ibid., recitals 227, 231.

1453 Cf. *supra* note 558; Probst, ibid.; *Widmer* accepts 'European law oriented' comparative interpretation, cf. Widmer, ibid., recital 232.

and conditions; the opportunity to take notice suffices.[1454] However, the terms that were included by such global incorporation must not be unusual and surprising to the receiving party (*Ungewöhnlichkeitsregel*).[1455] This is especially likely if the receiving party was 'inexperienced, not acquainted to the customs of the respective industry or generally in a weaker position when the contract was concluded'.[1456] The individual's subjective position, i.e. knowledge regarding the customs of the respective industry play a decisive role in determining whether a term must be considered unfair.[1457] Thus, the assessment in each individual case must be based both on objective and subjective considerations.[1458]

The following terms have been held unusual by the Swiss Federal Court due to a violation of the *Ungewöhnlichkeitsregel*:[1459]

- An exclusion clause included in the agreement for a comprehensive vehicle damage insurance (*Vollkaskoversicherung*) that excluded coverage in case of a minor violation of traffic rules[1460]
- A limitation clause that provided for a loss of claim to daily sickness allowance for sickness due to work incapacity under collective insurance if the insured party later concludes an individual insurance policy[1461]

1454 Cf. Swiss Federal Court, *X S.A. v Banque Y* [2006] 4C.427/2005, recital 2.1; Swiss Federal Court, *Hanspeter Krattiger v Adolf Forster AG* [1983] BGE 109 II 452 (456); Swiss Federal Court, *Garage Cornavin S.A. v CFF* [1982] BGE 109 II 416 (418).

1455 Swiss Federal Court, *Hanspeter Krattiger v Adolf Forster AG* [1983] BGE 109 II 452 (456). As for the relationship between the *Ungewöhnlichkeitsregel* and Art. 8 S-UWG 2011, cf. Widmer, *supra* note 1420, recitals 368 et seq.

1456 Kathrin Klett and Christoph Hurni, 'Eckpunkte der bisherigen bundesgerichtlichen AGB-Geltungskontrolle' [2012] 30 (2) recht 80 (83).

1457 Schnyder, *supra* note 1424, 50.

1458 Ibid.; Gauch and others, *supra* note 1424, recital 1138 (with examples for surprising terms); Swiss Federal Court, *X Versicherungs-Gesellschaft v Schweizerische Unfallversicherungsanstalt (SUVA)* [2007] 4A_187/2007, recital 5.1; Widmer, *supra* note 1420, recitals 91 et seq. with a detailed overview.

1459 The list does not purport to be conclusive but aims to depict such clauses in an exemplary manner. The list is taken from, Probst, *supra* note 1424, recital 179.

1460 Swiss Federal Court, *A S.A. v S.* [1993] BGE 119 II 443 (446-447).

1461 Swiss Federal Court, *O v Compagnie d'assurances X* [2002] 5C.74/2002, recital 2 c).

- An exclusion clause with respect to the right to terminate the contract after the one-sided amendment of T&Cs by an insurance company[1462]
- A clause that authorises the construction management to approve the final invoice of the company under Art. 154 of the rules of the Swiss Society of Engineers and Architects 118 (*Schweizerischer Ingenieur- und Architektenverein*, SIA-118)[1463]
- An exclusion clause with respect to coverage under a business liability insurance for actions of temporary employees for minor but not severe negligence[1464]
- A clause providing a bank authorisation to disburse a savings account without an identity check[1465]
- A clause providing the reduction of coverage for existing insurance claims if the insurance company terminates the insurance contract[1466]
- A clause providing a 50% reduction of daily sickness allowance for psychological illness[1467]

In the following cases the Swiss Federal Court did not find terms to be unusual or surprising:[1468]

- A clause providing that the consumer has to bear the risk of loss or theft of a Euro check[1469]
- An exclusion clause contained in a contract for supplementary hospitalisation insurance in case of substance abuse or attempted suicide[1470]
- An exclusion clause contained in an insurance contract providing that claims have to be asserted within a limited period[1471]

1462 Swiss Federal Court, *Hanspeter Krattiger v Adolf Forster AG* [1983] BGE 109 II 452 (458).

1463 Swiss Federal Court, *A. and B. v X. Versicherungsgesellschaft AG* [2008] BGE 135 III 1, recitals 3.3-3.5.

1464 Swiss Federal Court, *X Versicherungs-Gesellschaft v Schweizerische Unfallversicherungsanstalt (SUVA)* [2007] 4A_187/2007, recitals 5.4 et seq.

1465 Swiss Federal Court, *B v Banque Z* [1990] BGE 116 II 459, recital 2 a).

1466 Swiss Federal Court, *A. v X. AG* [2009] BGE 135 III 225, recitals 1.3-1.5.

1467 Swiss Federal Court, *A. v X. AG* [2012] BGE 138 III 411, recitals 3.4-3.6.

1468 The list does not purport to be conclusive but aims to depict such clauses in an exemplary manner. The list is taken from Walker, *supra* note 1424, 58-59.

1469 Swiss Federal Court, *L. v Banque X.* [1996] BGE 122 III 373, 378 et seq.

1470 Swiss Federal Court, *X. v Y. Versicherung* [2004] 5C.134/2004, recital 4.3.

1471 Swiss Federal Court, *X. SA v Y. Compagnie d'Assurances* [2008] 4A_200/2008, recital 2.3.

- A waiver clause relating to the exclusion of warranty claims and their offset against the purchase price claim against an acquirer of such purchase price claim.[1472]

The low number of cases indicates a restrictive application of the *Ungewöhnlichkeitsregel*.[1473] Furthermore, a decision regarding the unfairness of a term does not unfold *erga omnes* effect; thus, the *inter partes* finding of unfairness in one individual case must not automatically be applied to another case.[1474]

II. Auslegungskontrolle

As opposed to the German 'unitary approach' which provides a special normative regime with respect to the interpretation of general terms and conditions, Swiss contract law does not treat such terms differently from other terms of the contract.[1475] Consequently, the interpretation of general terms and conditions follows the interpretative canons applicable to all contracts.[1476]

In this regard, Art. 18 Section 1 OR provides that the parties' congruent intentions form the basis of any interpretation. Accordingly, the wording of the contract marks the starting point of any interpretation.[1477] In addition, events preceding the conclusion of the contract, surrounding circumstances, the parties' behaviours before and after the conclusion of the contract, the contract's purpose and customary rules shall be considered;[1478] furthermore, general interpretative principles, such as the principle of good faith.[1479] As mentioned above, any ambiguity that cannot be resolved under the Swiss principles of contractual interpretation (*Unklarheitenregel*),

1472 Swiss Federal Court, *A. v Bank X.* [1983] BGE 109 II 213 (218).

1473 Widmer, *supra* note 1420, recital 95.

1474 Walker, *supra* note 1424, 58.

1475 Christoph Müller, Art 18. in Regina Aebi-Müller and Christoph Müller (eds), *Berner Kommentar zum schweizerischen Privatrecht Art 1-18 OR mit allgemeiner Einleitung in das Schweizerische Obligationenrecht*, recital 227; Probst, *supra* note 1424, recital 204.

1476 Walker, *supra* note 1424, 65-69. For a detailed depiction of Swiss principles of contractual interpretation, cf. Müller, ibid., recitals 17 et seq.; Wolfgang Wiegand, Art 18. in Heinrich Honsell, Nedim Peter Vogt and Wolfgang Wiegand (eds), *Basler Kommentar Obligationenrecht I Art 1-529 OR*, recitals 7 et seq.

1477 Wiegand, ibid., recitals 7, 18 et seq.

1478 Ibid. recitals 26-31.

1479 Ibid. recitals 34 et seq.

will lead to an interpretation *in dubio contra stipulatorem*.[1480] Under general Swiss private law each contract is evaluated according to the individual circumstances. Consequently, a term that is held unfair in one contract may be considered reasonable in another.

III. (offene) Inhaltskontrolle

If the term in question can pass the *Geltungskontrolle* and *Auslegungskontrolle* its content must be reviewed (*Inhaltskontrolle*)[1481] in light of Art. 8 S-UWG 2011 if the contract involves a consumer[1482]. In case Art. 8 S-UWG 2011 is applicable, the court must first evaluate whether there exists an imbalance between the parties' rights and obligations. Second, an evaluation of the significance of this imbalance must be established. In case the imbalance can be classified as significant, a third step evaluates whether such a significant imbalance is unjustified. If so, a fourth and last step shall reveal whether the significant imbalance contravenes the principle of good faith.[1483]

Nature of Art. 8 S-UWG 2011

While the previous sections on Swiss term control emphasised the individualistic approach under Swiss private law, the nature of Art. 8 S-UWG 2011 allowing either for individual or abstract term control proves more controversial.[1484] While some argue that Art. 8 S-UWG 2011 only provides for an abstract term control mechanism (under the Law of Unfair

1480 Cf. Walker, *supra* note 1424, 71.

1481 For a classification and scope of the (general) content review, cf. Widmer, *supra* note 1420, recitals 118 et seq., 133 et seq. and 146 et seq as well as Walker, *supra* note 1424, 81-87. The following analysis will focus on Art. 8 S-UWG 2011 as a control instrument especially in consumer cases. For other (more general) legal instruments (i.e. Art. 19 Section 2 OR) in this regard, cf. Widmer, ibid., recitals 354 et seq.

1482 In cases that do not involve a consumer Art. 2 S-UWG 1986/2011 may serve as a control mechanism regarding the unfairness of general terms and conditions, cf. Schnyder, *supra* note 1424, 42.

1483 For a similar four-step-scheme, cf. Probst, *supra* note 1424, recital 293. *Thouvenin* suggests a different order of examination which, however, does not materially deviate from the scheme adopted here, cf. Florent Thouvenin, Art 8. in Reto M. Hilty and Reto Arpagaus (eds), *Basler Kommentar UWG*, recital 99.

1484 For an overview see Lisa Aeschimann, 'Rundgang durch Art 8 UWG' [1st September 2014] Jusletter recital 12; Heiss, *supra* note 1424, recitals 173 et seq.;

Practices),[1485] others hold that Art. 8 S-UWG 2011 provides for an individual term control mechanism (similar to the Code of Obligations).[1486] The preparatory works reveal that the legislator intended for Art. 8 S-UWG 2011 to have an abstract effect.[1487] This makes sense especially in light of the market regulating purpose of the S-UWG; the legislator intends for unfair terms to be removed from the market. However, the preparatory works also reveal that the legislator, furthermore, explicitly includes an individual term control mechanism in the instrumental description of Art. 8 S-UWG 2011 especially referring to the principle of good faith underlying the norm.[1488]

While the wording of Art. 8 S-UWG 2011 may indicate an abstract scope of term control, it appears more convincing to allow for an individually scoped term control under Art. 8 S-UWG 2011 in light of the Swiss legislator's clearly formulated intention to include an individual term assessment as well as the principle of euro compatible interpretation. In this sense, Art. 8 S-UWG 2011 can be applied in both individual and abstract proceedings with different scopes of term control respectively.[1489]

Scope of Applicability: 'General Terms and Conditions'

An official definition of *Allgemeine Geschäftsbedingungen* does not exist under Swiss law. With reference to several legislative sources, case-law and literature they can be defined as

> unilateral, pre-formulated clauses which are intended for the use in multiple contractual agreements that can usually be considered a non-negotiable basis for the conclusion of the contract.[1490]

Thouvenin (2013), ibid., recitals 89 et seq.; Thouvenin (2012), *supra* note 1451, recitals 3 et seq.; Walker, *supra* note 1424, 110-113.

1485 According to *Thouvenin* this is the majority view, cf. Thouvenin (2013), ibid., recital 89.

1486 Heiss, *supra* note 1424, recital 173; Thouvenin (2013), ibid., recital 89.

1487 Swiss Federal Council (2009), *supra* note 1447, (6162).

1488 Ibid. (6179).

1489 Heiss, *supra* note 1424, recital 175; Markus Hess and Lea Ruckstuhl, 'AGB-Kontrolle nach dem neuen Art 8 UWG - eine kritische Auslegeordnung' [2012] 21 (9) AJP 1188 (1208). See also, however, Thouvenin (2013), *supra* note 1483, recitals 91, 92 (arguing that individual proceedings may only take into account general market conditions rather than individual circumstances).

1490 Probst, *supra* note 1424, recital 234. Similarly, Heiss, ibid., recitals 71 et seq. and Thouvenin (2013), *supra* note 1483, recital 78. For a detailed analysis regarding the Swiss definition of general terms and conditions, cf. Aeschimann, *supra* note 1484, 4 et seq., 116-118.

They, thus, form the opposite of individually negotiated agreements.[1491] The terms and conditions must actually be introduced to the market by using them in individual cases; it does not require specific intent by the user.[1492] Furthermore, the usage of general terms and conditions does not require authorship of the user.[1493]

Scope of Applicability: 'Consumer'

Art. 8 S-UWG 2011 only applies to contracts to the detriment of *consumers*. Neither the preparatory works nor the S-UWG itself contain a definition of the consumer. Generally, a uniform definition of the consumer does not exist under Swiss law. Therefore, the scope of the term 'consumer' must be determined in light of the purpose of Art. 8 S-UWG 2011.[1494] Borrowing from consumer concepts in other legal instruments (among them Art. 3 KKG 2001 or the UCTD), the consumer with respect to Art. 8 S-UWG 2011 can be defined as a natural person who acts for the purpose of satisfying personal or familial requirements *vice versa* not pursuing commercial or professional activities (cf. also Art. 15 (1) (c) Lugano Convention on jurisdiction and the recognition and enforcement of judgments in civil and commercial matters).[1495]

Scope of Applicability: Exemptions

Unlike the UCTD, the wording of Art. 8 S-UWG 2011 does not contain any explicit exemptions as to the scope of applicability. Nevertheless, legal academia argues that certain exemptions contained in the UCTD similarly

1491 Gauch and others, *supra* note 1424, recital 1118; Heiss, ibid., recital 80; Probst, ibid.

1492 Probst, ibid., recitals 235-236; Thouvenin (2013), *supra* note 1483, recital 134; Walker, *supra* note 1424, 118-121.

1493 Probst, ibid., recital 238.

1494 Thouvenin (2013), *supra* note 1483, recital 80; Widmer, *supra* note 1420, recitals 319, 320. For an overview of different consumer definitions, cf. Aeschimann, *supra* note 1484, recitals 8, 9; Thouvenin (2012), *supra* note 1451, recitals 15 et seq.; Walker, *supra* note 1424, 122-126.

1495 Cf. Thouvenin (2013), ibid., recitals 81 et seq. The positive rather than negative definition of the realm of 'private acting' is chosen due to an apparent preference for such a distinction under Swiss law, cf. Thouvenin (2013), ibid., recital 84. *Heiss*, on the other hand, assumes that the distinction between a positive and negative definition does not entail any practical effect. Eventually he would prefer a negative definition with reference to European legislation and treaties, cf. Heiss, *supra* note 1424, recital 119.

apply to Art. 8 S-UWG 2011.[1496] In this regard, neither the definition of the main subject matter of the contract nor price adequacy should be subject to term control under Art. 8 S-UWG 2011 because these terms are usually subject to individual negotiations.[1497] Furthermore, similar to Art. 1 Section 2 UCTD terms that repeat mandatory statutory norms are exempted from term control under Art. 8 S-UWG 2011.[1498]

'Significant Imbalance'

The legislative preparatory works do not contain much guidance on the 'imbalance' of a term.[1499] An imbalance must, thus, be evaluated according to criteria set by the judiciary,[1500] i.e. by way of comparison with dispositive statutory regulation[1501]. The imbalance must further be classified as significant meaning that it must be 'noticeable' and not merely composed of marginal disadvantages.[1502] According to *Probst*, significance can be assumed if the term(s) in question deviate(s) from mandatory statutory norms.[1503] In case of deviation from dispositive statutory norms, a qualitative and quantitative analysis must reveal more than a marginal disadvantage.[1504] The evaluation shall be based on the most detrimental interpretation possible.[1505]

1496 Cf. Heiss, ibid., recital 165 et seq. with further references and a differentiated analysis of such exemptions; Thouvenin (2013), ibid., recitals 93 et seq.

1497 Cf. Heiss, ibid., recital 165; Thouvenin (2013), ibid., recitals 95-97.

1498 Heiss, ibid., recital 172.

1499 Probst, *supra* note 1424, recitals 246-247; Widmer, *supra* note 1420, recitals 249-252.

1500 Probst, ibid., recital 248. See also Widmer, ibid, recital 384. Similar to the German term control as suggested by *Raiser*, cf. *supra* note 1239.

1501 Gauch and others, *supra* note 1424, recitals 1153b, 1153c; Probst, ibid., recitals 250-251 with supporting reference to *Aziz*, thus, in line with a euro compatible interpretative approach; see also Widmer, *supra* note 1420, recital 260 with further references. Unlike *Hess and Ruckstuhl* who oppose such comparison with reference to the legislative preparatory works, cf. Hess and Ruckstuhl, *supra* note 1489, (1197), but see Widmer, ibid., recitals 263, 264 with convincing arguments against such a position.

1502 Probst, ibid., recital 253 with reference to Swiss Federal Council (1983), *supra* note 1438, (1074).

1503 Probst, ibid., recital 254.

1504 For a detailed overview of criteria for such an assessment, cf. Hess and Ruckstuhl, *supra* note 1489, (1205-1206); Widmer, *supra* note 1420, recitals 268 et seq.

1505 Heiss, *supra* note 1424, recital 207; Probst, ibid., recitals 255-256.

'Unjustified'

Furthermore, the significant imbalance must be unjustified. The legislative preparatory works do not reveal a reason for the additional insertion in 2011. It has, thus, been concluded that it was simply copied from the German version of the UCTD which is the only one that requires a significant *and* unjustified imbalance.[1506] With reference to the German version of the UCTD, the CJEU does not appear to attribute any special importance to the criterion.[1507] While Switzerland is not legally bound by the UCTD or CJEU case-law in that regard, some authors still question the significance of the requirement of justification and conclude that the criterion was inserted by mistake.[1508] It has, however, also been brought forward that a term that causes a significant imbalance between the rights and obligations of the parties may be justified if it is compensated by other contractual clauses to the benefit of the consumer which limits the detriment caused by the alleged unfair term, i.e. by concrete advantages such as different price options depending on the degree of excluded liability.[1509] Generally, concepts with respect to compensation reveal that the detrimental and beneficial clauses must closely relate to each other.[1510] If such a link cannot be established a term will be classified as causing a significant and unjustified imbalance.

'Contrary to Good Faith'

Lastly, the significant and unjustified imbalance must contravene the principle of good faith. Oriented at Art. 3 UCTD, the requirement was inserted as a replacement of the requirement of 'misleadingness' (Art. 8 S-UWG 1986) and is considered broader, thus, covering a wider range of unfair terms in consumer contracts.[1511] However, the intention to broaden the

1506 Heiss, ibid., recital 209; Probst, ibid., recital 261; Thouvenin (2013), *supra* note 1483, recital 132; Walker, *supra* note 1424, 131-132.

1507 Cf. Probst, ibid.

1508 Heiss, *supra* note 1424, recital 209; Probst, ibid., recital 262; Thouvenin (2013), *supra* note 1483, recital 132; Walker, *supra* note 1424, 133. For an overview, cf. Aeschimann, *supra* note 1484, recital 15.

1509 Heiss, ibid., recital 211; Probst, ibid., recitals 267, 272. With reference to a reduced price as compensation, cf. Heiss, ibid.; Walker, *supra* note 1424, 138; Widmer, *supra* note 1420, recital 301.

1510 Hess and Ruckstuhl, *supra* note 1489, (1206); Aeschimann, *supra* note 1484, recital 13; Widmer, ibid., recital 299 with further references.

1511 Probst, *supra* note 1424, recital 277; Swiss Federal Council (2009), *supra* note 1447, (6179).

norm's scope also brought about a doubling effect. Art. 2 S-UWG 1986/2011 already provides for a breach of the principle of good faith in case of unfair behaviour. Thus, the wording of Art. 8 S-UWG 2011 merely indicates that an imbalance that contravenes the principle of good faith constitutes a breach of the principle of good faith.[1512] One could, thus, conclude that the requirement does not bear any independent meaning.[1513] However, by way of euro compatible interpretation in light of CJEU case-law the requirement can bear meaning as an independent criterion.[1514] In this light, a lack of concern for the consumer's legitimate interests constitutes a breach of good faith.[1515] The term user, therefore, contravenes the principle of good faith if he or she disloyally uses general terms and conditions which the consumer would not accept if he or she had known about the unfair term(s) at the time of conclusion of the respective agreement.[1516] In support of this argument, the Swiss Federal Council had explained that the explicit insertion of a requirement of good faith should enable a holistic assessment and appreciation of the parties' legitimate interests relating to the (unfair) term(s) in question in the course of the law-making process.[1517]

1512 Probst, ibid., recital 278. Cf. Jung, *supra* note 1440, 137 et seq. for the effect of overlapping principles of good faith in Art. 2 S-UWG 1986/2011 and Art. 2 Section 1 ZGB on and scope of interpretation of the criterion in Art. 8 S-UWG 2011.

1513 Probst, ibid. recital 280; Widmer, *supra* note 1420, recital 293. For an overview, cf. Aeschimann, *supra* note 1484, recital 16.

1514 Probst, ibid., recitals 280-281.

1515 Heiss, *supra* note 1424, recital 217 with reference to further theories regarding the requirement of good faith under Art. 8 S-UWG 2011.

1516 Probst, *supra* note 1424, recital 280. In this light, *Probst* suggests a different scheme of review, under which the requirement of good faith is evaluated before a possible justification of the term, cf. Probst, ibid., recital 283.

1517 Swiss Federal Council (2009), *supra* note 1447, (6179). The requirement is specifically mentioned with reference to the review of terms in individual proceedings. Cf. also Thouvenin (2012), *supra* note 1451, recitals 22 et seq. and 31 et seq. and Jung, *supra* note 1440, 142 et seq. providing guidance on possible breaches of the principle of good faith.

Examples

The preparatory legislative works[1518] as well as academia[1519] have mentioned exemplary clauses that could be covered by Art. 8 S-UWG 2011, for example: exclusion clauses relating to liability due to gross negligence, automatic prolongation clauses in fixed-term subscription contracts,[1520] jurisdiction clauses providing for a jurisdiction venue far away from the actual place of performance or only serving to complicate taking legal action on behalf of the consumer, penalty clauses and clauses providing for lump-sum damage compensation and clauses that shorten limitation periods. The examples closely resemble clauses contained in the UCTD's Annex which may also serve as a guideline as to which terms may be considered unfair under Art. 8 S-UWG 2011.[1521]

Legal Consequences

The court must consider the potential unfairness of a term *ex officio*.[1522] If a term is found unfair under Art. 8 S-UWG 2011, it will consequently be held void according to Art. 20 OR.[1523] Similar to Art. 6 UCTD, only the respective term is voided, while the rest of the agreement remains valid.[1524] Due to the intended broad consumer protection the term in question may not be amended according to the hypothesised intentions of the parties at the time of conclusion of the contract but will be voided in any case.[1525]

1518 National Council, Protocol of the Parliamentary Session on the 8 March 2011, AmtlBull. NR 2011, 1 (229).

1519 Walker, *supra* note 1424, 154 providing an overview of suggested unfair terms with reference to several other authors, especially François Bohnet, 'Art 8 UWG und unlautere Pozessklauseln' [2012] 8 (6) Schweizerische Zeitschrift für Zivilprozessrecht 517 (524-527), Jörg Schmid, 'Die Inhaltskontrolle Allgemeiner Geschäftsbedingungen: Überlegungen zum neuen Art 8 UWG' [2012] 148 (1) ZBJV 1 (12-13) and Guido Sutter and Florian Lörtscher, 'Klagerecht des Bundes gegen missbräuchliche AGB' [2012] 30 (4) recht 93 (101).

1520 Regarding automatic prolongation clauses, cf. Eva Maissen, AGB und automatische Vertragsverlängerung. in Alexander Brunner, Anton K. Schnyder and Andrea Eisner-Kiefer (eds), *Allgemeine Geschäftsbedingungen nach neuem Schweizer Recht*, 2.

1521 Sutter and Lörtscher, ibid.; Walker, *supra* note 1424, 153.

1522 Gauch and others, *supra* note 1424, recital 1155a.

1523 Probst, *supra* note 1424, recital 291; for a critical account, cf. Heiss, *supra* note 1424, recitals 244 et seq. For a general overview, cf. Aeschimann, *supra* note 1484, recital 18.

1524 Probst, ibid.; Thouvenin (2013), *supra* note 1483, recital 147.

1525 Heiss, *supra* note 1424, recital 249; Probst, ibid.; Thouvenin (2013), ibid., recital 146 (all with reference to CJEU case-law).

The judgment only binds the parties to the individual dispute and does not unfold *erga omnes* effect.[1526] The decision may, thus, only be cited as an analogous case but does not generally lead to the prohibition of the use of the respective unfair term.

C. Abstract Control Mechanisms relating to Unfair Terms in Consumer Contracts

While the S-UWG 1986 only provided for a right of action of competitors (cf. Art. 9 S-UWG 1986/2011)[1527], individual consumers (cf. Art. 10 Section 1 S-UWG 1986/2011, providing for individual term control) and consumer organisations (cf. Art. 10 Section 2 lit b. S-UWG 1986/2011) the revision of the S-UWG in 2011 added a right of action on behalf of the Swiss Federation (Art. 10 Section 3 lit. b S-UWG 2011). The sole rights of action on behalf of private actors did not appear to ensure an effective enforcement against unfair business practices.[1528] If a term is found unfair in abstract proceedings, the respective term must not be used anymore; a judgment unfolds *erga omnes* effect.[1529]

I. Consumer Organisations

Art. 10 Section 2 lit. b S-UWG 2011 grants a right of action to organisations of importance for the whole or regions of Switzerland which address consumer protection. However, the right of action on behalf of consumer organisations has proven to be disappointing. Swiss consumer organisa-

1526 Walker, *supra* note 1424, 153-154.

1527 While this appears as a compelling mechanism under a market-oriented approach to the control of unfair terms in consumer contracts, it does not appear as relevant as the other abstract control mechanisms (see below) because the bar for a competitor to raise a claim against the use of unfair terms is equally high as for individual consumers and will, thus, not be depicted further, also cf. Thouvenin (2013), *supra* note 1483, recital 137.

1528 Swiss Federal Council (2009), *supra* note 1447, (6160).

1529 Widmer, *supra* note 1420, recital 327; Hess and Ruckstuhl, *supra* note 1489, (1209) with an opposing view. Cf. Lucy Gordon-Vrba, AGB-Kontrolle durch Verbandsklagen der Konsumentenverbände. in Alexander Brunner, Anton K. Schnyder and Andrea Eisner-Kiefer (eds), *Allgemeine Geschäftsbedingungen nach neuem Schweizer Recht*, recitals 27-35 for an overview of possible claims by consumer organisations as well as their effect.

tions have, so far, not brought claims relating to unfair terms in consumer contracts to the courts.[1530] In this regard, the nature of Art. 8 S-UWG 2011 as explained above may constitute a cause of irritation due to which consumer organisations do not feel inclined to engage in abstract control procedures. The wording of Art. 8 S-UWG 2011 indicates preference for individual term control because it implies the need for an individual contractual relationship.[1531] Similarly consumer organisations may rather feel inclined to help consumers in individual proceedings rather than proceedings on an abstract level due to higher costs of abstract proceedings and the limited financial leeway of Swiss consumer organisations.[1532]

The enforcement of abstract term control could be more effective if Art. 8 S-UWG 2011 provided for a more abstract scope of term control, consumer organisations received more funding[1533] and the bar for abstract proceedings was lowered for consumer organisations[1534]. The Swiss Federal Council has suggested that instead consumer organisations could notify the responsible Swiss government agency of the use of unfair terms for the agency to prosecute such behaviour. However, it remains questionable whether such a shift towards administrative enforcement effectively prevents the use of unfair terms in Switzerland.[1535]

Apart from the right of action under Art. 10 S-UWG 2011, Swiss consumer organisations frequently publish guidance and warnings regarding the use of unfair terms on their websites.[1536] Most publications seek to guide consumers in order to empower them to detect and combat or avoid unfair terms. However, they also publish information on terms that have

---

1530 Heiss, *supra* note 1424, recital 256; Probst, *supra* note 1424, recital 299; Thouvenin (2013), *supra* note 1483, recital 138.

1531 Probst, ibid.

1532 Heiss, *supra* note 1424, recital 256; Arnold F. Rusch and Andreas Schirrmacher, 'Konsumentenorganisationen im AGB-Streit' [2013] 149 (9) ZBJV 683 (691). Partly due to the fact that unlike in Germany Swiss consumer organisations cannot claim reimbursement for warning notices from the user of unfair terms, cf. Rusch and Schirrmacher, ibid., (693).

1533 Probst, *supra* note 1424, recital 299.

1534 Rusch and Schirrmacher, *supra* note 1532, (701).

1535 Heiss, *supra* note 1424, recital 256 with reference to a statement by the Swiss Federal Council which is not accessible anymore. According to the Swiss Federal Council the relationship with Swiss consumer organisations remained 'informal and occasional' as of 31 March 2015.

1536 Stiftung für Konsumentenschutz, 'Allgemeine Geschäftsbedingungen AGB' (*konsumentenschutz.ch*) <https://www.konsumentenschutz.ch/themen/allgemeine-geschaeftsbedingungen-agb/> accessed 14 July 2019.

been found unfair by Swiss consumer organisations and were consequently subject to warning notices or similar requests, including

- In 2014 Swiss consumer organisations jointly issued warning notices to telecommunication corporations Swisscom, Orange and Sunrise with respect to unilateral variation clauses (regarding pricing, broadband, speed, network coverage and fees for paper invoices) without a cancellation right on behalf of the customers, unilateral cancellation rights at any time without substantial reasoning, penalty clauses and clauses that provided for an automatic prolongation of contracts.[1537] Two months later the warned telecommunication providers changed their general terms and conditions so the unilateral variation clause now includes a cancellation right on behalf of the customer, automatic prolongation clauses were abolished and cancellation rights for customers were added.[1538]
- In 2015 Swiss consumer organisations and the magazine *Beobachter* issued warning notices against 17 fitness centres with respect to automatic prolongation clauses, exclusion clauses relating to an extraordinary termination of the contract (i.e. in the cases of a move or accident), an exclusion clause relating to the transfer of the subscription to a third party and a total exclusion of liability.[1539] Only three fitness centres amended their general terms and conditions according to the demands in the warning notices.[1540] In the meantime the Swiss consumer organisations prepared a guideline for con-

1537 Stiftung für Konsumentenschutz, 'Unfaire Vertragsklauseln der Telekomfirmen im Visier' (*konsumentenschutz.ch*, 23 January 2014) <https://www.konsumentenschutz.ch/medienmitteilungen/2014/01/unfaire-vertragsklauseln-der-telekomfirmen-im-visier/> accessed 14 July 2019.

1538 Stiftung für Konsumentenschutz, 'Grosser Erfolg in der Mobiltelefonie' (*konsumentenschutz.ch*, 14 March 2014) <https://www.konsumentenschutz.ch/medienmitteilungen/2014/03/grosser-erfolg-in-der-mobiltelefonie/> accessed 14 July 2019.

1539 Stiftung für Konsumentenschutz, 'Fitnessverträge: Ungleiches Kräftemessen stoppen' (*konsumentenschutz.ch*, 13 March 2015) <https://www.konsumentenschutz.ch/medienmitteilungen/2015/03/fitnessvertraege-ungleiches-kraeftemessen-stoppen/> accessed 14 July 2019.

1540 Stiftung für Konsumentenschutz, 'Fitnesscenter: Mangelnde Bewegung im Kleingedruckten' (*konsumentenschutz.ch*, 28 May 2015) <https://www.konsumentenschutz.ch/themen/allgemeine-geschaeftsbedingungen-agb/fitnesscenter-mangelnde-bewegung-im-kleingedruckten/> accessed 14 July 2019.

sumers to detect unfair terms in subscription agreements and make it easier for them to compare different providers.[1541]
- In 2016 the Hörnli cabin (*Hörnlihütte*) amended a penalty clause under which customers could not retrieve a reservation fee in case of a cancellation after the intervention of a Swiss consumer organisation.[1542]
- In 2018 a Swiss consumer organisation requested the telecommunication provider Sunrise to amend a clause that excluded the termination of the contract in writing.[1543]

The publications indicate that businesses frequently react to the public pressure imposed on them by Swiss consumer organisations. In the majority of cases this pressure leads to the deletion or amendment of the unfair term in question.

II. The Swiss Federal Government

Art. 10 Section 3 lit b. S-UWG 2011 grants the Swiss Federation a right of action if 'the interests of several persons or a group of members of a certain sector or collective interests are threatened or violated' if the Swiss Federation considers such action necessary. According to Art. 1 of the Regulation regarding the Right of Action of the Swiss Federation with respect to the Unfair Commercial Practices Law (*Verordnung über das Klagerecht des Bun-*

1541 Stiftung für Konsumentenschutz, 'Fitnesscenter weiterhin auf Fairness trimmen' (*konsumentenschutz.ch*, 29 October 2015) <https://www.konsumentenschutz.ch/medienmitteilungen/2015/10/fitnesscenter-weiterhin-auf-fairness-trimmen/> accessed 14 July 2019; Stiftung für Konsumentenschutz, 'Fitnessstudios: Welche haben kundenfreundliche AGB?' (*konsumentenschutz.ch*, 18 January 2018) <https://www.konsumentenschutz.ch/themen/allgemeine-geschaeftsbedingungen-agb/fitnessstudio-listen-welche-fitnesscenter-haben-kundenfreundliche-agb/> accessed 14 July 2019.

1542 Stiftung für Konsumentenschutz, 'Annullierungsbedingungen der Hörnlihütte: Nur eine kleine Verbesserung' (*konsumentenschutz.ch*, 29 January 2016) <https://www.konsumentenschutz.ch/themen/allgemeine-geschaeftsbedingungen-agb/annullierungsbedingungen-der-hoernlihuette-nur-eine-kleine-verbesserung/> accessed 14 July 2019.

1543 Stiftung für Konsumentenschutz, 'Abstrus und kundenunfreundlich: Sunrise verbietet schriftliche Kündigungen' (*konsumentenschutz.ch*, 4 May 2018) <https://www.konsumentenschutz.ch/medienmitteilungen/2018/05/abstrus-und-kundenunfreundlich-sunrise-verbietet-schriftliche-kuendigungen/> accessed 14 July 2019.

des im Rahmen des Bundesgesetzes gegen den unlauteren Wettbewerb)[1544] the State Secretariat for Economic Affairs (SECO) represents the Swiss Federation in such proceedings. Beside the right of action, the Federal Government may inform the public of the unfair commercial practices of certain actors where such information is necessary to protect public interests (Art. 10 Section 4 S-UWG 2011). Rather than going to court, the SECO will in many cases issue a warning notice which often suffices as a preventative mean against unfair terms.[1545] The framework of S-UWG norms relating to abstract control mechanisms could offer an effective administrative mean to prevent the use of unfair terms in consumer contracts. The insertion of federal powers relating to abstract control mechanisms has generally been received positively by commentators.[1546] *Thouvenin* explicitly compares the aggregate Swiss provisions contained in Art. 10 Sections 3, 4 S-UWG 2011 to the authority of the OFT in the UK and praises such as simple, price efficient and transparent.[1547]

However, it is questionable whether in the absence of an effective abstract term control by Swiss consumer organisations, the SECO alone can ensure effective consumer protection in this regard.[1548] The right to action does not impose a duty on the Federal Government to assume a 'guardian function' with respect to unfair terms. This 'pro-active' task remains with the private consumer organisations.[1549] Thus, the Swiss approach with respect to administrative abstract control cannot be branded 'preventative' and differs from the Norwegian and British approaches in practice.

The following tables list the complaints received by the SECO between 2013 and 2018 as well as the number of warning notices that were consequently issued.

1544 Verordnung über das Klagerecht des Bundes im Rahmen des Bundesgesetzes gegen den unlauteren Wettbewerb (SR 241.3, 12 October 2011) (Translation by author).

1545 Probst, *supra* note 1424, recital 300; Swiss Federal Council (2009), *supra* note 1447, (6181-6182) referring to the limited resources available for enforcement measures (a court claim would only be reasonable in case of 20 or more complaints to the SECO.

1546 Cf. Sutter and Lörtscher, *supra* note 1520, (99); Thouvenin (2013), *supra* note 1483, recital 141.

1547 Thouvenin (2013), ibid.

1548 Heiss, *supra* note 1424, recital 256; Probst, *supra* note 1424, recital 300; Sutter and Lörtscher, *supra* note 1520, (99); Swiss Federal Council (2009), *supra* note 1447, (6181) referring to their own limited resources.

1549 Sutter and Lörtscher, ibid.

Year	Complaints against unfair terms	Total number of complaints[1550]	in %[1551]
2019[1552]	112	13,518	ca. 0.82
2018[1553]	50	14,775	ca. 0.34
2017[1554]	40	17,696	ca. 0.23
2016[1555]	57	25,875	ca. 0.22
2015[1556]	20	29,186	ca. 0.07
2014[1557]	21	13,235	ca. 0.16
2013[1558]	40	5,830	ca. 0.7

1550 Covering all areas in which the SECO has a right of action (for a full list, cf. the material quoted in the following footnotes).

1551 Meaning the share of complaints against unfair terms of the total number of complaints.

1552 SECO, 'Statistische Angaben 2019' (State Secretariat for Economic Affairs, 15 May 2020) <https://www.seco.admin.ch/seco/de/home/Werbe_Geschaeftsmethoden/Unlauterer_Wettbewerb/statistische_angaben.html> accessed 9 August 2020.

1553 SECO, 'Statistische Angaben 2018' (State Secretariat for Economic Affairs, 16 April 2019) <https://www.seco.admin.ch/seco/de/home/Werbe_Geschaeftsmethoden/Unlauterer_Wettbewerb/statistische_angaben.html> accessed 13 July 2019.

1554 SECO, 'Statistische Angaben 2017' (State Secretariat for Economic Affairs, 24 May 2018) <https://www.seco.admin.ch/seco/de/home/Werbe_Geschaeftsmethoden/Unlauterer_Wettbewerb/statistische_angaben.html> accessed 13 July 2019.

1555 Philippe Barman, 'Beschwerden wegen unlauteren Wettbewerbs erstmals rückläufig' [2017] 90 (5) Die Volkswirtschaft 37 (38).

1556 Philippe Barman, 'Beschwerden gegen unlautere Geschäftspraktiken nehmen weiter zu' [2016] 89 (5) Die Volkswirtschaft 53 (53).

1557 Philippe Barman, 'Starker Anstieg der Beschwerden zu unerbetenen Werbeanrufen im Jahr 2014' [2015] 88 (6) Die Volkswirtschaft 66 (66).

1558 Philippe Barman, 'Unlautere Geschäftspraktiken im Jahre 2013 – erneute Zunahme der Beschwerden' [2014] 87 (5) Die Volkswirtschaft 41 (42).

Year	Warning notices regarding unfair terms	Total number of warnings[1559]	in %[1560]
2019[1561]	1	50	2
2018[1562]	1	49	ca. 2.04
2017[1563]	3	56	ca. 5.36
2016[1564]	39	76	ca. 51.3
2015[1565]	1	45	ca. 2.2
2014	N/A	N/A	N/A
2013	N/A[1566]	N/A	N/A

The SECO explains that the high number of complaints in many different business areas compared to only one issued warning in 2019 was caused by many unsubstantiated claims which did not concern collective interests within the meaning of Art. 10 Section 3 S-UWG. The singular rise in cases in 2016 was caused by the SECO's actions against 35 banks with respect to fees for the balancing of bank accounts, the transfer of securities and the redemption of mortgages.[1567]

The total number of complaints to and consequently warning notices issued by the SECO remains low. Especially the fact that only a minority of complaints entails the issuing of a warning notice could indicate that businesses do not tend to use unfair terms in consumer contracts. However, it

1559 Covering all areas in which the SECO has a right issue warning notices (for a full list, cf. the material quoted in the following footnotes).

1560 Meaning the share of warning notices regarding unfair terms of the total number of warnings issued.

1561 SECO, *supra* note 1552.

1562 SECO, *supra* note 1553.

1563 SECO, *supra* note 1554.

1564 Barman, *supra* note 1555, (38).

1565 Barman, *supra* note 1556, (54).

1566 Data on the issuing of warning notices is not available for the years 2013 and 2014. *Heiss* refers to a statement of the Swiss Federal Council (which is not accessible anymore) according to which until the 31 March 2015 out of 72 complaints against unfair terms, 11 had been followed up by a warning notice. In eight cases the warning notice led to the desired improvement while two were still open and one remained unresolved, cf. Heiss, *supra* note 1424, recital 257.

1567 All the information in this paragraph has been kindly provided by a representative of the SECO by way of e-mail (13 August 2020).

could also indicate tight resources with respect to the administrative enforcement mentioned by commentators.[1568]

While formally a judgment resulting from proceedings between the SECO or consumer organisations and the user of unfair terms only inheres *inter partes* effect, a successful injunction also unfolds a protective effect for consumers as the term user must refrain from using the unfair term in the future.[1569] Furthermore, a similar effect can be achieved for analogous clauses due to the (presumed) publicity of such court proceedings.[1570]

III. Further Abstract Term Control

The Insurance Supervision Act (*Versicherungsaufsichtsgesetz,* hereinafter "VAG") introduced a preventative control mechanism of general terms and conditions in insurance contracts (*Allgemeine Versicherungsbedingungen,* hereinafter "AVB").[1571] Before a Swiss insurance company for direct insurance or reinsurance or a foreign insurance company (Art. 2 Section 1 lits. a, b VAG) commences activities on the Swiss market, such activities have to be approved by the Swiss Financial Market Supervisory Authority (FINMA). The application for approval must include the AVB that the insurance company intends to use in the Swiss market (Art. 4 Section 2 lit. r VAG). Furthermore, the FINMA shall generally protect insured parties from abuse by insurance companies and insurance intermediaries (Art. 46 Section 1 lit. f VAG) which includes the review of general terms and conditions (Art. 117 Section 1 lits. b, c Ordinance on the Supervision of Private Insurance Companies, *Verordnung über die Beaufsichtigung von privaten Versicherungsunternehmen*). Beside these preventative and administrative measures, Art. 8 S-UWG 2011 remains applicable in individual cases.

Furthermore, the Consumer Information Act (*Konsumenteninformationsgesetz,* hereinafter "KIG") provides that consumer organisations and representatives of respective industries shall conclude agreements with respect to the form and content of goods and certain services (Art. 3 KIG).[1572] In this regard the declarations must be clear and transparent, i.e. by using a

---

1568 Cf. *supra* note 1532.

1569 Probst, *supra* note 1424, recital 301; Sutter and Lörtscher, *supra* note 1520, (99).

1570 Probst, ibid.

1571 For an overview of VAG term control mechanisms, cf. Walker, *supra* note 1424, 175-189.

1572 For an overview of KIG term control mechanisms, cf. ibid. 189-193.

uniform order and wording.[1573] The mechanism shall ensure that general terms and conditions are formulated intelligibly and prevent an overload of court cases dealing with ambiguous terms (*Unklarheitenregel*).[1574] It has, however, remained largely ineffective as no comprehensive agreements on unfair terms under Art. 3 KIG have been concluded.[1575]

Under the Federal Act on Cartels and other Restraints of Competition (*Bundesgesetz über Kartelle und andere Wettbewerbsbeschränkungen*, hereinafter "KG") the Swiss Competition Commission (*Wettbewerbskommission*) intervenes where general terms and conditions are used by cartels and, thereby, suspends the principle of freedom of contract in certain branches of industries.[1576] In case the Swiss Competition Commission finds that a business practice (relating to general terms and conditions) violates competition rules (Arts. 15, 47 KG), the respective court will base its decision on the Competition Commission's assessment and accordingly hold the contract void under Art. 20 OR.[1577] This mechanism, thereby, combines abstract administrative and concrete judicial control of unfair terms; however, only where there exist cartels or market-dominating practices.

D. Unfair Terms in Consumer Contracts in Court Practice

A research of cases on unfair terms in consumer contracts[1578] showed a total of 105 results with respect to court cases that mentioned Art. 8 S-UWG. Of those 21 referred to Art. 8 S-UWG 2011 while all others dating before 2013 referred to Art. 8 S-UWG 1986. Of the 21 cases that mentioned Art. 8 S-UWG 2011 only three materially dealt with Art. 8 S-UWG 2011.[1579] Of the remaining 18 cases, two concerned special norms under insurance

1573 Brunner (2008), *supra* note 1419, 128. For an overview of KG term control mechanisms, cf. Walker, ibid., 194-214.

1574 Brunner (2008), ibid.

1575 Ibid. 128-129.

1576 Ibid. 131-132 (including examples for such interferences).

1577 Ibid. 130-131.

1578 In order to evaluate the impact that Art. 8 UWG 2011 has had on Swiss court practice, I conducted a case search on the 21 May 2019 using the Swiss legal database www.swisslex.ch (using the search term "241 – UWG – LCD – LCSI, Art. 8").

1579 Cantonal Court of Jura (*Tribunal cantonal du Canton de Jura*), *A AG v B* [2016] CC 112/2015; Supreme Court of Zürich (*Obergericht des Kantons Zürich*), *A v B AG* [2015] NP150010; Swiss Federal Court, *A v B GmbH* [2014] 4A_475/2013.

law[1580] and two only mentioned Art. 8 S-UWG 2011 briefly without discussing the norm.[1581] In the remaining 14 cases Art. 8 S-UWG 2011 was either not applicable, the cases concerned criminal proceedings or cases were dismissed on procedural grounds.

Regarding the three cases that discussed Art. 8 S-UWG 2011, one concerned a limitation clause that related to a maximum number of kilometres included in a car leasing contract. Each kilometre which exceeded this maximum number would be charged additionally. The court held that the clause could not be considered unfair under Art. 8 S-UWG 2011.[1582] Another concerned a term providing for a minimum five-year-duration of a software licence agreement. In case of early termination, the customer would not be eligible for a refund. This term was also held to be fair in light of Art. 8 S-UWG 2011.[1583] The third case dealt with a clause providing for the automatic prolongation of a gym contract. Here the court had to deal with the question whether Art. 8 S-UWG 2011 was actually applicable to a contract concluded before 2012. It was held that Art. 8 S-UWG 2011 does not unfold any retroactive effect. The clause was, furthermore, not considered unusual according to the *Ungewöhnlichkeitsregel*.[1584]

Due to the low number of cases that have been decided under Art. 8 S-UWG 2011 it is difficult to assess its impact and whether it has brought about positive changes with respect to the control of unfair terms. Further cases regarding terms that have been held unfair under the *Ungewöhnlichkeitsregel* (see pages 324 et seq.) and exemplary cases have been depicted above.

Lastly, it must be pointed out again that the general Swiss concept of unfair term control is based on an individualistic approach so that no general conclusion may be drawn as to the unfairness of a particular term. Rather than determining certain terms as 'generally unfair' each decision must take into account the individual circumstances of the case so that a term may be considered unfair in one case and fair in another.[1585]

1580 Swiss Federal Court, *A v Krankenkasse B* [2018] 4A_499/2018; Swiss Federal Court, *A v B AG* [2016] 4A_512/2015.

1581 Cantonal Court of Graubünden (*Kantonsgericht des Kantons Graubünden*), *X AG v Y* [2014] ZK2 14 3; Supreme Court of Zürich, *A v B AG* [2014] HG100147-O U03.

1582 Cantonal Court of Jura, *A AG v B* [2016] CC 112/2015, recitals 5.2 et seq.

1583 Supreme Court of Zürich, *A v B AG* [2015] NP150010, recitals 2.2 et seq.

1584 Swiss Federal Court, *A v B GmbH* [2014] 4A_475/2013, recitals 3 et seq.

1585 Cf. Walker, *supra* note 1424, 153-154.

E. Consumer Image

Unlike Swiss consumer credit legislation, Swiss legislation on unfair terms in consumer contracts reveals a mixed consumer image. On the one hand, the Swiss legislator refused to insert a special normative regime on unfair terms in consumer contracts in the Code of Obligations because the general Swiss contract law regime, especially with respect to freedom of contract, appeared to suffice. Later the Swiss legislator inserted a norm on unfair terms in consumer contracts in the Unfair Commercial Practices Law which – systematically – still does not regard the individual (imbalanced) relationship between a trader and a consumer. In this light, the Swiss approach to unfair terms in consumer contracts reveals a rational consumer image that does not require individual legislative intervention.

On the other hand, Art. 8 S-UWG 2011 specifically refers to an imbalanced relationship contrary to good faith and obviously took inspiration from the UCTD. Despite its location in the Unfair Commercial Practices Law, Art. 8 S-UWG 2011 refers to the individual imbalanced relationship between a trader and a consumer and appears to acknowledge the vulnerability of the weaker party especially in consumer contracts. Thereby, Swiss legislation on unfair terms in consumer contracts also appears to target the vulnerable consumer.

F. Interim Conclusion

Even after the introduction of Art. 8 S-UWG 2011 the Swiss provisions on unfair terms (in consumer contracts) remain fragmented. Unfair term control does not appear to be embedded as firmly in the institutional framework as in the other depicted legal systems. The location as well as unclear wording of the norm causes problems and leads to its seldom use both on an individual as well as abstract level. The fragmentation reveals an inherent struggle between the wish to preserve a rather libertarian concept of freedom of contract[1586] and providing means of material justice that prove to be necessary in light of a development of mass consumer contracts. This is reflected in reluctant case-law with respect to the development of means of material justice to combat unfair terms rather than drawing back to a

1586 Cf. *supra* note 1421.

basic concept of freedom of contract[1587] as well as the refusal to implement a more general norm in the Code of Obligations[1588]. The legislative result proves unsatisfactory; located somewhere between the Unfair Commercial Practices Law and the Code of Obligations and worded so broadly that it is difficult to ascertain the unfairness of a term in advance. At the same time Art. 8 S-UWG 2011 and its legal consequences bear striking similarities with the UCTD. Under the principle of euro compatible interpretation, CJEU case-law could, thus, serve as a guideline to determine the (un-) fairness of terms.

It must be noted positively that the Swiss legislator has included norms for the abstract control of terms by consumer organisations and the Swiss Federal Government. While legal practice shows that not a lot of cases are subject to abstract proceedings, the public investigation and issuance of warning notices appears to unfold a deterrent effect. The Swiss approach, however, neither appears effective under EU law parameters nor under the parameters of this dissertation.

As Switzerland is not formally bound by EU law, EU parameters are not applicable in this case. Regarding the parameters of this dissertation, while it must be positively noted that Switzerland introduced abstract term control competence on behalf the Swiss Federal Government and consumer organisations, these means of collective term control, nevertheless, appear ineffective. On the one hand, mainly consumer organisations are tasked with preventative actions and collective term control. They often appear to lack the necessary funding to conduct these tasks. On the other hand, the Swiss Federal Government does not assume a similar 'guardian role' but remains passive and only deals with a small number of cases per year. The SECO does not assume a pro-active role with respect to collective term control but rather leaves this task with private consumer organisations. While the deterrent effect of warning notices and public investigations must be acknowledged, the system of collective term control is not structured effectively in Switzerland. The lack of case-law and relatively small number of proceedings by the SECO and consumer organisations illustrates a lack of institutionalisation of unfair term control under Swiss law as well as guidance for businesses which are unlikely to save transaction costs in this regard.

1587 Schnyder, *supra* note 1424, 47-49 with reference to Swiss Federal Court, *Tonwerke Thayngen AG v Fussballclub Lohn* [1997] BGE 123 III 292.

1588 Jung, *supra* note 1440, 130-132, 163.

G. Comparative Analysis

UCTD	UK	Germany	Norway	Switzerland
Transparency Test	Section 61 CRA 2015	§§ 305c, 307 BGB	§ 37 No. 3 Contracts Act	*Unklarheitenregel*
Fairness Test	Section 68 CRA 2015	§ 307 BGB	§§ 36, 37 Contracts Act	Art. 8 S-UWG 2011
List of Terms	Schedule 2 CRA 2015	§§ 308, 309 BGB	Preparatory Works	-
Abstract Control	Section 70, Schedules 3 and 5 of the CRA 2015	§§ 1, 3 UKlaG	§ 22 Marketing Control Act	Art. 10 S-UWG 2011

Under the Swiss bilateral model, the UK would not be bound by European legislation on unfair terms in consumer contracts. It shall now be determined whether the legal systems of Switzerland, the UK – and to a lesser extent in Norway and Germany – are comparable and whether Swiss legislation on unfair terms in consumer contracts may serve as a role model for similar UK legislation.

Switzerland is the only jurisdiction among those compared in this work that has not come under an obligation to implement the Unfair Contract Terms Directive. While the UK, Germany and Switzerland 'started off' with the same concept of *contra preferentem* they took very different turns when it comes to modern legislation on term control. It appears that the Swiss legislator was reluctant due to concerns to interfering with the doctrine of freedom of contract too much. The revision of Art. 8 S-UWG 2011 was inspired by the UCTD. Similar to the German and Norwegian norms on unfair terms (in consumer contracts), Art. 8 S-UWG 2011 only applies to non-individually negotiated contracts. Similar to the UK and German implementation of the UCTD, the main clauses relating subject matter of the contract and the adequacy of the price are excluded from the scope of applicability. There does not exist a grey or black list of terms under Swiss law. The underlying consumer definitions of all four depicted systems are largely the same.

As has been pointed out in the comparative analysis regarding consumer credit regulation, the legal systems of Switzerland and the UK are comparable especially regarding the rather liberal approach to economic policy which is less interventionist than in Germany and Norway. However, unlike the UK legislator that took action in the 1970s the Swiss legislator remains reluctant to introduce a comprehensive term control mechanism.

The unfair term control under Swiss law differs from that in the UK insofar as it is embedded in the regular Swiss legal regime on contract law.

It, thereby, resembles the German regulatory regime on unfair terms. It is also similar to German – and Norwegian – law in that it is closely related to the duty of good faith which underlies Swiss private law. The explicit explanation of the Swiss Federal Council regarding 'good faith' as an element of Art. 8 S-UWG 2011 as allowing for a 'holistic assessment' comes close to the English understanding of the term with respect to unfair terms.

However, while Germany introduced a special regulatory regime for unfair terms in the 1970s, the Swiss legislator refrained from introducing such a regime to the Law of Obligations but assumed that the regular legal regime on contract law would equally suffice regarding the contractual interpretation of unfair terms in T&Cs. Similarly, the Swiss legislator refrained from introducing a general clause such as § 36 under Norwegian law. In that way, the Swiss model of unfair term control also deviates from term control under English law, as in the UK at least the special character of exclusion and limitation clauses was recognised in the 1970s and consequently a special Act of Parliament was introduced. The Swiss legislator rather stuck to general rules of contract interpretation and insisted on the rigorous prevalence of applicability basic principles of contract law, such as freedom of contract longer than the other legal systems compared. While the UK moved forward, Switzerland was reluctant to change the law. Unlike in Germany, the UK and Norway, the Swiss legislator also did not introduce a legislative instrument clearly embedded in a system of legal norms aimed at the regulation of private or contract law but inserted Art. 8 S-UWG in the Unfair Commercial Practices Law. This causes an inherent ambiguity of the norm's systematic character which does not exist under the other compared legislative regimes.

Materially, similar to Germany and Norway most proceedings have concerned insurance cases and most such cases have been held unfair as part of the *Ungewöhnlichkeitenregel*, meaning outside the scope of Art. 8 S-UWG 2011. Like under German and Norwegian court and tribunal case-law such cases have included limitation clauses with respect to health insurance policies.

Systematically, Swiss legislation on unfair terms provides for standing of consumer organisation as well as the Swiss Federal Government. It, thus, bears similarities both the with Norwegian and UK systems relying on administrative control as well as the German system relying mainly of private actors. Similarly to Germany, Swiss law also includes special (preventative) competences on behalf of the FINMA (comparable to the German BaFin) and the Federal Cartel Office. Unlike the CMA and Norwegian Consumer

Authority the Swiss SECO has remained largely passive and does not assume an interventionist or 'guardian' function. It can, thus, not be said that the Swiss system of term control by the Federal Government has turned out as effective as the work of the CMA and the Norwegian Consumer Authority. The public and media-effective investigation of cases and guidelines regarding unfair terms still rests with private consumer organisations, thus, bringing the Swiss system of collective control closer to the German approach. The issues dealt with by consumer organisations are similar to court case-law both in the UK and Germany, i.e. Swiss consumer organisations have investigated gym providers (i.e. with respect to clauses preventing an extraordinary termination in case of, *inter alia*, an accident and exclusion clauses) as well as telecommunication providers, both areas which have arisen under court case-law in the UK and/or Germany. The numbers of successful cases upon the issue of warning notices indicates that businesses are likely to comply with the demands by consumer organisations and the SECO. However, the low number of cases dealt with could also indicate tight resources of both consumer organisations and the SECO regarding unfair term investigation. The dual Swiss approach to collective term control, therefore, does not appear as effective as such term control under Norwegian and English law where administrative authorities assume a much more pro-active role with respect to term control.

While the Swiss have aimed at maintaining their own system of term control, they have also moved toward an adaptation of the UCTD. To prevent 'too much interference' with the Swiss Code of Obligations they inserted a norm on unfair terms in consumer contracts in the Unfair Commercial Practices Law which caused ever more confusion. Furthermore, the means of collective term control try to achieve a balance between private and public control of terms which has failed in practice as both institutional legs of collective term control appear to lack resources and it does not become quite clear how competences are allocated. If the SECO does not assume a pro-active role for itself where does it actually see itself in the framework of collective term control? Is it responsible for a competent government agency to outsource a large part of collective term control to private actors where there exists an overlap of competences? This uncertainty shows that the Swiss systematic approach to term control is an unlikely candidate to serve as an example for legislation on unfair terms in consumer contracts. It is, furthermore, unlikely that the material term control under Art. 8 S-UWG 2011 serves as an example for the UK after Brexit. The norm itself does not appear to deviate from EU law and the scope of applicability is even narrower than under the CRA 2015 in that it only applies to non-individually negotiated terms. While the Swiss approach appears more independent than the other depicted systems because the Swiss legislator is not under a duty to implement the UCTD, it can be concluded that through autonomous adaptation the Swiss legislator has decided to, nevertheless, follow the European example. It is, thus, likely that the Swiss control of unfair terms will develop closely connected to CJEU case-law even though Swiss courts are not formally bound by such decisions. It is unlikely that Switzerland introduces regulation on unfair terms in consumer contract independently from the EU. The Swiss approach of inserting a norm in the Unfair Commercial Practices Law to cover both individual and collective term control without a grey or black list to provide guidance on the application of the norm is unlikely to serve as inspiration for UK regulation on unfair terms in consumer contracts.

Part IV: Conclusions – New found Freedom for the UK?

Chapter 14: New European Models?

The dissertation aims to answer three questions: Is European law really so foreign from UK and English law so it has to be removed from or changed within the existing regulatory system? Would the Norwegian or Swiss models of European cooperation serve as inspiration for future cooperation? And can regulatory approaches in Germany, Norway, and Switzerland be considered more effective and, thus, serve as inspiration for future regulation? This chapter draws conclusions regarding the first two questions.

A. *Foreign European Law?*

The foregoing analyses of English law have revealed that the European Directives on consumer credit and unfair terms in consumer credit have become firm parts of English law. The alleged foreign character cannot be confirmed. The British legislator was never merely a recipient of European legislation. The European institutions offer several opportunities of influence. Thus, for example consumer credit legislation has been influenced heavily by prior British legislative efforts.

While in the beginning the implementation of the consumer credit directive may have appeared unnecessary because the CCA 1974 had already been introduced earlier and the UCTD allegedly introduced foreign concepts to English contract law both legal instruments are fully integrated in UK legislative instruments today. Integration also took place by way of further development of regulation. For example, the requirement to conduct a creditworthiness assessment prior to consumer lending was introduced by European legislation. This requirement has recently been developed further by the FCA. Especially the UCTD that is presumably more foreign than European legislation on consumer credit is now fully incorporated in the CRA 2015. It cannot be said that the standards set by the European legislator limit the legislator in Westminster. The British legislature rather took unfair term control further by adding presumably unfair terms to the list under Schedule 2 of the CRA 2015 and adding competences for the CMA. Unfair term control in consumer contracts has, thereby, become full part of English law rather than an imposed and unwanted add on. This is also illustrated by the willingness of the UK Supreme Court to analyse decisions of the CJEU and to discuss and incorporate the consequences in their judgments (see i.e. *ParkingEye Ltd v Beavis*). This leads to the conclusion that at least with respect to consumer law European legislation cannot generally be regarded as foreign to UK or English law.

B. (Inspiration for) Future European Cooperation

The second question concerns alternative models that could serve as inspiration after the final departure from the European Union. The analyses portrayed two alternative systems: the Norwegian EEA-model (I.) and the Swiss bilateral model (II.). In the meantime, the EU and the UK also entered into a trade and cooperation agreement (provisionally) on the 30th December 2020 (III.). Nevertheless, comparative insights from other models of European partnership may still serve as inspiration for future dealings between the UK and the EU.

I. The Norwegian Model

Through EEA-Membership the UK would not be part of the customs union but would be bound by most EU legislative acts. The only areas that are excluded are the fields of agriculture and fisheries, the Monetary Union as well as justice and home affairs. The *Norwegian* model would, however, also include 130 further associating agreements, i.e. on the Schengen agreement. In total Norway has, thereby, adapted 75% of its own policies under EU-cooperation. Furthermore, the EFTA Court shall ensure that EEA-rules are adhered. This means that Norway is indirectly bound by CJEU case-law as the EFTA Court follows CJEU case-law in most cases. Thus, the formal freedom Norway has achieved does not mean that they are free from following EU rules. Especially in the field of consumer law the Norwegian legislator is bound to implement EU rules. Therefore, the Norwegian model would not offer much leeway with respect to changes to EU derived rules in the UK.

The EEA-model works for Norway due to the specific societal circumstances. It offers Norway formal freedom from 'foreign rule'. Considering the country's history as part of Denmark and Sweden for a long time, this feature is important to the self-understanding of Norwegians. The formal freedom does not, however, mean independence from EU rules. As part of

Scandinavia, it is clear to Norwegians that adaptation of EU rules to ensure (economic) cooperation with its neighbours is inevitable. Therefore, Norway had already adapted EU rules before the EEA was founded.

If the UK seeks total independence from EU rules the EEA will not serve as a model for future cooperation. Especially the EFTA Court ensures a mostly harmonious interpretation of EU rules in accordance with CJEU case-law. However, the Norwegian example shows that adaptation of EU rules eventually becomes inevitable to ensure smooth cooperation with its European neighbours. The EEA offers an institutionalised model of cooperation and would offer the UK room in the areas of agriculture and fisheries as well as justice and home affairs. In the areas of consumer credit and unfair terms in consumer contracts the UK would, however, be bound by EU Directives.

II. The Swiss Model

The Swiss model leaves more room to legislate independently from the EU. Notably, the legislator is not bound by non-cross border European consumer legislation. Switzerland is only bound by EU rules insofar as they concern areas dealt with in bilateral agreements. Nevertheless, the KKG 1993, Art. 8 S-UWG and the principle of euro compatible interpretation show that the Swiss legislator and courts seek guidance from EU law even in areas that do not concern cross-border matters. Furthermore, the Swiss example illustrates the difficulties associated with a model based on bilateral agreements. Today, there exist over 120 agreements that need to be administered and updated. The efforts regarding a new Institutional Agreement reveal that the administration of a large number of single and specific agreements is difficult and requires a lot of negotiations and resources. At the same time, Switzerland is dependent on functioning trade relations with its European neighbours. The Swiss experience shows that such a relationship assumes a lot of resources to administer. An institutionalisation of relations with the EU, therefore, appears desirable.

III. The Trade and Cooperation Agreement

On the 30th December 2020 representatives of the EU (and European Atomic Energy Community) and the UK signed the TCA. The TCA entered into force on the 1st May 2021.[1589] The UK is now neither a member of the customs union nor the single market.[1590]

The deal sets out rules and guidance, *inter alia*, on trade, transport/aviation, fisheries, energy, competition and state aid, security, law enforcement, joint programmes and dispute resolution regarding the terms of the agreement. Furthermore, the TCA establishes the Partnership Council (Art. INST.1) which comprises representatives of the UK and the EU. The Partnership Council must convene at least once a year (Section 2) and shall 'oversee the attainment of the objectives of [the TCA] and of any supplementing agreement' (Section 3). In addition, several joint Committees (Art. INST.2) which, *inter alia*, assist the Partnership Council and Working Groups (Art. INST.3) which, *inter alia*, assist the Committees are established. Other forms of bilateral cooperation include the Parliamentary Partnership Assembly (Art. INST.5) and the Civil Society Forum (Art. INST.8).

The Partnership Council and Specialised Committees also serve as institutions for dispute resolution for certain matters under the TCA (Arts. INST.10 Section 3; 13 Section 7). Beside proceedings in front of the Partnership Council or Specialised Committees the parties of the TCA may also seek a forum under other international agreements (Art. INST.12) or an arbitration procedure (Arts. INST.14 to 20). The CJEU does not play a role except with respect to the participation in EU programmes (Art. UNPRO.4.4).

The TCA remains vague regarding consumer protection. The parties recognise their mutual autonomy regarding consumer protection.[1591] However, they also desire a high level of consumer protection.[1592] The following table sets out areas of consumer protection mentioned in the TCA:[1593]

1589 The TCA was ratified by the House of Commons on the 30th December 2020 (cf. European Union (Future Relationship) Act 2020) but was only approved by the European Parliament on the 27th April 2021 and the Council of the European Union on the 29th April 2021.

1590 Northern Ireland still adheres to EU rules related to the customs union and the single market for goods while remaining part of the customs territory of the UK, cf. Protocol on Ireland/Northern Ireland (31 January 2020), Annex 2.

1591 Recital 7 of the TCA, cf. also Arts. SERVIN.1.1(2), SERVIN.5.39.(1)(b), DIGIT.3, ENER.4, GRP.1(3)(f) TCA.

1592 Recital 12 of the TCA, cf. also Arts. DIGIT.1, DIGIT.13(1), AIRTRN.22, COMPROV.11 TCA, Annex TBT-2, Art. 3.

1593 Not including mere definitions of consumer or consumer related terms or relating to consumer transactions.

Norm	Subject Area	Agreement
Art. TBT.8(2)(a)	technical barriers to trade	mandatory marking or labelling of products shall only require information which is relevant for consumers or users of the product or information that indicates that the product conforms to the mandatory technical requirements
Art. TBT.9(1)(3-6)	technical barriers to trade	cooperation on market surveillance, compliance and the safety of non-food products for the facilitation of trade and for the protection of consumers [...] and exchange of information in the area of non-food product safety and compliance to protect, *inter alia*, consumers
Art. CUSTMS. 7	customs and trade facilitation	adoption of or maintaining risk management systems for customs controls to, *inter alia*, reduce threats to security and safety of the parties and, *inter alia*, their consumers
Art. SERVIN.1.1(2)	services and investment	reaffirmation of the right to regulate within their territories to achieve legitimate policy objectives, such as: [...] consumer protection [...]
Art. SERVIN.5.17(b)	services and investment (delivery services)	prevention of unjustified differentiation between consumers with respect to tariffs or other terms and conditions for the supply of a service subject to a universal service or a postal monopoly
Art. SERVIN.5.36(1)	services and investment (telecommunication services)	cooperation and promotion of transparent and reasonable rates for international mobile roaming services [...] to enhance consumer welfare
Art. SERVIN.5.39(1)(b)	services and investment (financial services)[1594]	nothing in the TCA shall prevent parties from adopting or maintaining measures for prudential reasons, such as [...] ensuring the integrity and stability of a party's financial system
Art. SERVIN.5.40	services and investment (financial services)	protection of consumers' confidential information
Art. SERVIN.5.41	services and investment (financial services)	the parties shall make their best endeavours to ensure that, *inter alia*, internationally agreed standards in the financial services sector for regulation and supervision are implemented and applied in their territory

1594 Financial services include consumer credit (Art. SERVIN.5.38(a)(ii)(B)).

Norm	Subject Area	Agreement
Art. DIGIT.	digital trade	objective to facilitate digital trade, to address unjustified barriers to trade enabled by electronic means and to ensure an open, secure and trustworthy online environment for businesses and consumers
Art. DIGIT.3	digital trade	reaffirmation of the right to regulate within their territories to achieve legitimate policy objectives, such as: [...] consumer protection [...]
Art. DIGIT.13(1)	digital trade	ensuring adoption of or to maintain measures to ensure the effective protection of consumers engaging in electronic commerce transactions, including, *inter alia*, prohibition of charging consumers for unsolicited goods, provision of clear and thorough information and granting consumers access to redress for breaches
Art. DIGIT.13(2)	digital trade	entrusting consumer protection agencies [...] with adequate enforcement powers and recognising the importance of cooperation between these agencies in order to protect consumers and enhance online consumer trust
Art. DIGIT.16(1)(c)	digital trade	exchange of information on regulatory matters in the context of digital trade addressing consumer protection
Art. IP.55(2)(f)(j)	intellectual property	cooperation to raise consumers' public awareness regarding intellectual property measures
Art. ENER.4	energy	preservation of each party's right to adopt, maintain and enforce measures necessary to pursue legitimate public policy objectives, such as, *inter alia*, consumer protection consistent with provisions of the TCA
Art. ENER.28	energy	possibility of regulation of price of the domestic supply to consumers of electricity or natural gas for each party to achieve public policy objectives and only if clearly defined, transparent, non-discriminatory and proportionate
Art. GRP.1(3)(f)	good regulatory practice and cooperation	each party may define or regulate its own levels of protection in pursuit of its public policy objectives such as, *inter alia*, consumer protection
Art. AIRTRN.22	air transport	objective of achieving a high level of consumer protection; ensuring that effective and non-discriminatory measures are taken to protect the interests of consumers in air transport; consulting each other on any matter related to consumer protection

Norm	Subject Area	Agreement
Art. COMPROV.11	basis for cooperation	the parties endeavour to cooperate on current and emerging global issues of common interest such as, *inter alia*, consumer protection
Annex TBT-2, Art. 3	medicinal products	objective to promote, *inter alia*, high levels of consumer protection where relevant, by promoting regulatory approaches in line with the relevant international standards
Annex TBT-3, Art. 7(1)	chemicals	recognising that voluntary cooperation on chemicals regulation can facilitate trade in ways that benefit, *inter alia*, consumers
Annex TBT-5, Art. 4(2)	trade in wine	a party may require the display of a date of minimum durability on products that on account of the addition of perishable ingredients could have a shorter date of minimum durability than would normally be expected by the consumer

The table shows that the parties of the TCA mainly reaffirm their joint goal of a high level consumer protection while at the same time reiterating their respective autonomy with respect to legislation on consumer protection. This concept leaves the UK a lot of leeway to re-shape consumer protection rules.

The TCA only mentions consumer credit as part of financial services which constitutes one of the shorter sections of the TCA. Art. SERVIN.5.39 Section 1 TCA specifically provides that the UK is not prevented from adopting measures for 'prudential reasons' such as ensuring the 'stability of [their] financial system'. As the analysis concerning consumer credit has shown, imposing stricter rules on access to consumer credit may well serve the goal to improve the stability of the financial system by reducing the threat of overburdening by unsecured consumer credit. Such tighter restrictions would arguably also not conflict with internationally agreed standards in the financial services sector (cf. Art. SERVIN.5.41 TCA). Under the TCA the UK is, thus, not bound by EU consumer credit regulation anymore.

Regarding unfair terms in consumer contracts in particular the TCA only sets out concrete rules regarding digital trade (Art. DIGIT.13 Section 1), which is arguably the most important area of consumer transactions. The non-exhaustive list of information that must be provided to the consumer ('when they act through intermediary service suppliers, regarding their identity and contact details, the transaction concerned, including the main characteristics of the goods or services and the full price inclusive of all applicable charges, and the applicable consumer rights'), however, does not appear nearly as detailed as the UCTD or regulation under the CRA 2015. Notably, Art DIGIT.13 Section 2 TCA especially emphasises the role of consumer agencies – the CMA respectively – which appears to affirm the UK's focus on institutional term control. The TCA does not require the UK to adhere to the UCTD or any other future EU term control mechanisms in the future. The TCA also provides for the acknowledgment of basic rules 'to ensure a level playing field for open and fair competition between the parties and that ensure that trade and investment take place in a manner conducive to sustainable development' (Art. 1.1 Section 1 Part 2 Title XI TCA). They also recognise, however,

> that the purpose of this Title is not to harmonise the standards of the Parties. The Parties are determined to maintain and improve their respective high standards in the areas covered by this Title.[1595]

Each party, thereby, maintains their own competition law to address anti-competitive business practices (Art. 2.2 Section 1 Part 2 Title XI TCA). Each party is also allowed to 'provide for exemptions from its competition law in pursuit of legitimate public policy objectives, provided that those exemptions are transparent and are proportionate to those objectives' (Art. 2.2 Section 3 Part 2 Title XI TCA). These sections reveal that the UK is also not bound by the Unfair Commercial Practices Directive anymore.

If the UK intends to change legislation, the rules on good regulatory practice and regulatory cooperation (Part 2 Title X) under the TCA have to be observed. It must be noted that the rules on good regulatory practice in the TCA are not construed to 'achieve any particular regulatory outcome' (Art. GRP.1 Section 2 lit. c TCA) and shall especially not 'affect the right of a party to regulate its own levels of [consumer protection]' (Art. GRP.1 Section 3 lit. f TCA). The rules on good regulatory practice and regulatory cooperation under the TCA include

- that the parties shall implement internal coordination or review processes or mechanisms with respect to regulatory measures and make such processes publicly available (Arts. GRP.4, 5 TCA),
- that the parties shall provide early information on planned major regulatory measures and ensure proper public consultation and impact assessments on the matter (Arts. GRP.6 to 8 TCA),
- that the parties shall conduct retrospective evaluations of regulatory measures (Art. GRP.9 TCA),

1595 Art. 1.1 Section 4 Part 2 Title XI TCA.

- that the parties shall each keep a publicly available regulatory register (Art. GRP.10 TCA),
- -that the parties shall endeavour to exchange information on their good regulatory practices, especially in the Trade Specialised Committee on Regulatory Cooperation (Arts. GRP.11, 13 TCA) and
- that the parties may 'engage in regulatory cooperation activities on a voluntary basis, without prejudice to the autonomy of their own decision-making and their respective legal orders' (Art. GRP.12 TCA).

Any intended changes regarding rules on consumer credit as well as unfair terms in consumer contracts should follow such procedural requirements. The possibility of regulatory cooperation, furthermore, offers a forum of exchange to work together in enhancing consumer protection measures.

Chapter 15: Amending Consumer Legislation?

Historic and comparative analyses and an evaluation under economic parameters were conducted which brought about the following results regarding the question which of the regulatory approaches in the UK, Germany, Norway and Switzerland can be considered most effective and, thus, may serve as inspiration for future regulation.

A. Consumer Credit Regulation

Since the final departure from the EU the UK is not bound by EU consumer credit regulation anymore.

As has been presumed, consumer credit legislation has long been a part of UK and English law. Developments regarding consumer credit on the European stage have been influenced by the UK legislator. The move toward more consumer protection and growing focus on a vulnerable and individualised consumer image indicate that the UK will and should not lower standards of consumer protection with respect to consumer credit, i.e. by going back to the 'Crowtherian' information model. The history of consumer credit regulation in the UK indicates that UK law – unlike i.e. German consumer credit legislation – has been shaped much by the national legislator and would have likely moved in a similar regulatory direction outside the EU. The departure from the EU offers an opportunity to resolve possible conflicts between Sections 140A et seq. CCA 1974 and the UCTD.

The comparative analysis has revealed that the UK has traditionally been a fore runner of consumer credit legislation while Germany and Norway rather appear as recipients of such. Switzerland turned from being a late runner and recipient of EU legislation into a fore runner of modern consumer credit legislation more recently. The most likely source of inspiration will be provided by the fellow fore runner of consumer credit legislation, Switzerland.

Current Norwegian consumer credit regulation is an unlikely source of inspiration for UK consumer credit regulation. However, current Norwegian re-assessments of consumer credit legislation may provide valuable insights for the UK legislator if a more interventionist consumer lending policy shall be pursued in the future. Both the German and Swiss models that focus on rules on creditworthiness assessments appear most effective under the parameters of this work. Especially the Swiss model could serve as a model for future UK legislation. While the German model only provides for rights of redress of the borrower regarding the individual credit agreement, the Swiss policy focusses on strict and comprehensive rules on creditworthiness assessment and harsh penalties for creditors in case of non-compliance. The economic analysis has revealed that the Swiss approach proves most effective. It also revealed that the UK has recently pursued a more efficient consumer credit policy by introducing stricter rules on creditworthiness assessments which led to desirable economic outcomes. This leads to the conclusion that regulatory systems that focus on access restrictions based on individual creditworthiness assessments prove more efficient than those that are based on an informative approach.

I, therefore, hereby recommend to maintain consumer credit regulation with respect to pre-contractual information and creditworthiness assessment duties. The departure from the EU, furthermore, offers the opportunity to introduce a regulatory framework which is rather targeted at the vulnerable consumer. The Swiss approach to consumer credit regulation could, thereby, serve as source of inspiration.

B. Regulation of Unfair Terms in Consumer Contracts

Since the departure from the EU the UK is not bound by EU regulation on unfair terms in consumer contracts and relevant provisions of the Unfair Commercial Practices Directive anymore.

It was originally presumed that the UCTD may constitute EU legislation that was 'imposed' on the UK with an underlying principle of good faith which may be considered a foreign concept under English law. However, the analyses have shown otherwise.

While the principle of good faith had been and is still disputed by some English lawyers as a concept under English law it has been shown that traces of considerations of clearly defined fairness and good faith have appeared under English law long before the implementation of the UCTD and that especially good faith under the UCTD can be defined in light of guidance by CJEU case-law. English courts have, meanwhile, defined factors to consider under the concept of good faith and thereby started to fit it uniquely into common law case-law. It has also been shown that it is wrong to assume that the implementation of the UCTD remains problematic because the Directive relies on civil law concepts of term control despite court case-law that may indicate otherwise (i.e. *Abbey National*). Term control under Swiss law exemplifies that a different understanding of term control does not necessarily depend on the notion of a civil law or common law system. Furthermore, since the introduction of the CRA 2015 the overlap and legal uncertainty created by the parallel regimes of the UCTA 1977 and the UTCCRs 1994/1999 has been cleared.

The analysis has shown that the UK places emphasis on collective rather than individual term control which results in less 'visible' decisions regarding term control. However, under the parameters of this dissertation the UK approach has proven highly effective. The CMA (formerly OFT) is a well-established administrative authority with long-standing experience regarding the control of unfair terms. By publishing guidelines and advising businesses, they can prevent the use of unfair terms. As an investigative public authority, they can remove unfair terms quickly to the benefit of all consumers. The departure from the EU enables the UK legislator to implement Schedule 7 CRA 2015 which would provide for even further reaching enhanced consumer protection, including enhanced competences of the CMA. It can, thus, be concluded from the historic analysis of UK unfair term regulation that English law may have once appeared as an unlikely candidate for the implementation of term control measures based, *inter alia*, on notions of good faith and fairness. However, the UK approach focussing on collective rather than individual term control has proven very effective and has since been well-established in the UK.

The comparative analysis has revealed that with respect to individual term control none of the depicted legal systems serve as inspiration for future legislation and that the UK approach to term control appears most effective under the economic parameters set out in this work. Only Norway has introduced an administrative authority which is comparable to the CMA. The Norwegian discursive approach to collective term control could prove informative for the CMA.

I, therefore, recommend to maintain the current framework of regulation on unfair terms in consumer contracts under the CRA 2015. Furthermore, the departure from the EU offers the opportunity to implement enhanced consumer measures which (possibly) would have conflicted with the Unfair Commercial Practices Directive before.

Annex 1 OECD Figures on GDP per Capita and Trust Rates

Figure 1: Development of GDP per capita (in USD) in OECD countries 1998-2018. Highlighted countries: Norway, Germany, United Kingdom and Switzerland (OECD average = black line).

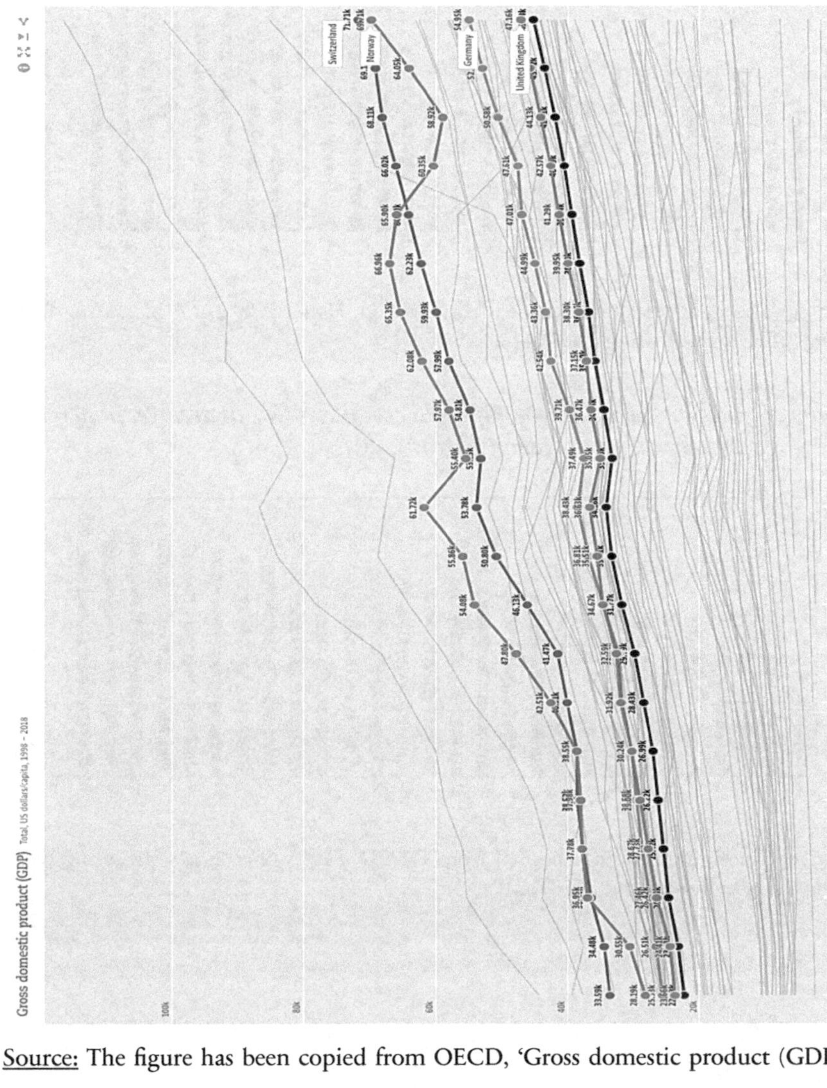

Source: The figure has been copied from OECD, 'Gross domestic product (GDP)'

(*OECD Data*, 2018) <https://data.oecd.org/gdp/gross-domestic-product-gdp.htm> accessed 31 August 2019.

Figure 2: Interpersonal trust among OECD countries (Mean average, from 0 (you do not trust any other person) to 10 (most people can be trusted), 2013).

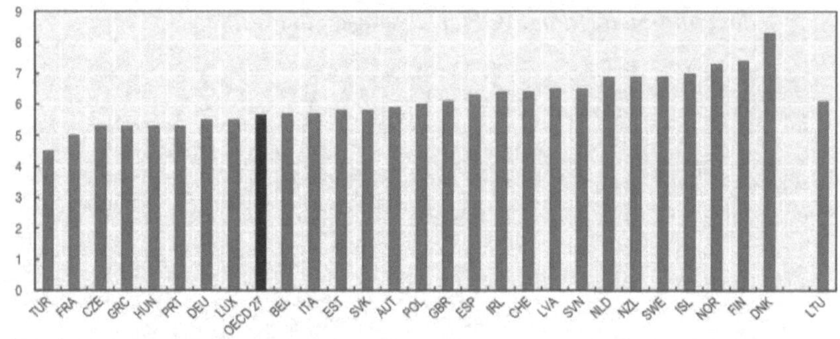

Source: The figure has been copied from OECD, *How's Life? 2017: Measuring Well-being* (OECD Publishing 2018) 448.

Figure 3: Trust in the police among OECD countries (Mean average, from 0 (no trust at all) to 10 (complete trust), 2013).

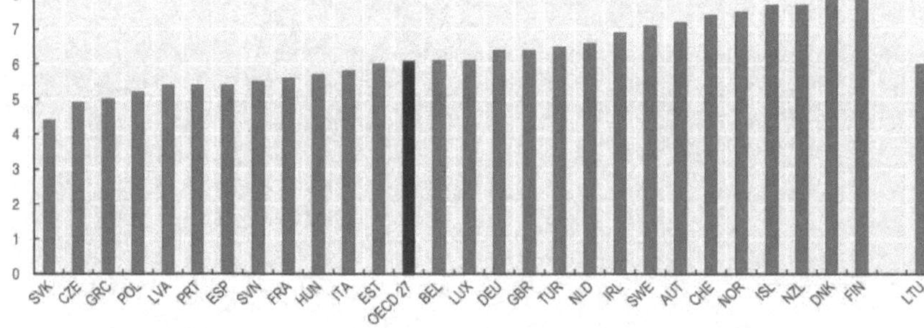

Source: The figure has been copied from OECD, *How's Life? 2017: Measuring Well-being* (OECD Publishing 2018) 450.

Figure 4: Trust in the national government among OECD countries (Proportion of the population responding "yes" to a question about confidence in the national government, 2014-2016 average).

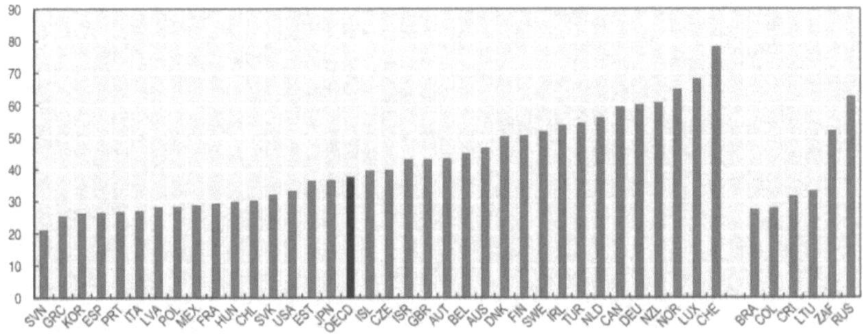

Source: The figure has been copied from OECD, *How's Life? 2017: Measuring Well-being* (OECD Publishing 2018) 453.

Annex 2 Statistics relating to Consumer Credit

Table 1: Outstanding Consumer Loans and Total Outstanding Loans to private individuals per 31 December (millions) and proportion of Outstanding Consumer Loans in relation to Total Outstanding Loans to private individuals (%)

Year	**UK (GBP, million)**[1596]			**Germany (EUR, million)**		
	Total	Consumers	*% (ca.)*	Total[1597]	Consumers[1598]	*% (ca.)*
2019	1,678,653	225,373	*13.42*	1,288,420	238,009	*18.47*
2018	1,628,879	220,096	*13.51*	1,228,423	233,662	*19.02*
2017	1,579,042	209,500	*13.26*	1,192,250	237,916	*19.95*
2016	1,518,220	194,134	*12.78*	1,150,112	231,158	*20.09*
2015	1,468,445	180,079	*12.26*	1,111,647	224,556	*20.20*
2014	1,426,164	170,224	*11.94*	1,078,627	221,996	*20.58*

1596 Anonymous, 'Data Viewer' (*Bank of England*) <https://www.bankofengland.co.uk/boeapps/database/fromshowcolumns.asp?Travel=NIxSTxTAxSUx&FromSeries=1&ToSeries=50&DAT=RNG&FD=1&FM=Jan&FY=2015&TD=31&TM=Dec&TY=2020&FNY=&CSVF=TT&html.x=87&html.y=52&C=O1S&C=O23&Filter=N> accessed 2 June 2020. Outstanding Student Loans are not included. Consumer lending includes loans and advances to individuals through credit cards and personal loans.

1597 Anonymous, 'Zeitreihe BBK01PQ3002: Kredite an inländische wirtschaftlich unselbständige und sonstige Privatpersonen / insgesamt / Alle Bankengruppen' (*Bundesbank*) <https://www.bundesbank.de/dynamic/action/de/statistiken/zeitreihen-datenbanken/zeitreihen-datenbank/723452/723452?tsTab=0&tsId=BBK01.PQ3002&listId=www_s104_vjkre_35&id=0> accessed 2 June 2020.

1598 Anonymous, 'Zeitreihe BBK01PQ3150: Sonstige Kredite an inländische wirtschaftlich unselbständige und sonstige Privatpersonen / insgesamt / Alle Bankengruppen' (*Bundesbank*) <https://www.bundesbank.de/dynamic/action/de/statistiken/zeitreihen-datenbanken/zeitreihen-datenbank/723452/723452?tsTab=0&listId=www_s104_vjkre_43&id=0&tsId=BBK01.PQ3150> accessed 2 June 2020. Consumer credit comprises instalment credit and overdraft credit to private individuals.

Table 1: continuation

Year	Norway (NOK, million)			Switzerland (CHF, million)		
	Total[1599]	Consumers	*% (ca.)*	Total[1600]	Consumers[1601]	*% (ca.)*
2019	3,623,514	178,300[1602]	*4.92*	n/a	8,113.342	*n/a*
2018	3,456,636	114,332[1603]	*3.30*	891,203	7,657.284	*0.86*
2017	3,263,840	102,326[1604]	*3.13*	867,172	7,238.902	*0.84*
2016	3,066,498	90,202[1605]	*2.94*	841,905	7,058.323[1606]	*0.84*
2015	2,884,065	78,145[1607]	*2.71*	820,280	7,171.961	*0.87*
2014	2,716,230	75,494[1608]	*2.78*	799,365	7,276.111	*0.91*

1599 Anonymous, '06718: Domestic loan debt, by borrower, lender and currency (NOK million) 1987M12 - 2020M04' (*Statistisk sentralbyrå*) <https://www.ssb.no/en/statbank/table/06718/> accessed 2 June 2020.

1600 Anonymous, 'Forderungen und Verpflichtungen des Sektors private Haushalte und POoE' (*Schweizerische Nationalbank*) <https://data.snb.ch/de/topics/uvo#!/cube/frsekphupooe?fromDate=2007&toDate=2018&dimSel=D0(BES),D1(T5,HYP,KON,UKR),D2(T6)> accessed 2 June 2020.

1601 ZEK, Jahresbericht 2019, page 12; ZEK, Jahresbericht 2017, page 12. Not including leasing contracts.

1602 Anonymous, 'Nøkkeltall' (*Gjeldsregisteret*) <https://www.gjeldsregisteret.com/pages/nokkeltall> accessed 2 June 2020.

1603 The Financial Supervisory Authority of Norway, Resultatrapport for finansføretak 2019 (17 February 2020), page 16.

1604 The Financial Supervisory Authority of Norway, Resultatrapport for finansføretak 2018 (14 February 2019), page 24.

1605 Ibid.

1606 In 2016 the maximum chargeable interest rates of consumer loans was reduced from 15% to 10% (and 12% for credit cards), Verordnung zum Konsumkreditgesetz (VKKG), changed on the 10 December 2015 (effective on the 1 July 2016).

1607 The Financial Supervisory Authority of Norway, Resultatrapport for finansføretak 2017 (5 March 2018), page 27.

1608 The Financial Supervisory Authority of Norway, Resultatrapport for finansføretak 2016 (21 February 2017), page 28.

Table 2: Annual growth rates of Loans compared to the prior year based on the data of Table 1 (ca. %)

Year	UK		Germany		Norway		Switzerland	
	Total	Consumers	Total	Consumers	Total	Consumers	Total	Consumers
2019	3.06	2.40	4.88	1.86	4.83	(55.95)[1609]	n/a	5.95
2018	3.16	5.06	3.03	-1.79	5.91	11.73	2.77	5.78
2017	4.01	7.92	3.66	2.92	6.44	13.44	3.00	2.56
2016	3.39	7.81	3.46	2.94	6.33	15.43	2.64	-1.58
2015	2.96	5.79	3.06	1.15	6.18	2.89	2.62	-1.43

OECD Data on Disposable Income and Household Debt

The OECD statistics provide a basis for the comparison of median disposable incomes because the same methods are used in respective countries. The OECD defines household disposable income as follows:

> *'Disposable income is closest to the concept of income as generally understood in economics. Household disposable income measures the income of households (wages and salaries, self-employed income, income from unincorporated enterprises, social benefits, etc.), after taking into account net interest and dividends received and the payment of taxes and social contributions. Net signifies that depreciation costs have been subtracted from the income presented. "Real" means that the indicator has been adjusted to remove the effects of price changes. Household gross adjusted disposable income is the income adjusted for transfers in kind received by households, such health or education provided for free or at reduced prices by government and NPISHs. This indicator is presented both in terms of annual growth rates (for real net disposable income) and in terms of USD per capita at current prices and*

1609 In 2019 the Norwegian Debt Registry published new numbers on consumer credit in Norway which are considerably higher than the numbers published on consumer credit by the *finanstlisynet* before. As the Debt Registry was founded to achieve an overview of consumer debt in Norway the new numbers appear more realistic than prior statistics. The actual growth in consumer credit does not amount to 55.95%.

PPPs (gross adjusted disposable income). All OECD countries compile their data according to the 2008 System of National Accounts (SNA 2008).' [1610]

Table 3: Annual median equivalised disposable income in US dollars at PPP rates (and OECD rank)

Year	UK	Germany	Norway	Switzerland	OECD Ø
2016[1611]	22,488 (21)	26,667 (13)	36,744 (2)	36,360 (3)	23,042
2013[1612]	20,763 (20)	25,140 (14)	36,043 (3)	36,402 (2)	21,578
2010[1613]	23,200 (17)	24,200 (12)	32,400 (2)	31,300 (3)	20,400

Table 4: Household disposable income Net, Annual growth rate (%), 2015 – 2018[1614]

Year	UK	Germany	Norway	Switzerland
2018	1.92	1.95	1.98	1.32 (estimated)
2017	1.20	1.61	1.33	0.29 (estimated)
2016	0.54	2.96	-0.78	1.56 (estimated)
2015	4.96	2.39	4.44	1.36

1610 OECD, 'Household disposable income' (*OECD Data*) <https://data.oecd.org/hha/household-disposable-income.htm> accessed 2 June 2020.
1611 OECD, Society at a Glance (2019), page 75.
1612 OECD, Society at a Glance (2016), page 79.
1613 OECD, Society at a Glance (2014), page 87.
1614 Cf. *supra* note 1610.

Table 5: Household debt, Total, % of net disposable income, 2015-2018 (and OECD rank)[1615]

'Household debt is defined as all liabilities of households (including non-profit institutions serving households) that require payments of interest or principal by households to the creditors at a fixed date in the future. Debt is calculated as the sum of the following liability categories: loans (primarily mortgage loans and consumer credit) and other accounts payable. The indicator is measured as a percentage of net household disposable income.'

Year	UK	Germany	Norway	Switzerland
2018	141.5% (11)	95.31% (20)	239.17% (3)	223.03% (4)
2017	142.76% (11)	95.15% (21)	236.86% (3)	222.41% (4)
2016	141.82% (11)	94.76% (21)	230.87% (3)	217.77% (4)
2015	138.48% (12)	95.01% (21)	220.95% (3)	214.89% (4)

Default, Repayment Problems, Debt (Collection) Proceedings, Over-indebtedness and Individual Insolvencies

Table 6: Default of and problems with respect to the processing of consumer loans

The compared countries do not gather the same data on losses relating to consumer loans. While there are numbers available regarding the proportion of write-offs in the UK ('write-offs') and consumer defaults in Norway, there are only numbers available regarding the proportion of payment arrears for Germany ('keine ordnungsgemäße Rückzahlung') and Switzerland ('Zahlungsrückstände'). Nevertheless, these proportionate numbers provide an indication of consumer loans that are not paid back properly or not at all.

1615 OECD, 'Household debt' (*OECD Data*) <https://data.oecd.org/hha/household-debt.htm#indicator-chart> accessed 2 June 2020.

Year	UK[1616]	Norway[1617]	Germany	Switzerland[1618]
	Losses	*Defaults*	*Payment arrears*	
2019	1.7%	ca. 9%	2.3%[1619]	n/a
2018	1.6%	ca. 7%	2.2%[1620]	n/a
2017	1.0%	ca. 6%	2.2%[1621]	5.1% (2.5%)[1622]
2016	n/a	ca. 5.5%	2.4%[1623]	n/a
2015	n/a	ca. 5%	2.5%[1624]	n/a
2014		ca. 4.5%		n/a
2013		ca. 5%		2.3%

Table 7: Debt (Collection) Proceedings and annual growth (ca. %)

An official statistic relating to debt collection could not be found for the UK. Therefore, the available numbers on county court judgments for debt against consumers (CCJs) are used to provide an overview of debt proceedings against consumers. The numbers of newly initiated debt collection proceedings for Germany and Switzerland stem from private debt collectors' organisations. The numbers for Norway are published annually by the finanstilsynet. The numbers for Germany, Norway and Switzerland do not solely relate to proceedings against consumers.

1616 James Cherowbrier, 'Share of consumer credit loan write-offs in the United Kingdom (UK) 2017-2022' (*Statista*, May 2019) <https://www.statista.com/statistics/793375/consumer-credit-loan-write-offs-united-kingdom/> accessed 19 June 2020.

1617 Norges Bank, *supra* note 884, page 12.

1618 Anonymous, 'Verschuldung' (*Bundesamt für Statistik*) <https://www.bfs.admin.ch/bfs/de/home/statistiken/wirtschaftliche-soziale-situation-bevoelkerung/einkommen-verbrauch-vermoegen/verschuldung.html> accessed 19 June 2020 (2017: including interest on or the payback of leasing contracts, consumer loans, loans, credit cards, instalments or mortgages for second homes. 2013: not including mortgages for second homes).

1619 SCHUFA (2019), *supra* note 844, page 3.

1620 SCHUFA, SCHUFA Kredit-Kompass 2018: Empirische Untersuchung der privaten Kreditaufnahme in Deutschland (April 2018), page 3.

1621 SCHUFA (2017), *supra* note 845, page 4.

1622 2.5% regarding consumer credit only, cf. Nicole Rütti, 'Die Verschuldung der Privathaushalte steigt markant' (*Neue Zürcher Zeitung*, 8 October 2019) <https://www.nzz.ch/wirtschaft/schweizer-privathaushalte-verschuldung-waechst-durch-tiefe-zinsen-ld.1508545> accessed 19 June 2020.

1623 SCHUFA, SCHUFA Kredit-Kompass 2016: Empirische Untersuchung der privaten Kreditaufnahme in Deutschland (May 2016), page 4.

1624 SCHUFA, SCHUFA Kredit-Kompass 2015: Empirische Untersuchung der privaten Kreditaufnahme in Deutschland (May 2015), page 4.

Year	**UK[1625]**		**Germany[1626]**		**Norway[1627]**		**Switzerland**	
	CCJs	*growth*	*New orders for debt collection/growth*					
2019	1,080,944	*2.25%*	20,600,000	*-7,62%*	10,092,175	*1.04%*	n/a	*n/a*
2018	1,057,198	*-2.28%*	n/a	*n/a*	9,988,350	*15.76%*	834,183[1628]	*8.30%*
2017	1,081,852	*21.69%*	n/a	*n/a*	8,628,741	*9.87%*	770,275[1629]	*-13.62%*
2016	889,001	*27.98%*	22,300,000	*n/a*	7,853,808	*5.24%*	891,748[1630]	*-0.45%*
2015	694,627	*3.49%*	n/a	*n/a*	7,463,011	*5.80%*	895,823[1631]	*18.11%*
2014	671,224		n/a	*n/a*	7,054,162		758,444[1632]	

Table 8: Over-indebtedness of private individuals

The statistics for each country are based on different definitions of over-indebtedness. All data has been collected and consolidated by private organisations.

- UK (The Money Advice Service)
  The definition of 'over-indebted' was derived from the same two questions within the FinCap and YouGov surveys. Respondents must have answered either:
  i. I find meeting my monthly bills/commitments a heavy burden; and/or
  ii. I have missed bill payments in three or more months out of the last six months.
- Germany (Creditreform)

1625 Anonymous, 'Registry Trust CCJ Region Data' (*data.gov.uk*, 15 April 2020) <https://data.gov.uk/dataset/4f2b1abf-4dcd-47f6-8b8b-5a2ec306e076/registry-trust-ccj-region-data> accessed 19 June 2020.

1626 Anonymous, 'Die deutsche Inkassobranche in Zahlen' (*Bundesverband Deutscher Inkasso-Unternehmen e.V.*) <https://www.inkasso.de/presse/branchenstudie> accessed 19 June 2020.

1627 Stein Tore Næprud, 'Statistikk for inkasso' (*The Financial Supervisory Authority of Norway*, 21 April 2017) <https://www.finanstilsynet.no/analyser-og-statistikk/statistikk-for-inkasso/> accessed 19 June 2020.

1628 Verband Schweizer Inkassotreuhandinstitute, Betriebsstatistische Erhebung 2019.

1629 Verband Schweizer Inkassotreuhandinstitute, Betriebsstatistische Erhebung 2018.

1630 Verband Schweizer Inkassotreuhandinstitute, Betriebsstatistische Erhebung 2017.

1631 Ibid.

1632 Verband Schweizer Inkassotreuhandinstitute, Betriebsstatistische Erhebung 2016.

Over-indebtedness occurs when the debtor is highly unlikely to be able to pay the sum of his due payment obligations over a long period of time and neither assets nor credit facilities are available to him to cover his livelihood. It is measured according to negative features including data from official debtor registers (failure to submit a statement of assets), private insolvencies, undisputed debt collection cases involving private individuals and sustained payment defaults. In a minimum definition, sustained payment defaults are defined by at least two, but usually several unsuccessful reminders from several creditors.

- Switzerland (CRIF)
  In order to determine the CRIF debtor ratio, all private individuals who were subject to debt collections from the date of continuation requests, bankruptcies and loss notes were considered. CRIF consolidates the payment experiences of over 10,000 companies from all over Switzerland.
- No official statistics with respect to over-indebtedness could be found for Norway.

Year	UK[1633]	Germany[1634]	Norway	Switzerland[1635]
2019	n/a	10%	n/a	6.13%
2018	17.2%	10.04%	n/a	6.1%
2017	15.9%	10.04%	n/a	5.6%
2016	16.1%	10.06%	n/a	5.3%

1633 Anonymous, 'Levels of Over-Indebtedness in the UK' (*The Money Advice Service*) <https://www.moneyadviceservice.org.uk/en/corporate/a-picture-of-over-indebtedness-in-the-uk> accessed 19 June 2020.

1634 Creditreform, Schuldneratlas Deutschland: Überschuldung von Verbrauchern, Jahr 2019 (14 November 2019), page 5.

1635 Anonymous, 'Schuldnerquote in der Schweiz nochmals leicht angestiegen' (*CRIF*) <https://www.crif.ch/news-und-events/news/2019/februar/schuldnerquote-2019/> accessed 19 June 2020. Statista Research Department, 'Schuldnerquote in der Schweiz von 2015 bis 2019' (*Statista*, February 2019) <https://de.statista.com/statistik/daten/studie/829280/umfrage/schuldnerquote-in-der-schweiz/> accessed 19 June 2020.

Table 9: Total numbers of individual insolvencies per year and in relation to the official population of the respective country (%)

Year	UK[1636]		Germany[1637]		Norway[1638]		Switzerland[1639]	
	Total	*% (ca.)*[1640]	Total	*% (ca.)*[1641]	Total	*% (ca.)*[1642]	Total	*% (ca.)*[1643]
2019	138,477	*0.21*	65,700	*0.08*	1,012	*0.02*	1,189	*0.01*
2018	129,729	*0.20*	67,740	*0.09*	1,125	*0.02*	1,284	*0.02*
2017	112,682	*0.17*	71,960	*0.09*	1,102	*0.02*	1,144	*0.01*
2016	103,018	*0.16*	77,260	*0.09*	1,236	*0.02*	1,154	*0.01*
2015	91,879	*0.14*	80,220	*0.09*	1,134	*0.02*	1,169	*0.01*
2014	114,240	*0.18*	86,460	*0.11*	1,369	*0.03*	1,269	*0.02*
2013	118,621	*0.18*	91,360	*0.12*	1,311	*0.03*	1,281	*0.02*

1636 Anonymous, 'Individual Insolvency Statistics Releases' (*gov.uk*, 30 July 2019) <https://www.gov.uk/government/collections/individual-insolvency-statistics-releases> accessed 19 June 2020.

1637 Creditreform, Insolvenzen in Deutschland (10 December 2019), page 1 (estimate numbers for 2019).

1638 Anonymous, '10790: Bankruptcies, by type of bankruptcy and industry (SIC2007) (M) 2009K1 - 2020K1' (*Statistisk sentralbyrå*) <https://www.ssb.no/en/statbank/table/10790/> accessed 19 June 2020.

1639 Anonymous, 'Betreibungen und Konkurse' (*Bundesamt für Statistik*, 6 April 2020) <https://www.bfs.admin.ch/bfs/de/home/statistiken/industrie-dienstleistungen/unternehmen-beschaeftigte/unternehmensdemografie/konkurse.html> accessed 19 June 2020.

1640 Official population figures of the UK per year (numbers for 2019 not yet available, thus, the numbers for 2018 were used), cf. Neil Park, 'United Kingdom population mid-year estimate' (*Office for National Statistics*, 29 June 2019) <https://www.ons.gov.uk/peoplepopulationandcommunity/populationandmigration/populationestimates/timeseries/ukpop/pop> accessed 19 June 2020.

1641 Official population figures of Germany per year, cf. Anonymous, 'Bevölkerung: Deutschland' (*Statistisches Bundesamt*) <https://www-genesis.destatis.de/genesis/online?operation=previous&levelindex=2&step=2&titel=Ergebnis&levelid=1592569839159&acceptscookies=false#abreadcrumb> accessed 19 June 2020.

1642 Official population figures of Norway per year, cf. Anonymous, '07459: Population, by sex and one-year age groups (M) 1986 – 2020' (*Statistisk sentralbyrå*) <https://www.ssb.no/en/statbank/table/07459/> accessed 19 June 2020.

1643 Official population figures of Switzerland per year (provisional numbers for 2019), cf. Anonymous, 'Bevölkerung: Stand und Entwicklung' (*Bundesamt für Statistik*) <https://www.bfs.admin.ch/bfs/de/home/statistiken/bevoelkerung/stand-entwicklung.html> accessed 19 June 2020.

Bibliography

Commentaries and Edited Books

Aebi-Müller, Regina; Müller, Christoph	Berner Kommentar zum schweizerischen Privatrecht Art 1-18 OR mit allgemeiner Einleitung in das Schweizerische Obligationenrecht (Stämpfli Verlag 2018)
Arnesen, Finn; Haukeland Fredriksen, Halvard; Graver, Hans Petter; Mestad, Ola; Vedder, Christoph	Agreement on the European Economic Area - A Commentary (CH Beck/Hart/Nomos/ Universitetsforlaget 2018)
Arnesen, Finn; Rognstad, Ole-Andreas; Kolstad, Olav	EØS-Rett (Universitetsforlaget 2011)
Barker, Theo; Drake, Michael	Population and Society in Britain 1850-1980 (Batsford Academic and Educational 1982)
Ballhaus, Werner; Gelhaar, Wolfgang; Kessler, Heinrich; Metzger, Hans-Robert; Weber, Reinhold	Das Bürgerliche Gesetzbuch mit besonderer Berücksichtigung der Rechtsprechung des Reichsgerichts und des Bundesgerichtshofs – Kommentar, Band II, 2. Teil (12th edn, Walter de Gruyter 1978)
Baudenbacher, Carl	The Handbook of EEA Law (Springer 2016)
Beale, Hugh	Chitty on Contracts (33rd edn, Sweet & Maxwell 2018)
Bjarup, Jes	Reason, Emotion and the Law - Studies in the Philosophy of Axel Hägerström (Ph.D. thesis at the University of Edinburgh, Press of the Faculty of Law, University of Aarhus 1982)
Blaurock, Uwe; Goldschmidt, Nils; Hollerbach, Alexander	Das selbstgeschaffene Recht der Wirtschaft (Mohr Siebeck 2005)
Breuss, Fritz; Cottier, Thomas; Müller-Graff, Peter-Christian	Die Schweiz im europäischen Integrationsprozess (Nomos/Helbing Lichtenhahn Verlag 2008)

Brouard, Sylvain; Costa, Olivier; König, Thomas	The Europeanization of Domestic Legislatures - The Empirical Implications of the Delors' Myth in Nine Countries (Springer 2012)
Brunner, Alexander; Schnyder, Anton K.; Eisner-Kiefer, Andrea	Allgemeine Geschäftsbedingungen nach neuem Schweizer Recht (HAVE) (Schulthess 2014)
Brussani, Mauro; Mattei, Ugo	The Cambridge Companion to Comparative Law (Cambridge University Press 2012)
Church, Clive H.	Switzerland and the European Union - A close, contradictory and misunderstood relationship (Routledge 2007)
Craig, Paul; De Búrca, Gráinne	The Evolution of EU Law (Oxford University Press 2011)
Diamond, Peter; Vartiainen, Hannu	Behavioral Economics and Its Applications (Princeton University Press 2007)
EFTA Court	The EEA and the EFTA Court - Decentred Integration (Hart Publishing 2014)
	Judicial protection in the European economic area: international conference by the EFTA Court on 17 June 2011 (German Law Publishers 2012)
Emmenegger, Susan	Kreditrecht SBT 2010 (Helbing Lichtenhahn Verlag 2010)
Emmett, Ross B.	The Elgar Companion to the Chicago School of Economics (Edward Elgar Publishing 2010)
Eriksen, Erik O.; Fossum, John Erik	The European Union's Non-Members - Independence under hegemony? (Routledge 2015)
Fauchald, Ole Kristian; Jakhelln, Henning; Syse, Aslak; Fleischer, Carl August	Dog fred er ej det beste: Festskrift til Carl August Fleischer på hans 70-årsdag (26 august 2006) (Universitetsforlaget 2006)
Faure, Michael; Stephen, Frank	Essays in the Law and Economics of Regulation: In Honour of Anthony Ogus (Intersentia 2008)

Fossum, John Erik; Eriksen, Erik Oddvar	Det Norske paradoks: om Norges forhold til Den europeiske union (Universitetsforlaget 2014)
Frønes, Ivar; Kjølsrød, Lise	Særtrykk av Det norske samfunn (bind 1, 2, og 3) for BSS130 - Samfunnsstruktur i endring, Universitetet i Stavanger (Gyldendal Akademisk 2017)
	Det norske samfunn (4th edn, Gyldendal Akademisk 2003)
Gammelgaard, Karen; Holmøyvik, Eirik	Writing Democracy - The Norwegian Constitution 1814-2014 (Berghahn 2015)
Halbeisen, Patrick; Müller, Margrit; Veyrassat, Béatrice	Wirtschaftsgeschichte der Schweiz im 20. Jahrhundert (Schwabe Verlag 2012)
Hatje, Armin; Müller-Graff, Peter-Christian	Enzyklopädie Europarecht: Europäisches Organisations- und Verfassungsrecht (Nomos/ DIKE/facultas.wuv 2014)
Hausheer, Heinz; Walter, Hans Peter	Berner Kommentar zum schweizerischen Privatrecht, Band I: Einleitung und Personenrecht (Art. 1-9 ZGB) (Stämpfli Verlag 2012)
	Berner Kommentar zum schweizerischen Privatrecht, Band VI: Obligationenrecht – Der Konsumkredit (Stämpfli Verlag 2007)
Heizmann, Reto; Loacker, Leander D.	UWG Kommentar (DIKE Verlag 2018)
Hestermeyer, Holger P.; König, Doris; Matz-Lück, Nele; Röben, Volker; Seibert-Fohr, Anja; Stoll, Peter-Tobias; Vöneky, Silja	Coexistence, Cooperation and Solidarity: Liber Amicorum Rüdiger Wolfrum (Martinus Nijhoff Publishers 2012)
Hilty, Reto M.; Arpagaus; Reto	Basler Kommentar UWG (Helbing Lichtenhahn Verlag 2013)
Hjelmeng, Erling; Hagstrøm, Viggo	Ugyldighet i privatretten: minnebok for Viggo Hagstrøm (Fagbokforlaget 2016)
Honsell, Heinrich; Vogt, Nedim Peter; Wiegand; Wolfgang	Basler Kommentar Obligationenrecht I Art 1-529 OR (6th edn, Helbing Lichtenhahn Verlag 2015)

Honsell, Heinrich; Zäch, Roger; Hasenböhler, Franz; Harrer, Friedrich; Rhinow, René	Privatrecht und Methode: Festschrift für Ernst A. Kramer (Helbing Lichtenhahn Verlag 2004)
Jenssen, Anders Todal; Valen, Henry	Brussel midt imot (Ad notam Gyldendal, 1995)
Jung, Peter; Spitz, Philippe	Stämpflis Handkommentar UWG (2nd edn, Stämpfli Verlag 2016)
Kahnemann, Daniel; Slovic, Paul; Tversky, Amos	Judgment under uncertainty: heuristics and biases (Cambridge University Press 1982)
Karpen, Ulrich; Xanthaki, Helen; Mader, Luzius	Legislation in Europe: A Comprehensive Guide for Scholars and Practitioners (Hart Publishing 2017)
Kelly-Louw, Michelle; Nehf, James P.; Rott, Peter	The Future of Consumer Credit Regulation: Creative Approaches to Emerging Problems (Ashgate 2008)
Kramer, Ernst A.	Schweizerisches Privatrecht, Band 10: Konsumentenschutz im Privatrecht (Helbing Lichtenhahn Verlag 2008)
	Zur Theorie und Politik des Privat- und Wirtschaftsrechts: Beiträge aus den Jahren 1969-1996 (CH Beck, Helbing & Lichtenhahn, Manzsche Verlags- und Universitätsbuchhandlung 1997)
Kristensen, Peer Hull; Lilja, Kari	Nordic Capitalisms and Globalization - New Forms of Economic Organization and Welfare Institutions (Oxford University Press 2012)
Krüger, Wolfgang; Rauscher, Thomas	Münchener Kommentar zur ZPO (5th edn, CH Beck 2017)
	Münchener Kommentar zur ZPO (4th edn, CH Beck 2013)
Larouche, Pierre; Chirico, Filomena	Economic Analysis of the DCFR (Sellier european law publishers 2010)
Leczykiewicz, Dorota; Weatherill, Stephen	The Images of the Consumer in EU Law: Legislation, Free Movement and Competition Law (Hart Publishing 2016)

Legrand, Pierre; Munday, Roderick	Comparative Legal Studies: Traditions and Transitions (Cambridge University Press 2003)
Letto-Vanamo, Pia; Tamm, Ditlev; Mortensen, Bent Ole Gram	Nordic Law in European Context (Springer 2019)
Lessenich, Stephan; Nullmeier, Frank	Deutschland - eine gespaltene Gesellschaft (Campus Verlag 2006)
Lilleholt, Kåre	Knophs Oversikt over Norsk Rett (Universitetsforlaget 2013)
Logemann, Jan	The Development of Consumer Credit in Global Perspective: Business, Regulation and Culture (Palgrave Macmillan 2012)
Meller-Hannich, Caroline; Höland, Armin	Abschlussbericht gemäß § 5 sowie Anhang B „Gliederung der Berichte" des Vertrags vom 16.11.2009: Evaluierung der Effektivität kollektiver Rechtsschutzinstrumente für Verbraucher im nationalen Recht und rechtliche Bewertung ausgewählter Ansätze zu ihrer Fortentwicklung, Az.: 514-06.01-2809HS011 (2011)
Micklitz, Hans-W.; Domurath, Irina	Consumer Debt and Social Exclusion in Europe (Ashgate 2015)
Müller-Graff, Peter-Christian; Mestad, Ola	The Rising Complexity of European Law (BWV Berliner Wissenschafts-Verlag 2014)
Müller-Graff, Peter-Christian; Selvig, Erling	European Law and National Constitutions (Berliner Wissenschafts-Verlag 2016)
	The European Economic Area – Norway's Basic Status in the Legal Construction of Europe (Berlin Verlag/Tano Aschehoug 1997)
Reich, Norbert; Micklitz, Hans-W.; Rott, Peter; Tonner, Klaus	European Consumer Law, Ius Communitatis Series, Volume 5 (2nd edn, Intersentia 2014)
Reimann, Mathias; Zimmermann, Reinhard	The Oxford Handbook of Comparative Law (2nd edn, Oxford University Press 2019)
Roth, Herbert	Staudinger BGB (Sellier-de Gruyter 2018)

Säcker, Franz Jürgen; Rixecker, Roland; Oetker, Hartmut; Limperg, Bettina	Münchener Kommentar zum Bürgerlichen Gesetzbuch (8th edn, CH Beck 2018/2019)
Solvang, Trond	SIMPLY 2016: Scandinavian Institute of Maritime Law Yearbook (MarIus nr 482) (Universitetet i Oslo, Scandinavian Institute of Maritime Law 2016)
Statistisk Sentralbyrå	Economic Survey 4/2001 (Statistisk Sentralbyrå 6 December 2001)
Twigg-Flesner, Christian	Research Handbook on EU Consumer and Contract Law (Edward Elgar Publishing 2016)
Ulmer, Hans; Brandner, Hans Erich; Hensen Horst-Diether	AGB-Recht Kommentar (12th edn, Verlag Dr. Otto Schmidt 2016)
Westermann, Harm Peter	Erman: Bürgerliches Gesetzbuch (10th edn, Verlag Dr Otto Schmidt 2000)
Whittaker, Simon; Zimmermann, Reinhard	Good faith in European contract law (Cambridge University Press 2000)
Zamir, Eyal; Teichman, Doron	The Oxford Handbook of Behavioral Economics and the Law (Oxford University Press 2014)

Monographs

Abelshauser, Werner	Deutsche Wirtschaftsgeschichte: Von 1945 bis zur Gegenwart (2nd edn, CH Beck 2011)
Arbia, Ali	The Road not Taken Europeanisation of Laws in Austria and Switzerland 1996-2005 (Studies and Working Papers, No. 1, Graduate Institute of International and Development Studies Geneva 2008)
Arnesen, Finn; Stenvik, Are	Internasjonalisering og juridisk metode - Særlig om EØS-rettens betydning i norsk rett (2nd edn, Universitetsforlaget 2015)
Atiyah, Patrick S.	An Introduction to the Law of Contract (5th edn, Clarendon Press 1995)
	Essays on Contract (Clarendon 1986)

Aubert, Vilhelm	Rettens sosiale funksjon (Universitetsforlaget 1976)
Aveyard, Stuart; Corthorn, Paul; O'Connell, Sean	The Politics of Consumer Credit in the UK, 1938-1992 (Oxford University Press 2018)
Barnikol, Michael	Die Schutzinstrumente des schweizerischen Konsumkreditrechts (Stämpfli Verlag 2014)
Bennion, Francis	Understanding Common Law Legislation (Oxford University Press 2009)
Benson, John	The Rise of Consumer Society in Britain 1880-1980 (Longman 1994)
Blandhol, Sverre	De Beste Grunner - Reelle hensyn i juridisk argumentasjon (Gyldendal Juridisk 2013)
Brownsword, Roger	Contract Law: Themes for the Twenty-First Century (2nd edn, Oxford University Press 2006)
Cole, Daniel, H.; Grossman, Peter Z.	Principles of Law and Economics (2nd edn, Wolters Kluwer Law & Business/Aspen Publishers 2011)
Coote, Brian	Exception Clauses (Sweet & Maxwell 1964)
Eckhoff, Torstein; Helgelsen, Jan	Rettskildelære (5th edn, Universitetsforlaget 2001)
Eisenhardt, Ulrich	Deutsche Rechtsgeschichte (7th edn, CH Beck 2018)
Egli, Patricia	Introduction to Swiss Constitutional Law (DIKE 2016)
Epiney, Astrid; Metz, Beate; Pirker, Benedikt	Zur Parallelität der Rechtsentwicklung in der EU und in der Schweiz - ein Beitrag zur rechtlichen Tragweite der „Bilateralen Abkommen" (Schulthess 2012)
Finlay, Steven	Consumer Credit Fundamentals (Palgrave Macmillan 2005)
Fleischer, Carl August	Rettskilder og juridisk metode (Ad Notam Gyldendal 1998)
Fossum, John Erik; Graver, Hans Petter	Squaring the circle on Brexit - Could the Norway Model Work? (Bristol University Press 2018)

Frommelt, Christian; Gstöhl, Sieglinde	Rapport #18 – Liechtenstein and the EEA: the Europeanization of a (very) small state (Europautredningen 2011)
Gauch, Peter; Schluep, Walter R.; Rey, Heinz; Schmid, Jörg; Emmenegger, Susan	Schweizerisches Obligationenrecht (10th edn, Schulthess Juristische Medien AG 2014)
Gehler, Michael	Deutschland: Von der Teilung bis zur Einigung 1945 bis heute (Böhlau Verlag 2010)
Geißler, Rainer	Die Sozialstruktur Deutschlands (7th edn, Springer 2014)
Gelpi Rosa-Maria; Julien-Labruyère, François	The History of Consumer Credit: Doctrines and Practices (Macmillan 2000)
von Gierke, Otto	Die soziale Aufgabe des Privatrechts (Springer 1889)
Giertsen, Johan	Avtaler (3rd edn, Universitetsforlaget 2017)
Gstöhl, Sieglinde	Reluctant Europeans: Norway, Sweden and Switzerland in the Process of Integration (Lynne Rienner Publishers 2002)
Haukeland Fredriksen, Halvard	Rapport #3 - EU/EØS-rett i norske domstoler (Europautredningen 2011)
Hellwege, Phillip	Allgemeine Geschäftsbedingungen, einseitig gestellte Vertragsbedingungen und die allgemeine Rechtsgeschäftslehre (Mohr Siebeck 2010)
Hodne, Bjarne	Norsk Nasjonalkultur - En kulturpolitisk oversikt (Universitetsforlaget 1994)

Holden, Steinar; Balstad, Jan; Bergesen, Finn jr.; Bergo, Jarle; Bjørgen, Randi; Blankholm, Aud; Cappelen, Ådne; Ellingsen, Anne-Grete; Lorentsen, Lorents; Meland, Heidi; Reymert, Morten; Skard, Halvdan; Skjærvø, Jan; Skarheim, Petter; Indgjerd Værdal, Kirsten; Wilhelmsen, Randi; Aanonsen, An-Magritt; Skjæveland, Arent; Jachwitz Andersen, Harald; Aslaksen, Rune; Berg, Erling; Dølvik, Bjørn; Forbord, Are; Hoff, Ingrid; Kongsrud, Per Mathis; Johansen, Morten Petter; Bolstad Pettersen, Erik; Skeie, Inge; Wasenden, Ole Christian; Aasdalen, Helga Brigitte; Åvitsland, Geir	En strategi for sysselsetting og verdiskaping (NOU 2000:21, Norges Offentlige Utredninger 2000)
Huguenin, Claire	Obligationenrecht - Allgemeiner und Besonderer Teil (2nd edn, Schulthess 2014)
Husa, Jaakko	A New Introduction to Comparative Law (Hart Publishing 2015)
Jahan, Selim; Palanivel, Thangavel; Kovacevic, Milorad; Assa, Jacob; Bonini, Astra; Calderon, Cecilia; Hsu, Yu-Chieh; Lengfelder, Christina; Mukhopadhyay, Tanni; Nayyar, Shivani; Rivera, Carolina; Tapia, Heriberto	Human Development Indicators and Indices: 2018 Statistical Update (United Nations Development Programme 2018)
Jenni, Sabine	Switzerland's Differentiated European Integration - The Last Gallic Village? (Palgrave Macmillan 2016)

Johnson, Paul	Saving and spending: the working-class economy in Britain, 1870-1939 (Clarendon 1985)
Jørgensen, Tanja	Forbrugerkredit: retligt og retspolitisk (Thomson Reuters 2010)
Kley, Andreas	Verfassungsgeschichte der Neuzeit - Grossbritannien, die USA, Frankreich, Deutschland und die Schweiz (2nd edn, Stämpfli Verlag 2008)
Kölz, Alfred	Neuere Schweizerische Verfassungsgeschichte - Ihre Grundlinien in Bund und Kantonen seit 1848 (Stämpfli Verlag 2004)
Kolb, Eberhard; Schumann, Dirk	Die Weimarer Republik (Oldenbourg Grundriss der Geschichte, Band 16) (8th edn, R. Oldenbourg Verlag 2013)
Kramer, Ernst A.	Juristische Methodenlehre (5th edn, Stämpfli Verlag 2016)
Lippstreu, Constanze	Wege der Rechtsangleichung im Vertragsrecht: Vollharmonisierung, Mindestharmonisierung, optionales Instrument (Mohr Siebeck 2014)
Little, Tikus	Scottish contract law essentials (Edinburgh University Press 2015)
Locher, Horst	Das Recht der Allgemeinen Geschäftsbedingungen (CH Beck 1980)
Lundmark, Thomas	Charting the divide between common and civil law (Oxford University Press 2012)
Marthinussen, Hans Fredrik; Oftedal Broch, Lars; Nandrup Dahl, Karl; Krosshaug, Walborg; Nyborg, Kjell; Scheel, Herman; Valle, Øystein; Vigeland, Rolf	Kredittkjøp m.v. (NOU 1977:12, Norges Offentlige Utredninger 1977)

Matre, Ståle René — Forbrukerkredittdirektivet (2008/48/EF) – Forholdet til kredittgivers frarådingsplikt etter finansavtaleloven § 47 (Universitetet i Oslo, Norwegian Open Research Archives (NORA) 2011)

McKendrick, Ewan — Contract Law: Text, Cases and Materials (8th edn, Oxford University Press 2018)

Misic, Alexander; Töpperwien, Nicole — Constitutional Law in Switzerland (2nd edn, Stämpfli Publishers 2018)

Moen Jünge, Lisa-Mari — EØS-rettens tjenere – Om norske domstolers plikt til å anvende EØS-rett ex officio (Universitetet i Oslo, Scandinavian Institute of Maritime Law, MarIus nr. 487, 2017)

Morsey, Rudolf — Die Bundesrepublik Deutschland: Entstehung und Entwicklung bis 1969 (Oldenbourg Grundriss der Geschichte, Band 19) (5th edn, R. Oldenbourg Verlag 2007)

Natland Wabakken, Marie — Om standardiseringen av en rettslig standard – En analyse av forbrukeravtaledirektivet og forholdet til avtaleloven § 36 (Universitetet i Oslo, Scandinavian Institute of Maritime Law, MarIus nr. 494, 2017)

Nebbia, Paolisa — Unfair contract terms in European law: a study in comparative EC law (Hart Publishing 2007)

Neidhart, Leonhard — Die politische Schweiz - Fundamente und Institutionen (Verlag Neue Zürcher Zeitung 2002)

Nipperdey, Thomas — Deutsche Geschichte 1800-1866: Bürgerwelt und starker Staat (CH Beck 2013)

Deutsche Geschichte 1866-1918: Machtstaat vor der Demokratie (Band II) (CH Beck 2013)

O'Connell, Sean — Credit and Community: Working-Class Debt in the UK since 1880 (Oxford University Press 2009)

OECD	How's Life? 2017: Measuring Well-being (OECD Publishing 2018)
	OECD Economic Surveys: Switzerland (OECD Publishing 2017)
Oesch, Matthias	Switzerland and the European Union - General Framework, Bilateral Agreements, Autonomous Adaptation (DIKE/Nomos 2018)
	Europarecht - Band I: Grundlagen, Institutionen, Verhältnis Schweiz-EU (Stämpfli Verlag 2015)
Ogus, Anthony	Costs and cautionary tales Economic insights for the law (Hart Publishing 2000)
Örücü, Esin; Nelken, David	Comparative Law - A Handbook (Hart Publishing 2007)
Pedersen, Thomas	European Union and the EFTA Countries - Enlargement and Integration (Pinter Publishers 1994)
Posner, Richard A.	The Problems of Jurisprudence (Harvard University Press 1990)
Raiser, Ludwig	Das Recht der allgemeinen Geschäftsbedingungen (Hanseatische Verlagsanstalt 1935)
Ramsay, Iain	Consumer Law and Policy: Text and Materials on Regulating Consumer Markets (3rd edn, Hart Publishing 2012)
Rehbinder, Manfred	Allgemeine Geschäftsbedingungen und die Kontrolle ihres Inhalts (J. Schweitzer Verlag 1972)
Reifner, Udo	Handbuch des Kreditrechts - Verbraucherkredit und Realkredit (CH Beck 1991)
	Alternatives Wirtschaftsrecht am Beispiel der Verbraucherverschuldung - Realitätsverleugnung oder soziale Auslegung im Zivilrecht (Luchterhand 1979)
Reifner, Udo; Weitz, Ewald; Uesseler, Rolf	Tatsachen zum Verbraucherschutz im Konsumentenkredit - Ergebnisse einer rechtswissenschaftlichen Lehrveranstaltung (JCB Mohr (Paul Siebeck) 1978)

Rödder, Andreas	Die Bundesrepublik Deutschland 1969-1990 (Oldenbourg Grundriss der Geschichte, Band 19A) (R. Oldenbourg Verlag 2004)
Sassatelli, Roberta	Consumer Culture: History, Theory and Politics (SAGE Publications Ltd 2007)
Sæbø, Rune; Forgaard Andreassen, Cammilla; Gjedrem, Jo; Grinaker, Anna; Haraldsen, Jan Fredrik; L'Abée-Lund, Sven; Skofteland, Helga; Wang; Per Sigvald	Kredittavtaler – Gjennomføring i norsk rett av forbrukerkredittdirektivet (2008/48/EF) m.m. (NOU 2009:11, Norges Offentlige Utredninger 2009)
von Savigny, Carl Friedrich	System des heutigen Römischen Rechts (Band 1) (Veit und Comp. 1840)
Schieren, Stephan	Großbritannien: Eine Einführung in das politische System (Wochenschau Verlag 2010)
Schöllgen, Gregor; Kiessling, Friedrich	Das Zeitalter des Imperialismus (Oldenbourg Grundriss der Geschichte, Band 15) (5th edn, R. Oldenbourg Verlag 2009)
Sejersted, Fredrik; Bargem Stubholt, Liv Monica; Dølvik, Jon Erik; Seierstad, Dag; Ulltveit-Moe, Karen Helene; Arbo, Peter; Bøckman Finstad, Fredrik; Sjursen, Helene; Aarebrot, Frank; Hansen Bundt, Kate; Rye, Lise; Tallberg, Jonas	Utenfor og innenfor – Norges avtaler med EU (NOU 2012:2, Norges Offentlige Utredninger 2012)

Selvig, Erling; Breck, Olav; Dalsøren, Ottar; Dyrhaug; Sverre; Elvestad, Kjersti; Gjelsvik, Eystein; Dordi Gjønnes, Arnhild; Fegth Knutsen, Øivind; Løining, Øystein; Løfsgaard, Anne-Lise; Melsom, Per; Nesheim, Anne; Nordkvist, Solveig; Nyberget, Astrid; Rikheim, Erling G.; Ryel, Marius; Skomsvold, Rolf A.; Skrede, Kristin; Stalheim, Per Anders; Synnøve Taraldsrud, Liv; Øverli, Bente	Frarådningsplikt i kredittkjøp – Utredning nr. 17 fra Banklovkommisjonen (NOU 2007:5, Norges Offentlige Utredninger 2007)
Selvig, Erling; Nyhagen, Bernt; Christiansen, Per; Fidjestøl, Asbjørn; Fusdahl, Ragnhild; Dordi Gjønnes, Arnhild; Graver, Kjersti; Halvorsen, Jan A.; Klemetsen, Berit; Kobberstad, Tor; Løining, Øystein; Melsom, Per; Myhre, Frank; Nygaard Ottesen, Eva; Prebensen, Inger E.; Raknerud, Evlyn; Skomsvold, Rolf A.; Stalheim, Per Anders; Vannebo, Olav; Steen, Sven Iver; Bøthun, Else M.; Klouman, Hans Henrik	Finansavtaler og finansoppdrag – Utredning nr. 1 fra Banklovkommisjonen (NOU 1994:19, Norges Offentlige Utredninger 1994)
Smith, Adam	An Inquiry into the Nature and Causes of the Wealth of Nations (Methuen & Co 1776)
Smith, Carsten	Bankrett og Statsstyre (Universitetsforlaget 1980)
	Statsliv og rettsteori (Universitetsforlaget 1978)

Sollohub, Maria	National Identity and the Norwegian EC Debate (Master Thesis, University of Southampton 1994)
Steinberg, Jonathan	Why Switzerland (3rd edn, Cambridge University Press 2015)
Steunenberg, Bernhard; Voermans, Wim	The transposition of EC directives: a comparative study of instruments, techniques and processes in six member states (Universiteit Leiden 2006)
Stoffels, Markus	AGB-Recht (3rd edn, CH Beck 2015)
Strand, Lena; Sveen, Mia	Utlånspraksis for forbrukslån - En kvalitativ studie av finansinstitusjoners utlånspraksis (Norges Handelshøyskole 2017)
Stray Rysddal, Anders C.	Economic Analysis of Law & Scandinavian Legal Realism - A Theory of Fact (Draft Edition) (NORAS Research Program on Banking, Capital and Society 1992)
Tayler, William James	A treatise on the differences between the laws of England and Scotland relating to contracts: including marriage considered as a contract affecting property, and marriage settlements (T & T Clark 1849)
von Unruh, Georg-Christoph	Eidsvoll: Das norwegische Grundgesetz von 1814 als konstitutionelles Modell (Schleswig-Holsteinische Landesbibliothek 1977)
Vahl, Marius; Grolimund, Nina	Integration ohne Mitgliedschaft - Die bilateralen Verträge der Schweiz mit der Europäischen Gemeinschaft (Schulthess 2007)
Vogenauer, Stefan	Die Auslegung von Gesetzen in England und auf dem Kontinent (Band II) (Mohr Siebeck 2002)
Walker, Nadia	Kontrolle von Konsumenten-AGB unter besonderer Berücksichtigung der Inhaltskontrolle nach Art 8 UWG (St Galler Schriften zur Rechtswissenschaft, Universität St Gallen (Band 26), DIKE 2015)

Wende, Peter — Grossbritannien 1500-2000 (R Oldenbourg Verlag 2001)

Wendell Holmes, Oliver — The Common Law (45th edn, Little, Brown and Company 1923)

Widmer, Esther — Missbräuchliche Geschäftsbedingungen nach Art 8 UWG: Unter besonderer Berücksichtigung der Allgemeinen Geschäftsbedingungen von Banken (DIKE Verlag 2015)

Wieacker, Franz — Privatrechtsgeschichte der Neuzeit unter Berücksichtigung der deutschen Entwicklung (2nd edn, Vandenhoeck & Ruprecht 1967)

Williamson, Oliver E. — The Economic Analysis of Institutions and Organisations - in General and with Respect to Country Studies (OECD Economics Department Working Papers, No. 133), 1993

Zweigert, Konrad; Kötz, Hein — Introduction to Comparative Law (3rd edn, Clarendon Press 1998)

Journal Articles

Aeschimann, Lisa — 'Rundgang durch Art 8 UWG' [1st September 2014] Jusletter

Akerlof, Geroge — 'The Market for 'Lemons': Quality Uncertainty and the Market Mechanism' [1970] 84 Quarterly Journal of Economics 488-500

Albors-Llorens, Albertina — 'Competition and Consumer Law in the European Union: Evolution and Convergence' [2014] 33 (1) Yearbook of European Law 163-193

Ali, Paul; Ramsay, Ian; Read, Cate — 'Behavioural Law and Economics: Regulatory Reform of Consumer Credit and Consumer Financial Services' [2014] 43 Common Law World Review 298-343

Ambühl, Michael; Scherer, Daniela — 'Zum Entwurf des Institutionellen Abkommens: Auf der Suche nach einem Interessenausgleich' [4th February 2019] Jusletter

Averitt, Neil W.; Lande, Robert H. 'Consumer Sovereignty: A Unified Theory of Antitrust and Consumer Protection Law' [1997] 65 Antitrust Law Journal 713-756

Bakos, Yanis; Marotta-Wurgler, Florencia; Trossen, David R. 'Does Anyone Read the Fine Print? Consumer Attention to Standard-Form Contracts' [2014] 43 (1) The Journal of Legal Studies 1-35

Baldus, Bianca; Siedler, Rainer 'Kompensation von „Streuschäden" im Bankgeschäft nach § 8 UWG?' [2018] 18 (10) BKR 412-420

Barman, Philippe 'Beschwerden wegen unlauteren Wettbewerbs erstmals rückläufig' [2017] 90 (5) Die Volkswirtschaft 37-38

'Beschwerden gegen unlautere Geschäftspraktiken nehmen weiter zu' [2016] 89 (5) Die Volkswirtschaft 53-54

'Starker Anstieg der Beschwerden zu unerbetenen Werbeanrufen im Jahr 2014' [2015] 88 (6) Die Volkswirtschaft 66-67

'Unlautere Geschäftspraktiken im Jahre 2013 – erneute Zunahme der Beschwerden' [2014] 87 (5) Die Volkswirtschaft 41-43

Bårdsen, Arnfinn 'Noen refleksjoner om Norges Høyesterett og EFTA-domstolen' [2013] 52 (8) Lov og Rett 535-546

Baudenbacher, Carl 'EFTA-domstolen og dens samhandling med de norske domstolene' [2013] 52 (8) Lov og Rett 515-534

Beckmann, Martin; Waßmuth, Guido 'Die Musterfeststellungsklage (Teil II)' [2019] (3) WM 89-96

Bernitz, Ulf 'What is Scandinavian Law? Concept, Characteristics, Future' [2007] 50 Scandinavian Studies in Law 13-29

Bjarup, Jes 'The Philosophy of Scandinavian Legal Realism' [2005] 18 (1) Ratio Juris 1-15

Bohnet, François	'Art 8 UWG und unlautere Pozessklauseln' [2012] 8 (6) Schweizerische Zeitschrift für Zivilprozessrecht 517-528
Bright, Susan	'Winning the battle against unfair contract terms' [2000] 20 (3) Legal Studies 331-352
Brownsword, Roger; Adams, John N.	'The Unfair Contract Terms Act: a decade of discretion' [1988] 104 LQR 94-119
Bull, Henrik	'The EEA Agreement and Norwegian Law' [1994] 5 (12) European Business Law Review 291-297
Bunte, Herrmann-Josef	'Folgenbeseitigungsanspruch nach dem UWG bei unzulässigen AGB-Klauseln?' [2016] (20) ZIP 956-961
Coase, Ronald H.	'The Problem of Social Cost' [1960] 3 Journal of Law and Economics 1-44
	'The Nature of the Firm' [1937] Economica 386-405
Cordero-Moss, Giuditta	'Ulike trekk ved norsk og engelsk kontraktsrett' [2016] 51 (5) Jussens Venner 276-302
Eidsand Kjørven, Marte	'Anvendelse av avtaleloven § 36 ved salg av finansielle instrumenter til forbruker; kommentar til Rt 2012, s. 355 (Lognvik)' [2012] 51 (7) Lov og Rett 387-406
Epiney, Astrid	'Der Entwurf des Institutionellen Abkommens Schweiz – EU: Überblick und erste Einschätzung' [17th December 2018] Jusletter
Epiney, Astrid; Hehemann, Lena	'Die Tragweite des Institutionellen Abkommens im Bereich der Arbeitnehmerentsendung' [8th April 2019] Jusletter
Eriksen, Erik Oddvar	'EØS, Norge og demokratiet' [2009] 35 (3) Kritisk Juss 230-243
Ernst, Wolfgang	'Fremde Richter – damals und heute' [2013] 22 (9) AJP 1374-1377

Faure, Michael G.; Luth, Hanneke A.	'Behavioural Economics in Unfair Contract Terms - Cautions and Considerations' [2011] 34 Journal of Consumer Policy 337-358
Frankenberg, Günter	'Critical Comparisons: Re-thinking Comparative Law' [1985] 26 (2) Harvard International Law Journal 411-455
Goff, Robert	'Commercial Contracts and the Commercial Court' [1984] Lloyd's Maritime and Commercial Law Quarterly 382-393
Goldberg, Victor	'Institutional Change and the Quasi-Invisible Hand' [1974] 17 (2) The Journal of Law & Economics 461-492
Graver, Hans Petter	'Mission Impossible: Supranationality and National Legal Autonomy in the EEA Agreement' [2002] 7 European Foreign Affairs Review 73-90
Graver, Kjersti	'A study of the Consumer Ombudsman institution in Norway with some references to the other Nordic countries I: Background and description' [1986] 9 (6) Journal of Consumer Policy 1-23
Häcker, Birke	'Das englische Common Law – Eine Einführung' [2014] JuS 872-876
Harbo, Tor-Inge	'The European Economic Area Agreement: A Case of Legal Pluralism' [2009] 78 Nordic Journal of International Law 201-223
Hart, Dieter	'Allgemeine Geschäftsbedingungen und Justizsystem' [1971] 4 (3) Kritische Justiz 269-277
Haukeland Fredriksen, Halvard	'One Market, Two Courts: Legal Pluralism vs Homogeneity in the European Economic Area' [2010] 79 Nordic Journal of International Law 481-499
	'The EFTA Court 15 years on' [2010] 59 (July 2010) International and Comparative Law Quarterly 731-760

Herresthal, Carsten	'Die richtlinienkonforme und die verfassungskonforme Auslegung im Privatrecht' [2014] JuS 289-298
Hess, Markus; Ruckstuhl, Lea	'AGB-Kontrolle nach dem neuen Art 8 UWG - eine kritische Auslegeordnung' [2012] 21 (9) AJP 1188-1212
Howells, Geraint	'The European Union's Influence on English Consumer Contract Law' [2017] 85 The George Washington Law Review 1904-1952
Husa, Jaakko	'Farewell to Functionalism or Methodological Tolerance?' [2003] 67 (3) The Rabel Journal of Comparative and International Private Law 419-447
Hveem, Dag Jørgen; Nyhus, Ellen Katrine	'Frarådingsplikten: Til bankens eller forbrukerens beste?' [2013] 30 (4) Praktisk økonomi & finans 53-65
Kahnemann, Daniel	'New Challenges to the Rationality Assumption' [1994] 150 (1) Journal of Institutional and Theoretical Economics 18-36
Kalamees, Piia; Lilleholt, Kåre; Sein, Karin	'Responsible Lending in Estonian and Norwegian Law' [2015] (1-2) EuCML 29-38
Kessler, Friedrich	'The Contracts of Adhesion - Some Thoughts about Freedom of Contract Role of Compulsion in Economic Transactions' [1943] 43 Columbia Law Review 629-642
Kinander, Morten	'Trenger man egentlig 'reelle hensyn'?' [2002] (4) Lov og Rett 224-241
Klett, Kathrin; Hurni, Christoph	'Eckpunkte der bisherigen bundesgerichtlichen AGB-Geltungskontrolle' [2012] 30 (2) recht 80-85
Kohler, Emilie	'Influences du droit européen sur la législation suisse: analyse des années 2004 à 2007' [31 August 2009] Jusletter
Koller, Thomas	'Einmal mehr: Das Bundesgericht und seine verdeckte AGB- Inhaltskontrolle' [2008] 17 (8) AJP 943-953

Leff, Arthur	'Unconscionability and the Crowd-Consumers and the Common Law Tradition' [1970] 31 University of Pittsburgh Law Review 349-358
Lilleholt, Kåre	'Application of General Principles in Private Law in the Nordic Countries' [2013] 20 Juridica International 12-19
	'Revitalisering av generalklausulen?' [2013] 126 (4-5) Tidsskrift for rettsvitenskap 550-566
Logemann, Jan	'Americanization through Credit? Consumer Credit in Germany, 1860s-1960s' [2011] 85 (3) Business History Review 529-550
Mackay Cooper, Thomas	'The Common and the Civil Law A Scot's View' [1950] 63 (3) Harvard Law Review 468-475
Maiani, Francesco	'Legal Europeanization as Legal Transformation: Some Insights from Swiss "Outer Europe"' [2008] EUI Working Paper MWP No 2008/32
Mak, Vanessa	'Review of the Consumer Acquis: Towards Maximum Harmonization?' [2009] (1) European Review of Private Law 55-73
Mak, Vanessa; Braspenning, Jurgen	'*Errare humanum est*: Financial Literacy in European Consumer Credit Law' [2012] 35 (3) Journal of Consumer Policy 307-332
Meier, Isaak; Siegwart, David	'Ombudsstellen für Konsumentenstreitigkeiten' [2012] 21 (11) AJP 1523-1545
Micklitz, Hans-W.	'Do Consumers and Businesses Need a New Architecture of Consumer Law? A Thought Provoking Impulse' [2013] 32 (1) Yearbook of European Law 266-367
Myrvang, Christine	'På kreditt og avbetaling – en kulturhistorie om nye markedspraksiser' [2007] 86 (1) Historisk Tidsskrift 57-82

North, Douglass C. 'Transaction Costs, Institutions, and Economic Performance' [1992] An International Center for Economic Growth Publication 1-32

Notter, Markus 'Institutionelles Rahmenabkommen - ein europapolitischer Zwischenruf' [2019] 21 (1) EUZ - Zeitschrift für Europarecht 4-9

Oesch, Matthias 'Die bilateralen Abkommen Schweiz-EU und die Übernahme von EU-Recht' [2017] 26 (5) AJP 638-652

Raiser, Ludwig 'Vertragsfreiheit heute' [1958] 13 (1) JZ 1-8

Reimann, Mathias 'The Progress and Failure of Comparative Law in the Second Half of the Twentieth Century' [2002] 50 American Journal of Comparative Law 671-700

Riesner, Sabine 'Sisyphusaufgabe: Vereinbarkeit von effektivem kollektiven Verbraucherschutz mit der Vermeidung einer kommerziellen Klageindustrie?' [2019] (32) ZIP 1507-1515

Rott, Peter 'Thesen zur Durchsetzung des Verbraucherschutzrechts durch die BaFin' [2019] (26) WM 1189-1196

Rusch, Arnold F.; Schirrmacher, Andreas 'Konsumentenorganisationen im AGB-Streit' [2013] 149 (9) ZBJV 683-704

Schillig, Michael 'Inequality of bargaining power versus market for lemons: legal paradigm change and the Court of Justice's jurisprudence on Directive 93/13 on unfair contract terms' [2008] 33 (3) European Law Review 336-358

Schmid, Jörg 'Die Inhaltskontrolle Allgemeiner Geschäftsbedingungen: Überlegungen zum neuen Art 8 UWG' [2012] 148 (1) ZBJV 1-22

Schöbi, Felix 'Die neue Verbraucherkreditrichtlinie und das Konsumkreditgesetz' [1 September 2008] Jusletter

Schultheiß, Tilman	'Der Folgenbeseitigungsanspruch bei unwirksamen AGB' [2019] (1) WM 9-16
Slagstad, Rune	'Norwegian Legal Realism since 1945' [1991] 35 Scandinavian Studies in Law 215-233
Smith, JA Clarence	'Legislative Drafting: English and Continental' [1980] 1 (1) Statute Law Review 14-22
Strang, Johan	'Two Generations of Scandinavian Realists' [2009] 32 (1) Retfærd 62-82
Sundlisæter Skinner, Marianne	'Norwegian Euroscepticism: Values, Identity or Interest' [2012] 50 (3) Journal of Common Market Studies 422-440
Sunstein, Cass; Jolls, Christine; Thaler, Richard H.	'A Behavioral Approach to Law and Economics' [1998] 50 Stanford Law Review 1471-1550
Sutter, Guido; Lörtscher, Florian	'Klagerecht des Bundes gegen missbräuchliche AGB' [2012] 30 (4) recht 93-101
Teubner, Gunther	'Legal Irritants: Good Faith in British Law or How Unifying Law Ends Up in New Divergences' [1998] 61 MLR 11-32
Thaler, Richard H.	'Behavioral Economics: Past, Present, and Future' [2016] 106 (7) American Economic Review 1577-1600
Thouvenin, Florent	'Art 8 UWG: Zur Strukturierung eines strukturlosen Tatbestandes' [29 October 2012] Jusletter
Tversky, Amos; Kahnemann, Daniel	'Rational Choice and the Framing of Decisions' [1986] 59 (2) The Journal of Business 251-258
	'Advances in Prospect Theory: Cumulative Representation of Uncertainty' [1992] 5 Journal of Risk and Uncertainty 297-323
Whitman, James Q.	'Consumerism Versus Producerism: A Study in Comparative Law' [2007] 117 (3) Yale Law Journal 340-406

Cases

Europe

CJEU judgment C-266/18, *Aqua Med sp. z o.o.v Irena Skóra* [2019]

CJEU judgment C-118/17, *Zsuzsanna Dunai v ERSTE Bank Hungary Zrt* (*Dunai*) [2019]

CJEU judgment C-58/18, *Michel Schyns v Belfius Banque SA,* [2019]

CJEU judgment C-176/17, *Profi Credit Polska S.A. w Bielsku Białej v Mariusz Wawrzosek* (*Profi Credit*) [2018]

CJEU judgment C-421/14, *Banco Primus SA v Jesús Gutiérrez García* (*Banco Primus*) [2017]

CJEU judgment C-186/16, *Ruxandra Paula Andriciuc and Others v Banca Românească SA* (*Andriciuc*) [2017]

CJEU judgment C-154/15, *Francisco Gutiérrez Naranjo v Cajasur Banco SAU, Ana María Palacios Martínez v Banco Bilbao Vizcaya Argentaria SA (BBVA), Banco Popular Español SA v Emilio Irles López and Teresa Torres Andreu* (*Gutiérrez*) [2016]

CJEU Joined Cases C-381/14 and C-385/14, *Jorge Sales Sinués and Youssouf Drame Ba v Caixabank SA and Catalunya Caixa SA (Catalunya Banc S.A.)* (*Sales Sinués and Drame Ba*) [2016]

CJEU judgment C-119/15, *Biuro podróży 'Partner' Sp. z o.o, Sp. komandytowa w Dąbrowie Górniczej v Prezes Urzędu Ochrony Konkurencji i Konsumentów* (*Biuro podróży 'Partner'*) [2016]

CJEU judgment C-377/14, *Ernst Georg Radlinger and Helena Radlingerová v Finway a.s.* [2016]

CJEU judgment C-143/13, *Bogdan Matei and Ioana Ofelia Matei v SC Volksbank România SA* (*Matei*) [2015]

CJEU judgment C-96/14, *Jean-Claude Van Hove v CNP Assurances SA* (*Van Hove*) [2015]

CJEU judgment, C-226/12, *Constructora Principado SA v José Ignacio Menéndez Álvarez* (*Álvarez*) [2014]

CJEU judgment C-449/13, *CA Consumer Finance SA v Ingrid Bakkaus, Charline Bonato, née Savary, Florian Bonato* [2014]

CJEU judgment C-26/13, *Árpád Kásler and Hajnalka Káslerné Rábai v OTP Jelzálogbank Zrt* (*Kásler*) [2014]

CJEU judgment C-565/12, *LCL Le Crédit Lyonnais SA v Fesih Kalhan* [2014]

CJEU judgment C-470/12, *Pohotovosť s. r. o. v Miroslav Vašuta (Pohotovost)* [2014]

CJEU judgment C-169/14, *Juan Carlos Sánchez Morcillo and María del Carmen Abril García v Banco Bilbao Vizcaya Argentaria SA* [2014]

CJEU judgment C-488/11, *Dirk Frederik Asbeek Brusse und Katarina de Man Garabito gegen Jahani BV* (*Asbeek*) [2013]

CJEU judgment C-415/11, *Mohamed Aziz v Caixa d'Estalvis de Catalunya, Tarragona i Manresa (Catalunyacaixa)* (*Aziz*) [2013]

CJEU-judgment C-92/11, *RWE Vertrieb AG v Verbraucherzentrale Nordrhein-Westfalen eV* (*RWE*) [2013]

Cf. also CJEU judgment C-618/10, *Banco Español de Crédito SA v Joaquín Calderón Camino* [2012]

CJEU judgment C-472/10, *Nemzeti Fogyasztóvédelmi Hatóság v Invitel Távközlési Zrt* (*Invitel*) [2012]

CJEU Case C-453/10, *Jana Pereničová and Vladislav Perenič v SOS financ spol. s r. o.* (*Pereničová*) [2012]

in CJEU judgment C-137/08, *VB Pénzügyi Lízing Zrt. v Ferenc Schneider* (*Pénzügyi*) [2010]

CJEU judgment C-40/08, *Asturcom Telecomunicaciones SL v Cristina Rodríguez Nogueira* (*Asturcom Telecomunicaciones*) [2009]

CJEU judgment C-243/08, *Pannon GSM Zrt. v Erzsébet Sustikné Győrfi* (*Pannon*) [2009]

ECJ judgment C-168/05, *Mostaza Claro v Centro Móvil Milenium SL* (*Mostaza Claro*) [2006].

ECJ judgment C-70/03, *Commission of the European Communities v Kingdom of Spain* [2004]

ECJ judgment C-237/02, *Freiburger Kommunalbauten GmbH Baugesellschaft & Co. KG v Ludger Hofstetter and Ulrike Hofstetter* [2004]

ECJ judgment C-473/00, *Cofidis SA v Jean-Louis Fredout* [2002]

ECJ judgment C-372/99, *Commission of the European Communities v Italy* [2002]

ECJ judgment C-478/99, *Commission of the European Communities v Kingdom of Sweden* [2002]

ECJ judgment C-144/99, *Commission of the European Communities v The Netherlands* [2001]

ECJ judgment C-240-C-244/98, *Océano Grupo Editorial SA v Murciano Quinter and Salvat Editores SA v Sánchez Alcón Prades* (*Océano*) [2000]

ECJ judgment C-67/96, *Albany International BV v Stichting Bedrijfspensioenfonds Textielindustrie (Albany)* [1999]

ECJ Case C-321/97, *Ulla-Brith Andersson and Susannne Wåkerås-Andersson v Svenska staten (Andersson)* [1999]

ECJ judgment C-210/96, *Gut Springenheide and Rudolf Tusky v Oberkreisdirektor des Kreises Steinfurt – Amt für Lebensmittelüberwachung* [1998]

ECJ judgment C-479/93, *Andrea Francovich v Italian Republic (Francovich)* [1995]

ECJ Opinion 1/92 (10 April 1992), ECR I-2825

ECJ Opinion 1/91 (14 December 1991), ECR I-6079

ECJ judgment C-148/84, *Deutsche Genossenschaftsbank v SA Brasserie du Pêcheur (Brasserie de Pecheur)* [1985]

EFTA Court judgment E-7/18, *Fosen Linjen AS v AtB AS (Fosen Linjen II)* [2019]

EFTA Court judgment E-16/16, *Fosen-Linjen AS v Atb AS (Fosen Linjen I)* [2017]

EFTA Court judgment E-28/15, *Jabbi* [2016]

EFTA Court judgment E-14/15, *Holship* [2016]

EFTA Court judgment E-11/12, *Beatrix Koch, Dipl. Kfm. Lothar Hummel and Stefan Müller v Swiss Life (Liechtenstein) AG (Koch)* [2013]

EFTA Court judgment E-3/12, *Staten v/Arbeidsdepartementet v Stig Arne Jonsson (Jonsson)* [2013]

EFTA Court judgment E-02/11, *STX Norway Offshore AS m.fl. v Staten v/ Tariffnemnda (STX)* [2013]

EFTA Court judgment E-18/11, *Irish Bank* [2012]

EFTA Court judgment E-18/10, *ESA v Norway* [2011]

Joint EFTA Court judgments E-9/07 and E-10/07, *L'Oreal* [2008]

EFTA Court judgment E-2/06, *ESA v Norway* [2007]

EFTA Court judgment E-3/02, *Paranova v Merck & Co., Inc. and Others (Paranova)* [2003]

EFTA Court judgment E-4/01, *Karlsson* [2002]

EFTA Court judgment E-8/00, *LO* [2002]

EFTA Court judgment E-1/99, *Storebrand Skadeforsikring AS v Veronika Finanger (Finanger I)* [1999]

EFTA Court judgment E-9/97, *Sveinbjörnsdóttir* [1998]

EFTA Court judgment E-5/97, *European Navigation* [1998]

EFTA Court judgment E-2/97, *Mag Instrument Inc. v California Trading Company Norway, Ulsteen (Mag Lite)* [1997]

EFTA Court judgment E-1/94, *Restamark* [1994]

England & Wales

African Export-Import Bank and others v Shebah Exploration and Production Co Ltd and others [2018] 1 WLR 487

Ailsa Craig Fishing Co Ltd v Malvern Fishing Co Ltd and Another [1983] 1 WLR 964

Air Transworld Limited v Bombardier Inc [2012] EWHC 243 (Comm)

Allcard v Skinner [1886-90] All ER Rep 90

Andrew Brothers (Bournemouth), Limited v Singer and Company, Limited [1934] 1 KB 17

Arnold v Britton and others [2015] AC 1619

Avrora Fine Arts Investment Limited v Christie, Manson & Woods Limited [2012] EWHC 2198 (Ch)

Barclay's Bank plc v O'Brien [1994] 4 All ER 417

Boustany v Pigott (1995) 69 P. & C.R. 298

BP Gas Marketing Ltd v La Société Sonatrach, Sonatrach Gas Marketing UK Limited [2016] EWHC 2461 (Comm)

British Fermentation Products Ltd v Compair Reavell Ltd [1999] 2 All ER (Comm) 389

Carter v Boehm [1766] 2 Burrow 1905

Casehub Ltd v Wolf Cola Ltd [2017] EWHC 1169 (Ch)

Chapelton v Barry Urban DC [1940] 1 KB 532

Charterhouse Credit Co Ltd v Tolly [1963] 2 QB 683

Chester Grosvenor Hotel Co Ltd v Alfred McAlpine Management Ltd [1991] 56 BLR 115

Christopher Doran, Joanne Doran v Paragon Personal Finance Limited [2018] 6 WLUK

Chubb & Bruce v Dean & Anr [2013] EWHC 1282 (CH)

CIBC Mortgages Ltd v Pitt [1994] 4 All ER 433

Curtis v Chemical Cleaning and Dyeing Co. Ltd [1951] 1 KB 805

Director General of Fair Trading v First National Bank plc [2001] UKHL 52

Fomento de Construcciones y Contratas SA v Black Diamond Offshore Ltd [2016] EWCA Civ 1141

Foxtons Ltd v O'Reardon [2011] EWHC 2946 (QB)

Fry v Lane (1880) 40 Ch.D. 312

Greenclose Ltd v National Westminster Bank plc [2014] EWHC 1156 (Ch)

Greenlands Trading Ltd & Anor v Girolama Pontearso [2019] EWHC 278 (Ch)

Grogan v Robin Meredith Plant Hire & Anor [1996] CLC 1127

Harbutt's "Plasticine" Ltd v Wayne Tank and Pump Co Ltd [1970] QB 447

Harrison v Shepherd Homes Ltd [2011] EWHC 1811 (TCC)

Homburg Houtimport BV v Agrosin Private Ltd (The Starsin) [2003] 2 All ER 785

Hurstanger Ltd v Wilson [2007] 4 All ER 1118

ING Bank NV v Ros Roca SA [2011] EWCA Civ

Interfoto Picture Library Ltd v Stiletto Visual Programmes Ltd [1989] QB 433

Investors Compensation Scheme Ltd v West Bromwich Building Society & Ors. [1997] CLC 1243

John Lee & Son (Grantham) Ltd v Railway Executive [1949] 2 All ER 581

Karsales (Harrow) Ltd v Wallis [1956] 1 WLR 936

K/S Victoria Street (a Danish Partnership) v House of Fraser (Stores Management) Limited and others [2011] EWCA Civ 904

Link Financial Limited v Mrs Teresa North Wilson [2014] EWHC 252 (CH)

Lloyds Bank Ltd v Bundy [1974] 3 All ER 757

London North Securities Ltd v Meadows [2005] EWCQ Civ 956

Lukoil Asia Pacific Pte Ltd v Ocean Tankers (Pte) Ltd [2018] 1 CLC 94

Maple Leaf Macro Volatility Master Fund and others v Jacques Rouvroy, Krzystof Trylinski [2009] EWHC 257 (Comm)

Mark Alan Holyoake and others v Nicholas Anthony Christopher Candy and others [2017] EWHC 3397 (CH)

Marks & Spencer plc v BNP Paribas Securities Services Trust Co (Jersey) Ltd [2015] UKSC 72

Michael Carney, Roberta Carney and others v N M Rothschild & Sons Limited [2018] EWHC 958 (Comm)

Mid Essex Hospital Services NHS Trust v Compass Group UK and Ireland Ltd [2013] EWCA Civ 200

Multiservice Bookbinding Ltd. and others v Marden [1978] 2 WLR 535

Munkenbeck & Marshall v Harold [2005] EWHC 356 (TCC)

Mylcrist Builders Ltd v Buck [2008] EWHC 2172 (TCC)

National Westminster Bank plc v Morgan [1985] 1 All ER 821

O'Brien v MGN Ltd [2002] CLC 33

Office of Fair Trading v Abbey National plc [2009] UKSC 6

Office of Fair Trading v Abbey National plc [2009] EWCA Civ 116

Office of Fair Trading v Ashbourne Management Services Ltd [2011] EWHC 1237 (Ch)

Office of Fair Trading v Foxtons Ltd [2009] EWHC 1681 (Ch)

Olley v Marlborough Court Ltd. [1949] 1 KB

Overseas Medical Supplies Ltd v Orient Transport Services Ltd [1999] CLC 1243

Paragon Mortgages Limited v Robert McEwan-Peters, Rachel Frances McEwan-Peters [2011] EWHC 2491 (Comm)

Parker v South Eastern Railway [1877] 2 CPD 416

ParkingEye Ltd v Beavis [2015] UKSC 67

Persimmon Homes Limited and others v Ove Arup & Partners Limited, Ove Arup & Partners International Limited [2017] EWCA Civ 373

Petromec Inc v Petroleo Brasileiro SA Petrobas and others (No. 3) [2005] EWCA Civ 891

Phillips Products Ltd v Hyland [1987] WLR 659

Photo Production Ltd v Securior Transport Ltd [1980] AC 827

Pilgrim Rock Ltd v Mr. Iwaniuk [2019] EWHC 203 (Ch)

Plevin v Paragon Finance Ltd [2014] UKSC 61

Prenn v Simmonds [1971] 1 WLR 1381

The Prince's Case (1606) 8 Co Rep 13b, 77 ER 496

Rainy Sky SA & Ors v Kookmin Bank [2011] 2 CLC 923

R. & B. Customs Brokers Co Ltd v United Dominions Trust Ltd v Saunders Abbott (1980) Ltd [1988] 1 WLR 321

Robert Shaw v Nine Regions Limited [2009] EWHC 3514 (QB)

Royal Bank of Scotland v Etridge (No. 2) [2001] 4 All ER 449

Saunders v Anglia Building Society [1971] AC 1004

Savills (UK) Ltd v Blacker [2017] EWCA Civ 68

Schwartz v Barclays Bank plc [1995] Lexis Citation 2066

Shafik Rahman and others v HSBC Bank plc [2012] EWHC 11 (Ch)

Smith v Eric S. Bush [1990] AC 831

St Albans City and District Council v International Computers Ltd [1997] FSR 251

Stephen West and Carol West v Ian Finlay Associates [2014] EWCA Civ 316

Strydom v Venside Ltd. [2009] All ER (D) 135 (Aug)

Suisse Atlantique Société d'Armement Maritime SA v NV Rotterdamsche Kolen Centrale [1967] 1 AC 361

Timeload Ltd v British Telecommunication plc [1995] EMLR 459

Titan Steel Wheels Limited v The Royal Bank of Scotland plc [2010] EWHC 211 (Comm)

Transocean Drilling UK Ltd v Providence Resources plc (The GSF Arctic III) [2016] EWCA Civ 372

Upendra Rasikdal Patel v Vithalbhai Bikabhai Patel [2009] EWHC 3264 (QB)

Walford v Miles [1992] 2 AC 128

Wallis, Son & Wells v Pratt & Haynes [1911] AC 394

Whitecap Leisure Ltd v John H. Rundle Ltd [2008] EWCA Civ 429

Wood v Capita Insurance Services Ltd [2017] AC 1173

Yam Seng Pte Ltd v International Trade Corporation Ltd [2013] EWHC 111 (QB)

Zealander & Zealander v Laing Homes Ltd (2000) 2 TCLR 724

Germany

German Federal Constitutional Court, order of the court on the 15 January 1958 (Lüth), reference number: 1 BvR 400/51, BVerfGE 7, 198

German Federal Supreme Court, judgment of the 9 July 2019, reference number: XI ZR 53/18, NJW-RR 2020, 116

German Federal Supreme Court, judgment of the 12 September 2017, reference number: XI ZR 590/15, NJW 2017, 3649

German Federal Supreme Court, judgment of the 16 February 2016, reference number: X ZR 97/14, NJW 2016, 2404

German Federal Supreme Court, judgment of the 13 January 2016, reference number: IV ZR 38/14, VuR 2016, 145

German Federal Supreme Court, judgment of the 10 December 2014, reference number: IV ZR 289/13, WM 2015, 223

German Federal Supreme Court, judgment of the 9 December 2014, reference number: X ZR 85/12, VuR 2015, 350

German Federal Supreme Court, judgment of the 13 May 2014, reference number: XI ZR 405/12, NJW 2014, 2420

German Federal Supreme Court, judgment of the 13 May 2014, reference number: XI ZR 170/13, WM 2014, 1325

German Federal Supreme Court, judgment of the 31 July 2013, reference number: VIII ZR 162/09, NJW 2013, 3647

German Federal Supreme Court, judgment of the 13 November 2012, reference number: XI ZR 500/11, NJW 2013, 995

German Federal Supreme Court, judgment of the 25 July 2012, reference number: IV ZR 201/10, NJW 2012, 3023

German Federal Supreme Court, judgment of the 31 May 2012, reference number: I ZR 45/11, NJW 2012, 3577

German Federal Supreme Court, judgment of the 8 February 2012, reference number: XII ZR 42/10, NJW 2012, 1431

German Federal Supreme Court, judgment of the 7 December 2010, reference number: XI ZR 3/10, NJW 2011, 1801 (*Schwäbisch Hall*)

German Federal Supreme Court, judgment of the 16 June 2014, reference number: IV ZR 257/03, VuR 2005, 22

German Federal Supreme Court, judgment of the 30 November 2004, reference number: XI ZR 200/03, NJW 2005, 1275

German Federal Supreme Court, judgment of the 13 July 1994, reference number: IV ZR 107/93, NJW 1994, 2693

German Federal Supreme Court, judgment of the 2 March 1994, reference number: IV ZR 109/93, NJW 1994, 1534

German Federal Supreme Court, judgment of the 30 November 1993, reference number: XI ZR 80/93, NJW 1994, 318

German Federal Supreme Court, judgment of the 14 July 1987, reference number: X ZR 38/86, NJW 1987, 2818

German Federal Supreme Court, judgment of the 4 November 1964, reference number: VIII ZR 46/63, NJW 1965, 246

German Federal Supreme Court, judgment of the 17 February 1964, reference number: II ZR 98/62, NJW 1964, 1123

German Federal Supreme Court, judgment of the 29 October 1956, reference number: II ZR 79/55, NJW 1957, 17

OLG Munich, judgment of the 21 July 2020, reference number: MK 2/19, BeckRS 2020, 19794

OLG Dresden, judgment of the 17 June 2020, reference number: 5 MK 1/20, juris

OLG Dresden, judgment of the 22 April 2020, reference number: 5 MK 1/19, VuR 2020, 306

OLG Munich, judgment of the 15 October 2019, reference number: MK 1/19, BeckRS 2019, 24323

OLG Stuttgart, judgment of the 20 March 2019, reference number: 6 MK 1/18, BKR 2019, 298

OLG Brunswick, judgment of the 12 December 2018, reference number: 4 MK 2/18, BKR 2019, 294

OLG Munich, judgment of the 12 October 2017, reference number: 29 U 4903/16, ZIP 2018, 213

OLG Dresden, judgment of the 10 April 2018, reference number: 14 U 82/16, WM 2018, 1304

OLG Brandenburg, judgment of the 26 April 2017, reference number: 4 U 178/15, juris

OLG Düsseldorf, judgment of the 28 April 2016, reference number: I-6 U 152/15, 6 U 152/15, WM 2017, 664

OLG Düsseldorf, judgment of the 22 September 2015, reference number: I-20 U 46/15, 20 U 46/15, juris

OLG Schleswig, judgment of the 3 July 2012, reference number: 2 U 12/11, BeckRS 2012, 15906

OLG Brandenburg, judgment of the 25 June 2003, reference number: 7 U 36/03, BeckRS 2003, 30321643

OLG Düsseldorf, judgment of the 18 July 2002, reference number: 6 U 218/01, BeckRS 2002, 6241

OLG Düsseldorf, judgment of the 31 October 1996, reference number: 6 U 206/9, BeckRS 9998, 15202

OLG Munich, judgment of the 30 March 1995, reference number: 29 U 4222/94, 29 U 4222/94, NJW-RR 1995, 1467

LG Ravensburg, decision of the 7 July 2020, reference number: 2 O 84/20, juris

LG Essen, judgment of the 26 February 2009, reference number: 10 S 356/08, BeckRS 2009, 9904

Imperial Court of Justice, judgment of the 14 August 1941, reference number: II 49/41, RGZ 168, 321

Imperial Court of Justice, judgment of the 15 December 1933, reference number: VII 292/33, RGZ 143, 24

Imperial Court of Justice, judgment of the 26 October 1921, reference number: I 132/21, RGZ 103, 84

Imperial Court of Justice, judgment of the 15 May 1920, reference number: I 25/20, RGZ 99, 107

Imperial Court of Justice, judgment of the 11 October 1918, reference number: VII 114/18, RGZ 94, 29

Imperial Court of Justice, judgment of the 11 November 1913, reference number: VII 281/13, RGZ 109, 299

Imperial Court of Justice, judgment of the 13 December 1912, reference number: VII 228/12, RGZ 81, 117

Norway

Norwegian Supreme Court, *AtB AS v Fosen-Linjen AS* [2019] HR-2019-1801-A

Norwegian Supreme Court, *Holship Norge AS v Norsk Transportarbeiderforbund* [2016] HR 2016, 2554

Norwegian Supreme Court, *A v Danica Pensjonsforsikring AS* [2014] Rt. 2014, 379

Norwegian Supreme Court, *HelgelandsKraft AS v Sigurd Einar and others* [2014] Rt. 2014, 351

Norwegian Supreme Court, *Ivar Petter Røeggen v DNB Bank ASA (Røeggen)* [2013] Rt. 2013, 388

Norwegian Supreme Court, *STX OSV AS and others v Staten v/Tariffnemnda (STX)* [2013] Rt. 2013, 258

Norwegian Supreme Court, *Aronsen Holding AS and others v Fokus Bank, filial av Danske Bank A/S (Fokus Bank)* [2012] Rt. 2012, 1926

Norwegian Supreme Court, *Halvor Lognvik, Harald Lognvik v Storebrand Bank ASA (Lognvik)* [2012] Rt. 2012, 355

Norwegian Supreme Court, *Smestad Nye Handelshus AS v Anne Juvet* [2012] Rt. 2012, 1537

Norwegian Supreme Court, *Kristin Amalia Ellingsen and others v Sørkedalsveien 9 AS (Nye Major)* [2011] Rt. 2011, 670

Norwegian Supreme Court, *Naturbetong AS v Erik O. Jacobsen (Krusesgate)* [2011] Rt. 2011, 679

Norwegian Supreme Court, *Tønnevoldsgate 30 AS v Are Groheim Berntsen and others* [2006] Rt. 2006, 1715

Norwegian Supreme Court, *A v Staten v/Justisdepartementet (Finanger II)* [2005] Rt. 2005, 1365

Norwegian Supreme Court, *A v Gjensidige NOR Sparebank ASA* [2004] Rt. 2004, 156

Norwegian Supreme Court, *Paranova AS v Merck & Co Inc, Merck, Sharp & Dohme B.V. og MSD (Norge) AS (Paranova)* [2004] Rt. 2004, 904

Norwegian Supreme Court, *Storebrand Skadeforsikring AS v Veronika Finanger (Finanger I)* [2000] Rt. 2000, 1811

Norwegian Supreme Court, *Gerd Eriksen and others v Løten kommune* [1997] Rt. 1997, 1965

Norwegian Supreme Court, *Oljearbeidernes Fellessammenslutning v Staten v/ Kommunal- og arbeidsdepartement (OFS)* [1997] Rt. 1997, 580

Norwegian Supreme Court cases *Heidi Gilde and others v Olav Moksnes and others (Selsbak)* [1990] Rt. 1990, 284

Norwegian Supreme Court, *Staten v/Forsvarsdepartementet v Andreas Røstad (Røstad)* [1988] Rt. 1988, 276

Frostating Court of Appeal, *Fosen-Linjen AS v Atb AS (Fosen Linjen)* [2018] LF-2015-187242

Borgarting Court of Appeal, *Christian Corneliussen v Norwegian Air Shuttle ASA* [2016] LB-2015-37187

Borgarting Court of Appeal, *STX* [2012] LB-2010-60176-2

Switzerland

Swiss Federal Court, *A v Krankenkasse B* [2018] 4A_499/2018

Swiss Federal Court, *A v B AG* [2016] 4A_512/2015

Swiss Federal Court, *A.A. und B.A. gegen Migrationsamt und Sicherheitsdirektion des Kantons Zürich* [2015] BGE 142 II 35

Swiss Federal Court, *X v Y AG* [2014] 5A_114/2014

Swiss Federal Court, *A v B GmbH* [2014] 4A_475/2013

Swiss Federal Court, *X. and Mitb. v Migrationsamt und Sicherheitsdirektion des Kantons Zürich* [2013] BGE 139 II 393

Swiss Federal Court, *X v Bank Y* [2013] BGE 139 III 201

Swiss Federal Court, *A. v X. AG* [2012] BGE 138 III 411

Swiss Federal Court, *Eidgenössisches Volkswirtschaftsdepartement v Swisscom (Schweiz) AG and Swisscom (Schweiz) AG v Wettbewerbskommission* [2011] BGE 137 II 199

Swiss Federal Court, *X. and Mitb. v Migrationsamt Kanton Aargau* [2009] BGE 136 II 329

Swiss Federal Court, *X. and Y. v Sicherheitsdirektion und Regierungsrat des Kantons Zürich* [2009] BGE 136 II 5

Swiss Federal Court, *A. v X. AG* [2009] BGE 135 III 225

Swiss Federal Court, *A. and B. v X. Versicherungsgesellschaft AG* [2008] BGE 135 III 1

Swiss Federal Court, *X. SA v Y. Compagnie d'Assurances* [2008] 4A_200/2008

Swiss Federal Court, *C. v Caisse de compensation des banques suisses ainsi que Tribunal des assurances du canton de Vaud (H 31/06)* [2008] BGE 133 V 329

Swiss Federal Court, *X Versicherungs-Gesellschaft v Schweizerische Unfallversicherungsanstalt (SUVA)* [2007] 4A_187/2007

Swiss Federal Court, *X S.A. v Banque Y* [2006] 4C.427/2005

Swiss Federal Court, *Bosshard Partners Intertrading AG v Sunlight AG* [2005] BGE 131 II 271

Swiss Federal Court, *X. v Y. Versicherung* [2004] 5C.134/2004

Swiss Federal Court, *Öffentliche Arbeitslosenkasse des Kantons Solothurn v Metallbau X. GmbH* [2003] BGE 129 III 335

Swiss Federal Court, *O v Compagnie d'assurances X* [2002] 5C.74/2002

Swiss Federal Court, *A. v Schweizerische Bundesanwaltschaft, Eidgenössisches Justiz- und Polizeidepartement und Schweizerischen Bundesrat* [1999] BGE 125 II 417

Swiss Federal Court, *Tonwerke Thayngen AG v Fussballclub Lohn* [1997] BGE 123 III 292

Swiss Federal Court, *L. v Banque X.* [1996] BGE 122 III 373

Swiss Federal Court, *SBG v BK Vision AG* [1995] BGE 121 III 219

Swiss Federal Court, *A S.A. v S.* [1993] BGE 119 II 443

Swiss Federal Court, *B v Banque Z* [1990] BGE 116 II 459

Swiss Federal Court, *X. v Bundesamt für Polizeiwesen* [1984] BGE 110 Ib 1

Swiss Federal Court, *Hanspeter Krattiger v Adolf Forster AG* [1983] BGE 109 II 452

Swiss Federal Court, *A. v Bank X.* [1983] BGE 109 II 213

Swiss Federal Court, *Garage Cornavin S.A. v CFF* [1982] BGE 109 II 416

Swiss Federal Court, *Bosshard Partners Intertrading AG v Sunlight AG* [1979] BGE 105 II 49

Cantonal Court of Jura, *A AG v B* [2016] CC 112/2015

Cantonal Court of Vaud [2016] Journal des tribunaux (Droit Cantonal), JdT 2016 III, 184-187

Supreme Court of Bern, *A v B* [2016] ZK 16 148

Supreme Court of Zürich, *A v B AG* [2015] NP150010

Supreme Court of Zürich, *A v B AG* [2014] HG100147-O U03

Cantonal Court of Graubünden, *X AG v Y* [2014] ZK2 14 3

Supreme Court of Bern, *A AG v B* [2013] ZK 13 320

Supreme Court of Bern, *Student X v Bank Y* [2012] ZK 12 269

Supreme Court of Thurgau [2010] Rechenschaftsbericht des Obergerichts des Kantons Thurgau an den Grossen Rat, RBOG 2010, 108-111

Cantonal Court of Fribourg [2008] Freiburger Zeitschrift für Rechtsprechung, RFJ 2008, 78-82

Websites

Anonymous, 'Betreibungen und Konkurse' (*Bundesamt für Statistik*, 6 April 2020) <https://www.bfs.admin.ch/bfs/de/home/statistiken/industrie-dienstleistungen/unternehmen-beschaeftigte/unternehmensdemografie/konkurse.html> accessed 19 June 2020

Anonymous, 'Individual Insolvency Statistics Releases' (*gov.uk*, 30 July 2019) <https://www.gov.uk/government/collections/individual-insolvency-statistics-releases> accessed 19 June 2020

Anonymous, 'Die Mehrheit der Schweizer Stimmbevölkerung unterstützt das institutionelle Abkommen' (*Presseportal.ch*, 31 March 2019) <https://www.presseportal.ch/de/pm/100002276/100826461> accessed 17 April 2019

Anonymous, 'The 1994 Referendum on Norwegian Membership of the EU' (*Statistisk Sentralbyrå*, 6 March 1995) <https://www.ssb.no/a/histstat/nos/nos_c235.pdf> accessed 17 November 2019

Anonymous, 'Data Viewer' (*Bank of England*) <https://www.bankofengland.co.uk/boeapps/database/fromshowcolumns.asp?Travel=NIxSTxTAxSUx&FromSeries=1&ToSeries=50&DAT=RNG&FD=1&FM=Jan&FY=2015&TD=31&TM=Dec&TY=2020&FNY=&CSVF=TT&html.x=87&html.y=52&C=O1S&C=O23&Filter=N> accessed 2 June 2020

Anonymous, '06718: Domestic loan debt, by borrower, lender and currency (NOK million) 1987M12 - 2020M04' (*Statistisk sentralbyrå*) <https://www.ssb.no/en/statbank/table/06718/> accessed 2 June 2020

Anonymous, '10790: Bankruptcies, by type of bankruptcy and industry (SIC2007) (M) 2009K1 - 2020K1' (*Statistisk sentralbyrå*) <https://www.ssb.no/en/statbank/table/10790/> accessed 19 June 2020

Anonymous, '07459: Population, by sex and one-year age groups (M) 1986 – 2020' (*Statistisk sentralbyrå*) <https://www.ssb.no/en/statbank/table/07459/> accessed 19 June 2020

Anonymous, 'Consumerism' (*Lexico Dictionaries English*) <https://www.lexico.com/en/definition/consumerism> accessed 27 August 2019

Anonymous, 'Free Trade Agreements and Trade Relations by Country' (*EFTA*) <http://www.efta.int/free-trade/free-trade-agreements> accessed 17 November 2019

Anonymous, 'EFTA Trade Statistics' (*EFTA*) <http://trade.efta.int/#/overview/EFTA/WORLD/2017/HS2> accessed 17 November 2019

Anonymous, 'Taking back control from Brussels' (*Vote Leave*) <http://www.voteleavetakecontrol.org/briefing_control.html> accessed 17 November 2019

Anonymous, 'Zeitreihe BBK01PQ3002: Kredite an inländische wirtschaftlich unselbständige und sonstige Privatpersonen / insgesamt / Alle Bankengruppen' (*Bundesbank*) <https://www.bundesbank.de/dynamic/action/de/statistiken/zeitreihen-datenbanken/zeitreihen-datenbank/723452/723452?tsTab=0&tsId=BBK01.PQ3002&listId=www_s104_vjkre_35&id=0> accessed 2 June 2020

Anonymous, 'Zeitreihe BBK01PQ3150: Sonstige Kredite an inländische wirtschaftlich unselbständige und sonstige Privatpersonen / insgesamt / Alle Bankengruppen' (*Bundesbank*) <https://www.bundesbank.de/dynamic/action/de/statistiken/zeitreihen-datenbanken/zeitreihen-datenbank/723452/723452?tsTab=0&listId=www_s104_vjkre_43&id=0&tsId=BBK01.PQ3150> accessed 2 June 2020

Anonymous, 'Bevölkerung: Deutschland' (*Statistisches Bundesamt*) <https://www-genesis.destatis.de/genesis/online?operation=previous&levelindex=2&step=2&titel=Ergebnis&levelid=1592569839159&acceptscookies=false#abreadcrumb> accessed 19 June 2020

Anonymous, 'Forderungen und Verpflichtungen des Sektors private Haushalte und POoE' (*Schweizerische Nationalbank*) <https://data.snb.ch/de/topics/uvo#!/cube/frsekphupooe?fromDate=2007&toDate=2018&dimSel=D0(BES),D1(T5,HYP,KON,UKR),D2(T6)> accessed 2 June 2020

Anonymous, 'Nøkkeltall' (*Gjeldsregisteret*) <https://www.gjeldsregisteret.com/pages/nokkeltall> accessed 2 June 2020

Anonymous, 'Verschuldung' (*Bundesamt für Statistik*) <https://www.bfs.admin.ch/bfs/de/home/statistiken/wirtschaftliche-soziale-situation-bevoelkerung/einkommen-verbrauch-vermoegen/verschuldung.html> accessed 19 June 2020

Anonymous, 'Bevölkerung: Stand und Entwicklung' (*Bundesamt für Statistik*) <https://www.bfs.admin.ch/bfs/de/home/statistiken/bevoelkerung/stand-entwicklung.html> accessed 19 June 2020

Anonymous, 'Registry Trust CCJ Region Data' (*data.gov.uk*, 15 April 2020) <https://data.gov.uk/dataset/4f2b1abf-4dcd-47f6-8b8b-5a2ec306e076/registry-trust-ccj-region-data> accessed 19 June 2020

Anonymous, 'Die deutsche Inkassobranche in Zahlen' (*Bundesverband Deutscher Inkasso-Unternehmen e.V.*) <https://www.inkasso.de/presse/branchenstudie> accessed 19 June 2020

Anonymous, 'Levels of Over-Indebtedness in the UK' (*The Money Advice Service*) <https://www.moneyadviceservice.org.uk/en/corporate/a-picture-of-over-indebtedness-in-the-uk> accessed 19 June 2020

Anonymous, 'Schuldnerquote in der Schweiz nochmals leicht angestiegen' (*CRIF*) <https://www.crif.ch/news-und-events/news/2019/februar/schuldnerquote-2019/> accessed 19 June 2020

Bank of England, 'Household credit' (*Bank of England*, 11 January 2019) <https://www.bankofengland.co.uk/statistics/visual-summaries/household-credit> accessed 21 September 2019

Barne- og likestillingsdepartement, 'Saksgang: Gjeldsinformasjonsloven' (*Regjeringen*, 18 October 2018) <https://www.regjeringen.no/no/dokument/dep/bld/sak/saksgang-gjeldsinformasjonsloven/id2608025/> accessed 17 November 2019

Baudenbacher, Carl, 'Fosen Fiasco – Now the ball is in the Norwegian Supreme Court's field' (*anbud365.no*, 5 July 2019) <https://www.anbud365.no/regelverk/fosen-fiasco-now-the-ball-is-in-the-norwegian-supreme-courts-field/> accessed 16 August 2019

Berglund, Nina, 'Sparks fly over the EU energy union' (*NewsinEnglish.no - Views and News from Norway*, 12 March 2018) <http://www.newsinenglish.no/2018/03/12/sparks-fly-over-eu-energy-union/> accessed 17 November 2019

Breievne, Harald, 'One of ten norwegians say yes to Acer' (*Norway Today - Small and Big News from Norway*, 16 March 2018) <http://norwaytoday.info/news/one-ten-norwegians-say-yes-acer/> accessed 17 November 2019

Bundeskanzlei, 'Volksabstimmung vom 06.12.1992' (*Volksabstimmungen*, 15 April 2019) <https://www.bk.admin.ch/ch/d/pore/va/19921206/index.html> accessed 16 April 2019

Bundesministerium für Justiz und Verbraucherschutz, 'Verbraucherrechtstage 2016: Neue Wege in der Durchsetzung des Verbraucherrechts' (*Bundesministerium für Justiz und Verbraucherschutz*, 15 April 2016) <https://www.bmjv.de/SharedDocs/Artikel/DE/2016/ 04152016_Verbraucherrechtstage.html> accessed 16 October 2019

CMA, 'COVID-19: CMA to investigate cancellation policy concerns' (*Competition and Markets Authority*, 30 April 2020) < https://www.gov.uk/government/news/covid-19-cma-to-investigate-cancellation-policy-concerns> accessed 28 August 2020

CMA 'Statement on coronavirus (COVID-19), consumer contracts, cancellation and refunds (Updated 28 August 2020)' (*Competition and Markets Authority*, 30 April 2020) <https://www.gov.uk/government/publications/cma-to-investigate-concerns-about-cancellation-policies-during-the-coronavirus-covid-19-pandemic/the-coronavirus-covid-19-pandemic-consumer-contracts-cancellation-and-refunds> accessed 28 August 2020

CMA, 'Unfair terms won't protect your business' (*Competition and Markets Authority*) <https://fairterms.campaign.gov.uk> accessed 30 September 2019

FCA, 'FCA launches review of the Credit Information Market' (Financial Conduct Authority, 27 June 2019) <https://www.fca.org.uk/news/press-releases/fca-launches-review-credit-information-market> accessed 19 September 2019

Forbrukerklageutvalget, http://www.forbrukertvistutvalget.no/om-forbrukerklageutvalget/, accessed 17 November 2019

Forbrukertilsynet, 'Forbrukertilsynets veiledning om avtalevilkår for digitale tjenester' <https://www.forbrukertilsynet.no/lov-og-rett/veiledninger-og-retningslinjer/forbrukertilsynets-veiledning-om-avtalevilkar-digitale-tjenester> accessed 17 November 2019

FOS, 'Annual Review 2018/2019 (Banking and borrowing)' (*Financial Ombudsman Service*, May 2019) <https://annualreview.financial-ombudsman.org.uk> accessed 22 September 2019

FOS, 'How is the Financial Ombudsman Service funded?' (*The Financial Ombudsman Services*) <https://www.financial-ombudsman.org.uk/faqs/rules-powers-information-us/financial-ombudsman-service-funded> accessed 21 September 2019

FOS, 'How we make decisions' (*The Financial Ombudsman Services*) <https://www.financial-ombudsman.org.uk/who-we-are/make-decisions> accessed 21 September 2019

Institut für Mittelstandsforschung Bonn, 'Unternehmensbestand' (*Institut für Mittelstandsforschung Bonn*) <https://www.ifm-bonn.org/statistiken/unternehmensbestand/#accordion=0&tab=0> accessed 6 October 2019

Næprud, Stein Tore, 'Statistikk for inkasso' (*The Financial Supervisory Authority of Norway*, 21 April 2017) <https://www.finanstilsynet.no/analyser-og-statistikk/statistikk-for-inkasso/> accessed 19 June 2020

Norges domstoler, 'Tingrettene' (Norges Domstoler) <https://www.domstol.no/no/Om-domstolene/De-alminnelige-domstolene/Tingrettene/> accessed 17 November 2019

OECD, 'Gross domestic product (GDP)' (*OECD Data*, 2018) <https://data.oecd.org/gdp/gross-domestic-product-gdp.htm> accessed 31 August 2019

OECD, 'Household debt' (*OECD Data*) <https://data.oecd.org/hha/household-debt.htm> accessed 2 June 2020

OECD, 'Household disposable income' (*OECD Data*) <https://data.oecd.org/hha/household-disposable-income.htm> accessed 2 June 2020

Office for National Statistics, 'Who does the UK trade with?' (*Office for National Statistics*, 3 January 2019) <https://www.ons.gov.uk/businessindustryandtrade/internationaltrade/articles/whodoestheuktradewith/2017-02-21> accessed 9 November 2019

Park, Neil, 'United Kingdom population mid-year estimate' (*Office for National Statistics*, 29 June 2019) <https://www.ons.gov.uk/peoplepopulationandcommunity/populationandmigration/populationestimates/timeseries/ukpop/pop> accessed 19 June 2020

Plecher, H., 'United Kingdom: Distribution of gross domestic product (GDP) across economic sectors from 2007 to 2017' (*Statista*, 9 August 2019) <https://www.statista.com/statistics/270372/distribution-of-gdp-across-economic-sectors-in-the-united-kingdom/> accessed 9 November 2019

Rütti, Nicole, 'Die Verschuldung der Privathaushalte steigt markant' (*Neue Zürcher Zeitung*, 8 October 2019) <https://www.nzz.ch/wirtschaft/schweizer-privathaushalte-verschuldung-waechst-durch-tiefe-zinsen-ld.1508545> accessed 19 June 2020

SECO, 'Statistische Angaben 2018' (State Secretariat for Economic Affairs, 16 April 2019) <https://www.seco.admin.ch/seco/de/home/Werbe_Geschaeftsmethoden/Unlauterer_Wettbewerb/statistische_angaben.html> accessed 13 July 2019

Statista Research Department, 'Schuldnerquote in der Schweiz von 2015 bis 2019' (*Statista*, February 2019) <https://de.statista.com/statistik/daten/studie/829280/umfrage/schuldnerquote-in-der-schweiz/> accessed 19 June 2020

SECO, 'Statistische Angaben 2017' (State Secretariat for Economic Affairs, 24 May 2018) <https://www.seco.admin.ch/seco/de/home/Werbe_Geschaeftsmethoden/Unlauterer_Wettbewerb/statistische_angaben.html> accessed 13 July 2019

Statista, 'Anteil der Wirtschaftssektoren an der Bruttowertschöpfung in Deutschland im Jahr 2018' (*Statista*, 20 August 2019) <https://de.statista.com/statistik/daten/studie/36846/umfrage/anteil-der-wirtschaftsbereiche-am-bruttoinlandsprodukt/> accessed 6 October 2019

Statista Research Department, 'Höhe der Konsumentenkredite an private Haushalte in Deutschland von 1991 bis zum 1. Halbjahr 2019 (in Milliarden Euro)' (*Statista*, 15 August 2019) <https://de.statista.com/statistik/daten/studie/6814/umfrage/hoehe-der-konsumentenkredite-in-deutschland/> accessed 6 November 2019

Statista Research Department, 'Kredite der Banken in Deutschland an Unternehmen und Privatpersonen von 2001 bis zum 2. Quartal 2019 (in Milliarden Euro)' (*Statista*, 15 August 2019) <https://de.statista.com/statistik/daten/studie/72495/umfrage/kredite-der-banken-in-deutschland-an-unternehmen-und-privatpersonen/> accessed 6 November 2019

Statista Research Department, 'Monatliche Ausgaben privater Haushalte in Deutschland für die Tilgung und Verzinsung von Konsumentenkrediten von 2009 bis 2017 (in Euro)' (*Statista*, 25 January 2019) <https://de.statista.com/statistik/daten/studie/538659/umfrage/monatliche-ausgaben-privater-haushalte-fuer-tilgung-und-verzinsung-von-konsumentenkrediten/> accessed 6 November 2019

Statistisches Bundesamt, 'Bevölkerungsstand' (Destatis - Statistisches Bundesamt, 2 October 2019) <https://www.destatis.de/DE/Themen/Gesellschaft-Umwelt/Bevoelkerung/Bevoelkerungsstand/Tabellen/zensus-geschlecht-staatsangehoerigkeit-2019.html;jsessionid=27F71E6A61A501E0C6DDD1C7E43CF22D.
internet741> accessed 14 October 2019

Statistisk sentralbyrå, 'Population and population changes' (*Population*, 22 February 2019) <https://www.ssb.no/en/befolkning/statistikker/folkemengde/aar-per-1-januar> accessed 12 November 2019

Stiftung für Konsumentenschutz, 'Allgemeine Geschäftsbedingungen AGB' (*konsumentenschutz.ch*) <https://www.konsumentenschutz.ch/themen/allgemeine-geschaeftsbedingungen-agb/> accessed 14 July 2019

Stiftung für Konsumentenschutz, 'Fitnessstudios: Welche haben kundenfreundliche AGB?' (*konsumentenschutz.ch*, 18 January 2018) <https://www.konsumentenschutz.ch/themen/allgemeine-geschaeftsbedingungen-agb/fitnessstudio-listen-welche-fitness-center-haben-kundenfreundliche-agb/> accessed 14 July 2019

Stiftung für Konsumentenschutz, 'Abstrus und kundenunfreundlich: Sunrise verbietet schriftliche Kündigungen' (*konsumentenschutz.ch*, 4 May 2018) <https://www.konsumentenschutz.ch/medienmitteilungen/2018/05/abstrus-und-kundenunfreundlich-sunrise-verbietet-schriftliche-kuendigungen/> accessed 14 July 2019

Stiftung für Konsumentenschutz, 'Annullierungsbedingungen der Hörnlihütte: Nur eine kleine Verbesserung' (*konsumentenschutz.ch*, 29 January 2016) <https://www.konsumentenschutz.ch/themen/allgemeine-geschaeftsbedingungen-agb/annullierungsbedingungen-der-hoernlihuette-nur-eine-kleine-verbesserung/> accessed 14 July 2019

Stiftung für Konsumentenschutz, 'Fitnesscenter weiterhin auf Fairness trimmen' (*konsumentenschutz.ch*, 29 October 2015) <https://www.konsumentenschutz.ch/medienmitteilungen/2015/10/fitnesscenter-weiterhin-auf-fairness-trimmen/> accessed 14 July 2019

Stiftung für Konsumentenschutz, 'Fitnesscenter: Mangelnde Bewegung im Kleingedruckten' (*konsumentenschutz.ch*, 28 May 2015) <https://www.konsumentenschutz.ch/themen/allgemeine-geschaeftsbedingungen-agb/fitnesscenter-mangelnde-bewegung-im-kleingedruckten/> accessed 14 July 2019

Stiftung für Konsumentenschutz, 'Fitnessverträge: Ungleiches Kräftemessen stoppen' (*konsumentenschutz.ch*, 13 March 2015) <https://www.konsumentenschutz.ch/medienmitteilungen/2015/03/fitnessvertraege-ungleiches-kraeftemessen-stoppen/> accessed 14 July 2019

Stiftung für Konsumentenschutz, 'Grosser Erfolg in der Mobiltelefonie' (*konsumentenschutz.ch*, 14 March 2014) <https://www.konsumentenschutz.ch/medienmitteilungen/2014/03/grosser-erfolg-in-der-mobiltelefonie/> accessed 14 July 2019

Stiftung für Konsumentenschutz, 'Unfaire Vertragsklauseln der Telekomfirmen im Visier' (*konsumentenschutz.ch*, 23 January 2014) <https://www.konsumentenschutz.ch/medienmitteilungen/2014/01/unfaire-vertragsklauseln-der-telekomfirmen-im-visier/> accessed 14 July 2019

Swiss Federal Statistical Office, 'Bevölkerungsentwicklung 2018: Provisorische Ergebnisse' (*Federal Statistical Office*, 9 April 2019) <https://www.bfs.admin.ch/bfs/en/home/statistics/population/effectif-change.assetdetail.7926998.html> accessed 13 April 2019

Swiss Federal Statistical Office, 'Verschuldung' (Art und Kumulierung von Schulden) (*Federal Statistical Office*) <https://www.bfs.admin.ch/bfs/de/home/statistiken/wirtschaftliche-soziale-situation-bevoelkerung/einkommen-verbrauch-vermoegen/verschuldung.html> accessed 26 April 2019

Swiss Federal Statistical Office, 'Überblick Schweiz' (*Federal Statistical Office*) <https://www.bfs.admin.ch/bfs/de/home/statistiken/raum-umwelt/bodennutzung-bedeckung/ueberblick-schweiz.html> accessed 13 April 2019

UK Parliament, 'Hire Purchase Act 1938' (parliament.uk) <https://www.parliament.uk/about/living-heritage/transformingsociety/electionsvoting/case-study-radical-politicians-in-the-north-east/from-the-parliamentary-collections/education-act-1944/> accessed 17 September 2019

Urmersbach Bruno, 'Die 20 größten Exportländer weltweit im Jahr 2018 (in Milliarden US-Dollar)' (*Statista*, 21 May 2019) <https://de.statista.com/statistik/daten/studie/37013/umfrage/ranking-der-top-20-exportlaender-weltweit/> accessed 9 November 2019

Utenriksdepartement, 'Financial Contributions' (Norway and the EU) <https://www.norway.no/en/missions/eu/areas-of-cooperation/financial-contribution/> accessed 17 November 2019

Official Reports and Declarations

Bank of England, Credit Conditions Survey, Survey Results 2019 Q2 (21 June 2019)

Bank of England, Financial Stability Report, July 2019, Issue No. 45

Bank of England, Financial Stability Report, June 2018, Issue No. 43

Bank of England, Financial Stability Report, June 2017, Issue No. 41

Barne- og likestillingsdepartementet, Lov om gjeldsinformasjon ved kredittvurdering av privatpersoner (gjeldsinformasjonsloven), Prop. 87 L (2016-2017)

Beauftragte der Bundesregierung für die neuen Bundesländer, Jahresbericht der Bundesregierung zum Stand der Deutschen Einheit 2019 (August 2019)

Bundesamt für Justiz, Liste qualifizierter Einrichtungen gemäß § 4 des Unterlassungsklagengesetzes (UKlaG) (1 July 2019)

Bundesamt für Justiz, Liste der Verbraucherschlichtungsstellen (as of 2 January 2019)

Bundesminister der Justiz, Vorschläge zur Verbesserung des Schutzes der Verbraucher gegenüber Allgemeinen Geschäftsbedingungen, Zweiter Teilbericht der Arbeitsgruppe beim Bundesminister für Justiz (March 1975)

Bundesminister der Justiz, Vorschläge zur Verbesserung des Schutzes der Verbraucher gegenüber Allgemeinen Geschäftsbedingungen, Erster Teilbericht der Arbeitsgruppe beim Bundesminister für Justiz (March 1974)

Bundesministerium für Justiz und Verbraucherschutz, Referentenentwurf für den Entwurf eines Gesetzes zur Änderung des EG-Verbraucherschutzdurchsetzungsgesetzes (27 May 2019)

Bundesrat, Bericht betreffend die Verhandlungen über ein institutionelles Abkommen zwischen der Schweiz und der EU (26 May 2021)

Cherowbrier, James, 'Share of consumer credit loan write-offs in the United Kingdom (UK) 2017-2022' (*Statista*, May 2019) <https://www.statista.com/statistics/793375/consumer-credit-loan-write-offs-united-kingdom/> accessed 19 June 2020.

CMA, Unfair contract terms guidance: Guidance on the unfair terms provisions in the Consumer Rights Act 2015, CMA37 (31 July 2015)

CMA, Unfair contract terms guidance: Guidance on the unfair terms provisions in the Consumer Rights Act 2015, CMA37, Annex A (31 July 2015)

Council conclusions on a homogeneous extended single market and EU relations with Non-EU Western European countries, General Affairs Council meeting, Brussels (16 December 2014)

Council conclusions on EU relations with EFTA countries, 3060th General Affairs Council Meeting, Brussels (14 December 2010)

Council of States, Protocol of Parliamentary Session on the 17 March 2011, AmtlBull. StR 2011, 1

Creditreform, Insolvenzen in Deutschland (10 December 2019)

Creditreform, Schuldneratlas Deutschland: Überschuldung von Verbrauchern, Jahr 2019 (14 November 2019)

Deutsche Bundesbank, Schlichtungsstelle bei der Deutschen Bundesbank Tätigkeitsbericht 2018 (3 January 2019)

Deutsche Bundesbank, Schlichtungsstelle bei der Deutschen Bundesbank Tätigkeitsbericht 2017 (3 January 2018)

Deutsche Bundesbank, Schlichtungsstelle bei der Deutschen Bundesbank Tätigkeitsbericht 2016 (11 January 2017)

Deutscher Bundestag, Entwurf eines Gesetzes zur Einführung einer zivilprozessualen Musterfeststellungsklage, BT-Drs. 19/2439 (4 June 2018)

Deutscher Bundestag, Entwurf eines Gesetzes zur Umsetzung der Wohnimmobilienkreditrichtlinie, BT-Drs. 18/5922 (7 September 2015)

Deutscher Bundestag, Entwurf eines Gesetzes zur Umsetzung der Verbraucherkreditrichtlinie, des zivilrechtlichen Teils der Zahlungsdiensterichtlinie sowie zur Neuordnung der Vorschriften über das Widerrufs- und Rückgaberecht, BT-Drs. 16/11643 (21 January 2009)

Deutscher Bundestag, Beschlußempfehlung und Bericht des Rechtsausschusses zum Entwurf eines Gesetzes über Verbraucherkredite, zur Änderung der Zivilprozeßordnung und anderer Gesetze, BT-Drs. 11/8274 (25 October 1990)

Deutscher Bundestag, Entwurf eines Gesetzes zur Regelung des Rechts der Allgemeinen Geschäftsbedingungen (AGB-Gesetz), BT-Drs. 7/3919 (6 August 1975)

Lord Geoffrey Crowther, Consumer Credit: Report of the Committee Vol. 1 ('Crowther Report') (Her Majesty's Stationery Office 1971)

Solemn Declaration on European Union, Stuttgart, 19 June 1983, Bull. EC 6-1983

European Commission, Report from the Commission to the European Parliament and the Councilon the implementation of Directive 2008/48/EC on credit agreements for consumers, COM(2020) 963 final (5 November 2020)

European Commission, Guidance on the interpretation and application of Council Directive 93/13/EEC of 5 April 1993 on unfair contract terms in consumer contracts, COM(2019) 5325 (22 July 2019)

European Commission, Evaluation of the Consumer Credit Directive (Directive 2008/48/EC) Summary report - public consultation, Ares(2019)3218540 (16 May 2019)

European Commission, Evaluation Road Map regarding the Evaluation of the consumer credit directive, Ares(2018)3472049 (29 June 2018)

European Commission, A New Deal for Consumers, COM(2018) 183 final (11 April 2018)

European Commission, EU Consumer Policy strategy 2007-2013: Empowering consumers, enhancing their welfare, effectively protecting them, COM(2007) 99 final (13 March 2007)

European Commission, Green Paper on the Review of the Consumer *Acquis* (2007/C 61/01)

European Commission, Amended proposal for a Directive of the European Parliament and of the Council on credit agreements for consumers amending Council Directive 93/13/EC, COM (2005) 483 final (23 November 2005)

European Commission, Proposal for a Directive of the European Parliament and of the Council on the harmonisation of the laws, regulations and administrative provisions of the Member States concerning credit for consumers, COM (2002) 443 final (11 September 2002)

European Commission, Report from the Commission on the implementation of Council Directive 93/13/EEC of 5 April 1993 on unfair terms in consumer contracts, COM(2000) 248 final (27 April 2000)

European Commission, Report on the operation of Directive 87/102/EEC, COM (95) 117 final (11 May 1995)

Kommission der Europäischen Gemeinschaften, Vorschlag für eine Richtlinie des Rates über mißbräuchliche Klauseln in Verbraucherverträgen, KOM(90) 322 endg. – SYN 285 (3 September 1990)

FCA, Review of retained provisions of the Consumer Credit Act: Final report (March 2019)

The Financial Supervisory Authority of Norway, Resultatrapport for finansføretak 2019 (17 February 2020)

The Financial Supervisory Authority of Norway, Resultatrapport for finansforetak 2018 (22 August 2019)

The Financial Supervisory Authority of Norway, Retningslinjer for forsvarlig utlånspraksis for forbrukslån - oppsummering av undersøkelse om finansforetakenes gjennomføring, Saksnr. 18/568 (12 June 2018)

The Financial Supervisory Authority of Norway, Resultatrapport for finansforetak 2017 (5 March 2018)

The Financial Supervisory Authority of Norway, Resultatrapport for finansføretak 2016 (21 February 2017)

Finansdepartement, Finansmarkedsmeldingen 2016–2017, Meld. St. 34 (2016-2017)

FOS, Data in more depth (May 2019)

FOS, Annual Review 2017/2018 (30 May 2018)

FOS, Annual Review 2016/2017 (June 2017)

FOS, Annual Review 2015/2016 (May 2016)

FOS, Annual Review 2014/2015 (May 2015)

Hagen, Marius; Turtveit, Lars-Tore; Vatne, Bjørn Helge, Norges Bank Aktuell Kommentar: Sterk vekst i forbrukslån, Nr. 1/2017

Justis- og politidepartementet, Endringer i finansavtaleloven mv. (gjennomføring av direktiv 2008/48/EF om kredittavtaler for forbrukere mv.), Prop.65 L (2009-2010)

Justiskomiteen, Innstilling fra justiskomiteen om lov om finansavtaler og finansoppdrag (finansavtaleloven), Innst. O. Nr. 84 (1998-1999), Ot.prp. nr. 41 (1998-99)

Justis- og politidepartementet, Om lov om endring i avtaleloven, Ot. prp. nr. 89 (1993-1994)

Justis- og politidepartementet, Om lov om lovvalg i forsikring, lov om gjennomføring i norsk rett av EØS-avtalens vedlegg V punkt 2 om fri bevegelighet for arbeidstakere m.v innenfor EØS og lov om endringer i enkelte lover som følge av EØS-avtalen, Ot. prp. nr. 72 (1991-1992)

Justis- og politidepartementet, Om lov om kredittkjøp m.m., Ot. prp. nr. 38 (1984-1985)

Justis- og politidepartementet, Om lov om endringer i avtaleloven 31 mai 1983 nr. 4 m.m. (generell formuerettslig lempingsregel), Ot. prp. nr. 5 (1982-1983)

Justis- og politidepartementet, Om utfærdigelse av en lov om kjøp paa avbetaling, Ot. prp. nr. 36 (1916)

The Law Commission and the Scottish Law Commission, Unfair Terms in Consumer Contracts: Advice to the Department for Business, Innovation and Skills (March 2013)

The Law Commission and the Scottish Law Commission, Unfair Terms in Contracts, Law Com No. 292, Scot Law Com No. 199 (February 2005)

The Law Commission and the Scottish Law Commission, Unfair Terms in Contracts: A Joint Consultation Paper, Law Com. Consultation Paper No. 166, Scot. Law Com Consultation Paper No. 119 (3 July 2002)

The Law Commission and the Scottish Law Commission, Exemption Clauses Second Report, Law Com. No. 69, Scot. Law Com No. 39 (5 August 1975)

NAO, Report by the Comptroller and Auditor General: The Office of Fair Trading Progress in Protecting Consumers' Interests (6 March 2003)

NAO, Report by the Comptroller and Auditor General: The Office of Fair Trading: Protecting the Consumer from Unfair Trading Practices (2 December 1999)

National Council, Protocol of the Parliamentary Session on the 8 March 2011, AmtlBull. NR 2011, 1

Norges Bank, Financial Stability Report 2019 – Vulnerabilities and Risks (2019)

OECD, Regions and Cities at a Glance – Germany (5 March 2019)

OECD, Regions and Cities at a Glance – Norway (5 March 2019)

OECD, Regions and Cities at a Glance – Switzerland (5 March 2019)

OECD, Regions and Cities at a Glance – United Kingdom (5 March 2019)

OECD, Society at a Glance (2019)

OECD, Society at a Glance (2016)

OECD, Society at a Glance (2014)

OFT, Guidance on unfair terms in tenancy agreements, OFT356 (1 September 2005)

OFT, Guidance on unfair terms in holiday caravan agreements, OFT734 (1 September 2005)

OFT, Guidance on unfair terms in home improvements contracts, OFT737 (1 March 2005)

OFT, Guidance on unfair terms in package holiday contracts, OFT668 (1 March 2004)

OFT, Guidance on unfair terms in consumer entertainment contracts, OFT667 (1 December 2003)

OFT, Guidance on unfair terms in care home contracts: A guide for professional advisers, OFT635 (1 October 2003)

OFT, Guidance on unfair terms in health and fitness club agreements OFT373 (1 April 2002)

President John F. Kennedy, Special message to Congress on Protecting Consumer Interest (15 March 1962)

SCHUFA, SCHUFA Kredit-Kompass 2019: Empirische Untersuchung der privaten Kreditaufnahme in Deutschland (Mai 2019)

SCHUFA, SCHUFA Kredit-Kompass 2018: Empirische Untersuchung der privaten Kreditaufnahme in Deutschland (April 2018)

SCHUFA, SCHUFA Kredit-Kompass 2017: Empirische Untersuchung der privaten Kreditaufnahme in Deutschland (Mai 2017)

SCHUFA, SCHUFA Kredit-Kompass 2016: Empirische Untersuchung der privaten Kreditaufnahme in Deutschland (May 2016)

SCHUFA, SCHUFA Kredit-Kompass 2015: Empirische Untersuchung der privaten Kreditaufnahme in Deutschland (May 2015)

Statistisches Bundesamt, Außenhandel: Rangfolge der Handelspartner im Außenhandel der Bundesrepublik Deutschland (2018)

Storting Library, The Storting and the EEA Agreement – Factsheet from the Storting Library (July 2019)

Swiss Banking Ombudsman, Jahresbericht 2018

Swiss Banking Ombudsman, Jahresbericht 2017

Swiss Banking Ombudsman, Jahresbericht 2004, 'Volljährig und damit eigenverantwortlich'

Swiss Federal Council, Botschaft zum Finanzdienstleistungsgesetz (FIDLEG) und zum Finanzinstitutsgesetz (FINIG), 4 November 2015, Bundesblatt Nr. 50, 8901

Swiss Federal Council, Botschaft zur Änderungn des Bundesgesetzes gegen den unlauteren Wettbewerb, 2 September 2009, Bundesblatt 2009 Nr. 38 6151

Swiss Federal Council, Botschaft betreffend die Änderung des Bundesgesetzes über den Konsumkredit, 14 December 1998, Bundesblatt 1999 III 3155

Swiss Federal Council, Bericht über die Stellung der Schweiz im europäischen Integrationsprozess, 24 August 1988, Bundesblatt, 140. Jahrgang, Band III, 249

Swiss Federal Council, Botschaft zu einem Bundesgesetz gegen den unlauteren Wettbewerb, 18 May 1983, Bundesblatt 1983 II 1009

Swiss Federal Council, Botschaft über ein Konsumkreditgesetz, 12 June 1978, Bundesblatt 1978 II 485

Swiss Federal Council, Botschaft des Bundesrates an die Bundesversammlung betreffend den Entwurf zu einem Bundesgesetz über den Abzahlungs- und den Vorauszahlungsvertrag, 26 January 1960, Bundesblatt 1960 I 523

Swiss Federal Council, Bericht des Bundesrates an die Bundesversammlung zum Postulat betreffend Bekämpfung des Wuchers im Kleinkreditwesen, 6 September 1946, Bundesblatt 1946 III 85

UK Government (Department of Trade and Industry), Fair, Clear and Competitive: The Consumer Credit Market in the 21st Century (White Paper), December 2003

The United Nations Guidelines for Consumer Protection (UNGCP) (General Assembly resolution 39/248 of the 16 April 1985, revised by the General Assembly resolution 70/186 of the 22 December 2015)

Verband Schweizer Inkassotreuhandinstitute, Betriebsstatistische Erhebung 2019

Verband Schweizer Inkassotreuhandinstitute, Betriebsstatistische Erhebung 2018

Verband Schweizer Inkassotreuhandinstitute, Betriebsstatistische Erhebung 2017

Verband Schweizer Inkassotreuhandinstitute, Betriebsstatistische Erhebung 2016

ZEK, Jahresbericht 2019

ZEK, Jahresbericht 2017